Friar Gate Chapel, Derby. Royal Arms.

ROYAL COMMISSION ON THE HISTORICAL MONUMENTS
OF ENGLAND

An Inventory of

Nonconformist
CHAPELS
and
MEETING-HOUSES
in Central England

LONDON · HER MAJESTY'S STATIONERY OFFICE

©Crown copyright 1986
First published 1986

ISBN 0 11 701181 9

Printed for Her Majesty's Stationery Office by Acolortone Ltd. Dd 736262 **C10** 4/86

TABLE OF CONTENTS

LIST OF ILLUSTRATIONS

(illustrations are exterior photographs unless otherwise stated)

All photographs except those distinguished by an asterisk were taken by members of the photographic staff of the Royal Commission on the Historical Monuments of England. The majority of those asterisked were taken by the author of this volume. Copies of all photographs have been deposited in the collection of the National Monuments Record.

CHAIRMAN'S FOREWORD

The published Inventories of the Royal Commission began in 1910 with the county of Hertford. The unfortunate omission from that volume of the oldest Friends' meeting-house in the country, of 1670 in Hertford, illustrates the scant regard which was then paid to early nonconformist buildings. Their consideration was further constrained by the terminal date of 1700 which was laid down in the original Royal Warrant. Although this date was subsequently amended to 1714, and a few meeting-houses found their way into successive volumes, it was not until 1946 that the Commission was empowered to report on more recent monuments.

Since then more serious consideration has been possible, and several examples have been named as being of exceptional interest. The extension of the Commission's brief in 1955 to include the general recording of buildings which are threatened with demolition has focussed attention on the urgent need for a more complete survey of some potentially vulnerable categories. Of these the subject of the present volume is one.

Nonconformist chapels and meeting-houses have for too long been regarded as the poor relations of parish churches. The new appreciation of their historical and architectural interest, which is now manifest, will be reflected, it is hoped, in an increased sense of respect and care by those to whom they are entrusted. Social and economic forces, however, have been depleting the stock of these buildings at an alarming rate. The national need for a detailed study of them has been met in the work of which this Inventory is an example.

This Commission was fortunate in having at its disposal an initial survey which was begun privately by one of its staff, Mr C. F. Stell. This formed the foundation of the much more comprehensive record which is now completed.

The field investigation of buildings throughout the whole of England required to create this record was the work of Mr Stell. His endeavours have resulted in a survey of over four thousand examples of nonconformist architecture. To him also must be credited the text of this published Inventory and the measured drawings and sketches which illustrate it. The Commissioners are indebted to him for work which he has done with such care and scholarship over a period of many years.

The great bulk of the record prevents its publication as a whole. This Inventory is restricted to Central England. The Commissioners nevertheless recognize that nonconformist chapels and meeting-houses of outstanding importance throughout England need to be identified without delay. They have therefore issued a White Paper which specifies all those buildings which they deem 'especially worthy of preservation'.

The present Inventory as a work of reference will be found to include every major monument in the area defined. Inevitably, some minor buildings will have escaped notice and others would benefit from reappraisal. The volume should, therefore, be regarded not so much as a final statement but rather as a stimulus to further research. To this end the county sections are also being made available as separate offprints.

The archive which results from this survey will be available in the National Monuments Record at the Royal Commission's offices, 23 Savile Row, London W1.

FERRERS

PRINCIPAL MONUMENTS

List of monuments described in this Inventory that are recommended by the Commissioners as being 'most worthy of preservation'. (For the complete list for England see the Forty-second Interim Report of this Commission, Command No. 9442, 1985.)

Monument numbers, in brackets, are followed by page references.

Buckinghamshire

Amersham. Friends' meeting-house, Whielden Street. (4) 3.

Chalfont St Giles. Friends' meeting-house, Jordans. (21) 7.

Chenies. Particular Baptist chapel. (23) 11.

Haddenham. Baptist chapel. (40) 17.

Sherington. Congregational chapel. (76) 24.

Waddesdon. Strict Baptist chapel, Waddesdon Hill. (87) 25.

Winslow. 'Keach's Meeting-house'. (96) 27.

Derbyshire

Belper. Field Row Chapel. (13) 33.

Chesterfield. Elder Yard Chapel. (39) 37.

Chinley, Buxworth and Brownside. Chinley Chapel. (43) 39.

Middleton and Smerill. Former Congregational chapel, Middleton by Youlgreave. (111) 52.

Gloucestershire

Bristol. 'Buckingham Chapel', Baptist, Queens Road. (16) 62.

Bristol. 'The New Room', Broadmead. (26) 68.

Bristol. Lewin's Mead Meeting-house. (32) 70.

Cirencester. Friends' meeting-house, Thomas Street. (62) 80.

Kingswood. Whitefield's Tabernacle, Park Road. (90) 85.

Marshfield. The Old Meeting-house, High Street. (101) 89.

Painswick. Friends' meeting-house, Vicarage Street. (122) 92.

Stroud. Former Methodist chapel, Acre Street. (142) 97.

Tewkesbury. The Old Baptist Chapel, Church Street. (145) 98.

Winterbourne. Frenchay Chapel. (161) 102.

Winterbourne. Friends' meeting-house, Frenchay. (162) 104.

Herefordshire

Almeley. Friends' meeting-house, Almeley Wooton. (2) 107.

Bromyard. Congregational chapel, Sherford Street. (6) 108.

Leominster Borough. Baptist chapel, Etnam Street. (29) 111.

Leicestershire

Hinckley. The Great Meeting-house, Stockwell Head. (29) 121.

Leicester. The Great Meeting-house, East Bond Street. (44) 125.

Leicester. Former Baptist chapel, Belvoir Street. (45) 126.

Leicester. Evington Chapel, Evington. (48) 127.

Long Whatton. General Baptist chapel, Diseworth. (52) 128.

Market Harborough. Congregational chapel, High Street. (60) 129.

Swepstone. Congregational chapel, Newton Burgoland. (79) 132.

Northamptonshire

Daventry. Congregational chapel, Sheaf Street. (20) 138.

Northampton. Castle Hill Meeting-house. (47) 145.

Potterspury. Congregational chapel. (54) 146.

Weedon Bec. Congregational chapel, Church Street. (68) 149.

Wellingborough. Congregational chapel, High Street. (71) 151.

Nottinghamshire

Kirkby-in-Ashfield. General Baptist chapel, Kirkby Woodhouse. (23) 157.

Mansfield. The Old Meeting-house, Stockwell Gate. (30) 158.

Newark. Wesleyan chapel, Barnby Gate. (36) 160.

ACKNOWLEDGEMENTS

The writer is indebted to many friends and acquaintances who have greatly encouraged and materially assisted in the preparation of this volume. To those immediate members of his family who have suffered from the disruptive and all-pervading demands of enthusiasm no mere acknowledgement can suffice.

Especial thanks are due to Mr David Butler whose unrivalled knowledge of Friends' meeting-houses has been made freely available throughout this work and who has kindly read the relevant entries. Grateful acknowledgement is also made to Dr Arnold Baines for his comments on Baptists in Buckinghamshire; to Mr Roger Evans for reading through the Buckinghamshire inventory; to Mr David Barton for his assistance with the Derbyshire text; to Mr John Steane and Mr E. F. J. Eustace for commenting on the Oxfordshire entries and for making available the results of their researches into the nonconformist buildings of that county; to Mr J. H. Lenton for reading the Shropshire text, and to Mr Robert Sherlock for assistance in preparing the Staffordshire section.

Much help and encouragement has been received from members of the Baptist Historical Society, in particular the late Dr Ernest Payne, the Strict Baptist Historical Society through its secretary Mr Kenneth Dix, the United Reformed Church History Society and its predecessors, the Congregational Historical Society and the Historical Society of the Presbyterian Church of England through its officers Dr Clyde Binfield and Mr A. G. Esslemont, the Unitarian Historical Society through its secretary the Rev. Andrew Hill, and the Wesley Historical Society through its former general secretary the Rev. Thomas Shaw and its editor Mr E. A. Rose. Mr Godwin Arnold, whose publication on 'Early Meeting Houses' provided an initial stimulus to this work, has generously corresponded on a variety of topics, and Mr Roger Thorne has given invaluable assistance in unravelling the many strands of Methodist history.

To all ministers, church officers and others who, when called upon often without warning to permit an inspection of their premises, responded with almost uniform kindness further thanks must be extended; without such co-operation the task would have been impossible. The staff of Dr Williams's Library have, as always, been unfailingly courteous and helpful over a period of many years.

Of the staff of the Royal Commission particular thanks are due to Dr Bridgett Jones, who inspected the contents of numerous record offices; to Mrs Glenys Popper for undertaking many of the more onerous aspects of editing; to Miss Lizbeth Gale, who helped in compiling the Index, and to the Chief Photographer Mr R. Parsons and to Mr T. Rumsey and all the photographic staff for their constant assistance. Without their efforts this work could not have been completed.

C.F.S.

EDITORIAL NOTES

Denominational names used are generally those in use when the buildings were erected. Methodist chapels appear under the name of the original society where this could be ascertained. Presbyterian and Congregational chapels now used by the United Reformed Church (URC) are so indicated in the text. No general attempt is made to distinguish the present grouping of continuing Congregational or Baptist congregations not involving a change in their principal designation; most of the latter, where not otherwise stated, will be found to be of Particular Baptist origin. Unitarian and Free Christian congregations appear under their proper historical appellations.

The name 'meeting-house' or 'chapel' although not generally given should be assumed to be included as appropriate in the heading of each entry. The designation 'church', as increasingly applied indiscriminately to ecclesiastical structures, is avoided as incorrect and tending to ambiguity in the present context. 'Former' indicates that the building is now used by another stated denomination or for other purposes. Closure or demolition is noted where this could reliably be determined but in view of the time which has elapsed since many of the records were made further changes will inevitably be found to have taken place.

The measured drawings are reproduced to uniform scales of 12 and 24 feet to the inch (1:144 and 1:288) with a few sketch plans to an approximate scale of 48 feet to the inch. Sequence hatching has been adopted throughout: the original or principal work is indicated by solid black, secondary work by crossed hatching and later minor additions by single-line hatching; where necessary this is more fully explained in the accompanying text. Dimensions are quoted in the text for monuments built prior to 1800; these are internal unless otherwise stated, the length of the principal axis of the original pulpit or rostrum being given first. A conversion table for Imperial/metric measurements is given below.

Historical information concerning the origins and development of individual congregations necessarily derives in the main from published sources. The accuracy of these varies considerably and although they have been used with caution some errors may remain. Corrections or comments on any statement in this Inventory will be gratefully acknowledged.

Boundary Changes. In order to avoid unnecessary and prolonged delay in the publication of material which has been gathered over many years and because of the continued unsettled state of local government boundaries particularly as regards the metropolitan counties of which the West Midlands falls within the scope of the present volume, this Inventory is arranged by historical counties under civil parishes, the names and boundaries being taken as those obtaining immediately prior to local government reorganization in 1974. The principal changes affecting the area covered by this volume are indicated on the map (p. xviii); these include the removal of Bristol and much of south Gloucestershire to form part of a new administrative county of Avon, and parts of Staffordshire, Warwickshire and Worcestershire in the vicinity of Birmingham to form the West Midlands. The counties of Hereford and Worcester have been united under their combined names and Leicestershire and Rutland under the name of the former. A few parishes in south Buckinghamshire and north Nottinghamshire have been transferred to adjacent counties. Many parishes in north Berkshire south of the river Thames, which have been added to Oxfordshire, and Tintwistle in Cheshire, added to Derbyshire, will appear under their historical counties in subsequent volumes. Changes within the area of the present Inventory are indicated in italics under the county headings or beside individual parish names. Berkshire parishes now transferred to Oxfordshire in which monuments have been recorded are as follows: Abingdon; Aston Tirrold; Bourton; Buckland; Childrey; Cholsey; Draycot Moor; Drayton; Fernham; Frilford; Fyfield and Tubney; Great Faringdon; Grove; Kingston Lisle; Longcot; Longworth; South Moreton; Uffington; Wallingford; Wantage; Wootton. Accounts of the monuments found in these parishes will be available in the Oxfordshire Sites and Monuments Record, Woodstock, and in the National Monuments Record, London.

Conversion Table

1 inch = 25.4 mm

1 foot (12 inches) = 304.8 mm

1 yard (3 feet) = 914.4 mm

1 mile (1760 yards) = 1.6 km

PREFACE

Nonconformity cannot be confined simply to matters of bricks and mortar. Any serious study of the buildings of English religious dissent must assume in both author and reader an understanding and respect for the conditions from which arose the need for such constructions. This is not, however, the place nor does the writer claim any particular qualification to discourse at length upon the rich and varied history of nonconformity. The growth of the various denominations loosely united here under the general, if sometimes reluctantly accepted, title of 'nonconformist', and their principal differences, will be discussed in a future volume. A considered account of the architectural quality, the planning, and the construction of chapels and meeting-houses may also confidently be promised as may individual accounts of the distinct categories of fittings which, in such relatively simple structures, assume a more than usual importance. An inventory of nonconformist communion plate is also in preparation and only select references have been included here.

The denominational scope of this survey embraces all Protestant nonconformists as this term is generally and most widely accepted. The principal religious groups excluded are therefore the Church of England, whose buildings have long been a primary field of study for architectural historians, and the Roman Catholic church and the Jewish community the buildings of both of which still await more detailed examination. Of the denominations included the Methodist church is by far the largest in membership and in the number of chapels it possesses. Baptists and Congregationalists (the latter now largely included in the United Reformed Church) also figure in considerable numbers. Some smaller denominations, such as the Quakers (Religious Society of Friends) and Unitarians, possess buildings which, for historical reasons, are of a significance disproportionate to the statistics of membership.

The discretionary terminal date of 1850 which has been adopted by the Commission in recent years has here been extended to 1914 to include a limited number of monuments of more recent date. Particular attention has, however, been paid to structures built prior to 1800 which, with few exceptions, have been recorded with traditional completeness. The more notable meeting-houses of this early period which have been demolished since c.1940 are also listed, but, with the exception of these, no building is included in the Inventory which has not been personally visited by the author. All buildings of 1801–50 which were inspected are also included though in less detail, but only certain of the more prominent examples from the subsequent period are described. Although the location of buildings worthy of inspection has been no easy matter it can reasonably be claimed that no major chapel or meeting-house dating from before 1850 has been omitted.

The counties now chosen for publication provide illustrations of the great variety in date and type of building common throughout much of England. It will be noticed that there is a relative scarcity of chapels of distinction in the regions close to the Welsh border whereas the formerly rich manufacturing districts of the Cotswolds still possess an inheritance which, in spite of inevitable losses, remains almost an *embarras de richesse*. The more rugged hills of the Peak District shelter chapels where the memory of long departed preachers is yet cherished and the fame of munificent benefactors remains undiminished. In many of the larger towns the great meeting-houses of once wealthy and influential congregations bear a sad and decaying witness to their former glory, some still carrying the tattered banners of hope, others closed and the despair of owners and planners alike. In the countryside small chapels and meeting-houses abound, of all dates but particularly of the 19th century when the prospect of two or more chapels in the smallest of villages was viewed not only with equanimity but as an outward sign of grace to which no objection could properly be made.

Between the Baptists of Buckinghamshire and the Quakers of Gloucestershire, the Independents of Northamptonshire and the Primitive Methodists of Staffordshire, the Presbyterians, the Unitarians, and all the other groups represented here, runs the uniting thread of a modest lack of ostentation in many of their buildings; this, coupled with traditional building materials, lends them an unquestionable charm. It will be apparent from the present volume that no single class of building other than the houses of the people themselves is, in its many and varied forms, its range of date and its use of materials, more representative of the life and aspirations of a considerable body of the inhabitants of these islands.

CHRISTOPHER STELL

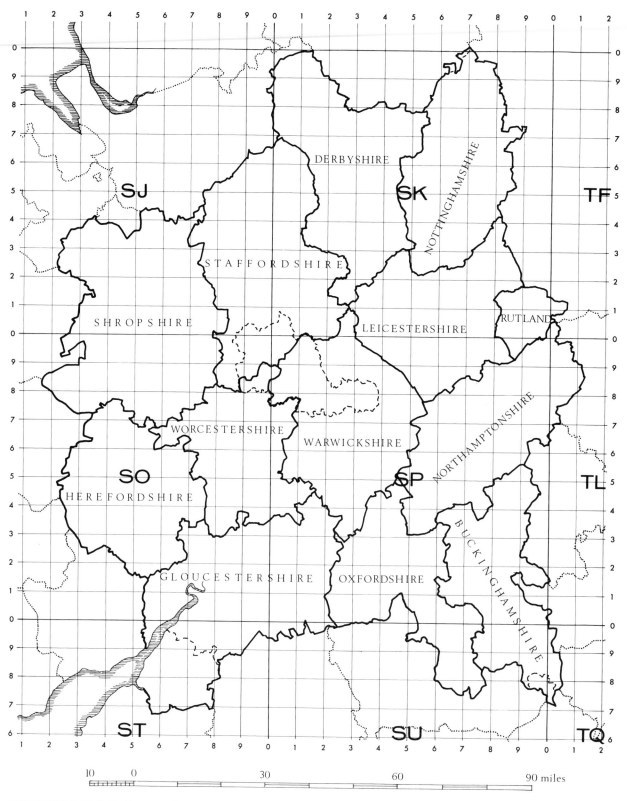

10   0   30   60   90 miles

COUNTY BOUNDARIES. The boundaries of county areas within the present volume are indicated by continuous lines. Alterations resulting from the formation of the counties of Avon and West Midlands and other minor changes are shown by broken lines.

AN INVENTORY OF
NONCONFORMIST CHAPELS AND MEETING-HOUSES
IN CENTRAL ENGLAND

BUCKINGHAMSHIRE

Religious dissent in Buckinghamshire can be traced back to the 14th century when John Wycliffe was rector of Ludgershall (1368–74) and the lasting influence of his itinerant preachers in this and neighbouring counties is evident. At the end of the following century a Lollard revival occured, notably in the southern Chilterns around Amersham and High Wycombe, and in the early 16th century severe penalties were inflicted on its adherents at the instigation of the Bishop of Lincoln; in 1521 six persons were burnt alive at Amersham and in 1532 Thomas Harding of Chesham suffered a similar fate. A little over a century later scattered groups of Baptists began to form themselves into churches of which the General Baptist churches at Winslow (96) and 'Cuddington' (33) were among the earliest. The remarkably complete early records of the Upper Meeting in Amersham (2) are of particular interest in illustrating the provision made for meetings in the difficult years following the Restoration. Comparable evidence, also from Amersham, exists of the sufferings of the Quakers in a part of the county where, with the adherence of several persons of note, Friends' meetings received considerable support in the late 17th and early 18th century.

The Friends' meeting-house in Amersham (4) is an outstanding example of the development of an existing cottage into a meeting-house, enlarged to satisfy increasing needs in the 18th century, closed during the later 19th-century recession which affected many Friends' meetings, and subsequently reopened. In the meeting-house at Jordans (21) the county possesses by contrast one of the most notable buildings of its kind, purpose-built in 1688 and externally little changed from that date. The requirements of a much smaller town meeting of 1727 are to be seen at Aylesbury (9), while work of the end of the century is represented by the meeting-house at Chesham (27) of 1796.

Baptist meeting-houses predominate among the older monuments in the county although only one, at Winslow (96), can be ascribed to the 17th century; 'Keach's Meeting-house' has passed through the hands of two distinct churches and although internally altered in the early 19th

century it remains one of the principal monuments of this denomination. No early 18th-century Baptist buildings remain although the demolished General Baptist chapel at Aylesbury (7), of 1733, is noted below. Apart from fragmentary remains at Wendover (89) and of a large meeting-house at Olney (71) the second oldest Baptist chapel in the county is at Chenies (23), of 1778. Here much interest lies in the subsequent enlargement of the building which, in spite of reseating, is one of the major nonconformist monuments in the county. The Upper Meeting-house at Amersham (2), of 1779, has suffered severely by conversion, but the Lower Meeting-house (3), largely of c.1783, although internally disfigured, remains remarkable for the elaboration of the entrance front. The smaller Strict Baptist chapel at Waddesdon Hill (87), of 1792, is also notable though it, too, has been partly refitted. The total loss of earlier meeting-houses by subsequent rebuilding, a particular characteristic of the 19th century, is nowhere more apparent than in Chesham (24–6) where two long-established Baptist congregations and the Independent, originally Presbyterian, meeting now occupy buildings of 1901–2, 1897 and 1885–6 respectively.

Several Presbyterian congregations which originated in the late 17th or early 18th century in the principal towns experienced those doctrinal changes to which the denomination was especially prone, either to die out or to emerge as Congregational churches. In several instances their meeting-houses passed into the use of these re-formed congregations, but only at Buckingham (16) does any major portion of an early 18th-century Presbyterian meeting-house survive. At Aylesbury (8) a chapel built in 1788 for a newly-formed Independent congregation was demolished in 1981 having passed through a variety of uses. Small former Congregational chapels of 1791 and 1800 remain at Burnham (19) and at Beaconsfield (10) but their design is not notable.

Only a few early 19th-century chapels call for comment, that of the Baptists at Haddenham (40), of 1809, for its size and materials, and that of the Strict Baptists at Ivinghoe (54), of c.1813, for a wide-fronted plan of an exceptionally late date; the conversion of a barn at Great Horwood (37) is also of interest as an example of a once common means of providing for a newly formed congregation. The Congregational chapel at Marlow (61), of 1839–40, by James Fenton is one of the few buildings in the county to which an architect's name can be ascribed, a building in the Classical style of which Great Missenden (39), of 1838, is another example. Equally effective but less elaborate are the Congregational chapels at Sherington (76) and Stony Stratford (99), of 1822 and 1823, clearly by the same hand.

The mid 19th century is represented at High Wycombe (48) and Slough (78) by chapels of moderate size in the Romanesque and Gothic styles respectively, but no important major monuments of the later 19th century were recorded. The Primitive Methodist chapels at Stokenchurch (82), of 1896, and Stewkley (81), of 1903, are, however, of a suitable if strident design which cannot be passed by in silence, the more so in a county not notable for its Methodist architecture.

The principal building material in the county is brick, which appears from an early date and is seen at its best in the Friends' meeting-house at Jordans (21). Where flint was freely available, throughout the Chilterns, this was used in conjunction with brick quoins and bonding-courses; the earliest part of the chapel at Speen (56) is constructed entirely of flint. Stone walling, not much found except in the north-western parts of the county, occurs at the Old Meeting-house, Buckingham (16) in 1726. The most unusual and very localized material in the county is wichert, a form of cob walling, found in the district around Haddenham where the Baptist chapel (40) is probably the largest surviving building to be constructed in this manner; the Wesleyan chapel (42) is also of this material, and some indication of the use of wichert was also noted at Ford (33). Roofs are generally covered with tiles, but slates, introduced in the early 19th century, have frequently been used as a replacement.

AKELEY

(1) WESLEYAN (SP 709378). Dated 1829.

AMERSHAM

(2) THE UPPER MEETING-HOUSE (SU 956972). A Baptist congregation, in existence by 1669, separated in 1675–6 from the church with which it had previously been in communion and was constituted a separate society. The church thus formed insisted on the General Baptist tenet of 'laying on of hands' at baptism (Hebrews vi.1–2) but otherwise appears initially to have maintained its principal links with the Particular party. In the early 18th century a change in attitude resulting in membership

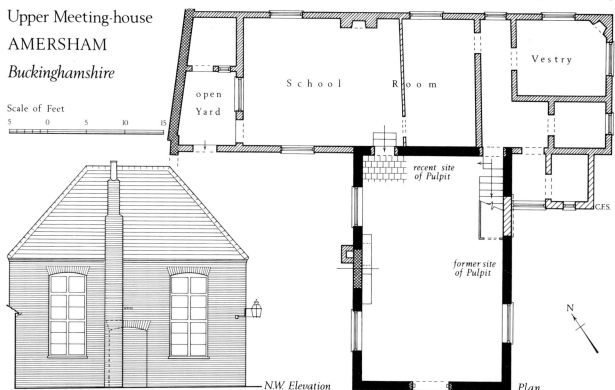

Upper Meeting-house
AMERSHAM
Buckinghamshire

Scale of Feet
5 0 5 10 15

open Yard

School Room

Vestry

recent site of Pulpit

former site of Pulpit

C.F.S.

N

— N.W. Elevation

Plan

of the General Baptist Association led c.1740 to a Particular Baptist secession (see (3) below), the seceders claiming to be the original church whose rights had been usurped by the opposite faction. By the end of the 18th century the cause was very weak and in 1823 the building passed to seceders from the Lower Meeting, of increasingly Calvinistic tendency, who continued to use it for a century, and, after a brief period of occupation by Brethren, sold it in 1944.

The site was bought by the newly-formed church in February 1676 for use as a burial-ground, meetings being held in part of a private house. Use of that building was denied in the following year and a meeting-house was immediately erected on the burial-ground at a cost of £26 and opened 30 December 1677. Some difficulty over meeting the full cost of the building seems to have caused the site to be left in the hands of the former owners, the first existing deed of 1 May 1685 being the transfer from them to two members of the church who in August 1685 placed the property in trust as a burial-ground, referring also to 'two bays of building' which, although not legally admissable at that date, clearly comprised the meeting-house. The meeting-house was placed in trust in 1702 and registered in 1707.

The existing building, now converted to a private house, was built in 1779 on the site of its predecessor, the entire cost being met by John Harding, one of the trustees. It is a small rectangular building with walls of red brick in Flemish bond and a hipped tiled roof, standing on a concealed site 80 yards SW of the Lower Meeting-house. The NW front has a small stone tablet above the former doorway inscribed with the date of erection. Two windows in the SE wall flanked the original site of the pulpit. In the late 19th century a new doorway was inserted at the SW end and the interior was refitted; in 1906 land was bought at the opposite end on which was built a low annexe comprising Sunday-school rooms and a vestry. The interior (18¼ft by 28¼ft) has been entirely altered and a floor inserted.

Inscription: on king-post of roof-truss 'H.W. 1779'. *Monuments*: in burial-ground (1) James Harding, 1799, Jonas Harding, 1804, Sarah Harding, 1830, and Caroline Harding, 1904; (2) Rev. John Cocks, 9 years minister, 1850; (3) John Harding, 1803, and Sarah his wife, 1797; (4) Mrs Ann Morten, 1820, and her daughters Ann, wife of John Grimsdale, 1812, and Charlotte, wife of John Statham, 1812. (The original church book is now in the care of the Berkhamsted Baptist Church. The Trust Deeds were inspected (1967) through the kindness of Mrs Jon Walley, Stone House, Penn, Bucks. All monuments destroyed and three principal windows altered since 1967)

Stell (1977) 23–6: Whitley (1912).

(3) THE LOWER MEETING-HOUSE, High Street (SU 956973). Particular Baptists who seceded from the Upper Meeting c.1740 began to hold services in a cottage at Woodrow (1½ miles WSW) followed by the erection there of a meeting-house. Soon after the appointment of Richard Morris to the pastorate meetings were commenced at his house in Amersham, close to the present site, which he registered in July 1777. Before 1781 a small chapel was built described in the trust deeds as 27ft long and 20ft wide standing 56ft up from the street, parts of which may be incorporated into the existing building. In 1783 a fund was opened 'to erect a more commodious building' on part of Richard Morris's 'great yard' and this date has been generally accepted as that of the present structure although some of the details could date from the early 19th century.

The meeting-house, which stands behind other property on the SW side of the street, has brick walls and a hipped slated roof. The wide front wall is of two distinct building phases; the first the three bays to the left (28¼ft long), the second the two bays to the right. The arches of the three doorways and two windows on the ground floor have keystones decorated with female heads. In each side wall are two small circular windows at gallery level. The rear is three-sided with round-arched windows in the angles. Above the roof is a decagonal lantern with urn finial. The interior has a circular domed ceiling; the rear wall is treated as a wide rounded apse opposite which is a balustraded gallery front of matching shape breaking forward slightly at the centre. Plain boarded pews in the gallery and box-pews below are contemporary with the building but the pulpit and surrounding seating date from the late 19th century. (Interior refitted c.1980)

The *British School* attached to the rear of the chapel is of similar materials, in two stories; a cast-iron tablet above a side doorway is dated 1842.

Monuments: in burial-ground at rear, in use from 1784, (1) James Rogers, 1797, headstone; (2) Martha Bateman, 1806, *et al.*, table-tomb; (3) William Morten, 1832, *et al.*, sarcophagus-shaped monument within contemporary railed enclosure, the iron railings having lotus flower finials (railings destroyed since 1967); (4) Richard Morris, 1817, Martha, his wife, 1811, and Elizabeth Morris.

Stell (1977) 23–6.

(4) FRIENDS, Whielden Street (SU 956971). Friends occupancy of this site is believed to date from c.1660, when part of an orchard 'at the town's end' was given by Edward Perot or Parret for use as a burial-ground. The funeral of Perot in 1665 was notorious for its forcible interruption and the arrest of many of the mourners, following which the coffin was left lying all day in the public road and finally interred in a remote corner of the steeple-house yard. In 1669 meetings were being held at Isaac

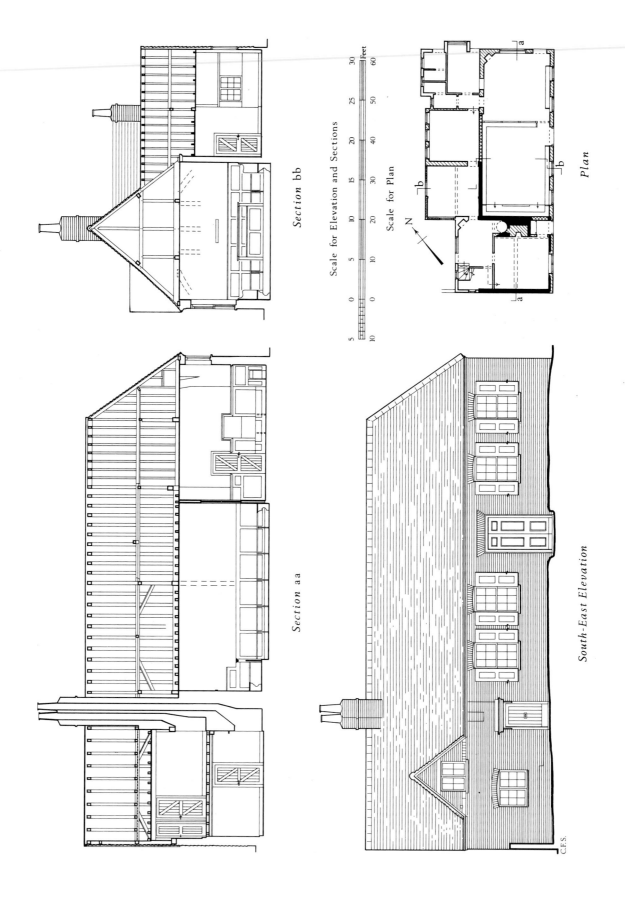

Section bb

Section aa

Scale for Elevation and Sections

Scale for Plan

Plan

N

South-East Elevation

C.F.S.

The Friends' Meeting-house in Whielden Street, AMERSHAM, *Buckinghamshire*

Penington's house, Woodside Farm (RCHM *Buckinghamshire* II (1912) 13–14), demolished *c*.1970, but in 1689 'part of Joseph Winch's house' was registered for meetings and this evidently relates to the earliest section of the present building. It originated *c*.1600 as a timber-framed cottage of one storey and attics with two principal rooms and a central chimney-stack. By 1689 the NE room had been enlarged by one bay to form a meeting-house, also of timber-framed construction, and about this time a gabled wing was added at the rear. In the late 18th century the meeting-house was further extended to the NE in brickwork, refronted and entirely refitted, together with other enlargements at the back. In the early 19th century the cottage was also refronted in brickwork and further minor alterations and additions were made in 1957. During the second half of the 19th century the building was occupied by Wesleyans prior to the erection of their present chapel in 1899; it was reopened for Quaker use in 1917.

The meeting-house and cottage have a front wall of brick, gabled tile-hung SW end wall and gabled and weather-boarded rear wings. The roof is tiled, and hipped to the NE; some timber framing visible in 1967 internally at the rear of the middle bay of the meeting-house has since been concealed. The front wall apart from the cottage is symmetrical about a central doorway and has four windows with segmental heads of rubbed brick, hung sashes and external shutters with decorative iron fasteners. The interior (41ft by 17ft) is divided into two rooms by a screen with counter-weighted shutters. The principal room is lined with a dado of plain panelling, with wall benches and a stand at the SW end. The seating comprises open-backed benches with shaped ends.

The roof structure exhibits evidence of the various periods of enlargement. The former cottage bay at the SW end of the meeting-house has straight wind-braces below clasped purlins with remains of lime washing and of a former ceiling at collar-beam level. The centre bay is without wind-braces but is otherwise similar with common rafters laid flat and without a ridge-piece.

Crump, C.G., ed., *The History of the Life of Thomas Ellwood* (1900) 139 sqq.

ASTON ABBOTTS

(5) Former CONGREGATIONAL (SP 847201). Brick with hipped slate roof. Now two cottages, built 1839.

ASTWOOD

(6) Former CONGREGATIONAL (SP 953473). Brick and slate, pedimented front. Tablet dated 1826.

AYLESBURY

(7) Site of GENERAL BAPTIST, 40 Cambridge Street (SP 822141). A small brick and tile meeting-house registered in 1733 as 'newly erected . . . on part of the ground called Welches Mount' was demolished *c*.1938–40 and no traces now remain. The original church died out in the late 18th century and the building was occupied by a newly-formed Particular Baptist congregation which removed in 1828 to a new chapel in Walton Street (SP 820136) also now demolished (pulpit now in Ebenezer Chapel, Ripley, Surrey). Attempts to revive the General Baptist cause

failed and the old 'Baker's Lane' meeting-house was used by a variety of denominations including Wesleyans, 1829–31, and in the late 19th century by the Brethren.

Durley (1910) illus. opp. 8: Gibbs (1885) 447–52: Taylor (1818) I, 226 sqq., 327: Wood (1847) 230.

(8) Former INDEPENDENT, Castle Street (SP 817138). The chapel, built in 1788, was registered 22 August as the 'house of Thomas Poulton'. It served an Independent congregation until 1816 when services were transferred to the former Presbyterian 'Hale Leys Chapel' in High Street, of 1707, which was subsequently enlarged and, in 1874, rebuilt. Castle Street chapel was then used by Wesleyans, until the erection in 1837 of their chapel in Friarage Passage (demolished *c*.1965), as a Congregational Sunday-school and more recently as a social club. The burial-ground at the rear continued in use until *c*.1870. (Chapel demolished 1981)

The walls are of brick and the roof is tiled. The N end was built in the later 19th century probably replacing a cottage behind which the chapel was erected. The W wall behind the adjoining property has at the centre a wide round-arched window matched by a similar window in the E wall, and to each side a small octagonal window of early 19th-century type. Further rooms have been added against the S end.

The interior (55¾ft by 20ft including the front enlargement) has a late 19th-century N gallery. The roof is supported by four trusses with king-posts above collar-beams, and clasped purlins.

Inscription: on brick in W wall, S of centre window, 'TP 1788', for Thomas Poulton. *Monuments*: externally on W wall (1) large shaped tablet now decayed but formerly inscribed to Thomas Bates, 1791; (2) Robert Woodman, 1861, and Bithia his wife, 1860; W of chapel (3) Mary, wife of John Gunn, 1832; in burial-ground to S (4) William Gibbs, 1839, and John Rolls Gibbs, his brother, 1845, editor of *The Aylesbury News*; (5) Samuel Luke Gunn, 1830, son of [Rev.] William and Obedience Gunn; (6) Isaac Moss, 1825; (7) Eusebia, wife of Rev. William Slatyer, missionary, of Mandeville, Jamaica, 1840.

Gibbs (1885) 445–7 has full list of monuments.

(9) FRIENDS, Rickford's Hill (SP 818137). Meetings commenced in 1703 when premises fronting the street, now Nos. 9 and 11, were registered for worship. In 1726 additional land was

acquired at the rear and the present meeting-house erected in the following year. From 1836 until its reopening in 1933 the building was variously occupied; by a school, by a newly-formed Baptist congregation, and by the YMCA. The meeting-house stands concealed behind other property E of the 'Saracen's Head Inn' (RCHM *Buckinghamshire* I (1912) 32). It is a small rectangular building of brick with a hipped tiled roof. The SW front, of dark glazed headers with red brick dressings and a moulded brick eaves cornice, has a central segmental-arched entrance between windows with timber lintels; the NW window has been widened. A porch, added in the early 19th century, was removed when the building reverted to its original function. The SE end wall, now internal, is timber framed and may have been weatherboarded.

Friends' Meeting - house, AYLESBURY *Buckinghamshire*

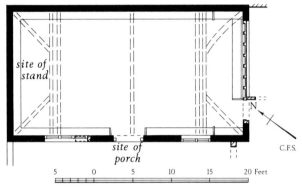

The interior (29¾ft by 15½ft) was formerly ceiled at tie-beam level and had a coved or moulded cornice; a modern ceiling at collar level leaves the roof structure partly exposed: three trusses with braces to clasped purlins, straight wind-braces from the central truss, and double tie-beams at the ends with dragon-beams in the corners. The walls are lined with a dado of plain panelling with an upper range of panels at the NW end with shaped cheeks against the adjacent walls marking the former site of the stand. Wall benches incorporate shaped ends next to the entrance, and at the SE end is a reset seat, perhaps from the front of the stand.

BEACONSFIELD

(10) BETHESDA CHAPEL (SU 944902). A Presbyterian meeting which existed in the early 18th century merged about 1740 with another congregation more Independent in character although retaining vestiges of a Presbyterian polity. Heterodox tendencies in the 'Old Meeting' led to the formation of a separate society for which 'Bethesda Chapel' was built in 1800. To the Congregational church (now URC) thus formed the remnant of the older meeting was later added and their meeting-house of c.1730 at Wycombe End was used for a time as a Sunday-school; it was demolished in 1904.

The original chapel (44ft by 22¾ft) standing behind its successor of 1875 is a plain building of brick with three round-arched windows in each side wall.

Monuments: reset against S boundary wall (1) George Healy, 1824, *et al.*; (2) William Henry Boddy, 1825, and Selina Margaretta Boddy, 1825; (3) Elizabeth Boddy, 1823, and Laura Elizabeth Boddy, 1823; (4) William Boddy, 1832; (5) Charlotte, wife of John Henry Micklem, 1834, and Charlotte their daughter, 1835; (6) William Mead, 1841; also, loose, three cast-iron grave markers, one dated 1864, by Haden, Warminster.

Summers, W.H., *A Centenary Memorial of the Congregational Church, Beaconsfield* (1900): Summers (1905) 2–9.

BIERTON WITH BROUGHTON

(11) STRICT BAPTIST, Bierton (SP 839157). The church was formed by William Bonham who registered a house for preaching in 1821. A second certificate also taken out in his name, dated 7 June 1831, probably relates to the present chapel of brick and slate originally aligned with a row of cottages but enlarged to the front in 1885. The original building erected or converted from a cottage in 1831 is almost entirely obscured by the later work but the interior retains the former cottage-like proportions with two doorways and two upper windows flanking the pulpit on the back wall. In 1885 a gallery in the front extension took the place of side galleries.

Monuments: in chapel (1) Ann Fleet, wife of Thomas Bonham, 1849, signed 'Whitehead, Aylesbury'; in burial-ground in front (2) William Bonham, 1853, and Mary his wife, 1850; (3) 'S.P.', 1837.

BLETCHLEY

(12) WESLEYAN, Mill Road, Water Eaton (SP 880330). Rendered brick and slate, gabled front; opened 1830.

BRADWELL

(13) WESLEYAN (SP 833396). Small plain building, rendered brick and slate; opened 1839.

BRILL

(14) CONGREGATIONAL (SP 654139). Tall gabled front with ball finials, 1839 (URC).

(15) WESLEYAN (SP 656137). Gabled front with urn finials, 1841.

BUCKINGHAM

(16) THE OLD MEETING-HOUSE, Well Street (SP 696339), built in 1726 for a Presbyterian, latterly Independent, congregation which had been formed c.1700. In spite of a secession in 1793 which resulted in the erection of the Congregational 'New Meeting-house' on the site of the present chapel of 1857 in Church Street (now URC), increased attendances necessitated enlargements in 1809, 1816, and again after 1839. About 1850 the two congregations united and the Well Street building was converted for use as schoolrooms and for mid-week meetings. It has long since passed into commercial use although the upper part was occupied for a time by a Brethren's Assembly.

The original building has walls of coursed rubble and a hipped tiled roof with central valley. In the early 19th century the front was brought forward by about 10ft and the present SE front of brick is entirely of that date, although perhaps incorporating some earlier dressings. The rear NW wall has two tall round-

Front facing Well Street.

arched windows, one retaining a decorative iron casement plate, flanking the site of the pulpit. Two small windows high in the side walls served the former gallery.

The interior (originally about 29ft by 33¾ft) has been much altered and the ground lowered by about 3ft to street level. Traces remain of a gallery around three sides, now floored over, and of early 19th-century staircases in the front corners. The *roof structure* of the original building remains complete and comprises two principal frames with queen-posts, bent principals and curved braces, with centre posts carrying a, possibly renewed, valley beam; half trusses with curved braces support the roof at the centre of each side and diagonally at each corner. The construction is closely comparable with that at Bicester, Oxfordshire (15) of 1728.

[Cannon A], *The Jubilee Manual of the Congregational Church, Buckingham, 1857-1907* [1907]: *CYB* (1858) 262; (1879) 298–9.

(17) Former BAPTIST, Moreton Road (SP 696341). Later Primitive Methodist, now the Salvation Army Hall, was built *c*.1842.

BUCKLAND

(18) Former WESLEYAN (SP 887125). Registered 1836 but perhaps built a few years earlier, Sunday-school added 1907. Now a house.

BURNHAM

(19) Former CONGREGATIONAL, Gore Road (SU 931828). 'Zion Chapel' was built in 1791 for a newly formed congregation which remained in membership with the Maidenhead church until 1827. In 1963–4 a new chapel (now URC) was built ¼ mile S and the former building passed to industrial use. The chapel is a plain timber-framed building with rendered walls and a hipped tiled roof. The front wall has a central entrance in a later gabled porch and two tall round-arched windows; one similar window occupies the centre of each side wall. The interior (44½ft by 20¼ft), perhaps enlarged, was refitted in the late 19th century.

Monuments: externally against W side wall (1) Daniel Winch, 1842; (2) Rev. George Newbury, 1849, nearly 20 years minister, and Mary his wife, 1841; (3) Eleanor Winch, 1844.

Hayns, D., *The Burnham Congregational Church* (1964): Summers (1905) 30-3.

CHALFONT ST GILES

(20) CONGREGATIONAL (SU 988933). Although the former rector, Thomas Valentine, died in 1665, several other ejected ministers were active in this locality in 1669 when Presbyterian meetings were reported as taking place at Mrs Fleetwood's house, which has been identified as 'Milton's Cottage'. The Presbyterian society thus formed built a meeting-house in 1721 on a site 100 yards E of the present chapel. By the end of the 18th century the cause was very weak but it was revived and transformed under subsequent Independent preachers. About 1854 the old meeting-house was demolished and replaced by the present plain building of brick and slate which was refronted in 1901. (URC)

The site of the old meeting-house, on the S side of the road W of the manse, has been cleared, but in the W boundary wall of the burial-ground behind it is a portion of brick walling which may have been part of a vestry. *Monuments*: in burial-ground (1) Rev. George Todhunter, 1825; (2) Mary, wife of William Dennis Jones, 1817; (3) Thomas Hart, 1829, Cicely his widow, 1835, and Hannah his daughter, 1832; (4) Mrs Rebeccca Keen, 1869 and Charles Keen, her nephew, 1862, wooden 'leaping board' with shaped posts.

A small wooden *model*, in the present chapel, believed to represent the former meeting-house shows a building of brick with two stages of windows, front of three bays with two doorways having canopies supported by shaped brackets, and two-bay sides; the interior fittings also depicted include a gallery around three sides and pulpit opposite the entrances. A description quoted by Summers referring to 'a square double-gabled structure . . . and two large supporting columns' is not confirmed by the model which has a plain hipped roof of single span, but this may represent a refashioning of *c*.1800.

Summers (1905) 34-8.

(21) FRIENDS, Jordans (SU 975911). Meetings of Quakers which from the late 1650s had been held at a number of different sites were by 1669 being conducted mainly at Jordan's Farm, the house of William Russell, with Isaac Penington as one of the principal members and William Penn, from 1672-7, as another. In 1671 a rood of ground 250 yards S of the farm was purchased by Thomas Ellwood and others for use as a burial-ground, to which additions were made to the N in 1761 and 1911. The land E of the burial-ground, on which the meeting-house stands, was acquired in 1688 and the building opened 30 September in that year, although not registered until 10 October 1689. Support seriously declined in the late 18th century and regular use ceased in 1798; annual meetings were held from 1851, and weekly meetings were resumed in 1910.

The meeting-house stands on a sloping site falling away gradually to the S but steeply to the east. The walls are of brickwork with a coved plaster eaves cornice and the hipped roof is covered with tiles. The S end is of two stories and along the E side at a lower level was a range of apparently contemporary stabling, heightened in 1867 by the addition of an upper room for women's business meetings and subsequently converted in 1930 and 1958 to provide alternative living accommodation. The W front and S end are in Flemish bond brickwork with glazed headers above a levelling course of irregular bond. The principal openings have flat-arched heads of rubbed brick. The W front has a central doorway with window above, two cross-framed windows to the N and two stories of windows to the S, all with external shutters and with leaded glazing and iron casements with ornamental fastenings in wood frames. One window in the N wall has a segmental-arched head, a rectangular wood frame of three lights with a transome and renewed shutters.

The interior (44¼ft by 20¼ft excluding the stabling) is divided by a screen with shutters; the principal room to the N (31¼ft long) has a plaster ceiling with coved surround and a brick floor. To the S is a smaller room at a lower level with a kitchen fireplace and former bread oven against the end wall and a room above, both rooms having shutters opening to the principal meeting-room. The fittings date in part from 1773 when the meeting-house was closed for several weeks for alterations. These include a dado of plain panelling which rises at the N end behind the stand and has been further heightened in the centre, obscuring the lower part of the N window. The stand has a partly-open front with an upper rail supported by dwarf balusters and with ball finials to the newels. Seating comprises wall benches and open-backed benches of several dates. *Monuments*: in burial-ground, erected 1862 on the approximate site of burials, include memorials to William Penn, 1718, Gulielma Maria (Springett) his first wife, 1694, and Hannah (Callowhill) his second wife, 1726, Isaac Penington, 1679, and Mary his wife, widow of Sir William Springett and mother of Gulielma Maria Springett, 1682, Thomas Ellwood, 1713, and Mary (Ellis) his wife, 1708.

Arnold (1960) 107, 123: Hayward, A.L., *Jordans, the Making of a Community* (1969): RCHM *Buckinghamshire* I (1912) 82.

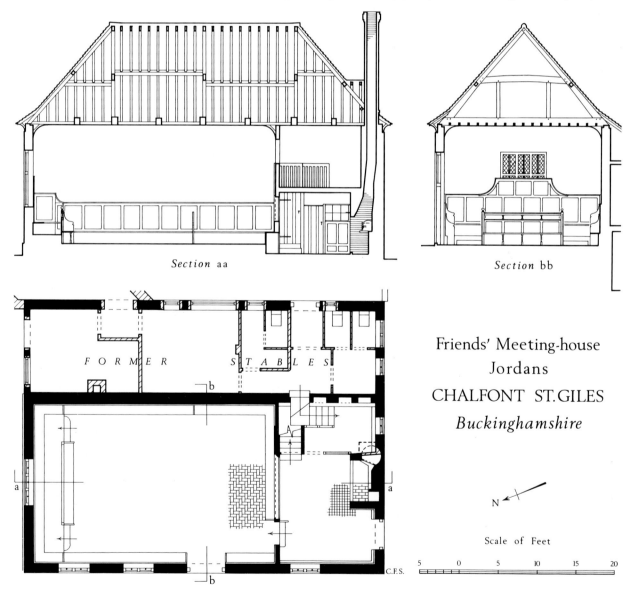

Section aa

Section bb

Friends' Meeting-house
Jordans
CHALFONT ST.GILES
Buckinghamshire

FORMER STABLES

N

Scale of Feet

5   0   5   10   15   20

C.F.S.

Exterior from SW.

Interior from SE.

(21) CHALFONT ST GILES. Friends' meeting-house, Jordans.

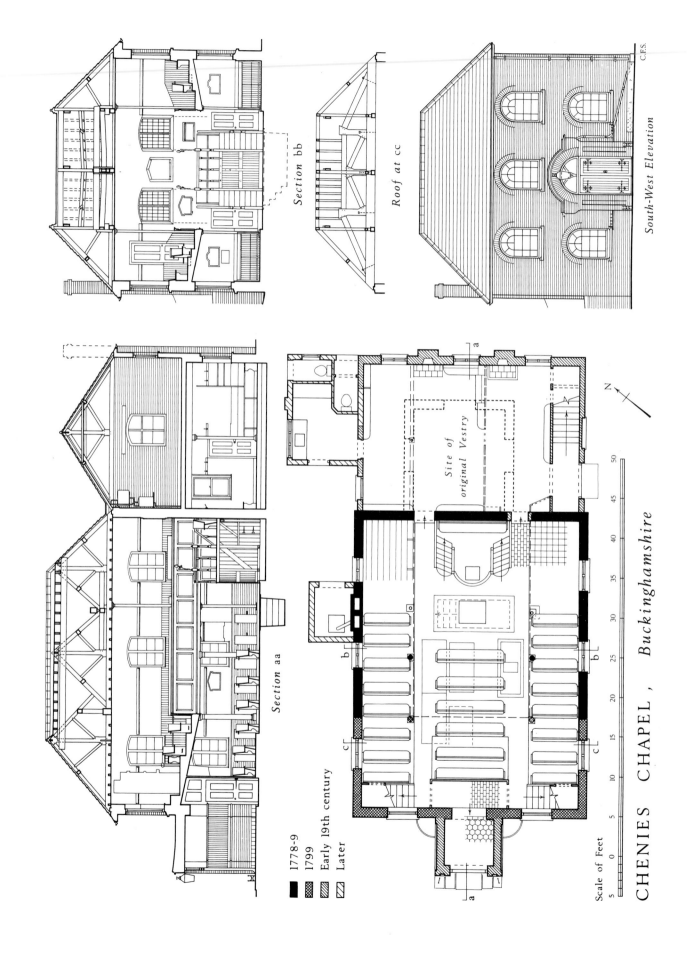

Section bb

Roof at cc

South-West Elevation

Section aa

Site of
original Vestry

N

1778-9
1799
Early 19th century
Later

Scale of Feet

5   0   5   10   15   20   25   30   35   40   45   50

CHENIES CHAPEL, *Buckinghamshire*

C.F.S.

CHALFONT ST PETER

(22) BAPTIST, Gold Hill (SU 996903). Brick with tall round-arched windows and a bell-cote; built 1870–1 on the site of a meeting-house registered 1792. The church, which until 1807 was Independent, was first formed in 1786 by a society originating c.1772–4. *Monument*: in chapel, Rev. David Ives, 1855, 29 years pastor, and Mary his wife, 1830.

Summers (1905) 297–8.

CHENIES

(23) PARTICULAR BAPTIST (TQ 021981). Although the rector, Benjamin Agas, was ejected in 1662 for nonconformity and several certificates attest the existence of nonconformist groups in the early 18th century, it was not until 1757, when William Bennett resigned as Baptist pastor in St Albans and moved to Chenies, that a regular congregation came to be formed here. A meeting-house, the location of which is not known, was fitted up in Green Street; for it the maintenance accounts survive and include references to a gallery and clock. In 1773 a lease was obtained of the present site, then part of an orchard, with permission to build a meeting-house when the need should arise. The building appears to have been ready by 8 October 1778 when a meeting-house certificate was issued; it was placed in trust for Particular Baptists in May 1779. The meeting-house was enlarged to the front in 1799. The rear vestry was rebuilt or enlarged in 1833 and again enlarged and a schoolroom built above it in 1841 although not completed until 1851; the front porch was built in 1838. Internal alterations included the provision of a baptistery in 1794, the insertion of two additional cast-iron columns in 1829 to support the roof, and a general replacement of the pulpit and seating in the late 19th century.

The chapel has brick walls and a hipped roof formerly with a central valley and presumably tiled but now altered and slated. The front wall, facing SW, is of 1799; of three bays with two tiers of round-arched windows and a round-arched doorway in the later porch. The side walls, originally of two bays with one bay added at the front, have two stages of segmental-arched windows with renewed frames. The NW wall has an original brick chimney breast central to the older bays, and the two lower windows flanking it are narrower than those above and have been designed as doorways; a plan of the chapel on the 1779 trust deed indicates a front entrance as at present and it is possible that these doorways represent part of an earlier design which was changed during building. The combined vestry and Sunday-school at the rear is of two stories and is separately roofed; the NE wall has three bays of segmental-arched windows separated by two chimney breasts. The SE entrance to the vestry has a flat canopy supported by shaped brackets.

The interior (originally 24ft by 28ft) has a flat plaster ceiling. The original NE wall, now internal, has two segmental-arched windows flanking the pulpit the cills of which have been raised and the inner jambs splayed. The gallery around three sides has a fielded panelled front extended to the SW in 1799 and supported by four turned wood columns, one replaced in cast-iron, and by two thin columns added in 1829. The columns and gallery fronts were marbled in green c.1910. The gallery staircases in the front corners replace staircases in the corresponding corners of the original structure. The vestry is divided by a panelled screen, part folding and part with a hinged shutter; the NW room has early 19th-century wall benches. The roof of the chapel is supported by king-post trusses with a braced queen-post truss on the line of extension. A lead flat now replaces the former valley.

Fittings – *Books*: miscellaneous titles published by the Religious Tract Society, some with book-plates 'Chenies Sunday School Library. Established by the Baptist Denomination June 1840'. *Boot-scrapers*: pair, flanking front entrance, wrought-iron, tall standards with knob finials, early 19th-century. *Clock*: on front of SW gallery, signed 'Pitt, Amersham', late 18th-century. *Collecting Shovels*: pair, wood, late 19th-century or later.

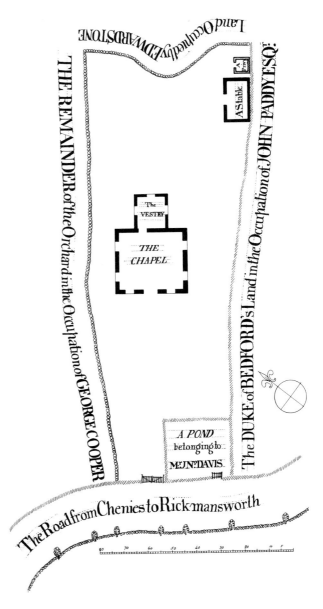

Plan of chapel and burial-ground from 1779 trust deed (scale in feet).

Front of 1799 from S.

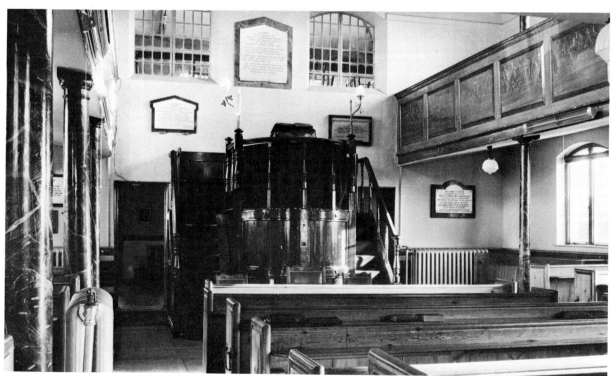

Interior from SW.
(23) CHENIES. Baptist chapel.

Communion Table: (former) with two legs and floor bearers, single drawer, late 18th-century. *Inscriptions*: on front of SW gallery 'Erected-1779.', repainted. On external brickwork, initials and dates – on front extension of SE wall, 1799; on NW wall of vestry, 1833; on SE wall of vestry, 1841; on NE wall below middle upper window, 1841, 1897.

Monuments and *Floorslabs*. *Monuments*: in chapel (1) Rev. Ebenezer West, 1836, 15 years pastor; (2) James Bates, 1849, 20 years deacon; externally on SE wall (3) Mrs Maria Bean, daughter of Mark and Mary White, 1836; against NE wall of vestry (4) Sarah, daughter of Richard and Martha Church, 1789; (5) John Johnson, 1787; (6) Ann, wife of James Body of Chenies Lodge, 1780; (7) Francis Morton, 1790; (8) Samuel Clark, 1810, and George Clark his great-grandson, 1829; (9) Sarah, wife of Thomas Jordan, 1780; N of vestry (10) Fanny, wife of John Abbee jun. of Chorleywood Brick Kiln, 1811, vault; against SE wall of vestry (11) Charlotte, wife of John Talbot, daughter of Thomas Dell, 1801; (12) John Talbot, 1820; in burial-ground SW of chapel (13) James Body of Chenies Lodge, 1840, Elizabeth his wife, 1851, their children Martha, 1838, Ann, wife of Thomas Davis, 1844, and Caroline, 1849, also Richard, son of Thomas and Ann Davis, 1838; (14) Rev. Joseph Caldwall Wyke, 1848; (15) Mary, wife of Rev. Benjamin Bartlett, 1842; (16) James White, 1845, with later inscription to Rebecca, his widow, 1884, headstone and slab in railed enclosure; loose, recovered from structural timbers of vestry floor, (17) pair of moulded wooden end-posts from 'leaping-board', inscribed 'E.S. 1796', 'W.S. 1798'. *Floorslabs*: (1) Rev. Morgan Jones LL.D., of Hammersmith, 1797, and Sarah his widow, 1808; (2) William Davis, the elder, 1799, and Mary his wife, 1780; (3) Thomas Dell, 1806, and Hannah his widow, 1830; (4) William Davis, 1819, John Davis Jones, 1838, Rev. William Lewis, (n.d.), and Ann his wife, widow of William Davis, 1853; (5) John Reeve, the elder, 1805.

Railings: in front of chapel, cast-iron, erected 1840. *Seating*: all pews renewed late 19th century, but some slight indications of former layout remain especially in gallery, where seat numbers on inside of fronts to side galleries are faintly visible below over-painting. Some open-backed benches of *c*.1850 remain in the Sunday-school, and one bench with boarded back and shaped arms, late 18th-century.

Ivimey IV (1830) 434–5: Urwick (1884) 219.

CHESHAM

(24) GENERAL BAPTIST, Broadway (SP 959017). A section of the Berkhamsted (Herts.) General Baptist church built a meeting-house in Chesham in 1712 known as the 'Star Meeting-house' which was enlarged in 1735 and 1835. The present chapel of 1901–2 is by J. Wallis Chapman.

B. Hbk (1902) 349–50: *Broadway Baptist Church, 1706–1956* [1956]: Taylor (1818) I, 229–31, 327 & II, 440–6: Wood (1847) 207.

(25) PARTICULAR BAPTIST, Red Lion Street (SP 960014). The Lower Meeting, formed in 1701 and a branch of the Hemel Hempstead (Herts.) church until 1707, occupied a meeting-

house on a concealed site behind buildings on the E side of the street. This was replaced in 1897 on an extension of the former site by the present chapel, latterly named 'Hinton', a Gothic building of brick by John Wills of Derby. Reset in the back wall are several bricks inscribed with names and the date 1797 from the former building.

B. Hbk (1898) 328–9: Webb, A.E. & Baines, A.H.J., *Hinton Baptist Church, Chesham; 250 Years of Baptist Witness* [*c*.1951].

(26) CONGREGATIONAL, Broadway (SP 961018). A congregation meeting in the early 18th century under the ministry of the Presbyterian Isaac Robinson appears to have adopted Independency under his successor William King. A new meeting-house

was built in 1724 which remained, although enlarged *c*.1820, until replaced in 1885–6 by the present Gothic building of flint with brick and stone dressings, designed by W.G. Habershon and Fawkner. (URC)

Fittings – *Clock*: given in 1727, now at Great Horwood, Bucks, see (37) below. *Monuments*: in chapel (1) Rev. John Hall, 1839; in schoolroom (2) John Graveney, 1818, and Margaret his wife, 1807; externally at rear (3) Rev. William Miller, 1830, and Philippa his widow, 1841; (4) Mrs Elizabeth Undey, 1796, Robert Earle, 1802, and Rev. H.B. Lees, 1850. *Plate*: includes a pair of cups, 1774, given by Mrs Ann Skottowe.

CYB (1886) 222–3: Summers (1905) 39–44.

(27) FRIENDS, Bellingdon Road (SP 959019). A meeting in existence by 1672 was held at various places including 'part of John How's house, in Chesham' which was registered in 1689. The place of meeting during the 18th century is not known, but a separate burial-ground had been provided at the present site by 1796, in which year it was agreed to build a new meeting-house on adjacent land then belonging to Thomas White. The building was reported to be well advanced early in 1798 and was completed by the spring of 1800. The building accounts survive and show a total cost of £455 1s.7¼d. including carpenters' bills of £258 12s. 6d. and bricklayers' bills of £137 2s. 4d. The porch was rebuilt and minor rooms added to the S in 1964.

The meeting-house has brick walls and a hipped tiled roof, segmental-arched windows with hung sashes and a brick dentil eaves cornice. The brickwork of the front S wall is in Flemish bond but elsewhere is in English bond with some glazed headers.

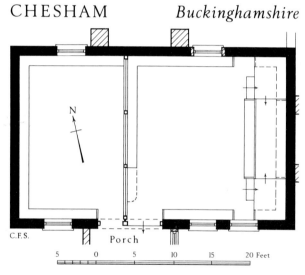

Friends' Meeting-house,
CHESHAM   *Buckinghamshire*

C.F.S.   Porch

5 0 5 10 15 20 Feet

The interior (34½ft by 20½ft) is divided into two rooms by a screen with three pairs of counter-weighted shutters. The principal room to the E has a stand at the E end with plain panelled front and fixed seat with shaped ends. Both rooms have wall-benches and are lined with a dado of plain panelling. The two doorways inside the porch have a late 18th-century frame and flush panelled doors.

Inscriptions on bricks in outer walls, initials and dates including: N wall at E end 'JP 1776', 'M.P.'; E wall S end '1796'; S wall E of porch, '·1·7·9·7', and built into modern porch four bricks one with 'M.P. 1806' perhaps the date of the former porch. *Monuments*: in burial-ground, some loose, flat rectangular stones with chamfered corners, from 1842.

Snell (1937).

CHOLESBURY-CUM-ST-LEONARDS

(28) BAPTIST, Buckland Common (SP 922072). Mid 19th-century front of flint with brick diaper.

CUBLINGTON

(29) WESLEYAN (SP 839222). Brick and slate with low-pitched gabled front of three bays. Dated 1850.

CUDDINGTON

(30) BAPTIST, Dadbrook (SP 739110). A General Baptist church of mid 17th-century origin based on Cuddington, later removed to Ford (see (33) below). The present chapel was built *c*.1831.

DATCHET   *Berkshire*

(31) Former BAPTIST, High Street (SU 987770). On E side of road N of level crossing; built 1841 for a church formed 1801 apparently at the house of the Duchess of Buccleuch which was registered as a Baptist meeting-house in that year. Refronted and converted to three shops after 1955. Former date-tablet, loose and broken, at rear of present chapel in London Road (SU 992772).

DENHAM

(32) WESLEYAN (TQ 040867). Small late 18th-century cottage, formerly part of a short terrace, is of brick and tile with remains of two stories of windows in the front wall, replaced by two round-arched chapel windows with entrance between in later porch. Perhaps converted *c*.1828 (in which year the house of John House, wheelwright, was registered for Wesleyans), although dated 1820 on a late 19th-century tablet.

Denham Methodist Church, 1820–1970 [n.d.].

DINTON-WITH-FORD AND UPTON

(33) GENERAL BAPTIST, Ford (SP 776092). 'The Church of Cuddington', as it was known in the 17th century, is first heard of in 1669 when Clement Hunt and William Bate of Dinton were reported to be 'teachers' and a conventicle was held in the

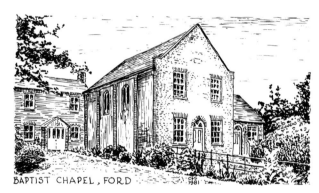

BAPTIST CHAPEL, FORD   1981

latter's house. Many preaching stations in the locality served by this church are mentioned in the earliest church book and it was not until 1716 that the principal activity became centred on Ford in the 'new built house of John Hunt' which was registered in July of that year. Although no certain evidence remains of this structure it may have been built of wichert and an undated, possibly mid 18th-century, account inserted into the church book 'for Repairs of the House' totalling £5 18s. 5d. includes the item 'paid for youlming nailess & spicks and hemp & diging of Whitch 5s. 3d'. A decline in support in the late 18th century resulting in a period of use by Particular Baptists was followed by a revival in interest and in 1818 by membership of the General Baptist New Connexion. Wood (1847) refers to an enlargement of the building in 1829 and it is said elsewhere to have been 'considerably enlarged' in 1852. It was largely refitted in 1884.

The chapel has walls of mixed materials, partly rendered, and a tiled roof half hipped to the rear. The lower part of the rear SE wall which may be wichert and parts of the NE side, possibly of rubble beneath the rendering, date from the 18th century, but the front bay and the upper parts of the walls are enlargements of the following century. A late 19th-century Sunday-school with slate roof stands against the SW side. The NW front is gabled, of Flemish bond brickwork with glazed headers and has a central doorway with fanlight and two tiers of sash windows. The NE side, divided into four bays by 19th-century brick pilasters, has two round-arched windows with Y-tracery. Two plain windows in the rear wall flank the pulpit.

The interior (35ft by 17¾ft) has a NW gallery with early 19th-century seating. The heightened side walls have thin panels of brickwork between strengthening pilasters.

Monuments: in chapel (1) Rev. William Hood, 1886, 46 years pastor, and Eliza his wife, 1874; SW of chapel (2) William Poole, 1834, and Ann, daughter of William and Elizabeth Poole, 1833.

B. Hbk (1877) 111–12: Whitley (1912): Wood (1847) 210.

DRAYTON PARSLOW

(34) BAPTIST, Chapel Lane (SP 839285). Built 1830, front bay 1883.

(35) Former PRIMITIVE METHODIST (SP 842288). Built 1847; date-tablet, replaced after erection of present chapel in 1912, now reads 'Carrington Hall, 1913'.

EDLESBOROUGH

(36) WESLEYAN (SP 974197). Purple brick with yellow brick dressings and slate roof; octagonal corner buttresses to gabled front formerly with pinnacles, lancet windows with cast-iron frames; built 1858. Original rostrum pulpit between front entrances with vestry behind, gallery opposite with screens to schoolroom beneath; box-pews.

GREAT HORWOOD

(37) CONGREGATIONAL (SP 772313). A Sunday-school commenced *c.*1819 by John Adey of Winslow led to the formation of an adult congregation for the increased needs of which a barn was fitted up 'as a school house and a place of worship', registered 24 March and opened 10 April 1821. A gallery was added two years later. A church was formed 13 February 1823 and Adey was formally instituted as pastor in the following year.

The chapel, built as a barn in the 18th century, has brick walls and a tiled roof. The original barn entrances remain visible in the N and S walls, the latter, with a segmental-arched brick head, is flanked by two tiers of rectangular ventilating slits; similar slits in the end walls and blocked doorways in the gables are also visible. When the barn was converted the N wall was partly rebuilt and a narrower doorway with wooden-columned porch replaced the principal entrance, pointed-arched windows were cut through the walls without the use of structural arches, and a rectangular window was inserted at the E end at the back of the gallery. The roof is supported by two trusses with double collar-beams and braces and clasped purlins; the ceiling is boarded.

The interior retains its original seating with shaped ends to open benches; the gallery seats have open backs, the ends of two of which rise to slender posts serving as candle sconces. The E gallery has a plain panelled front. Other fittings include – *Clock*: on gallery front, early 19th-century enamelled face, early 18th-century mechanism formerly belonging to the Independent

Congregational Chapel, GREAT HORWOOD
Buckinghamshire

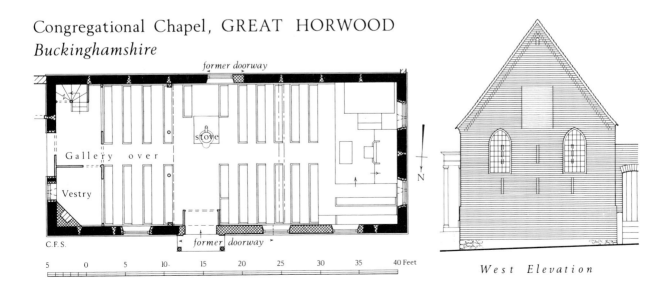

West Elevation

N front.

Interior from E.
(37) GREAT HORWOOD. Congregational chapel.

congregation in Chesham (26), inscribed 'A gift to the Congregat^n that was under the Care of the late Revd. Mr Isaac Robinson and is now Entrusted with Mr King presented by their hearty Wellwisher, Chesham March ye 7th 1727'; added later are the names of Thomas Jordan, Chas. Osborn, and the note 'Chesham for the Indepe't Chapel Great How'd Repaired Sept 4th 1823 John Adey'. *Pulpit*: panelled front with fluted corners, *c.*1821. *Table*: in vestry, small and plain with two legs and floor bearers, perhaps the former communion table.

   CYB (1971) 300–1: *NBAP* (1820) 14–15, (1821) 13–21, (1823) 18, (1824) 14, (1827) 17–18.

GREAT LINFORD

(38) Former CONGREGATIONAL (SP 853419). Three-bay front, dated 1833.

GREAT MISSENDEN

(39) BAPTIST, High Street (SP 894013). The chapel, set back behind other buildings on the W side of the street, was built 1838 for a church formed in 1778. The front wall, rendered in stucco, has a recessed, central entrance flanked by narrow gallery staircases behind the blind end-bays. Each side wall, of flint with brick dressings, has two windows to the chapel and one to a room at the back. The interior, now largely refitted, has a curved E wall behind the pulpit and a segmental gallery opposite with original cast-iron balustraded front.

(39) GREAT MISSENDEN. Baptist chapel.

HADDENHAM

(40) BAPTIST (SP 740086). A Particular Baptist church existed in Haddenham in 1655 in which year it sent representatives to a meeting of the Abingdon Association. The meeting-house was burnt down in 1701 but the congregation continued to meet and in 1734 the present site was acquired and a small chapel built; by 1773 the chapel appears to have closed and it was allowed to fall into decay. A fresh start was made and a house registered in 1799,

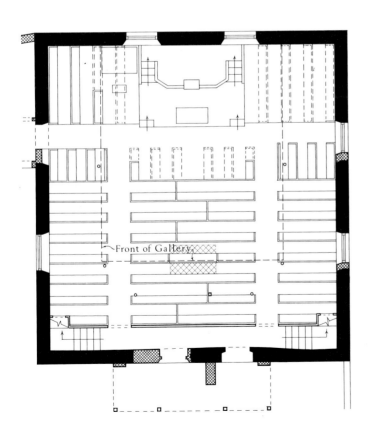

Front of Gallery

Baptist Chapel

HADDENHAM

Buckinghamshire

N

Scale of Feet

5   0   5   10   15   20   25

E side from burial-ground.

and in 1809 the existing chapel was built on the site of its predecessor.

The chapel is an almost square structure with rendered walls of wichert and a slate roof. The S front is gabled and has two entrances, that to the W re-sited closer to the other, and altered round-arched windows above. Two tiers of windows in the E wall have also been altered but one of the lower windows in the W wall retains its original proportions.

The interior (38¼ft by 36¾ft) has a plaster ceiling with a wide cove along the E and W sides. The S gallery is original and has a panelled front with applied pointed-arched ornament; side galleries were added soon after 1812 for the use of the Sunday-school children and have panelled fronts similar to the S gallery but lower, and contemporary seating with shaped ends and low backs. Other seating is of the late 19th century, the pulpit was replaced *c.*1948.

Fittings – *Chair*: formerley in pulpit, comb-back Windsor chair, top of back ?removed, late 18th-century. *Communion Table*: with turned legs and cusped arched pendants to upper rail, early 19th-century. *Inscription*: over E doorway in S wall, 'BUILT NOV. 1ST 1809 P.T.'. *Monuments*: in chapel (1) Rev. Peter Tyler, 1859, 'nearly 50 years pastor'; S of chapel (2) Peter Tyler, 1859, headstone in railed enclosure; (3) Jane, wife of John Tyler, 1813; (4) Hannah, wife of P. Tyler, 1819; (5) fragment of headstone with Corinthian pilasters and cherub's head below curved pediment. In burial-ground to E on opposite side of lane (6) William Duncombe, who 'gave this piece of land in 1832 for a burying place for Nonconformists who at that time were not allowed Christian burial in the churchyard', erected 1891. *Painting*: in vestry, portrait in oils by J. Forster of Rev. Peter Tyler, presented to him 18 February 1839; list of subscribers and bill for 4 gns, frame 2 gns and carriage 5s. pasted on back. *Plate*: includes a two-handled gadrooned cup of 1714.

(41) FRIENDS' BURIAL-GROUND (SP 742089). 'A poor cottage' near this site was used for meetings *c.*1710–1813. The surviving burial-ground which in 1968 was a small enclosure about 8 yards by 13 yards has since been entirely altered. Several reset monuments include a modern memorial to Edward Rose, 1704, Jane his wife, 1694, and others.

(42) WESLEYAN, High Street (SP 740085). Rendered walls of wichert partly faced at the front in rubble with brick dressings, and a slate roof. Gabled front of three bays with two tiers of round-arched windows, unusually tall lower windows and central doorway with fanlight. Tablet dated 1822. Small 'Wesleyan School' behind of 1842.

Dolbey (1964) 173–4.

HAMBLEDEN

(43) CONGREGATIONAL, Pheasant's Hill (SU 784874). 'Salem Chapel' was registered for Independents on 8 September 1807. The front wall is of brick, the sides of flint with brick dressings and the roof is slated. The gabled front of three bays formerly had two tiers of segmental-arched windows, now replaced by two wide pointed-arched windows, and a central doorway. The side wall facing the burial-ground has also been refenestrated and formerly had windows only in the rear bay which, before major alterations and refitting in the late 19th century, may have contained separate accommodation of two stories. (URC)

Summers (1905) 111–14.

(44) Former CONGREGATIONAL, Skirmett (SU 776902). Built 1824, now village hall.

Summers (1905) 112, 114.

HANSLOPE

(45) Former BAPTIST, Gold Street (SP 804468). The chapel, now used by Brethren, was built in 1809 for a church probably of high Calvinist persuasion which had ceased to meet by 1939. The walls are of coursed rubble with gabled sides and the roof is slated. The SW front of three bays with round-arched openings has a small date-tablet with chamfered cornice above the central entrance.

Fittings – *Monuments*: in chapel (1) Thomas Hindes, 1844, 'founder of the cause of God in this place' and donor of the present site, and Hannah his widow, 1859; (2) Emma Hindes, 1841, daughter of Richard and Mary Latimer, and three infants, marble tablet signed G. Wills, Blisworth. *Pulpit*: opposite entrance, rostrum incorporating early 19th-century fielded panels.

(46) BAPTIST, Long Street (SP 795478). Built 1845.

(47) WESLEYAN (SP 803469). Built 1828.

HIGH WYCOMBE

(48) TRINITY CHAPEL, Easton Street, High Wycombe (SU 871928). A Presbyterian congregation formed in the late 17th century, which later became Congregational, built a meeting-house in 1714 on the W side of Crendon Street 'at the North end, adjoining to the Charity Houses on the South' later described as 'an old fashioned building with gabled roofs and low ceiling, supported by four pillars'. In 1807 a major secession occurred led by the minister, and separate meetings were commenced in 'Ebenezer Chapel', a mediaeval building close to the grammar school, presumably part of the Hospital of St John the Baptist (see RCHM *Buckinghamshire* I (1912) 197). Trinity Chapel, built for this congregation in 1850 (the two churches reunited here in 1883), was designed by Charles Gray Searle. The S front, of squared rubble, is in the Romanesque style with

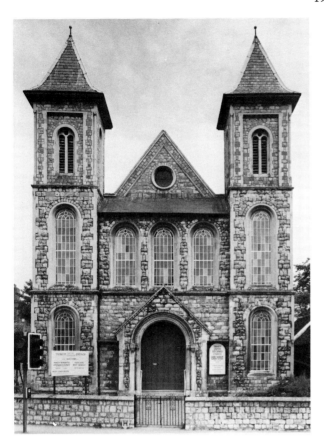

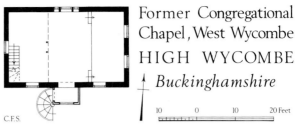

Former Congregational
Chapel, West Wycombe
HIGH WYCOMBE
Buckinghamshire

C.F.S.

10   0   10   20 Feet

The front faces S; a tripartite window lights the N side. *Inscriptions*: on bricks in S wall, initials and date 1808.
    Summers (1905) 100.

(50) Former WESLEYAN, West Wycombe (SU 831947). In lane off N side of main road. Flint with brick dressings and hipped tiled roof. The E front has a brick dentil eaves cornice. *Inscriptions*: on tile, centrally in front wall, 'I.BIGG/MASON 1815',

E front.

also on jambs of centre window and on quoins at N corner, date 1815 and names and initials. Superseded by present chapel, 100 yards E, in 1894, subsequently used as a workshop and latterly by Christadelphians.

ICKFORD

(51) Former BAPTIST (SP 650073). Rubble with half-hipped roof; built in the early 19th century for a church formed in 1825. The original entrance was at the E end, two sash windows faced the road. Now a cottage.

pyramidally roofed corner-towers and a gabled centre bay. The side walls are of brick and the roof is slated. (URC)
    CYB (1866) 309; (1882) 302: Summers (1905) 89–100.

(49) Former CONGREGATIONAL, West Wycombe (SU 830947). Concealed behind houses on the N side of the main road, the 'new meeting-house' registered for Independents 23 July 1808 has walls of flint with red brick dressings and a hipped tiled roof.

IVER

(52) STRICT BAPTIST, High Street, Colnbrook (TQ 026772). The chapel built in 1871–2 for a church formed in 1708 stands on the site of a meeting-house erected in 1754–5 on a former orchard behind the Swan Inn. The walls are of red brick with yellow brick and stone dressings, the front has a pediment with brick dentil cornices, two tall round-arched windows and a central doorway. In the upper schoolroom is an 18th-century painted wooden *chest* of three drawers with cupboard above, the door panels inscribed alternately in *Hebrew* and English '*I am the Lord thy God* which brought thee out of the land of Egypt out of the house of Bondage. *Thou shalt have no other Gods before me*' (Exodus xx.2–3). The inscription, which is ascribed to Alexander Cruden the concordancer, may refer to his release from a brief confinement at Chelsea in 1753 when he is believed to have stayed with his sister, Mrs Wild, of Middle Green, Langley.

Monuments: in chapel (1) William Rayner, 1839, Martha his wife, 1838, and his brothers Thomas, 1821, and Joseph, 1846; in burial-ground behind chapel, monuments of early 19th century and later include (2) Sarah, wife of Thomas Hanks, 1804, and two children; (3) Sophia Coleman, 1845, wife of William Coleman, pastor; (4) Rev. John Lloyd, 1801, six years pastor; (5) John Kimber, Ann his wife, and Mary their daughter, all 1802.

Kerridge, D.J., 'Our History', *Colnbrook Strict Baptist Chapel Newsletter*, nos 2–4 (1974–5).

(53) BAPTIST, West Square, Iver (TQ 036812). The small chapel occupies one half of a timber-framed, formerly weatherboarded, barn of the early 18th century, converted in the mid 19th century for an un-named denomination and the SE front rebuilt in stock brick. The NE end, rendered and altered at the front, now forms a cottage of one storey and attics.

IVINGHOE

(54) STRICT BAPTIST, Station Road (SP 944163). The Particular Baptist church formed in 1804 was gathered by George Clark, a 'tammy weaver' from Braunstone, Northants., later a 'navigator' on canal construction work near Tring, who became the first pastor. 'The dwelling house of William Watts . . . with the garden, and a piece of orchard on which to build a Meeting House and have a Burying Ground . . .' was bought 3 May 1813, the house of William Watts was registered 15 July 1813, and the chapel was opened 21 July 1813, the cost being met in part by donations and the balance paid for by fifty persons who each agreed to subscribe a penny a week. It was enlarged to the S in 1866 by the addition of a vestry and schoolroom.

The walls are of brick and the roof, originally slated, was re-covered in 1976 in dark concrete tiles. The wide W front is of three bays with two tiers of sash windows and a rendered porch of *c*.1830 with moulded stucco cornice and round-arched doorway with fanlight. The E wall has three upper windows, one centrally above the pulpit, and two taller intermediate windows at a lower level. The N end is covered by an early 19th-century cottage and the S end by the two-storied extension of 1866. The interior (24½ft by 42¼ft) has a gallery around three sides added *c*.1832 with plain panelled front supported by thin cast-iron columns; contemporary plain box-pews with numbered backs remain in the N gallery.

Fittings – Clock: on front of S gallery, reverse side of face is inscribed 'T.CLEMENT/TRING/Made in the Year 1816'. *Inscription*: on bricks at N end of W wall, 'WC + 1815', '1815 SP'. *Monuments*: in chapel (1) William Price, 1856, and Mary his wife, 1840; (2) William Collyer, 1879, pastor; in burial-ground (3) George Clark, 1831, 27 years pastor; (4) William Collyer, 1879, 48 years pastor, and Mary, his wife, 1895. *Pulpit*: against E wall, square panelled box with splayed front corners, supported by two tall thin wooden columns, early 19th-century.

[Collyer, W.], *The Everlasting Union of Christ and His Saints* (1832), funeral sermon including memoir of George Clark.

(55) Former WESLEYAN, Ivinghoe Aston (SP 952182). Dated 1831. Now a house.

LACY GREEN

(56) BAPTIST, Speen (SU 844998). 'Salem Chapel' was built in 1802 by Joseph Gibbons of Speen for a congregation gathered by preachers from Princes Risborough. A Particular Baptist church was formed in 1813. The chapel was enlarged to the E in 1817, principally to provide a vestry, and to the N in 1834. The walls are of flint rubble with brick dressings to the later parts only; the

roof is tiled and has a central valley. The original S front is symmetrical; the N wall, of 1834, has two round-arched windows flanking the pulpit and two tiers of windows at the E end.

The interior has a gallery around three sides; the roof is supported by three tall posts on the line of the original N wall.

Fittings – Inscriptions: on brick over SE doorway, 'T.G. 1817', other initials and this date on E jamb of doorway, at S corner, and in E wall. On N wall between main windows, stone tablet '18 T.A. 34' and tablet on N half of E wall 'J + T'. *Monuments*: in burial-ground opened 1838 and later enlarged, include two wooden 'leaping-boards' of 1878 and 1884 and head and foot-stones to the sculptor Eric Gill, 1940, and Mary Ethel his widow, 1961, carved by himself.

LITTLE BRICKHILL

(57) Former WESLEYAN (SP 909324). Gabled three-bay front, dated 1819.

LITTLE MISSENDEN

(58) BAPTIST, Little Kingshill (SU 894989). Built 1812. Flint with brick dressings. Much altered, and extended at ends.

LONG CRENDON

(59) BAPTIST (SP 696088). Built 1853. Brick and slate. Gabled front; central doorway with Tuscan pilasters and pediment.

LONGWICK-CUM-ILMER

(60) THE LITTLE CHAPEL, Longwick (SP 787050). The chapel, described in the trust deed of 13 November 1810 as 'lately erected', was not denominationally restricted although commonly regarded as Baptist and with two ministers of that denomination as trustees – John Hester of Princes Risborough and Peter Tyler of Haddenham. The building is small and set far back from the road; the walls are of coursed rubble with brick quoins and dressings and the roof is hipped and tiled. The NE

The Little Chapel, Longwick
LONGWICK-cum-ILMER
Buckinghamshire

front has a central entrance between two segmental-arched windows and a circular window above; there are two similar windows in the rear wall and in each end wall is a window set high up below the eaves. The interior, partly refitted in the late 19th century and later, has a gallery to the SE and an early 19th-century pulpit opposite with coved and moulded cornice.

MARLOW URBAN

(61) CONGREGATIONAL, Marlow (SU 846865). 'Salem Chapel' was built 1838–40 to the designs of James Fenton of Chelmsford for a church (now URC) formed in 1777. The former chapel which stood to the SE had been built in 1726 by a Presbyterian society originating about 1692 but which had ceased to meet by

the mid 18th century. The present chapel has walls of red brick with a facing of yellow brick to the front. The pedimented SE front is of three bays with two tiers of rectangular windows and a central doorway between paired pilasters. The interior, largely refitted in the late 19th century, has a rear gallery with children's seating divided and each half accessible separately from two staircases. There are Sunday-school rooms below the chapel.

Fittings – *Benefaction Tablet*: on SW wall, recording gift of the ground for the present chapel by Col. Sir William Clayton Bart., M.P. for Marlow, 1838. *Monument*: in chapel on NE wall, to Daniel Humphreys and Sarah his wife, 1827.

RB XV (1947) 15; Summers (1905) 54–8.

MARSH GIBBON

(62) CONGREGATIONAL (SP 643229). Built 1853, contemporary open-backed benches with turned supports below arm rests. (Demolished since 1975)

MENTMORE

(63) BAPTIST, Ledburn (SP 905220). Dated 1840.

MOULSOE

(64) WESLEYAN (SP 911420). A low timber-framed range with thatched roof hipped to the W, built in the early 19th century,

WESLEYAN CHAPEL, MOULSOE

probably as cottages, and converted to a mission-hall in the late 19th century. An E gable and window added. (Demolished for road improvements since 1972)

NASH

(65) STRICT BAPTIST (SP 781344). A date of 1798 is claimed for the church meeting here which may be of Independent origin. The chapel which dates from the early 19th century was built by John King whose house was licensed for worship in 1823.

The walls are of brickwork in English bond and the roof is slated. The S wall facing a lane is blank; two windows with segmental-arched heads face N over the burial-ground and a similar but taller window in the E wall is set above the entrance. A lean-to vestry at the W end dates from the mid 19th century. In the late 19th century an E porch was added and the interior refitted.

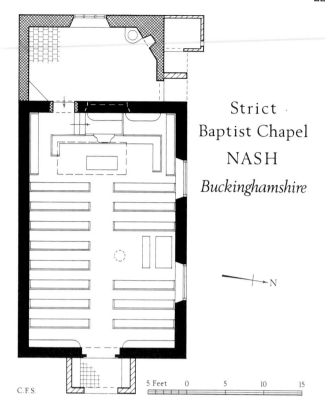

Strict
Baptist Chapel
NASH
Buckinghamshire

← N

5 Feet 0 5 10 15

C.F.S.

Monument: in chapel, over vestry door, to John King 'who died April 18th 1836 Aged 81. The chapel built on his premises he invested in the hands of trustees and by his will directed 700 pounds for the support of the Gospel in this his native place. Tho's Knighton, Jos'ph Stuchbery, Exors.'.

NBAP (1825) 15.

NEWPORT PAGNELL

(66) BAPTIST, High Street (SP 875438). A cottage of two bays W of the Rectory was converted for use as a meeting-house in 1717; a schoolroom was built on the forecourt in 1861. These buildings were demolished *c*.1960–5 and no reliable description has been found.

Bull (1900) 150–3.

(67) CONGREGATIONAL, High Street (SP 876438). The formerly Presbyterian congregation (now URC) originated with the ejection in 1662 of the vicar, Rev. John Gibbs, who in 1672 took out a licence as a Presbyterian preacher. A meeting-house said to have been 40ft square externally was built *c*.1700 and side galleries added in 1725. This was rebuilt in 1805–6, considerably enlarged in 1808, extended to the front in 1819 and to the rear in 1826–7. It was almost entirely demolished in 1880 and the present Gothic chapel by John Sulman built on the NW part of the site was opened in 1881.

A narrow rear extension dated 1826, of two stories with a schoolroom above vestries, remains freestanding behind the chapel; it has brick walls with a wide pedimented elevation to the SE of five bays with a former central entrance, a row of five

round-arched windows above a platband, and a blind lunette above. Several wall monuments, much decayed, have been reset externally. Some earlier masonry remains in the NW wall.

A nonconformist academy which flourished 1783–1850 was conducted in a house facing the High Street.

Bull (1900) 138–49: *CHST* IV (1909–10) 260–71, 305–22: *CYB* (1881) 464; (1887) 177–8: Ivimey II (1814) 79–86: Martin, R.G., *The Story of the Congregational Church, Newport Pagnell* [1960].

(68) Former FRIENDS, Silver Street (SP 87624380). Built 1863 on site of a skittle alley behind a former inn; sold 1929, now Pentecostal.

(69) WESLEYAN, High Street (SP 875439). Red brick front with oval tablet dated 1815. Original gallery at entrance otherwise refitted.

NORTH CRAWLEY

(70) Former CONGREGATIONAL (SP 928447). Brick and slate, blind circle above central doorway and oval tablet in pediment dated 1821. Interior square with arcaded side walls and rear gallery with original open-backed benches. (Closed *c*.1968, now converted to a house)

CONGREGATIONAL CHAPEL, NORTH CRAWLEY

OLNEY

(71) BAPTIST (SP 889513). The church, with which the name of John Sutcliff (pastor 1755–1814) is particularly associated and which is further notable for the ordination of the missionary William Carey, originated in the late 17th century when it appears to have included a considerable Independent element. The present chapel, largely rebuilt in 1893, has stone walls and a slate roof. The E front is entirely of this date but earlier masonry remains in the N wall and in the lower courses of the S side which was the original front of the building. Two date-stones reset in the S wall, of 1694 and 1763, relate to earlier structures.

Exterior from SW, before 1893.

Prior to the rebuilding the S wall was of eight bays with two tiers of windows, the two bays to the W probably being an enlargement of *c*.1800 and the remaining six bays with entrances in the end bays constituted the front of the 1763 meeting-house, with the tablet of that date centrally between the upper windows. The 1694 tablet may derive from a former meeting-house on this site. The surviving older masonry of the N wall confirms the secondary character of the W bays, to the E of which is a blocked doorway and below the cill of an upper window the date 1799. Until 1893 there was a pulpit with pedimented back

Interior from SE, before 1893.

centrally against the longer N wall and deep galleries at the E and W ends.

Fittings – *Inscriptions*: on S wall, tablets inscribed '1694', 'Enlarged 1763', 'Restored 1893'; on re-used stones in W wall 'IT 1763', 'HI', and on SW corner 'W.A'. *Monuments*: in chapel (1) John Sutcliff A.M., 1814, 39 years minister, white marble tablet with urn in low relief, on grey marble backing, signed 'Jno Barlow fecit, London'; externally on S wall (2) Christiana, daughter of William and Elizabeth Andrews, 1840; in burial-ground S of chapel (3) Thomas Palmer, 1768, Hannah his wife, 1765, *et al.*, elaborate table-tomb with shaped and fluted domical top and finial, in railed enclosure.

BQ XXX (1983) 26–37: Hewett, M.F., History of Olney Baptist Meeting *c*.1930, typescript in chapel.

(72) CONGREGATIONAL (SP 890516). A separate congregation was formed in 1718 by Independents who had belonged since 1691 to the church in Wellingborough, Northants., becoming after 1732 a branch church of Yardley Hastings, Northants. The present Gothic 'Cooper Memorial' chapel of 1879–80 by John Sulman, gutted by fire *c*.1965 but since restored, stands on the site of a meeting-house dated 1762 which had been enlarged to the rear in 1806 and to the front in 1818. The front wall of this latter date was of rubble with a wide gable having a blind lunette comparable with (98) below. (URC)

CYB (1879) 404–5: [Garner, J.J.], *History of the Congregational Church at Olney* [1930].

PENN

(73) Site of BAPTIST, Beacon Hill (SU 909930). Chapel built 1808–9, demolished since 1935; site now a garden with small burial-ground to south. Wall footings remain.

PRINCES RISBOROUGH

(74) BAPTIST, Bell Street (SP 809032). A doctrinal secession from the General Baptist church of Ford or 'Cuddington' led to the establishment of a Particular Baptist meeting in Princess Risborough *c*.1701 and the erection of a meeting-house in 1707 which was placed in trust for 'Peculiar Baptists'. This was superseded in 1804–5 by the present building which was extended to the rear and internally rearranged in 1814. The galleries were enlarged and extended in 1833 and about 1871 a vestry was added and the interior reseated.

The chapel has walls of flint with brick dressings, rendered at front and rear, and a hipped slated roof. The wide NW front has two tiers of segmental-arched windows; the original entrance, now covered by a modern brick porch, was central to the three right-hand bays with a fourth bay to the left including a secondary entrance. The NW end wall has two tiers of windows replacing a pair of larger windows which prior to 1814 flanked the pulpit and are now re-sited at the SE end. The SE extension is narrower than the front and has two pointed-arched windows in the end wall.

The interior has early 19th-century galleries around three sides with rooms below the NE gallery and a former baptistery below the opposite gallery. The tops of the side galleries are each carved with large numerals 1–16 and the NW gallery had square slots for music stands. *Monuments*: in chapel (1) John Bowler, 1811, slate tablet with urn in low relief; (2) John Webb, 1801, and Sarah his widow, 1802.

A *former Presbyterian meeting-house* (behind the 'George and Dragon' p.h.), perhaps early 18th-century, was demolished *c.*1950-7.

Baines, A.H.J. *et al.*, *Princes Risborough Baptist Church; A Short History of the Church 1707-1957* [1957].

SEER GREEN

(75) Former BAPTIST (SU 966918). now parish church hall; brick and slate with gabled E front. Built 1829, but since altered and enlarged, it passed to Sunday-school use after a new chapel (now a house) was built opposite in 1899. Low annexe built against the N side 1933.

Inscriptions: on tablet in gable, now erased, 'BAPTIST SUNDAY SCHOOL 1841 RES'D 1933'; on bricks on S wall, various initials including '18 T. W 29'.

SHERINGTON

(76) CONGREGATIONAL (SP 891463). Services commenced in the late 18th century through the efforts of the minister at Newport Pagnell, Rev. William Bull, who is said to have fitted up a barn for this purpose about 1782. The present chapel, registered

6 September 1822, is of brick and slate. The N front, of three bays in Flemish bond with glazed headers and stone dressings, has a central doorway with blind circular window above and shaped tablet in the pediment inscribed 'SHERRINGTON CHAPEL 1822'; on each side is a lower two-storied cottage with a hipped roof. The interior, which has no gallery, was refitted in the late 19th century. (URC)

(77) Former FRIENDS, Water Lane (SP 885464). A meeting in existence by 1662 was supported by Richard Hunt, a plough-wright, and met on his premises in Water Lane which were registered in 1689. Meetings ceased by the late 18th century and the meeting-house was later reported to have been converted into three cottages. A long narrow building of stone with a slate roof, 15ft by 52ft externally, formerly three cottages but now forming part of Nos. 38 and 40 Water Lane may represent the former meeting-house; it has no datable features.

Bull (1900) 134: Chibnall A.C., *Sherington: Fiefs and Fields of a Buckinghamshire Village* (1965) 210, 213-5, 280.

SLOUGH   *Berkshire*

(78) CONGREGATIONAL, Church Street (SU 977797). Stock brick with stone dressings and slate roof, in Gothic style, built 1852-3. Triple-gabled front formerly surmounted by tall

CONGREGATIONAL CHAPEL, Church Street, SLOUGH

pinnacles, wide two-centred arch to centre bay with recessed entrance; gabled buttresses and lancet windows to side walls. (Demolished 1981)

Summers (1905) 61-4.

SOULBURY

(79) WESLEYAN, Chapel Hill (SP 883272). Opened 1831.

STEWKLEY

(80) WESLEYAN, Chapel Square (SP 850263). Built 1839, enlarged to front *c.*1870 and original date-tablet reset.

(81) PRIMITIVE METHODIST, High Street (SP 854255). Red brick with contrasting white stone dressings, corner turret with pyramidal spire; quatrefoil tracery in large central window. Architect T. Colbourne, 1903.

STOKENCHURCH

(82) PRIMITIVE METHODIST (SU 760962). Similar in materials and some general details to the foregoing and presumably by the

PRIMITIVE METHODIST CHAPEL, STOKENCHURCH

same architect; round-arched windows, plate-tracery to window above porch, iron finials to front gable. Dated 1896.

THE LEE

(83) PRIMITIVE METHODIST, Lee Common (SP 908041). Flint with brick banding, dated 1839. Later schoolroom in front.

THORNBOROUGH

(84) Former INDEPENDENT, Lower End (SP 740337). Dated 1829, much altered for agricultural use.

(85) Former WESLEYAN, Chapel Lane (SP 745337). At end of row of cottages; rubble with hipped slate roof, built 1832 by William King and superseded by new chapel 1903. Altered three-bay front with two stories of domestic windows and

defaced tablet; before conversion to a house the front doorway and windows had pointed-arched heads with keystones and imposts.

TWYFORD

(86) CONGREGATIONAL (SP 663263). Built 1897, former chapel of c.1850 adjacent. (URC)

WADDESDON

(87) STRICT BAPTIST, Waddesdon Hill (SP 753150). A church was formed c.1788 and the chapel built by Francis Cox was registered on 4 August 1792, his name and the year of erection being inscribed on a brick above the entrance. The first meeting of the Buckinghamshire Baptist Association was held here in 1811.

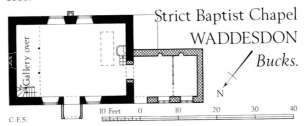

Strict Baptist Chapel
WADDESDON
Bucks.

The chapel stands on an isolated roadside site within a rectangular walled burial-ground. The walls are of flint rubble with brick dressings and some later rendering and the hipped roof is covered with tiles. A lower vestry was built at the SW end in the early 19th century and towards the end of that century a small porch was built over the main entrance and the interior partly rearranged. The NW front has a doorway between two plain sash windows, the sashes here and elsewhere probably superseding leaded casements which still survive in the vestry al-

(87) WADDESDON. Strict Baptist chapel.

though lacking their external shutters. The rear wall has two closely-set windows which flank the original site of the pulpit, and high in each end wall is a window to light a gallery.

The interior ($18\frac{1}{4}$ft by $28\frac{1}{2}$ft) has a gallery at the NE end with panelled front supported by two octagonal posts and contemporary seating. The pulpit, lowered and re-sited at the SW end with a baptistery in front, replaces a second gallery; the window above has been reduced in width. The vestry is divided by a wooden screen with removable shutters. The chapel roof has two original trusses with tie and collar-beams and framed purlins.

Monuments: in chapel, on SE wall (1) Rev. George Williams, 1828, 19 years pastor, oval tablet; in vestry (2) Francis Cox, 1803, and Esther his grand-daughter, 1803; (3) William Cox, 1844, and Olive his wife, 1836; (4) Francis Cox junior, 1831, and Olivia daughter of William and Catharine Cox, 1830; in burial-ground, headstones of early 19th century and later, also two wooden 'leaping-boards', one dated 1866.

(88) WESLEYAN, Waddesdon (SP 742169). Immediately NW of the present chapel of 1877, set back behind houses, is the former chapel of 1805, now the Sunday-school. Rubble walls with brick dressings and gabled roof covered with tiles; one round-arched window in E and W side walls, entrance at S end covered by extension.

Durley (1910) pl. opp. 14.

WENDOVER

(89) GENERAL BAPTIST, South Street (SP 869074). The church meeting in and about Cuddington in the late 17th century (see (33) above) included members from Wendover where the

Baptist Meeting-house,
WENDOVER   *Buckinghamshire*

North Elevation c.1770 (conjectural)

C.F.S.

5   0   5   10   15   20 Feet

provision of separate services is recorded in 1688 and later. The date at which the Wendover Baptists formed themselves into a church is not known, but it probably took place early in the 18th

century. Although a brief revival may have been experienced about 1770, by c.1796 the cause was very weak and meetings infrequent. Considerable congregations were gathered in the chapel c.1806–11 but this only resulted in the opening of a new Independent meeting-house and the re-awakening of the Baptist interest was left to a member of the Berkhamsted (Herts.) church, William Darvell, who became pastor c.1817.

The first chapel on the present site appears to have been 'a new erected building' registered as a meeting-house for Baptists in October 1735. Although this is said to have been enlarged 'before 1773' it seems more likely to have been rebuilt c.1770 and that work of this period forms the nucleus of the present building. This is of dark brick, heightened in the early 19th century and given a tiled roof gabled to E and W, but probably hipped originally. The N front is of three bays with central doorway and window above, now blocked, and two segmental-arched windows; two similar windows in the S wall set more closely together mark the former site of the pulpit. In 1833 the chapel was greatly enlarged to the W in yellow brick and slate and in 1883 the W front was rebuilt in white brick with red brick dressings and the gallery staircase rebuilt in a projection to the south. A Sunday-school at the E end built in 1894 stands on the site of a vestry of 1822.

The interior (originally $17\frac{1}{4}$ft by 28ft) was drastically refitted in 1883 and again in 1950 when also a larger porch was built at the W end. There is a W gallery. *Monument*: in chapel, to Mrs Mary Franklin, 1847, wooden tablet with painted inscription.

NBAP (1821) 11–13: Taylor (1818) II, 446: Wood (1847) 211.

WESTON TURVILLE

(90) UNION CHAPEL, School Lane (SP 854106). Baptist chapel, dated 1839; gabled front with small octagonal window above entrance. Sunday-school added at back in 1908.

(91) Site of FRIENDS (SP 861111). 'The Brills', a house on S side of road, timber-framed with a thatched roof, built in the 15th century, was the scene of Quaker meetings in the 17th century. In October 1689 a meeting-house certificate was issued for 'the orchard of George Brill's house' and a meeting-house believed to have stood S of the house existed until the early 19th century. A burial-ground 100 yards distant is also recorded.

Eland, G., 'A Meeting-place of the Early Quakers in Buckinghamshire', *RB* XI (1920–6) 11–24: RCHM *Buckinghamshire* I (1912) 316 (mon. 21) 'The Black Horse Inn': Snell (1937).

WEST WYCOMBE RURAL

(92) WESLEYAN, Moor Lane, Downley (SU 849953). Built 1824, greatly enlarged and original date-tablet reset.

WHITCHURCH

(93) WESLEYAN (SP 801209). Built 1844 replacing a chapel opened 1808; refronted.

Durley (1910) pl. opp. 22.

WING

(94) WESLEYAN, Church Street (SP 882226). Red brick and slate. Dated 1847.

WINGRAVE WITH ROWSHAM

(95) CONGREGATIONAL, Wingrave (SP 868189). Built 1832 for a church (now URC) formed in 1805. Brick walls, rendered W front and hipped slate roof. Two tiers of windows with renewed frames; round-arched doorway with fanlight and small date-tablet above. W gallery with a panelled front and applied mouldings, supported by two thin iron columns. Reseated late 19th century.

Fittings – *Bootscrapers*: pair, wrought-iron with single end standard. *Monuments*: in chapel (1) John Grace, 1844, 'one of the principal founders and supporters of this religious interest . . .'; (2) Jane, wife of Augustis (*sic*) Lines of Aston Abbots, 1826.

WINSLOW

(96) KEACH'S MEETING-HOUSE (SP 769274). A General Baptist church was in existence in Winslow by 1654 in which year John Hartnoll was sent as messenger to the General Assembly of that denomination. In 1658 Benjamin Keach, a native of Stoke Hammond, then aged 18, commenced preaching in this district. He associated particularly with the church in Winslow, remaining there, though suffering grave legal penalties in 1664 for preaching and publishing, until 1668 when he removed to London and adopted Calvinist views. The episcopal returns of 1669 list Baptist meetings in Winslow at the houses of Eliot, a carpenter, and Foster, a baker, with other meetings in the surrounding villages, at which the principal preachers were John Hartnoll, thatcher, of North Marston, and William Giles, shop-keeper. No licences were issued under the 1672 Indulgence but meetings presumably continued; meeting-house certificates were taken out in 1689 and 1693 perhaps for this congregation, and in 1690 the church was represented at a meeting of 'the five churches' of Buckinghamshire General Baptists, held at Bierton. References to the congregation continue until about 1777 when the minister, James Hall, following Keach's example of a century earlier, left the church 'having become a Calvinist'. Attendance then declined sharply and the church was dissolved. Sporadic preaching by visiting Baptist and Independent ministers continued and the Bedfordshire Union of Christians took an interest in the place *c.*1799 which resulted in the formation of an Independent cause in 1800, initially sharing in the use of the building. A revival of support for Baptist principles under the influence of visiting Calvinistic preachers led in 1807 to the formation of a Particular Baptist Church, the varied fortunes of which may be briefly stated – from a sudden short-lived influx of Independent seceders between 1827 and 1830, a secession 1838–40 which left the cause almost deserted, and a sudden revival 1847–9 under the ministry of a gifted foreman bricklayer, to another decline, re-formation of the church in 1862 and its extinction in the 20th century. An unsuccessful attempt to re-establish the cause was made in 1937.

The meeting-house, which stands concealed behind other property close to the cattle market, and variously described as in Pillar's Ditch, Bell Alley, or Market Walk, was built in 1695. A deed of 5 July 1696 refers to the building as 'lately erected and

North Elevation

Section aa

Keach's Meeting-house
WINSLOW
Buckinghamshire

N

Scale of Feet

5   0   5   10   15   20   25

Gallery over

C.F.S.

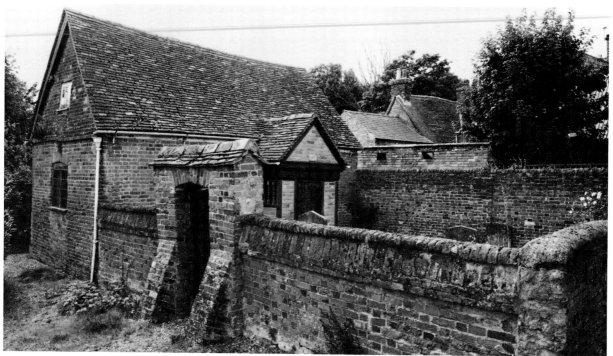

Exterior from NE.

Interior from E.
(96) WINSLOW. Keach's Meeting-house.

built, with the porch, courts, brick wall...commonly called...the Meeting house...standing next to a garden belonging to the dwelling house of the said Joseph Harding on the west end, and the barn of the said Samuel Norman (late Leaches) standing on the North side thereof and a close of the said William Gyles the elder on the South and East, on most of which said close the ground was lately taken upon which the said Meeting house and brick wall is erected...'.

The building is a small rectangular structure with walls of red brick in Flemish bond and a tiled roof gabled to E and west. The N front has two small rectangular windows with leaded glazing and external shutters; between them is a timber-framed porch with a moulded cornice and pulvinated frieze around three sides and gable to the N, the side walls have open upper panels with twisted balusters. Most of the porch woodwork was renewed c.1958. In the gable is a small stone tablet with recut or renewed inscription 'WMG/1695', for William and Mary Gyles. The S wall has two segmental-arched windows and a later brick buttress between. The E wall has a two-course brick platband below the gable, a segmental-arched window below, converted to a doorway c.1827 but now restored, and a small window inserted into the gable. The W wall has a similar platband cut across by two upper windows inserted in 1824 to light the pulpit; centrally below is a blocked window with flat soldier-arched head, probably of 1695.

The interior (23ft by 15¼ft) has been altered at various dates, and the fenestration appears to require the pulpit, now at the W end, to have been originally between the windows of the longer S wall; the present arrangement probably dates from the beginning of the 19th century. A gallery built at the E end in 1827 as a temporary measure to accommodate the influx of Independent seceders has an open cross-braced front supported by two posts replacing a central post, and a steep staircase to the north. The roof, ceiled at collar level and with straight wind-braces below clasped purlins, has a single truss E of centre supported by wall-posts and curved brackets; the removal of a tie-beam appears to be indicated by a minute of 26 October 1821: 'Our Meeting house underwent a Repair the Roof was stripd New Lathd and Retiled and the Large Beam which went across the Meeting was taken a way And Converted into Severall Purposes such as the Posts which are on Each Side of the Meeting the Window Lineings Pulpitt Stairs Back to table Pew and Box to put the Books in...'.

A small *burial-ground* on the N side of the meeting-house is surrounded by a brick boundary wall, that to the E being of the late 17th century with moulded brick coping and a central gateway with segmental-arched head.

Fittings – *Communion Table*: with turned baluster legs, 17th-century, drawer added early 19th century. *Monuments* and *Floorslabs*. *Monuments*: in chapel (1) William Yeulett, 1873, Baptist pastor at Eaton Bray; (2) Benjamin Keach, 1704 [erected 1962]; (3) George Whichello, 1915; in burial-ground (4) Dinah and Sarah Delafield, sisters, 1775. *Floorslabs*: (1) Sarah (Morley) widow of William Gyles, 1726; (2) Grace, daughter of Thomas and Grace Alldridge, 1726; (3) Sarah, 1728, and Dick, 1737, children of Thomas and Sarah Foster; (4) Martha (Norman)

widow of Thomas Burch, 1731, Samuel Norman, 1735, and Martha his widow, 1742; (5) Daniel Gyles senr., 1747, Mary his wife, 1734, and Frances Collier her sister, 1734, with later inscription to William Matthews, 1860, and Mary his wife, 1856. *Pulpit*: centrally at W end, square with plain panelled front and shelf with shaped brackets, c.1800. *Seating*: Box-pews N and S of pulpit flanking table-pew, c.1800, altered; open-backed benches at E end, early 19th-century; against E wall, desks with hinged tops and four lead ink-wells, for use of Sunday-school commenced 1824.

Arnold (1960) 107, 113, figs 19 & 20: Clear, A., *The Kings Village in Demesne or A Thousand Years of Winslow Life* (1894): Crosby II (1739) 185–209; III (1740) 143–4; IV (1740) 268–314: *NBAP* (1828) 20; (1829) 23–4: [Prickett, A.] *1695; or Old Winslow Chapel, Buckinghamshire* [c.1936]: RCHM *Buckinghamshire* II (1913) 341: Whitley (1912) 7.

WOBURN SANDS

(97) Former FRIENDS, Hogsty End (SP 928355). In 1672 Quakers bought a 'modest thatched house' on this site for use as a meeting-house. Photographs show it as a long, probably timber-framed, building with a tiled roof and a 17th-century brick chimney-stack at one end. This was replaced in 1901 by a gabled building of brick, closed 1947 and now used as a library. A small burial-ground at the back has monuments dating from 1801.

Architectural Review XCIX (April 1946) 109: Godber, J., *Friends in Bedfordshire and West Hertfordshire* (1975) pl. 1b: *The Friend*, 31 Dec. 1897 & 20 Dec. 1901.

WOLVERTON

(98) BAPTIST, Horsefair Green, Stony Stratford (SP 788403). The chapel was built in 1823 for a church formed in 1657. The walls are of brick with stone dressings and the roof is slated. The

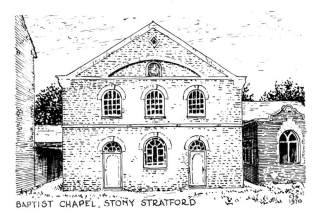

BAPTIST CHAPEL, STONY STRATFORD
Front before alteration.

SE front, of red brick with yellow brick headers, is partly obscured by a wide porch erected since 1970. The side walls have been refenestrated and the interior largely refitted.

(99) CONGREGATIONAL, Wolverton Road, Stony Stratford (SP 789404). A congregation initially gathered by students of New-

CONGREGATIONAL CHAPEL, STONY STRATFORD

port Pagnell Academy was formed into a church October 1815 and the present chapel of brick and slate opened June 1823.

(100) WESLEYAN, Silver Street, Stony Stratford (SP 787403). Opened 1844.

WOOBURN

(101) STRICT BAPTIST, Wycomb Lane, Wooburn Green (SU 913887). Small with three-bay gabled front; built 1836.

(102) CONGREGATIONAL, Cores End (SU 903873). A palace of the Bishops of Lincoln, notorious for the imprisonment there in the early 16th century of Lollards from Amersham and Chesham, became in 1658 the principal seat of Philip fourth Lord Wharton. Here, after the Restoration, shelter was given to various eminent nonconformist divines and in 1690 a meeting-house certificate was taken out for the building. Subsequent registrations of houses in Wooburn point to a continuance of dissent throughout the 18th century, although the present church only originated in 1768 with the preaching of Thomas Grove who had been expelled from Oxford for engaging in methodistical practices.

The present chapel built in 1804 to replace one of 1781 was extended to the front and refitted in 1881. Schoolrooms at the rear were built c.1860. The chapel has brick walls with rendered dressings at the front and a slate roof. The NW front has a pediment over three bays, the lower entablature being broken at the centre by a wide round-arched window above a gabled porch; the bays are divided by Corinthian pilasters paired at the ends, the latter surmounted by short parapets with ball finials. The sides were originally of three bays and the former front wall had two tiers of round-arched windows below a pediment.

Fittings – *Inscriptions*: below front windows, two oval tablets (1) inscribed 'BETHEL The original House and ground were given by the Rev. T. GROVE. 1768. The Chapel was Taken down and rebuilt by public Subscription 1804'; (2) recording the enlargement and reseating in 1881; set in boundary wall SE of chapel, tablet inscribed 'This wall is part of the barn in which the founder of the church the Rev. T. Groves first held services 1768'. *Monuments*: in chapel (1) Thomas English, 1809, 31 years pastor, Mary his wife, 1794, and Elizabeth Sneath, her sister, 1800; (2) Rev. Samuel Weston, 1856, 24 years minister, and Mary his widow, 1857; (3) Rev. Joshua Harrison, 1831, and Mary his wife, 1831; inside front porch (4) Thomas Bennett, 1802, and Elizabeth his widow, 1806; externally against SE wall (5) Ann East 179[ ], Ann, daughter of William and Mary East, 1795, and Mary Poole, 1795.

Dale, B., *The Good Lord Wharton* (1906) 75–6, 83: *RB* IV (1871–7) 20: Summers (1905) 81–9.

(102) WOOBURN. Congregational chapel, before 1881. Late 19th-century print.

Although nonconformist congregations existed in many towns in the county by the end of the 17th century the most notable evidence of early dissent is to be found in the Peak district where William Bagshawe, the ejected vicar of Glossop, exercised an itinerant ministry, encouraging the formation of separate societies such as Bradwell (24), Chinley (43) and Great Hucklow (77), and earning for himself the title of 'The Apostle of the Peak'. Of the meeting-houses subsequently erected for these congregations, that at Chinley, of 1711, is particularly remarkable for the completeness of its fittings and for some resemblance to the slightly earlier Cheshire group of chapels at Knutsford, Macclesfield and Dean Row. Chesterfield (39) and Derby (51) possessed two large and impressive town chapels of the late 17th century, the former of 1694 with a carefully designed elevation although altered internally, the latter of 1698, demolished during the course of this survey, having a plain exterior but with the rare feature of two stone columns to support the equally unusual roof structure. The much smaller meeting-house of 1722 in Bolsover (17) is exceptionally complete in spite of internal refitting and is an outstanding example of the requirements of a modest urban congregation. At Charlesworth (37) dissenters had the use of a mediaeval chapel until 1797 when it was replaced by the present large but internally much altered building. Quakers also appeared in significant numbers in the late 17th century, the site of their meeting-house at Tupton (135) dating from 1677, but both here and at Low Leighton (118) where a meeting-house was built in 1717 the surviving early remains are no more than fragmentary. The oldest complete Friends' meeting-house in the county is at Toadhole Furnace (127), of 1743, but neither this nor the next oldest, at Monyash (115), of 1771, have continued in their original use.

Most of the existing 18th-century chapels date from the second half of the century and include buildings of all the larger denominations. The Moravian settlement at Ockbrook (120), commenced in 1751, is of interest although not laid out with quite the usual degree of regularity. The earliest Methodist preaching-house in the county, at Derby (55) in St Michael's Lane, visited by John Wesley in 1765, has been demolished, but the nearly contemporary building at Crich (49) where he preached in the following year still remains; the chapel at Hayfield (85), of 1782, is also of note in spite of much later alteration. Baptist chapels mainly belong to the General Baptist churches which

joined the New Connexion after 1770; the earliest, though fragmentary, being at Melbourne (109), others which retain late 18th-century walling are at Bradwell (25), Ilkeston (98) and Smalley (129). At Loscoe (48) the Particular Baptist church occupies a former Presbyterian meeting-house. To those Presbyterian societies where Unitarianism prevailed, notably Derby and Chesterfield, must be added Belper (13) where the industrialist Jedediah Strutt proved a timely benefactor. The interest of manufacturers in religious provision was also to be seen at Matlock Bath where Cromford Chapel (106), now demolished, was built for the employees of Richard Arkwright; although intended for established worship it soon became one of the few Independent chapels in England supported by Lady Glenorchy. The Countess of Huntingdon's Connexion is represented at Ashbourne where a former Presbyterian chapel (6) formed a convenient meeting place.

Many small three-bay chapels, mainly of the Wesleyan and Primitive Methodist Connexions, are typical of the early 19th century: of these Winster (143), of 1837, is the most unusual, with a pair of Venetian windows; other more typical examples being at Parwich (123) and Sutton on the Hill (122). The larger Wesleyan chapels at Ticknall (134) and Belper (15) are also notable, but the most remarkable, in King Street, Derby, is one of several important chapels in that town to have suffered demolition – a group which also included the octagonal New Jerusalem chapel (56) in the same street. An interesting and informed use of the Gothic style is found at Middleton (111) where the Congregational chapel owes its existence to the patronage of Thomas Bateman, grandfather of the noted antiquary of that name whose unusual monument lies in a field behind the chapel and who himself designed a small chapel nearby in Youlgreave (149) in the Romanesque manner. Other essays in the Romanesque are at Alfreton (2) and at Little Longstone (103) also for the Congregationalists. The Gothic Revival is further illustrated by the Wesleyan chapel in Buxton (35), of 1849, and by the Congregational chapel in Belper (14), of 1871.

A group of chapels built in the mid 19th century by John Smedley of Matlock for congregations of Wesleyan Methodist Reformers which in 1864 joined the United Methodist Free Churches show the liturgical aspirations of this patron whose efforts even extended to the provision of a revised Prayer Book for use in these buildings. At Somercotes (4) and at Holloway (58) a distinct nave and chancel was provided, both chapels having towers, a feature repeated in a more substantial manner at Butts (9), and even the smallest of the group, at Bonsall (19), has a bell-cote. The continuance of the Georgian tradition is found at its simplest in the later Friends' meeting-houses, where Bakewell (10), of 1852, is essentially little different from Derby (54), of 1808, and the General Baptist meeting-house at Netherseal (116), of 1840, is similarly conservative in its design. More positive Renaissance elements appear in the heavily rusticated Primitive Methodist chapel at Coal Aston (61), of 1866, and are at their highest

development at Eckington (65) where the influence of a wealthy patron is again in evidence.

The county is well provided with building materials and good stone is readily available in the upland areas. In the south near the River Trent brick is generally used, the earliest chapels in Derby being of this material, as is the chapel further north at Loscoe (48), of 1722. Although thatch was formerly used none now survives, some stone slates remain but have more often been replaced by Welsh slate. Tiles are found in the south and at Weston upon Trent (140) is a single instance of the use of pantiles.

ALFRETON

(1) BAPTIST, Swanwick (SK 404535). Built and registered as a meeting-house in 1796 and enlarged to the front in 1828. The walls were rendered, window frames renewed and the interior largely refitted in the late 19th century or later. The walls are of brickwork and the roof is slate-covered and gabled to N and south. The W front of three bays with two tiers of plain windows with splayed lintels has a wide central doorway with semi-circular arch, keystone inscribed with the dates of erection and enlargement, and blind tympanum above double doors. Two round-arched windows in the E wall flank the pulpit. The interior (originally 23½ft by 42ft) is now square and has an early 19th-century W gallery.

Fittings – *Monuments*: in front of chapel (1) George Haslam, 1823, Mary his wife, 1815, and Hannah their daughter, 1814; (2) John Haslam, 1842, Hannah his widow, 1848, and Mary their daughter, 1824, two slate headstones in railed enclosure; (3) Francis Skerritt, 1807; (4) Jonathan Cartlidge, 1806, and Mary his widow, 1821. *Pulpit*: incorporates early 19th-century work.

(2) CONGREGATIONAL, Church Street (SK 408557). Brick and slate with gabled stone front, in Romanesque style by G.C. Gilbert of Nottingham; built 1850 on a new site for a church which originated in the late 17th century. The N front has two tiers of windows, a NW tower formerly surmounted by a spire, with an entrance in the lower stage, and a second entrance at the NE corner. The interior is divided by E and W arcades with clerestorey lighting and has a small wheel window above the NE entrance, of nine lights filled with coloured glass. (URC)

CYB (1850) 197; (1855) 260–1.

(3) WESLEYAN, Spring Road, Riddings (SK 432526). Brick and slate, three-bay front with open pediment and large panel inscribed in raised characters 'WESLEYAN/A.D. 1838.'

(4) WESLEYAN REFORM, Birchwood, Somercotes (SK 429540). The hand of the patron, John Smedley of Matlock, is apparent in this building of 1853 which has all the major attributes of a parish church: chancel, nave, and tower, although with a reversed orientation. The walls are of brick with stone dressings and the roofs are slated. The chancel, of three bays, and the slightly wider nave of four bays, have lancet windows with cast-

iron frames and coloured glass in marginal lights, between two-stage buttresses. The W window of the chancel has three graduated lancets. The E tower is of three receding stages with a porch, N doorway and gallery staircase in the lower stage, a circular panel for a clock face on the N side of the middle stage, lancets to the belfry and a battlemented parapet formerly with corner pinnacles.

A Sunday-school and vestry were built against the N side of the chancel in 1907 and an organ chamber has been added against the W bay of the nave on the S side. The nave and chancel are divided by a four-centred arch, the jambs now cut away and replaced by iron columns. A folding screen has been introduced into the chancel to separate the two W bays which now form a schoolroom. The nave has an open timber roof with queen-post trusses and a gallery at the E end. *Fontlet*: pottery, Winchester Cathedral type, *c*.1900.

(5) FREE METHODIST, Swanwick (SK 403534), dated 1850.

ASHBOURNE

(6) Former PRESBYTERIAN, St John Street (SK 181467). Presbyterian meetings conducted by visiting ministers were held fortnightly in the early 18th century. Towards the end of that century 'the old Presbyterian meeting-house, which had been

shut up for some time, was procured' for the use of a new congregation gathered by ministers of the Countess of Huntingdon's Connexion. A certificate dated October 1786 for 'an old erected building in Compton adjoining to Ashbourne' noted as 'set apart from [?for] Presbyterians' appears to relate to this transaction. In 1801 a new chapel was built in Derby Road (see below) and the former chapel passed to other uses including a period as a court-house.

The building standing on the S side of the street behind a mid 19th-century frontage incorporating a central entrance below three tall round-arched windows was formerly approached through Salt Alley at the W side. It has walls of brick and a slate roof, three round-arched windows in each side wall and two in the gabled S end; all except those to the E have inserted lintels. The chapel was much altered in the 19th century.

Seymour (1839) II, 279—80.

(7) SION CHAPEL, Derby Road (SK 181463). The congregation of the Countess of Huntingdon's Connexion, which had been formed at the old Presbyterian chapel, removed in May 1801 to the present chapel which was paid for by John Cooper a member of the committee of Spa Fields Chapel, London, and a native of Ashbourne. The pedimented front of three bays with a central open porch was greatly changed in the late 19th century by the conflation of two tiers of windows and the insertion of stone dressings. A row of single-storey *almshouses* alongside the chapel of similar materials, in two groups of three with round-arched doorways and windows, also erected by John Cooper, is dated 1800. (URC)

LRSP XI (1975) 85: Seymour (1839) II, 279–80.

ASHOVER

(8) PRIMITIVE METHODIST, Ashover Hay (SK 358612). Small wayside chapel of coursed rubble with roof of stone flags largely replaced by slates. Three-bay gabled front with tablet inscribed 'erected 1824, enlarged 1870'.

(9) Former WESLEYAN REFORM, Butts (SK 345634). Built by John Smedley *c*.1856 and now used as a studio, has walls of squared stone and a slate roof. Entrance at S end in base of a three-stage tower with two-centred arched doorway, blank shield-shaped stone tablet above and embattled parapet with corner pinnacles (removed); three lancet windows in side walls.

BAKEWELL

(10) FRIENDS, Chapel Lane (SK 218683). Squared stone walls and hipped slate roof. Wide E front with date 1852 on lintel of

middle window; porch later. Interior divided by renewed shutters, larger room to S with stand at S end, smaller room to N formerly with gallery over.

BARROW UPON TRENT

(11) BETHEL CHAPEL, Chapel Lane (SK 355285). Built 1839 for Independents, but now in Methodist use. Brick with hipped slate roof, pointed-arched doorway with intersecting glazing bars in fanlight, and large date-tablet above. Three lancet windows in side walls with cast-iron frames. Gallery at S end.

BASLOW AND BUBNELL

(12) WESLEYAN, School Lane, Baslow (SK 254725). Sunday-school dated 1822 has domestic front of three bays with external staircase at S end to upper room. Present chapel, 60 yards N, opened 1844.

BELPER

(13) FIELD ROW CHAPEL (SK 350479). Presbyterian meetings were held in Belper in 1672 at the house of Samuel Charles, ejected vicar of Mickleover. A regular congregation was formed by the end of the 17th century and several meeting-house certificates were issued which may relate to this society. The congregation, latterly Unitarian, was joined in the late 18th century by the manufacturer Jedediah Strutt who erected the present building in 1788.

The chapel, of squared stone with hipped slate roofs, was originally rectangular with the entrance at the S end; this has a

round-arched opening with triple keystone and above it, approached by an external cantilevered stone staircase, is a gallery doorway dated 1788, between two upper windows. Two round-arched windows in the N wall flank the former site of the pulpit beyond which is a low vestry. E and W wings were added to the chapel probably by 1800 and in a similar style.

The interior (originally 42ft by 23¾ft) has a S gallery. Box-pews rise steeply in the E and W wings and below the latter is a burial vault with 32 compartments, mostly empty.

Fittings – *Books: Forms of Prayer for the Use of a Congregation of Protestant Dissenters in Belper* (1823). *Monuments*: in chapel (1) Rebecca, wife of Rev. Rees Lewis Lloyd, and an infant daughter, 1849; (2) Jedediah Strutt, 1797, 'Founder of this chapel', William his brother, 1800, George Benson, his son, 1841, Catherina (Radford), wife of the last, 1842, and their children George Henry, 1821, Mary, 1828, John, 1858, and Anthony Radford, 1875; (3) Elizabeth, daughter of George Benson and Catherina Strutt, 1854. *Pulpit*: irregular octagon with two tiers of fielded panels and moulded cornice, late 18th-century.

Bolam (1962) 9–12: Evans (1897) 13.

(14) CONGREGATIONAL, Green Lane (SK 349478). Stone and slate with corner tower and broach spire, by George Woodhouse of Bolton, 1871. The former chapel of *c*.1798 stood behind.

CYB (1871) 406.

(15) WESLEYAN, Chapel Street (SK 347473). The chapel, a large square building opened in 1825, replaced one registered in 1798. The walls are of squared stone with an ashlar front and the

hipped roof, formerly slated, is now tiled. The E front is of five bays with a three-bay pedimented centre, porch with pilasters and pediment, and two tiers of plain sash windows. The rear wall has a later polygonal projection partly covering the sites of two former windows. W of the chapel is a brick Sunday-school dated 1841. *Monuments*: in burial-ground (1) Edward Bourne, 1814, and Sarah, daughter of Edward and Mary Bourne, 1815; (2) John Bourne, 1819, and John, his son, 1815; (3) William Bourne, 1819, and William his son, 1869; (4) William Bourne, 1823, and Edith his widow, 1828.

Dolbey (1964) 157–8 gives '1807' for this building.

(16) WESLEYAN, Kilbourn Road (SK 361479). 'Pottery Chapel', dated 1816, with shaped gable. Sunday-school adjacent to W dated 1878.

BOLSOVER

(17) THE OLD MEETING-HOUSE, High Street (SK 472705). Although an exceptionally early date has been claimed for the Congregational church recently meeting here there is no evidence for any regular congregation before the early 18th century. At that time John Thomas (d.1719), Presbyterian minister at Elder Yard, Chesterfield, held fortnightly services in Bolsover and these meetings were continued by Thomas Ibbetson, or Ebbisham, pastor of the Independent section at Elder Yard. The meeting-house described as 'a new erected house' was registered in July 1722. This is approached by a narrow alley running between High Street and Castle Street and was formerly concealed by buildings facing the adjacent streets. The original entrance was at the S end but about 1893, when a new chapel was built to the N linked to it by vestries, a lean-to extension was added against the S wall of the former meeting-house concealing the principal elevation. The older building, which then became a hall or Sunday-school, was repaired and refitted in 1912 with steel beams inserted to support the ceiling and to replace the internal lintels of the side windows. In 1981 following the closure of the church the adjacent structures were removed and the interior stripped prior to conversion to office use.

The walls are of brickwork with stone dressings and the roof, which has twin gables to N and S, is covered with tiles. The S front has a stone platband and quoins projecting slightly beyond

C.F.S.

South Elevation (Restored)

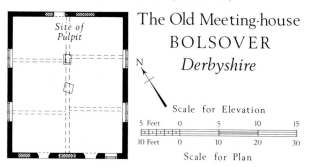

Site of Pulpit

N

The Old Meeting-house
BOLSOVER
Derbyshire

Scale for Elevation

5 Feet   0   5   10   15

10 Feet   0   10   20   30

Scale for Plan

S front and E side.

the brick face, two original doorways with stone jambs and lintels, perhaps formerly covered by canopies, and three windows below the platband, two of which have been blocked. The centre window was further altered, possibly in the early 19th century, when a doorway was pierced below it. There are no original openings above the platband. The N wall has two former windows set close together, slightly E of the main axis of the building, which flanked the pulpit; external brick labels above these windows have been cut away. The side walls each have two original windows with renewed frames and brick labels.

The interior (34¼ft by 28¼ft) does not appear to have had galleries nor any intermediate supports to the roof structure. The roof is supported by a principal valley-beam and two pairs of collar trusses with staggered tie-beams. Two irregular masonry foundations were revealed below the suspended floor, one at the centre of the building probably supported a heating stove, the other in front of the site of the pulpit may have supported a secondary post below a weak point in the roof timbers.

Fittings – *Chair*: in later chapel, oak, with carved and panelled back, late 17th-century. *Monuments*: in Old Meeting-house, on S wall (1) Rev. Thomas Ibbetson, d. 7 August 1723 aged 37, floor-slab reset in blocking of later central doorway; on N wall (2) Rev. John Ellaby, 1837; (3) Ann, 1873, and Julia, 1877, sisters of John Wardley.

BONSALL

(18) GENERAL BAPTIST (SK 279582). Rendered walls with stone dressings and dark tiled roof. The E front has cast-iron frames to windows and tablet above the entrance dated 1824. Two round-arched windows in the S wall flank the pulpit and two upper windows at the opposite end light the N gallery. Originally built as a preaching station for Wirksworth.

Monuments: against boundary wall E of chapel (1) John Amatt, 1842, and Sarah Ann his daughter, 1842; (2) Sarah, wife of George Cottrill, 1852.

(19) Former METHODIST REFORM (SK 279581). Built by John Smedley *c*.1850, now the Baptist Sunday-school. Rendered rubble walls with stone dressings, three-bay front with lancet windows and central porch, small bell-cote on N gable.

(20) Former PRIMITIVE METHODIST (SK 278584). Tablet dated 1852. Now Assembly of God.

BOYLESTONE

(21) Former WESLEYAN (SK 182359). Brick and slate, low gabled front to SE with a dentil cornice, segmental-arched entrance and small tablet dated 1809. Side walls each with two windows having stone dressings, round-arched heads, keystones and impost blocks. Pulpit at NW end, other fittings removed.

(22) PRIMITIVE METHODIST (SK 175357). Brick and slate with three-bay front, windows with splayed lintels and later gabled porch with tablet above original entrance dated 1846. Adjacent to right under same roof, a contemporary cottage, altered and extended to the front for Sunday-school use in 1931.

Inscriptions: on bricks in front wall, names and initials including J. Tunstall; S.L.; J. SMITH; J.B.; T.J.

BRACKENFIELD

(23) PRIMITIVE METHODIST, Woolley Moor (SK 369606). Stone and slate. Tablet above S entrance with date 1841 and initials JW.

BRADWELL

(24) THE OLD CHAPEL, Smithy Hill (SK 171812). A Presbyterian congregation gathered in the late 17th century by William Bagshaw 'the Apostle of the Peak' was said in 1695 to 'have prepared a more meet place to meet in'. The meeting-house was demolished by a 'popish mob' in 1715 and its successor is

GENERAL BAPTIST CHAPEL, BONSALL

Former PRESBYTERIAN CHAPEL BRADWELL

reported to have been 'destroyed by fire' in the mid 18th century. The present building, which may stand on the site of its predecessors, is dated 1754 and does not appear to incorporate any earlier work; the congregation was latterly Unitarian. The chapel has been used since 1968 as a Scout hall.

The walls are of coursed limestone rubble with gritstone dressings and the roof is covered with stone slates. The front E wall, the S half of which is partly covered by the end of an adjacent house, has a doorway with narrowly-chamfered jambs and lintel between two cross-framed windows with square stone mullions and transoms, the heads joined by a stone platband. A rectangular tablet above the entrance is inscribed with the date of erection. To the left of the gable is a smaller upper window to light a pulpit at the S end. The W wall has three windows similar to those in the front wall; the N and S gable walls are blank. The interior (approx. 36ft by 17ft) retains no original fittings. *Monuments*: see Great Hucklow (77).

Evans (1897) 30: Evans (1912) 19–22, 52, 95–101: *UHST* IV (1927–30) 279–80.

(25) Former GENERAL BAPTIST (SK 173813). A congregation formed *c*.1789, originally part of the church at Ashford but which became autonomous in 1811, died out by *c*.1840. The meeting-house, opened in October 1790 but not registered until 1803, passed to the Primitive Methodists for use as a Sunday-school. The original building (about 27½ft by 33½ft externally), of a single storey gabled to N and S, was heightened in 1853. The W front is of three bays with two original windows flanking a porch, and sash windows above. The E wall has two similar windows to the lower storey and traces of a blocked doorway near the S end. A small bell-cote of *c*.1854 with one bell stands on the N gable. *Monument*: to W, headstone with floral decoration, illegible, early 19th-century.

Evans (1912) 23, 25: Taylor (1818) II, 267–9, 369: Wood (1847) 208.

(26) WESLEYAN (SK 173811). Built 1807 replacing a preaching-house of 1768; altered and refitted 1891. The front of three bays has a simple pediment, quoins, and two tiers of round-arched windows. The central doorway is covered by a substantial stone porch of 1891.

Evans (1912) 22–5, 101–5.

(27) PRIMITIVE METHODIST (SK 173812). 'Bethlehem Chapel' was built in 1845 to supersede a smaller plain building of 1822 which had an earth floor covered with waste material from local lead mines. The chapel, enlarged in 1878, was closed after 1972 and the date-tablet defaced.

Evans (1912) 25, 105–9.

BRAILSFORD

(28) Former WESLEYAN (SK 247419). Tall building of brick with hipped tiled roof. Entrance at E end with rusticated flat arch and keystone, two round-arched windows with cast-iron frames and intersecting glazing bars and square tablet between with inscription 'WESLEYAN METHODIST CHAPEL 1821' (defaced since 1968).

(29) PRIMITIVE METHODIST (SK 254415). Three-bay front dated 1845.

BRAMPTON

(30) PRIMITIVE METHODIST, Cutthorpe (SK 347735). Three-bay front dated 1837; pyramidal roof.

(31) WESLEYAN, Wadshelf (SK 316709). Gabled front dated ?1834 with obelisk finials.

BRASSINGTON

(32) CONGREGATIONAL (SK 232545). Built *c*.1845 in a style of *c*.1600, has stone walls and a stone slate roof. A basement storey has an outer doorway and three windows between two-stage buttresses on the E side. The chapel above has stone-mullioned windows in the gabled N and S ends only, the former of three lights with a transom and the latter of three lights with raised transomed centre. The entrance is in a gabled porch at the S end. All gables have stone copings and shaped kneelers. (Closed *c*.1977, now village hall)

(33) PRIMITIVE METHODIST (SK 229543). Dated 1834.

BREADSALL

(34) WESLEYAN (SK 374396). Rendered brick and slate. Three-bay front with shaped gable, tablet dated 1826.

BUXTON

(35) WESLEYAN, Eagle Parade (SK 057732). Built in 1849 to replace a chapel of *c*.1797 which stood on Smithy Hill, of squared stone with a slate roof, in a 14th-century Gothic style. Some materials from the former building and timber from the race-course grandstand were employed in its erection. The architect was James Wilson of Bath. In 1880 transepts and a W vestry with organ and choir gallery above were added, to designs by R.R. Duke, and in 1895 under J. Bryden, the vestry was transformed into a chancel.

The original chapel comprised the present nave of three bays with two-stage buttresses between two-light traceried windows and a pierced parapet. The gabled E front with central entrance and four-light window above with reticulated tracery was formerly surmounted by a small bell-cote but this was altered in

1901 when the upper part of the front wall was rebuilt. A large traceried panel at the apex with the date 1849 is a replica, the original panel and parts of the window tracery remain in the garden of the manse, W of the chapel. The interior has an E gallery; N and S galleries were removed in 1880 and an arcade of three bays (removed 1970) was introduced in 1895 at the entrance to the chancel in place of a single arch above the former choir gallery.

Love-feast Cups: Pair, white glazed pottery with gilt decoration, straight sides and two handles, inscribed on two faces – (a) '*Whosoever drinketh of the water that I shall give him, he shall never thirst*', (b) '*The water that I shall give him shall be in him a well of water springing up into everlasting life*', 4⅛in., mid 19th-century. Also, pair of cups from former Methodist chapel at Brand Top, Hartington Upper Quarter, Derbys. (SK 044685), each inscribed '*Bran Top*', and of similar material, with rounded bowl on stem and two handles; one cup has the text (a) as above, the other '*Give me this water, that I thirst not*', 6¼in., mid 19th-century.

Woodhead, D.W., *Buxton Wesley Chapel; The Story of a Hundred Years, 1849–1949* [1949].

CHAPEL-EN-LE-FRITH

(36) PRIMITIVE METHODIST, Whitehough (SK 039821). West front of three bays with tablet dated 1840 above blocked doorway.

CHARLESWORTH

(37) CHARLESWORTH CHAPEL (SK 010928). This site is believed to be that of the mediaeval chapel of St Mary Magdalen which had almost fallen out of use by the mid 17th century. It appears to have been occupied from the later 17th century by a Presbyterian congregation perhaps the remnant of that ministered to by John Jones, curate in 1650, who was later a nonconformist preacher at Marple, Cheshire.

A certificate was issued in 1709 for 'a meeting-house of protestant dissenters in Glossop Dale called Charlesworth Chapel'. The present building dates from 1797 by which period the church had become Independent; it was drastically refitted in the late 19th century.

The chapel stands on a prominent site ½ mile E of the village

and is surrounded by a large burial-ground. The walls are of coursed rubble with ashlar dressings, quoins, and platband around the principal sides; the roof is covered with stone slates. The N and S ends are gabled; the N front, surmounted by a bellcote with one bell, has two doorways with wide architraves, a Venetian window between, another above, and plain windows over the entrances; a small tablet in the gable is inscribed 'CC/1797'. The side walls are of five bays with two tiers of windows, the S bay being possibly an extension. The S wall has a central window of three lights and a blocked Venetian window above.

The interior (61ft by 39ft) has a late 19th-century gallery around four sides with more recent minor rooms introduced beneath it at the S end. The upper part of the *pulpit*, of mahogany with a shaped front having quarter-round fluted columns at the corners, is of the late 18th century.

Monuments: in burial-ground, of 1797 and later, include some mid 19th-century table-tombs enclosed by ornamental cast-iron railings. *Miscellaneous*: in chapel, wood panel (8ft 11in. by 5in.) carved with monsters, scrollwork, and dated '17 B 03'.

Hosken, J.T., *Memorials of Charlesworth* [n.d.]: Mansfield, R., *Charlesworth Independent Chapel... 1798–1948* [1948].

(38) PARTICULAR BAPTIST (SK 008931). Square with coursed stone walls; tablet dated 1835 above central doorway.

PARTICULAR BAPTIST CHAPEL, CHARLESWORTH

CHESTERFIELD

(39) ELDER YARD CHAPEL (SK 383712). The congregation was in existence by 1681; its origins may in part be traced to the ejection in 1662 of the vicar, John Billingsley, and Thomas Ford or Forth, a lecturer in the parish. It included both Presbyterians and Independents who co-existed from 1703 to 1721 as two distinct churches using one building, the Independents continuing to support the surviving Presbyterian society until the appointment of an Arian minister in 1773 after which they seceded. The building was first referred to as 'Unitarian' in 1818.

The site for the chapel, on the S side of Saltergate 'in or near to a place called Ellar Yard', was bought in 1692 and the chapel erected by 1694 at the expense of Cornelius Clarke of Norton Hall, the cost being £229 10s. The walls are of sandstone, roughcast to S and W in 1818, with exposed stone dressings and

(39) CHESTERFIELD. Elder Yard Chapel, before removal of graveyard monuments.

the roof is hipped and covered with stone slates. The S front of five, now six, bays was originally symmetrical, the present E bay, on the site of a former vestry, was built in 1821 to house an organ gallery, converted to a chancel in 1896–7 and a S window inserted. The wall has rusticated quoins and a plain entablature; the three centre bays are pedimented and have a doorway with eared architrave and segmental pediment below a tablet inscribed 'This Chapel was erected in the Year of Our Lord 1694'. The windows each side of the entrance have square stone mullions and transoms, eared architraves and moulded cills. The W end has a secondary entrance between two tiers of two-light mullioned windows.

The interior (25ft by 50¼ft) was re-arranged in 1818 when the pulpit was removed from the N wall to the E end, and again drastically refitted in 1896–7 when the seating was renewed or remade and the E bay altered to its present form. A deep gallery with panelled front remains at the W end. The roof is supported by four king-post trusses of c.1694. (The interior was further altered in 1980 when the W gallery was extended forward and two stories of rooms constructed at that end)

Fittings – Clock: on N wall, with octagonal face, signed 'John Berry, London', c.1694. Inscription: painted on post below gallery, 'Tho: Mellor Pade for two Moyetys in this Seat. And Edw: Turner for one. 1694'. Monuments: in chapel, over S doorway (1) Rev. Thomas Astley, pastor 'above forty years', 1817; in gallery (2) Robert Malkin, Elisabeth his wife, and their children Henry and Mary, erected 1847; in burial-ground S of chapel (partly denuded since 1968) some flat slabs and loose stones remain, including (3) Mr Joseph Foolow, minister, 1707, and Anne his widow, 1707/8; (4) Ann Astley, 1807, and her sisters Catharine Astley, 1814, and Sarah, widow of Rev. John Atkinson,

vicar of Ribchester, 1820; (5) Jane (Gill) wife of Thomas Slater, apothecary, 1705; (6) Richard Slater, mercer, 1768; (7) Martha, widow of Rev. John Ashe of Ashford, 1749; (8) Mary, widow of Rev. Jonah Malkin, 1805, top of table-tomb; (9) Charles, son of James and Mary Margerson, 1837, et al., slate headstone.

Plate: includes a pair of cups of 1709. Pulpit: hexagonal with two tiers of fielded panels, on tapered stem and pillar with moulded cap, c.1694; re-sited without canopy and reduced in height.

Evans (1897) 46–7: Robson, D.W., Origins and History of Elder Yard Chapel, Chesterfield (1924): UHST v (1931–4) 324–5.

(40) CONGREGATIONAL, Rose Hill (SK 381712). Independent seceders from Elder Yard chapel formed themselves into a separate church in 1778 and appear to have opened a meeting-house in that year in a yard 'facing Swines Green'. The present chapel dated 1822 is of coursed stone. The front of three bays has a central entrance with Roman Doric columns supporting a stone entablature. The parapet, formerly raised in the centre, has been altered. (URC)

(41) FRIENDS, Saltergate (SK 382713). The first meeting-house on this site was built in 1696–7 and is described as standing at the N end of a small croft, behind what was probably an earlier cottage. The meeting-house was rebuilt in 1770 and in 1799 a proposal was made to enlarge the building by 3 yards to the E, in 1802 Joseph Storrs submitted his account for this work for £227 7s. 1d. An elevation before alteration and a plan and elevation of the proposed enlargement (Nottingham City Library: Q 330/1–3) show the 1770 meeting-house with gables to E and W ends, an entrance at the E end of the S front with a small square

S front.

window to the left and two taller windows beyond to the principal room. In the enlarged and refronted building a further bay was added to the E with a new doorway at that end of the rebuilt front wall and four uniform windows are shown to the left; the new roof was hipped. In the completed work three windows only were provided at the front, and the gallery stair, designed to be internal, was re-sited in a projection at the back.

The meeting-house has yellow sandstone walls of 1770 to N and W and brickwork of *c.*1800 to the S front and the E end; the roof is hipped and covered with stone slates. Three sash windows in the S front have splayed lintels with false voussoir joints and the S doorway has a stone surround incorporating a rectangular glazed panel. In the W wall are two similar windows with plain stone surrounds and two windows of like design in the E wall serve an upper room.

The interior (44¾ft by 22¾ft) has a very deep E gallery or upper room, the front closed by hinged shutters, and with a fireplace in the E wall. A passage at the E end below the gallery has a central doorway to the meeting-room flanked by detachable fielded-panelled shutters, on the N section of which is a removable hat-rail secured by early hand-wrought wing-nuts. The stand at the W end incorporates 18th-century fielded panels. The roof is supported by trusses with king-posts, queen-posts with raking braces, and butt-purlins.

Fittings include seven open-backed benches with turned

supports below arm-rests and a small library dating from the early years of the meeting: books include a late 17th-century edition of the *Journal* of George Fox, and his *Gospel Truth Demonstrated in a Collection of Doctrinal Books* (1706) inscribed 'This book is paid for by Chesterfield Monthly Meeting Cost 18s 8d', and other early Quaker works. A small burial-ground to the S contains 14 round-topped headstones of the late 19th century and later, other graves are marked by grass mounds.

The meeting-house was demolished and the site cleared *c.*1974; a modern tablet marks its approximate location.

(42) WESLEYAN, Saltergate (SK 38257130), 1870, with Ionic portico and pediment, replaces a chapel of 1795, enlarged 1828.

CHINLEY, BUXWORTH AND BROWNSIDE

(43) CHINLEY CHAPEL, Chapel Milton (SK 055820). The Presbyterian, latterly Independent, congregation which originated in the late 17th century met first at Ford Hall under the ministry of William Bagshawe, ejected Vicar of Glossop, later removing to a barn at Malcoff. The present chapel was erected in 1711. A structural failure in 1908 caused the rebuilding of the N wall and the upper part of the S wall, but apart from alterations to the heads of the upper windows on the S side the appearance is unchanged.

The walls are of coursed squared stone and the roof, gabled to E and W, is covered with stone slates. The S front is of six bays with two tiers of windows separated by a moulded stringcourse and segmental-arched doorways in the end bays, that to the E altered to a window but the other retaining its original nail-studded door. The windows are of two lights with chamfered cills and jambs but with square-fronted mullions. The upper windows have been raised, cutting through an upper string course, and the two middle windows have been given segmental-arched heads. Centrally in the W wall is a window of two segmental-arched lights and a similar window above, also with square-fronted mullions. The E wall was similarly fenestrated but the lower window was replaced *c.*1908 by a central doorway. In the N wall two windows with segmental-arched lintels flank the pulpit and to E and W are two-light windows above and below the ends of the galleries. A small vestry in the NE

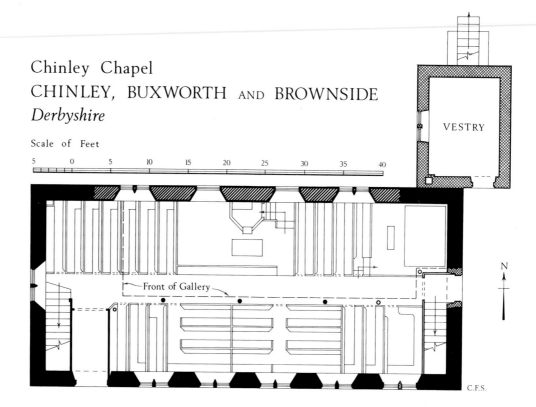

Chinley Chapel
CHINLEY, BUXWORTH AND BROWNSIDE
Derbyshire

Scale of Feet

5 0 5 10 15 20 25 30 35 40

VESTRY

─ Front of Gallery

N

C.F.S.

corner was added in the late 19th century.

The interior (23¾ft by 51½ft) has a gallery around three sides, altered at the E end to accommodate an organ first installed 1861. The gallery supports have been replaced by cast-iron columns but the front is original and has a dentil sub-cornice, fielded panels and moulded capping; the two staircases have shaped flat balusters. The ceiling, with four exposed tie-beams, and the superstructure of the roof, are of 1908.

Fittings – *Bell*: in bell-cote on W gable, 1959, replacing earlier bell now loose. *Benefaction Boards*: in gallery, three, (1) by Samuel Flood of Bowden, 1764, £200, part 'to be given to the Minister of Chinley Chapel for Permitting Six Poor Widows sitting Rent Free on the North Side of the said Chapel for Ever'; (2) by Thomas Moult of Chinley Naze, 1751, of £5 'to go towards repairing of this place'; (3) by Thomas Kirk of Shireoaks, of £50 paid to trustees 1782, interest to go to 'A Protestant Dissenting Minister Duly officiating at this Place and HE to be chosen by the Majority of the Said Trustees'. *Chandeliers*: three, brass, one of 8 branches surmounted by eagle, and two of 4 branches, purchased June 1783, cost £8 11s 10d.; also two candle sconces on N wall reset from former pulpit. *Inscriptions*: on plaster ceiling below S gallery, lozenge with scroll ornament, inscribed 'John Mellor George Mellor 1711'; on seat of pew 26 in SW corner, 'IP 1789', repeated three times.

Monuments: in burial-ground, many flat slabs, table-tombs and headstones of 18th century and later, (1) Josiah Bradbury of Combshead 1753, and Ann his widow, 1761; (2) John Bennet, 1759, [Methodist lay preacher] and Grace his widow, 1803; (3) [William] Sutcliffe, minister, [1805]; (4) Ann, widow of Samuel Waterhouse minister of Risley Chapel, Lancs., daughter of James Clegg, minister of Chinley Chapel, 1787, table-tomb; (5) James Clegg V.D.M., M.D., 1755, minister 53 years, *et al.*, table-tomb with brass shield-shaped tablet; (6) Benjamin Holland, minister at Burton upon Trent, 1795; (7) Ann, wife of Rev. William Harrison, daughter of John Cooper minister of Hyde, granddaughter of Samuel Angier, minister of Dukinfield, Cheshire, 1782, and William her son, 1756; (8) Rev. William Harrison, 27 years pastor, grandson of Cuthbert Harrison ejected minister of Kirkham, Lancs., 1783; (9) Rev. William Bennet, and Mary (Ewer), his wife, both 1821.

Plate: includes a cup of 1637. *Pulpit*: front of four irregular bays of late 17th-century panelling on new base with matching back-board, much restored; reputed to be the pulpit used at Malcoff, subsequently preserved at Ford Hall, presented 1931 and erected in place of former pulpit 1958. *Seating*: Chairs, three in communion space, one with arms, carved panelled backs, late 17th-century; pews in gallery and below, box-pews with fielded-panelled numbered doors and backs, one pew in NW corner marked 'Widow's Pew' and two to E marked 'Free'.

Simpson, W., *The History of Chinley Chapel* (1979): Thomas F.C., *Chinley Chapel, Celebration of the 250th Anniversary... 1711-1961* [1961].

S front.

Interior from SE.
(43) CHINLEY, BUXWORTH AND BROWNSIDE. Chinley Chapel, Chapel Milton.

(44) CONGREGATIONAL, Buxworth (SK 027824). Brierley Green Chapel at Buxworth (formerly Bugsworth) originated in 1826 with the erection of a building for use as a day-school and Sunday-school in which the minister of Chinley Chapel held regular services; a meeting-house certificate for its use by Independents was issued in May 1827. The school remained in an undenominational trust until 1890 when it was purchased by Congregationalists who erected the present chapel at the W end in 1906-7. The original building, with stone walls and stone slate roof, was formerly entered through a round-arched rusticated doorway at the E end. The S wall, of three bays with two tiers of sash windows, has a tablet inscribed 'This school was erected by Subscription in the Year 1826 Pro bono publico'. The interior, now of a single storey with E gallery and shutters at the W end opening to the chapel, may have been divided by a floor with accommodation above for resident teachers.

Bugsworth Independent Chapel, Derbyshire, Centenary Souvenir, 1827-1927 [1927].

(45) WESLEYAN, White Knowle (SK 051829). Coursed rubble with slate roof, gabled and rendered to E and W, built 1809. S front with central entrance and three segmental-arched upper windows. Two tiers of arched windows in end walls, and central round-arched window behind pulpit in N wall flanked by windows above and below the ends of the galleries. Box-pews. (Repaired after damage in fire of 1978)

CHURCH BROUGHTON

(46) PRIMITIVE METHODIST, Chapel Lane (SK 206337). Brick with original splayed door-lintel dated 1828 reset in later W porch; round-arched windows with cast-iron frames.

CLIFTON AND COMPTON

(47) Former PRIMITIVE METHODIST, Hanging Bridge (SK 161457). Three-bay front with blocked entrance, dated 1830. (Closed and tablet defaced *c.*1971-4)

CODNOR AND LOSCOE

(48) Former PRESBYTERIAN, Loscoe (SK 422478). Built in 1722 for a congregation which apparently originated under John Hieron, ejected Rector of Breadsall. Heterodox influences later in the 18th century led to a decline in support and the meeting-house came to be shared with and eventually transferred to a Baptist church whose first minister was ordained in 1784. The chapel is a square building of brick with a pyramidal slate roof. In 1848 the walls were heightened and the present E front erected; this has terminal pilasters and a moulded cornice, three upper windows and entrances below covered by a recent timber porch. The N and S walls were entirely refenestrated in 1848 and have each two tall round-arched windows, but traces of former openings remain visible. The W wall is partly covered by later buildings. *Inscriptions*: on front wall, below centre window, small square tablet 'F.T/1722' for Francis Tantum; centrally above cornice 'BAPTIST CHAPEL/AD 1848'.

CRICH

(49) METHODIST (SK 351537). John Wesley preached in the 'new house at Creitch' on 25 March 1766. The chapel, which is

of this period but with traces of alterations to the side walls and re-roofed *c.*1905, has walls of squared stone and a hipped slate roof. The S front has two doorways with deep lintels and a window between with altered frame and formerly with an external shutter; two upper windows have round-arched heads and wooden frames with intersecting glazing bars. The side walls have each two upper windows, also round-arched but with cast-iron frames, and two tall windows in the N wall flank the pulpit. The interior ($38\frac{3}{4}$ft by $26\frac{3}{4}$ft) has a gallery around three sides with numbered seating of the early 19th century. The pulpit, of the late 18th century, is supported by a substantial turned wood post. Other fittings are of the late 19th century and after.

Methodist Recorder, 28 Dec. 1905.

DENBY

(50) WESLEYAN, Copper Yard (SK 406468). Built by Joseph Bourne, a local potter; tablet in gable was originally inscribed 'WESLEYAN CHAPEL ANNO 1841'. The society supported the Methodist Reform movement in 1850. A red brick United Methodist Sunday-school dated 1909 stands to the right.

DERBY

(51) FRIAR GATE CHAPEL (SK 348363). The Presbyterian, latterly Unitarian, congregation was formed in the late 17th century and numbered amongst its first ministers Robert More, ejected curate of Brampton, Derbys. Early meeting-places are said to have included the chapel of St Mary-on-the-Bridge and a building in a yard on the E side of Irongate. The chapel in Friar Gate was built in or about 1698 which date appears on the Royal Arms and is the year in which the registers commence. About 1860 two small porches were added to the front and some alterations made to the interior. In 1862 two large Sunday-school rooms were built at the rear over part of the burial-ground. In 1890 the front porches were rebuilt, a pediment was added to the front, the rear rooms were rebuilt including the addition of an organ loft and choir gallery, and the interior further refitted.

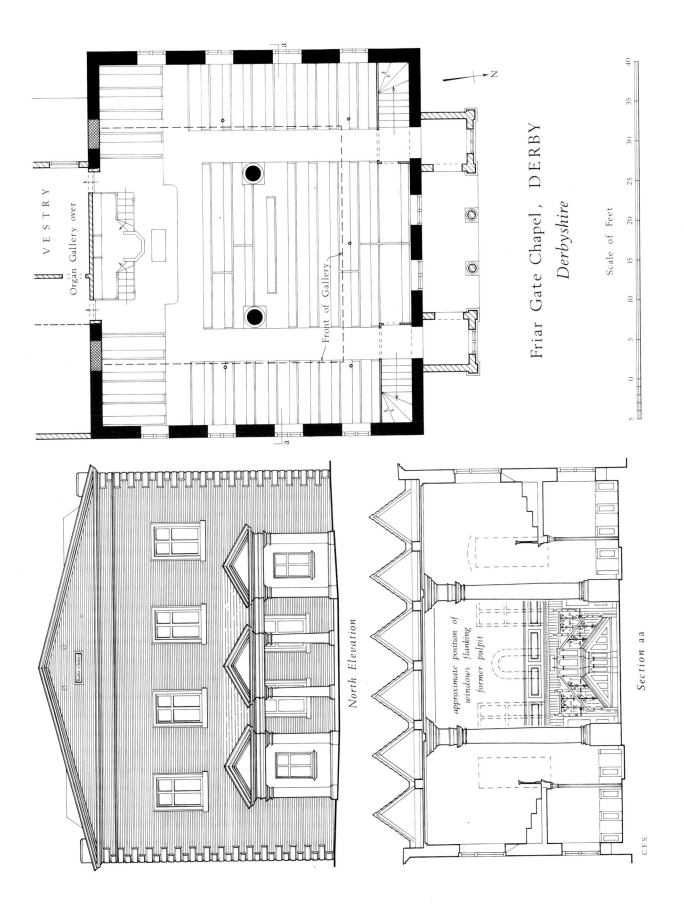

VESTRY

Organ Gallery over

Front of Gallery

a

a

N

Friar Gate Chapel, DERBY

Derbyshire

Scale of Feet

5 0   5   10   15   20   25   30   35   40

North Elevation

approximate position of
windows flanking
former pulpit

Section aa

C.F.S.

N front.

Interior from SW.
(51) DERBY. Friar Gate Chapel.

The chapel is a large plain building of brick with a low hipped and slated roof. The N front has stone quoins, two original doorways with two windows between and four above, with moulded stone surrounds and mullioned and transomed wooden frames introduced in the 19th century to match the side windows, replacing sashes which appear on an engraving of 1791. The wall was originally finished with a simple moulded stone cornice, without blocking course; in 1890 a brick pediment with stone dressings was added, with a string-course below and a tablet inscribed 'Gloria in excelsis'. The front porches, also of this date, have pedimented stone fronts and are joined by an open loggia with two Tuscan columns and a matching pediment. The E and W walls have each four bays of windows in two tiers, those to the E alone have structural flat-arched brick heads, and most have their original wooden frames with mullions and transom moulded internally but plain externally and flush with the wall face. The original moulded stone cornice also survives. The S wall formerly had two tall windows flanking a central pulpit and may have had other windows above or below the ends of the galleries of which slight indications remain at the W end. The pulpit windows were destroyed in 1890 by the construction of the organ and choir gallery.

The interior ($39\frac{1}{2}$ft by $45\frac{1}{4}$ft) is dominated by two massive stone columns of the Roman Doric order with entablature blocks which carry the principal beam of the roof and rise from square stone dies above the level of the former box-pews. The gallery around three sides was altered c.1860 when it was refronted and the supports replaced by cast-iron columns; it has a level plaster floor of the late 17th century above which stepped seating was built c.1860 and the window cills, formerly 2ft lower, were raised to match. The cills to the windows below the side galleries have also been raised. The pews and pulpit all date from the late 19th century as does the boarded ceiling. The roof comprises six hipped sections joined by a cross-roof at the front, all with simple triangular trusses, and with valleys discharging to the south.

Fittings – *Monuments*: in chapel on N wall below gallery (1) Isabella wife of Joseph Strutt, 1802, white marble tablet with enriched apron and cheeks, surmounted by a draped urn in low relief, on grey slate backing; SW of chapel (2) Sophia, daughter of Isaac and Sarah Pike, 1833, slate, signed Maskrey; (3) William Hodgson, 1849, and Mary, his widow, 1850; (4) Ellen . . . , 1830; (5) Sarah, wife of Edward Higginson, minister, 1832; (6) Margaret Evanson, 1823, and Dorothy Evanson, 1827; (7) Joseph Greatorex, 1827, and Elizabeth his widow, 1845, slate, signed E. Shenton; (8) Sarah, wife of George Tunnicliffe, 1831, slate, signed Evans. *Pictures*: in vestry (1) engraving of S front, 'G. Moneypenny Delin., R. Hancock Sc.', 1791; (2) photograph from NE in 1860; (3) watercolour of interior before 1890, c.1925 based on a photograph.

Plate: includes a pair of two-handled cups of 1724 and two two-handled cups of 1726 and 1731 formerly belonging to a congregation at Duffield. *Royal Arms*: oil on canvas, 4ft 11in. by 5ft 8in., in moulded wood frame, William III (1694–1702) with Royal cypher and date 1698 (see Frontispiece).

(Demolished 1974 and replaced by office block with small chapel on ground floor)

Birks, J., *Memorials of Friar Gate Chapel, Derby* [1893]: Bolam (1962) 17–22: Evans (1897) 67–9; *UHST* VI (1935–8) 58–60.

(52) Former GENERAL BAPTIST, Brook Street (SK 348367). General Baptist doctrines were first introduced into Derby in 1789 when the Rev. Dan Taylor preached his first sermon in Willow Walk, close to the present site. The chapel was built in 1802 but almost entirely rebuilt in 1814. In 1830 a secession resulted in the erection of a second chapel in Sacheverel Street. The original church removed in 1842 to a large mansion house in St Mary's Gate (now demolished) built in 1750 and converted to a chapel by James Fenton of Chelmsford. Brook Street Chapel later served as a home for a secession from Sacheverel Street Chapel, but by 1857 it had passed to a section of one of the Wesleyan Reform societies then in dispute over the proposed erection of a chapel in Becket Street. The chapel, still in Methodist use, has a front of squared stone of three bays with a narrow pediment, round-arched doorway and two tiers of plain windows with splayed and keyed lintels. A tablet above the entrance is now inscribed 'WESLEY CHAPEL'. The rear wall facing Willow Walk is of brick with a gable and upper windows similar to the front.

Alger (1901) 53–6, 110: Wood (1847) 192, 229, 233.

(53) Former INDEPENDENT, Green Hill (SK 352360). 'Marrowbones Chapel', nicknamed after three butchers who were principally concerned in its erection in 1816, apparently as a speculative venture, was purchased by Wesleyans c.1821 after the failure of the original congregation. The chapel was enlarged to the rear and a gallery added in the early 19th century, reseated in 1872 and further altered in 1893. The walls are of brick, with a late 19th-century rendered and pedimented front and round-arched windows above an altered porch.

Alger (1901) 86–8.

(54) FRIENDS, St Helen's Street (SK 349367). Friends' meetings, commenced in 1799 in a hired room in 'The Bell', were soon afterwards transferred to a large room in a former silk mill in the Irongate, converted to a meeting-house and registered in January 1800. The present site was acquired in 1804 and plans prepared by John Bevans. The meeting-house, dated 1808 and registered in January 1810 as 'lately erected', has squared sandstone walls and a hipped slate roof with moulded stone eaves cornice. The

front is symmetrical with a central entrance now covered by a later porch, date-tablet above and two segmental-arched windows to each side. The rear wall, partly covered by later rooms, has three similar windows. The interior is divided into two rooms by a wall, formerly with folding shutters, the front entrance opening directly into the larger room to the west.

(55) Former METHODIST, St Michael's Lane (SK 351367). On 20 March 1765 John Wesley wrote in his journal, 'M. Lewen took me in a post-chaise to Derby, where the new house was thoroughly filled; and the people behaved in a quite different manner from what they did when I was there last.'. The new

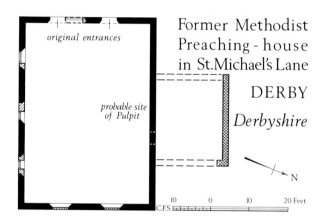

Former Methodist Preaching - house in St.Michael's Lane DERBY *Derbyshire*

preaching-house of *c*.1765 served its original purpose until 1805 when Wesleyans transferred their services to the first of two chapels in King Street, the second of which (built or reconstructed from the former in 1841 by James Simpson of Leeds), a notable building with a Doric portico between wings and five-bay pedimented facade behind, was demolished *c*.1968.

The St Michael's Lane building was subsequently used as a

malthouse and more recently for other commercial activity. It has brick walls and the roof, rebuilt *c*.1960, may have been hipped and tiled although E and W stepped gables and clerestorey lighting were provided in the early 19th century, probably on conversion to other uses. There are two tiers of windows in the S and W walls and two windows at the E end above the site of the former doorways; the upper windows have semicircular arches with keystones and impost blocks, the lower openings have flat-arched brick heads with keystones. The N wall, originally exposed, was later covered by a variety of buildings of which the earliest was an axial wing of stone with no openings to the chapel; the only possibly original opening in this wall remains as a small square blocking 1ft 8in. above the level of an inserted floor and slightly W of the centre which may have been a window to light the pulpit. The interior ($32\frac{1}{4}$ft by $45\frac{1}{2}$ft) has no original fittings. A substantially constructed plaster floor, later boarded, was introduced in the early 19th century. The fenestration provides for a gallery around E, W and S sides and a pulpit against the N wall. (Demolished 17 January 1973)

Alger (1901) 79–81: Alger, B.A.M., *King Street Wesleyan Chapel, Derby, a Centenary Memorial 1805-1905* [1905]: Dolbey (1964) 74–5, 154–6: *WHSP* XV (1925–6) 109–12.

(56) Former NEW JERUSALEM CHAPEL, King Street (SK 350368). The first 'Swedenborgian' society in Derby was established in 1814 by Rev. E. Madeley subsequent to the opening of a Sunday-school; a permanent chapel in London Street commenced 1818, reported 1820 to be nearly complete, was sold in

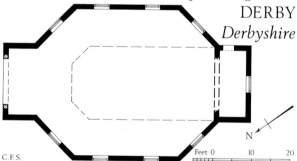

Former New Jerusalem Chapel, King Street DERBY *Derbyshire*

1836 to the Methodist New Connexion. A second congregation seems to have been gathered by James Robinson and the chapel in King Street 'lately erected by Mr. J. Robinson, at his own expense, was opened . . . on Sunday, the 18th of June [1820]'; Robinson was ordained 10 August 1820. About 1844 the King Street congregation removed to 'The New Jerusalem Chapel, Babington Lane' where the New Church Conference was held in 1847. King Street Chapel was then briefly occupied by Baptist seceders from a chapel in Agard Street but by 1849 the building was sold to George Wells as a Coach Manufactory whose firm, now motor engineers, still uses it.

The chapel is an elongated octagon with stone walls and a hipped slate roof, the pedimented front bay projects and has a

Venetian window above an altered entrance; there is a small vestry at the rear and two tiers of round-arched windows in the other six sides, the lower windows being partly blocked in stone leaving only lunettes. The original gallery remains. (Demolished *c*.1970)

Alger (1901) 62: Hindmarsh (1861) *passim*.

DETHICK LEA AND HOLLOWAY

(57) LEA CHAPEL (SK 330575). A Presbyterian congregation was meeting at 'Dethick-chappel' in the early 18th century and a meeting-house certificate issued July 1719 for the house of Thomas Nightingale at Lea may relate to the same society. The early history of Lea Chapel is obscure but it appears to have originated with Presbyterians, although now occupied by an Independent church. The chapel is a long, narrow building of sandstone with a slate roof. Three four-centred arched windows in the N wall with intersecting tracery indicate a major reconstruction of the early 19th century but masonry at the E end of this wall may be the remains of an early 18th-century building. A late 19th-century schoolroom covers part of the S side, to the E of which is a cottage, much altered or rebuilt in 1897 but incorporating a date-stone of 1671 in the S gable.

The interior of the chapel (43ft by 15¾ft) has a W gallery with early 19th-century panelled front, formerly approached by external stairs against the W wall. *Monuments*: in chapel (1) John Alsop of Lea Bridge, 1831, and Ann his wife, 1816; (2) Luke Alsop of Lea Hall, lead merchant, 1830, white marble tablet with urn, signed 'Watson fecit'.

(58) WESLEYAN REFORMERS, Holloway (SK 324565). Built by John Smedley in 1852 for liturgical services, altered and enlarged in 1879. It has stone walls and slate roofs, lancet windows and a porch centrally on the E side rising in three stages as a tower with pyramidal roof. On the E face of the middle stage is a circular stone panel for a clock face and two tablets below: 'C/I + S/1852'; 'ADDITION 1879'. The original building comprised a nave with chancel to the N with a principal window of three graduated lancets, and a four-centred chancel-arch. In 1879 a parallel nave was added alongside to the W with pulpit and organ recess at the W end, an E gallery was erected in the original nave and the chancel converted to a schoolroom. *Glass*:

the windows have borders of coloured glass in cast-iron frames; N window of chancel has a lozenge of plain multicoloured quarries at the centre of each light.

DOVERIDGE

(59) WESLEYAN (SK 122340). Brown brick and slate; gabled S front dated 1805. *Monument*: externally against S wall, John Deaville, 1853, local preacher, and Ann his widow, 1857.

DRAYCOTT AND CHURCH WILNE

(60) Former WESLEYAN, Draycott (SK 444332). Date-tablet obscured, 18[?3]0. Now Anglican.

DRONFIELD

(61) PRIMITIVE METHODIST, Coal Aston (SK 363796). Stone and slate; elaborately rusticated front with segmental tablet dated 1866.

(62) WESLEYAN, Dronfield Woodhouse (SK 329786). Gabled front with shaped kneelers; dated 1848.

DUFFIELD

(63) GENERAL BAPTIST, Town Street (SK 346429). The congregation originated in 1807 and opened a meeting-house in 1809 in a disused factory. The chapel, E of Duffield Hall, is of red brick with stone dressings to the N and W and of squared stone to the

other sides; the hipped roof has been re-covered with concrete tiles. The N doorway has a frieze with tablet dated 1830 and initials IT for James Taylor. The W wall has four tall round-arched windows; the E wall has two small round-arched upper windows, now blocked. A two-storied Sunday-school and vestry range was added to the S in 1877. *Monuments*: realigned W of chapel include (1) Arabella Stanley, 1834.

Taylor (1818) II, 365–8: Wood (1847) 207.

(64) Former WESLEYAN, Chapel Street (SK 346435). Squared stone walls and pyramidal slate roof. Ashlar NW front with terminal pilasters, plain plinth and moulded cornice. Central doorway dated 1843 with paired consoles, cornice and blank inscription-tablet, flanked by two plain sash windows. Three round-arched upper windows with platband joining the imposts. Now in industrial use.

ECKINGTON

(65) Former WESLEYAN (SK 428793). Opened April 1876; a

large building with stone walls and elaborate ashlar front of five bays with two Corinthian columns *in antis*, entablature with frieze inscribed 'IN MEMORIAM', and balustraded parapet with urns. Built in his memory by the family of George Wells, colliery owners. (Demolished *c.*1976)

(66) WESLEYAN, Ridgeway, The Moor (SK 402811). Low pedimented front and porch ornamented with crocketed pinnacles. Tablet in gable dated 1806; date 1901 on porch may refer to repairs or a refitting. *Monument*: at rear of vestry, Thomas Webster of Highlane, 1840, Hannah his widow, 1860, *et al.*, table-tomb.

EDALE

(67) WESLEYAN, Barber Booth (SK 113847). Methodist preaching was commenced *c.*1750 by David Taylor of Sheffield. The chapel dated 1811 has stone walls and a stone slate roof. The front wall has two upper and two lower windows with splayed lintels and a plain doorway to the right. A vestry has been added at one end. The interior is tall and has a gallery next to the entrance with panelled front and original seating. *Monuments*: in chapel (1) George Kirk Shirt, 1846, and Martha his widow, 1860; (2) Mary Kershaw, 1865, and Martha Shirt, 1872.

ELTON

(68) WESLEYAN (SK 222610). Tablets inscribed 'Wesleyan Methodist Chapel and Sunday School 1831' and 'Rebuilt 1923 enlarged'. Outer walls mainly 1831.

(69) PRIMITIVE METHODIST (SK 221609). Dated 1843.

(70) WESLEYAN REFORM (SK 223609). 'Ebenezer Chapel', built 1852, altered and porch added 1921. Entrance gates with stone piers and ball finials.

FINDERN

(71) WESLEYAN (SK 310305). Dated 1835.

FLAGG

(72) FLAGG CHAPEL (SK 135686), built 1838–9 for a Unitarian congregation. Rubble walls and slate roof with small bell-cote over front gable. Two-centred arched doorway in front and circular stone clockface above. Three lancet windows to each side wall and pointed lunette opposite entrance. *Monument*: in burial ground, to Rev. William Birks, 1863.

Evans (1897) 87–8.

FOOLOW

(73) WESLEYAN REFORM (SK 191769). Dated 1866; three-bay front of squared rock-faced stone and a hipped slate roof. Fittings include a pair of 17th-century chairs with turned legs and triple-arched backs.

GLOSSOP

(74) Former WESLEYAN, Wesley Street, Old Glossop (SK 043949). Gable with ball finial; tablet inscribed 'WESLEYAN CHAPEL AD 1813'. Now in commercial use.

(75) THE TABERNACLE, Manor Park Road, Old Glossop (SK 042944). The original chapel, later the Sunday-school, was built in 1836–7 for seceders from the foregoing who supported the

Wesleyan Methodist Association. A larger chapel was built alongside in 1860. Both buildings are now in commercial use.

(76) Former PRIMITIVE METHODIST, Shrewsbury Street (SK 031942). Built in 1855 and now in commercial use. Simple pedimented front with Venetian window above entrance. A tablet above the doorway has been obliterated. Tall round-arched windows divided by stone panels *c*.1885–8 when the chapel was refitted. The former Sunday-school behind was built in 1858.

GREAT HUCKLOW

(77) THE OLD CHAPEL (SK 179777). The Presbyterian, latterly Unitarian, congregation originated in the late 17th century under William Bagshawe whose brother was Lord of the Manor. The present chapel, built in 1796, has walls of ashlar to the S and W and rubble to N and east. The roof has been re-covered in

W wall.

concrete tiles. The E and W walls have each three round-arched windows. The N wall is gabled and has a square tablet with the date A.D. 1796. The S wall is largely covered by an extension of 1901 incorporating an entrance on the W side, gallery staircase and a stone bell-cote.

The interior (39¼ft by 27¼ft) entirely refitted in 1901, has a gallery at the S end; the N bay has been separated from the chapel by a thick wall to form a schoolroom. *Font:* artificial stone basin on moulded stem and square base, signed J. Armitage & Son, Manchester and Sheffield, mid 19th-century. *Monuments:* in vestibule (1) William Drabble, 1887, 'bellringer at this chapel for nearly 40 years' and Ellen his wife, 1874; also three monuments from The Old Chapel, Bradwell, Derbys. (24); (2) Rev. Robert Shenton, 1889; (3) William Evans of Smalldale, 1844; (4) Rev. Robert Shenton, 1889, and Selina his widow, 1891, loose headstone.

(78) WESLEYAN (SK 178778). Three-bay front with round-arched openings and pedimental gable with tablet dated 1806.

GREAT LONGSTONE

(79) WESLEYAN, Station Road (SK 199718). Opened 1843; entrance formerly between S windows. Schoolroom added to W incorporating new entrance.

HARTINGTON MIDDLE QUARTER

(80) WESLEYAN, Earl Sterndale (SK 091669). Three-bay front of ashlar, original gabled porch dated 1850.

HARTINGTON NETHER QUARTER

(81) PRIMITIVE METHODIST, Biggin (SK 156594). Rendered walls and tiled roof. Date 1842 reset.

HARTINGTON TOWN QUARTER

(82) WESLEYAN, Hartington (SK 130604). Rendered stone with ashlar dressings, slate roof. Dated 1809; schoolroom below.

HARTSHORNE

(83) Former GENERAL BAPTIST (SK 324212). Built 1845–6, pedimented front with defaced tablet.

HATTON

(84) WESLEYAN (SK 213309). Opened 1841. Brown brick and tile. Mostly concealed by front extension of late 19th century.

HAYFIELD

(85) METHODIST (SK 036869). Built in 1782 for a society which originated in the mid 18th century, the chapel, refitted *c*.1838 and *c*.1910, has stone walls with rusticated quoins, a platband at mid height and two tiers of round-arched windows with keystones and impost blocks; the slated roof formerly had a small

bell-cote at the front. The N front is gabled and originally had two round-arched doorways now altered to windows and two windows above; *c*.1910 a gabled porch was built and a Venetian window inserted above with a tablet at its base inscribed 'Wesleyan chapel erected A.D. 1782'. The side walls are of three bays; the rear wall is mostly covered by a later vestry and organ loft.

The interior (40½ft by 33¾ft), entirely refitted, has a gallery around four sides supported by cast-iron columns.

Dolbey (1964) 70–1.

HEAGE

(86) METHODIST (SK 369502). 'Ebenezer Chapel' of brick was built c.1840–50, of two bays with entrance at the S end. It was extended to the S and has a tablet dated 1855 above the present W doorway. The windows have round-arched heads and intersecting glazing bars.

HEANOR

(87) Former FRIENDS (SK 437464). The site was bought in May 1834 and a meeting-house built shortly afterwards. The building, closed 1936 and now used by the Pentecostal Church, has brick walls now rendered and a hipped slate roof. The broad N front has two windows with splayed lintels and a large gabled central porch. There is a stepped gallery and modern porch at the W end. In the front yard are several reset headstones of 1840 and later.

(88) WESLEYAN (SK 434466). Brick with three-bay front and re-built parapet with date 1839. Front masked by further building of 1974. Centenary Hall alongside dated 1804–1904. *Monument*: in remains of burial ground, George, son of George and Ann Bryan, born 1818, 'who by a wise but Mysterious Providence was suddenly removed into eternity while bathing in the river Trent at Gainsborough Septr. 7th 1840 . . . ', slate headstone.

HILTON

(89) WESLEYAN (SK 245307). Dated 1841. Brick with hipped tile roof. Stone arches to windows; later gabled porch.

HOLLINGTON

(90) PRIMITIVE METHODIST (SK 232398). Dated 1847. Three-bay front with splayed lintels.

HOPE

(91) WESLEYAN (SK 173836). Stone with hipped slate roof. Built 1835, enlarged.

HORSLEY

(92) WESLEYAN (SK 376445). Dated 1845. Ashlar walls and slate roof. Narrow gabled front with shaped kneelers.

HORSLEY WOODHOUSE

(93) WESLEYAN (SK 393449). Opened 1845. Three-bay pedimented front.

HULLAND

(94) WESLEYAN (SK 250466). Built c.1840. Three-bay S front with round-arched windows.

(95) PRIMITIVE METHODIST (SK 250463). Dated 1821.

HULLAND WARD

(96) PRIMITIVE METHODIST, Mercaston Lane (SK 268439). Dated 1827. Gabled three-bay front.

IBLE

(97) PRIMITIVE METHODIST (SK 250571). Basically early 19th-century but refitted in 1872.

ILKESTON

(98) Former GENERAL BAPTIST, South Street (SK 466415). In 1784 Baptists formerly meeting at Little Hallam removed to a new building in Ilkeston and in 1785 became independent of the Kegworth church to which they formerly belonged. In 1858 services were transferred to a new chapel in Queen Street (see below).

The former meeting-house on the E side of South Street, latterly used by Elim Pentecostal Church, is a plain structure of brick with rendered gabled front of three bays with two tiers of windows and a slated roof. The original building of 1784 (37¼ft by 25½ft externally) was enlarged to the E in 1842 by the addition of minor rooms, heightened and partly refronted. Two original wide windows remain in each side wall with coursed brick heads resting directly on the frames. The interior has a gallery around three sides added c.1795–8 but has otherwise been refitted. (Demolition proposed 1975)

Monuments: W of chapel (1) Elizabeth Seavern, 1812; (2) Ann Harrison, 1794; (3) Ann, wife of Philip Hardcastle 'an Itinerant Minister in the Methodist Connexion', 1811; (4) Mary (Newton), wife of George Blount, 1846; (5) Sarah (Newton), wife of George Blount of Lenton Lock, 1820; in derelict burial-ground E of chapel (6) William Barnes West, 1831, table-tomb; also four reset slate headstones to John Twells, 1833, Eliza Twells, 1829, Ann Twells, 1847, and Ann, wife of William Twells, 1850.

Taylor (1818) II, 156, 229–31, 342: Wood (1847) 191.

(99) GENERAL BAPTIST, Queen Street (SK 464416). Built in 1858 to replace the foregoing, it has rendered walls and a slate

roof. The sides and semicircular E front have a continuous plain arcade of fourteen bays with tall round-arched windows in each bay and a triple-arched porch partly covering its two front bays, with date-tablet above.

KIRK IRETON

(100) Former PRIMITIVE METHODIST (SK 268501). Now a Sunday-school. Three-bay front dated 1836.

KNIVETON

(101) Former WESLEYAN (SK 209502). Built c.1840; three-bay front with cast-iron window frames.

(102) PRIMITIVE METHODIST (SK 208501). Dated 1832.

LITTLE LONGSTONE

(103) CONGREGATIONAL (SK 188716). Built *c*.1844 for a congregation founded in that year. Walls of limestone with

rusticated sandstone dressings and a slated roof supported by two exposed king-post trusses. Gabled front, stone bell-cote.

LITTON

(104) WESLEYAN (SK 166751). Stone and slate. Dated 1834, re-built late 19th century, altered and refitted 1905.

LONG EATON

(105) GENERAL BAPTIST, Sawley (SK 471315). The first meeting-house at Sawley was an existing building given by Joseph Parkinson and fitted up by John Stenson; it was opened in 1783 as a preaching station of the church at Kegworth, Leics., but from 1785 was attached to the Castle Donington church. The present chapel, built in 1800–1 and enlarged to the front in 1843, has brick walls and a slate roof. The N front is gabled, of three bays with two tiers of windows, the upper ones round-arched, and a central doorway with half-round Tuscan columns and open pediment. A large tablet in the gable is inscribed with the dates of erection and enlargement. The side walls were originally of two bays with two tiers of windows; the rear wall has two tall round-arched windows flanking the pulpit.

The interior (originally 23ft by 32¼ft) has a N gallery of 1843 with panelled and balustraded front and slight central projection with clock. Some mid 19th-century box-pews remain with doors removed and capping altered.

Monuments: in chapel (1) Elizabeth widow of John Bonsall of Breaston, 1838; (2) John Bonsall, 1822; (3) Joseph Bowmer,

1832; (4) Martha, widow of William Parkinson, 1848; (5) William Parkinson, 1844; (6) Elizabeth (Parkinson) widow of William Fearson, 1849; (7) William Fearson, 1836; (8) Mary (Fearson) wife of Thomas Harriman, 1851; (9) Mary wife of C. Robe, 1848; in burial-ground, slate headstone (10) Catharine, wife of Thomas Topley, 1814, and Thomas their son, signed Booth & Johnson C. Don.; (11) Thomas Topley, 1846, signed T. Kiddey; (12) Thomas North Buttery son of John and Elizabeth Buttery, 1820; (13) John Buttery, 1840, and Elizabeth Buttery, 1831; (14) children of John and Elizabeth Stenton, John, Paul, and Mary, 1810, Sibyl, 1811, signed Booth & Johnson, C. Donington; (15) Joseph Parkinson, 1795, Grace his widow, 1817, and two sons, both Thomas, 1787, 1788, double headstone with rococo border and urn in low relief, traces of gilding, signed B. Pollard.

Taylor (1818) II, 156, 231, 343: Wood (1847) 191.

MATLOCK BATH

(106) LADY GLENORCHY'S CHAPEL (SK 294574), S of Masson Mill, was demolished *c*.1960–5. Built in 1777 as Cromford Chapel apparently for Anglican worship although the adjacent house was provided for the use of Samuel Need, one of Richard Arkwright's partners, who was an Independent. After Need's death in 1781 the house and chapel were bought by Lady Glenorchy who presented communion plate 'bearing her name and arms' to the newly-formed Independent congregation. The chapel stood N of the house and was of brick with four tall windows at the side facing the road.

Thompson (1967) 52–6.

(107) Former WESLEYAN, North Parade (SK 295584). Opened 1867; corner tower with pyramidal spire.

(108) Former PRIMITIVE METHODIST, Cromford (SK 294570). Dated 1853; brick with rusticated stone quoins.

MELBOURNE

(109) GENERAL BAPTIST, Chapel Street (SK 386254). The congregation originated about 1747 when the church at Barton in the Beans, Leics., (72), first sent itinerant preachers. Like its parent church, Melbourne was originally Independent and is so described on a 1753 marriage covenant, but both societies were General Baptist by 1760 when the daughter churches of Barton became autonomous; in 1770 Melbourne was one of the founders of the General Baptist New Connexion.

The first chapel, built in 1749–50, was enlarged in 1768 and heightened and galleries added in 1782, but it is said to have been 'virtually rebuilt' and enlarged in 1832; it was further enlarged in 1856 by the addition of an organ loft at the W end. The walls are of stone with later brickwork, rendered at the front and S side, and the roof is slate covered. The E front (39¼ft wide) is gabled and has two platbands above and below three upper windows; the lower openings which alone remain recognizable as work of 1750 (or possibly 1768) comprise two doorways with stone architraves and keystones and two windows between joined by a narrow panel with arched head. The side wall to the N, where exposed behind the adjacent buildings, is of 18th-century masonry to the lower half, of random rubble with some coursed stone near the W end. The interior, entirely refitted in

CONGREGATIONAL CHAPEL, MIDDLETON by Youlgreave CFS 1972

1832 and later, has a gallery around three sides. *School* to N, brick, built 1810, enlarged 1835, rebuilt 1852.

Fittings – *Books*: pulpit Bible, 1611, said to be now in Baptist Union Library, formerly belonging to Francis Smith, first ruling elder. *Monuments*: in burial ground at rear, many reset slate headstones, (1) Ann, wife of James Worstall, 1760; (2) Thomas Robinson, senior, 1768, John Robinson, 1760, Thomas Robinson, 1761, and Mary his wife, 1760, Daniel Robinson, 1763, *et al.*; (3) John Joseph son of James and Ann Newbold, 1845, with cherub in oval cartouche, signed Bagnall. *Organ*: bought 1856 from Great Meeting, Leicester.

Budge, T.L., *Melbourne Baptists, The Story of Two Hundred Years in Melbourne, Derbyshire* (1951).

(110) Former WESLEYAN, Church Street (SK 387252). Built 1826 replacing chapel of 1800, heightened and converted to Sunday-school 1870 when adjacent chapel was built.

MIDDLETON AND SMERRILL

(111) Former CONGREGATIONAL, Middleton by Youlgreave (SK 195634). Built 1826–7 by Thomas Bateman of Middleton

CONGREGATIONAL CHAPEL, MIDDLETON by Youlgreave 1972

Hall, foundation stone laid 1 September 1826 by his grandson Thomas Bateman junior. The walls are of ashlar and the roof is slated. The chapel is built on a sloping site with minor rooms below and a later house of three storeys attached to the rear. In the side walls are two tiers of windows, the upper chapel windows having four-centred arched heads of two lights with labels. The E front is gabled with a parapet which continues around the sides, and has a central doorway between lancet windows. The interior has two ranks of box-pews with a wide central aisle, and square pulpit on dwarf legs. *Monuments*: on W wall (1) Thomas Bateman of Lomberdale House and Middleton Hall, 1861, white marble tablet surmounted by low relief of Bronze Age urn resting on book 'Ten Years Diggings' and crest above; (2) Sarah, widow of Thomas Bateman, 1866, with lozenge of arms; in field W of chapel, in railed enclosure, monument to above (see p. 58), stone tomb-chest with coped lid carved with stem and stepped base of cross, and stone replica of Bronze Age urn at head. (Chapel closed 1972, sold 1978 for conversion to a house)

MILFORD

(112) GENERAL BAPTIST (SK 34984523). Dated 1849. Three bays with round-arched windows.

(113) Former WESLEYAN (SK 34984520). Date 1842 on defaced door-lintel.

(114) PRIMITIVE METHODIST, Shaw Lane, Hopping Hill (SK 349457). Date 1823 on oval tablet; altered 1883.

MONYASH

(115) Former FRIENDS (SK 150668). Built in 1771 to supersede a building of 1697, it was closed in 1892 and converted in 1969 for social purposes. The walls are of coursed limestone rubble and the roof is covered with tiles. The S front has a two-light mullioned window to the right of the entrance with another window above, probably renewed in the early 19th century, and further E is a taller sash window formerly with external shutters, also presumably a 19th-century alteration. The other walls have no original openings, the E and W ends are gabled and a large stable of stone with stone slate roof adjoins to the east.

The interior ($24\frac{1}{2}$ft by $15\frac{1}{4}$ft) has a gallery at the W end with sliding shutters and a fireplace in the W wall. The stand at the E end, removed by 1969 and loose in outbuilding, had an open

S front.

front with plain flat balusters. Burial-ground to W has a few uniform headstones of late 19th-century and after.

Lidbetter (1961) fig. 24.

NETHERSEAL

(116) GENERAL BAPTIST (SK 286131). The society established *c.*1826 as a branch of Austrey, Warwicks., became autonomous in 1829 and in 1840 formed a united church with Measham, Leics. The meeting-house built in 1840 has brick walls and a

hipped slate roof. The broad N front is in Flemish bond with glazed headers, the windows have cast-iron frames. The S wall is blank, the rendered W wall has two small pointed-arched windows at the upper level and the E wall has two similar windows below the gallery with a pair of plain windows above. The

fenestration appears to require two end galleries but there is now only a single E gallery, closed with shutters below the front, and a late 19th-century rostrum pulpit at the W end. *Monument*: loose in chapel yard, to John Copestake, 1844, and Martha his widow, 1856, slate headstone.

Wood (1847) 228, 231.

NEW MILLS

(117) CONGREGATIONAL, Mellor Road (SK 003862). Tablet inscribed 'PROVIDENCE CHAPEL 1823'. Much altered *c.*1900 (URC)

(118) FRIENDS, Low Leighton (SK 008856). Stone and slate, originally erected in 1717 but much rebuilt, probably on the old foundations, in the mid 19th century. The S front has three plain sash windows to right of entrance and two tiers of windows to the left; the E and W ends are gabled. The interior (54ft by 18¾ft) is divided by a thick wall, perhaps part of the original structure, into two parts; a large meeting-room to the E (34ft long) and a smaller two-storied section to the west. A stone reset in the E gable is dated 1717; the S door, boarded and nail-studded with strap hinges with fleur-de-lys terminals, is of the early 18th century.

(119) Site of METHODIST, High Street (SK 001858). A preaching-house of 1766 was superseded in 1810 by a chapel in St George's Road, 200 yards E, and in 1844 the former building was replaced by the present 'Wesleyan Day and Sabbath School', of stone and slate with gabled W front and porch with rusticated quoins, round-arched doorway and inscribed tablet. Above a window in the S wall is a reset keystone dated 1766. The chapel in St Georges Road was demolished before 1972 but the *burial-ground* remains with monuments including table-tombs of the early 19th century. The *pulpit* of *c.*1766 is now at Methodist Central Hall, Manchester.

OCKBROOK

(120) MORAVIAN (SK 421361). Moravian tenets were introduced here by Benjamin Ingham and Jacob Rogers and in 1739 Rogers commenced preaching in a barn lent by Isaac Frearson on whose land the settlement was subsequently built. The society was formed into a regular congregation in 1750 and the chapel built in 1751–2. Houses for the single brethren and single sisters were opened in 1759 and buildings for boys, and girls, day and boarding-schools were subsequently provided. In 1867 the brethren's house was replaced by a Sunday-school. The chapel was enlarged to the rear, heightened and refitted in 1875–6.

The main buildings of the settlement, of brick with slate roofs, are aligned on sloping ground facing SE with the chapel near the centre, houses of two and three stories to the right which include the former single sisters' house, and to the left the minister's house of three stories, dating from the mid 18th century, and a range of late 19th-century buildings of Ockbrook girls boarding-school. The chapel, of red brick with a stone plinth, has three principal windows at the front with doorways in the end bays, all with round-arched heads. The wall was heightened and a wide pediment and bell-cote added in 1875–6, the latter probably replacing a similar feature on the original

(120) OCKBROOK. Moravian Settlement. Chapel and adjoining houses from SE.

more steeply pitched roof. The rear wall, with similar fenestration to the front, is entirely of the late 19th century. The chapel (originally $24\frac{1}{4}$ft by $54\frac{1}{4}$ft) was widened in 1875–6 and the interior entirely refitted; the pulpit, formerly against the NW wall, was re-sited at the SW end facing a single gallery which replaced galleries at each end.

Fittings – *Monuments*: in burial-ground at rear, flat rectangular slate tablets, not numbered, typical examples being (1) J. Birch, 1752; (2) Mary Clark, 1787. The ground is divided into four parallel plots, with male and female burials respectively in two, one with the sexes separated in alternate rows, and one vacant. *Painting*: in vestry, portrait in oils of John Cennick at age 26, signed 'M. Jenkin fecit'.

Railings: in front of chapel, with acorn finials, late 18th-cen-

tury. *Sundial*: in front of chapel, stone pillar with moulded cap and base, horizontal dial, late 18th-century.

England (1888) 31–6.

(121) Former WESLEYAN, Borrowash (SK 418345). Tall building of square plan. Brick and slate; pedimented front of three bays with two tiers of round-arched windows, recessed centre bay rising to semicircular arch enclosing defaced tablet dated 1825. Superseded *c*.1902 and now in commercial use.

OSLESTON AND THURVASTON

(122) PRIMITIVE METHODIST, Lane Ends, Sutton on the Hill (SK 236347). Red brick and tile, with brick dentil cornice and shaped tablet dated 1838; later porch.

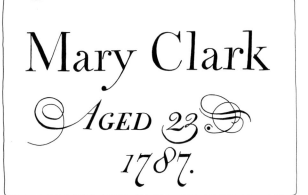

PRIMITIVE METHODIST CHAPEL, Lane Ends, OSLESTON & THURVASTON   1973

PARWICH

(123) WESLEYAN (SK 186544). Squared stone with slate roof. Three-bay front with tablet dated 1847 recut to 1849, and later porch. Gabled sides with external stairs to gallery at NW end.

PENTRICH

(124) Former PRESBYTERIAN (SK 389522). Although the vicar, Robert Porter, was ejected in 1662 there is no evidence to suggest that he was concerned in the establishment of the Presbyterian meeting here which in the early 18th century shared a minister with the congregation in Belper. The meeting-house of c.1700 altered in the mid 19th century, probably for another denomination, was derelict in 1970.

The building has walls of coursed rubble and the roof, gabled to N and S, has been re-covered in tiles. The W wall originally had a central entrance with chamfered jambs now partly blocked and a wooden window frame inserted; to each side is a window of three lights with square stone mullions. The E wall had three similar windows, but that in the centre has been altered to a doorway. There are two single-light windows in the S wall with pointed-arched heads, probably altered, and at the N end is a

later vestry and entrance. The interior ($42\frac{1}{4}$ft by $19\frac{1}{4}$ft) has no fittings, but a fireplace in the N wall with chamfered jambs and lintel may be original. (Demolished c.1971)

REPTON

(125) CONGREGATIONAL, Pinfold Lane (SK 308266). Built c.1837 for a church which claimed to have been formed in 1780; a certificate for meetings in a private house is dated January 1788. The chapel has three round-arched windows at the side, the entrance is in a later porch with gallery adjacent; one bay has been added at the opposite end. (URC).

RODSLEY

(126) WESLEYAN (SK 201404). Opened 1823. Brick with a hipped tile roof.

SHIRLAND AND HIGHAM

(127) Former FRIENDS, Toadhole Furnace (SK 389569). A small building of squared stone with a slate roof, formerly thatched, was built in 1743. Adjacent, to the E, is a cottage of two storeys with rendered walls which may be of a similar date but has been

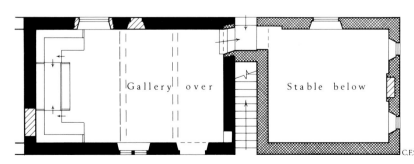

Former Friends' Meeting-house
at Toadhole Furnace
SHIRLAND AND HIGHAM
Derbyshire

Gallery over   Stable below

Scale of Feet

5   0   5   10   15   20

C.F.S.

entirely altered. A stable with women's meeting-house above of the later 18th century, similarly constructed, stands to the W separated from the main building by an external stair to the gallery. The N front has a doorway with deep lintel inscribed 'Matthew Hopkinson 1743' and a small two-light window to the left with a square mullion. The S wall has a small blocked window near the centre, and further E a large window has been inserted in the 19th century. The interior (24ft by 14¼ft) has two exposed beams supporting a deep gallery the front of which is closed by fielded panelled shutters. The stand and wall benches at the E end date from the 19th century. *Monument*: outside N doorway, to Matthew Hopkinson, 1747.

SHIRLEY

(128) WESLEYAN (SK 217412). Brick and tile. Three-bay front with splayed lintels; gabled sides. Tablet dated 1855.

SMALLEY

(129) GENERAL BAPTIST (SK 407446). The church, formerly linked with Ilkeston, separated in 1822. The meeting-house was built in 1790 and enlarged to the front and heightened in 1817. The walls are of brick and the hipped roof has been re-covered with concrete tiles. The side and rear walls of the original building remain (33¼ft by 24¼ft externally) with one wide segmental-arched window at each side and two altered windows at the rear. The front, extended by 12ft, has a central doorway and two tiers of windows. *Monuments*: in burial-ground (1) Elizabeth, wife of Christopher Harrison, 1796, stone headstone, signed 'Bradbury, Ashford'; also many slate headstones, including (2) William Carrington, 1833, *et al.*; (3) Elizabeth Woolley, 1807; (4) Ann, wife of William Kerry, 1838; (5) Joseph Harrison, 1825; (6) Anthony Weston, 1836, signed 'S. Kerry'; (7) Thomas and John Shaw, 1828; (8) Elizabeth Beeson, 1844; (9) John Smith, 1820, Mary his wife, 1813, and Sarah his widow, 1845; (10) Joseph Fletcher, 1826.

Taylor (1818) II, 229, 453: Wood (1847) 226.

SMISBY

(130) WESLEYAN (SK 350192). Dated 1845. Rendered brick and slate; front with open pediment.

SWADLINCOTE

(131) WESLEYAN, West Street (SK 299196). Opened 1837, later front with polygonal corners.

TANSLEY

(132) WESLEYAN, Church Street (SK 322596). Late 19th-century; tablet 'open'd December 25th 1829' reset.

TICKNALL

(133) GENERAL BAPTIST (SK 354239). A meeting-house built in 1795 was registered in January 1803 and described as a 'new building standing in Bucknall's yard on the South side of the street'. It was 'enlarged' in 1817 at a cost of £271. The present chapel, which appears to be a rebuilding of *c*.1817, has walls of red brick with some rubble in the S and E walls and a hipped tiled roof. The W front has a wide round-arched window between two smaller but similarly-arched windows and with a doorway

to the left. The pulpit is at the S end and gallery opposite.

Taylor (1818) II, 223: Wood (1847) 181.

(134) WESLEYAN, Chapel Street (SK 354241). Brown brick and slate with shaped gable and tablet dated 1815; hung sashes to front windows replaced since 1970. Square interior, gallery

around three sides with original seating, lower pews renewed in late 19th century, rostrum pulpit. *Collecting Shovel*; open box with short flat round-ended handle, early 19th-century. *Inscriptions*; on bricks left of entrance, initials and date 1815.

TUPTON

(135) Former FRIENDS, Nethermoor Road (SK 391653). A meeting-house built in 1677 was closed by the late 18th century and sold in 1806. The site is now occupied by a house of two stories with walls of stone with some rendered brickwork at the S end. Although largely of 19th-century date it includes in the N wall a small upper window with re-used jambs and cill; some of the walling may also be of an earlier period. Incorporated in the garden wall to the S is a stone dated 1673 and in an outhouse to the W are two inscribed stones, one 'IW/1707' and one with part of a funerary inscription.

TURNDITCH

(136) GREEN BANK CHAPEL (SK 302467), built in 1818 for a Congregational church formerly associated with Belper, has brick walls and tiled roofs. The original building has a gabled front with two former windows with splayed lintels and a central entrance. It was extended to one side and refitted in the later 19th century.

UNSTONE

(137) WESLEYAN (SK 377774). Dated 1847.

WENSLEY AND SNITTERTON

(138) WESLEYAN REFORM, Oaker Side (SK 275610). Three-bay front; tablet inscribed 'Wesleyan Methodist Reform Chapel 1854'. Stepped seating.

(139) WESLEYAN, Wensley (SK 262611). Built 1829, enlarged 1879.

WESTON UPON TRENT

(140) GENERAL BAPTIST, Trent Lane (SK 405279). Small chapel of brick with partly pantiled roof, built in 1845 as a preaching station of Castle Donington, Leics. (Derelict 1974)

(141) WESLEYAN (SK 402280). Three-bay front, tablet above former entrance with cherubs' heads supporting ogee canopy with finial, inscribed 'EBENEZER WESLEYAN CHAPEL 1846'.

WHALEY BRIDGE

(142) WESLEYAN, Buxton Road (SK 012812). Chapel dated 1867. Sunday-school attached dated 1821 with wall anchor 'W' at front for 'Wesleyan'.

WINSTER

(143) WESLEYAN, West Bank (SK 240605). Dated 1837. Stone with slate roof, N front of ashlar with plinth, quoins and round-arched doorway between Venetian windows. Two round-arched windows in the S wall and a blocked window high up at W end; pulpit against blank E wall.

(144) PRIMITIVE METHODIST, East Bank (SK 240604). Built 1823 but greatly enlarged in 1850. Some early 19th-century masonry remains on N side with evidence of successive enlargements.

(145) WESLEYAN REFORM, East Bank (SK 242605). Dated 1852; part of a continuous terrace of houses.

WIRKSWORTH

(146) CONGREGATIONAL, Middleton (SK 278560). Built in the late 19th century for a church formed in 1786. *Pulpit:* hexagonal with three tiers of fielded panels and stairs with turned balusters and moulded handrail; *c*.1695, removed from Castle Hill Meeting-house, Northampton in 1862; lowered and stairs altered.
    Deacon (1980) 76.

(147) Former WESLEYAN, Chapel Lane (SK 288541). Three-bay front; central doorway with arched hood of *c*.1900; original tablet above inscribed 'EBEN-EZER 1810'. (Partly demolished February 1983)

(145) WINSTER. Wesleyan Reform.

YEAVELEY

(148) CONGREGATIONAL (SK 184399). Dated 1814; refitted in the late 19th century; closed *c*.1970.

YOULGREAVE

(149) Former CONGREGATIONAL (SK 206640). Sandstone ashlar with stone slate roof, gabled front in Romanesque style dated 1853; designed and paid for by Thomas Bateman of Lomberdale House.

(150) WESLEYAN, Main Street (SK 208642). Built 1807 and enlarged to front 1907.

(151) WESLEYAN REFORM, Holywell Lane (SK 210642). Dated 1857; gabled front with rusticated quoins and lancet windows with wide external splays.

(111) MIDDLETON AND SMERRILL. Former Congregational chapel, Middleton by Youlgreave. Monument to Thomas Bateman.

Commerce and industry, which have been found to encourage independency in religious expression, were flourishing in several parts of the county in the 17th century and many societies of the older denominations came into existence at that time. Bristol, in the extreme south of the county, then a major seaport through which many groups of Puritans had left in the earlier years of the century to seek a new life in the American colonies, became the home of some of the oldest congregations; of these Broadmead (14), though lacking antiquarian interest in its buildings, makes recompense in the completeness and antiquity of its records. The woollen manufacturing area around Stroud also proved hospitable to new ideas, and travelling Quaker preachers soon attracted considerable support from amorphous groups of 'seekers' and others at Nailsworth (107), Painswick (122), and elsewhere throughout the county from Bristol (24) to Cirencester (62) and Broad Campden (55), leaving several notable meeting-houses in their wake of which those named are of particular interest. The early 19th-century meeting-house at Frenchay (162), on an older site, is also worthy of note.

The Old Baptist Chapel in Tewkesbury (145) is another reminder of a church which has existed from the mid 17th century although looking for its earliest support mainly amongst like-minded congregations to the north; the meeting-house, a converted timber-framed house hidden in a narrow alley, redolent of the clandestine meetings of a proscribed conventicle, is as enigmatic about its history as were the earlier professors about their place of meeting. A rare but slight reminder of the Seventh-day Baptists also exists nearby in the graveyard at Natton (2).

Presbyterian congregations which sprang up in many of the main centres of population following the Restoration are no longer represented by any notable chapels of that period; Barton Street Chapel, Gloucester (75), a plain brick building of 1699, entirely transformed in the late 19th century, has been demolished as has the much altered Old Chapel in Stroud (138), while the surviving Gosditch Street Chapel in Cirencester (59) also suffered a major 19th-century refitting at the hands of its Unitarian congregation. The early 18th-century Frenchay Chapel (161), however, although much altered about 1800, remains of especial importance for the provision of a prominent bell-tower above the entrance. The former chapel at Marshfield (101), of 1752, is a dignified and remarkably well-preserved building of its period, while in Bristol the rebuilt Lewin's Mead Meeting-house (32), of 1787–91, is of national importance.

Many of the leading figures in the Evangelical Revival of the 18th century were attracted to Gloucestershire as a fruitful field of activity. George Whitefield, a native of Gloucester, was responsible for forming Methodist societies in Bristol and Kingswood, which John Wesley was soon called to administer, and on becoming the leader of Calvinistic Methodists he encouraged the growth of further societies including Kingswood (90) and Rodborough (140), both of which have 'Tabernacles' of this period, the former being of particular architectural interest. John Wesley is especially remembered at Bristol where the New Room (26), partly of 1739 though enlarged and refashioned in 1748, is the oldest remaining Methodist preaching-house. Lesser known though still historically important is the former Methodist octagon chapel in Stroud (142), of 1763, the oldest survivor of a style of building for which Wesley expressed particular favour. Captain Thomas Webb, doyen of American Methodism, was closely connected with the erection of Portland Chapel, Bristol (27), in 1791–2, a building which in its overtly parochial character proclaimed Methodism's emancipation from the Anglican attachments of its founder and which is one of the more tragic architectural losses to have occurred during the course of this survey. The Rev. Rowland Hill is also associated with this county in the Tabernacle at Wotton-under-Edge (169) although only the house remains of the 18th-century structure. The Countess of Huntingdon is more evident in her encouragement of the work of Whitefield than in the few 19th-century chapels which still bear the name of her Connexion, but the comparable though less well-known Lady Glenorchy has left as one of her rare English chapels, Hope Chapel in Bristol (19), of 1786–8. John Cennick whose brief but active life was devoted to the furtherance of Moravian societies in Wiltshire and Ireland also began his work in Gloucestershire amongst the miners of Kingswood where is one of the few chapels of this denomination in the county (93), others being at Apperley (68) and Brockweir (86).

The impetus given by these and others of lesser fame to the growth and muliplication of societies of various denominations continued into the 19th century when it is particularly evident in the mining areas of the Forest of Dean and in the vicinity of Kingswood near Bristol. In

Cheltenham the needs of visitors to a popular watering place resulted in a rich variety of chapels which were an epitome of the architecture of early 19th-century dissent; of these Salem Chapel (40), of 1844, is an interesting example of the Gothic style. Although few outstanding Gothic Revival buildings were recorded, Buckingham Chapel in Bristol (16), of 1842, is unusually important as an exceptionally early and scholarly exercise for a Baptist church, while Highbury Chapel, Bristol (22), is notable as the earliest work of William Butterfield.

The grand Classical manner, found in the late 18th-century at Lewin's Mead Meeting-house (32) and in some degree at Uley (154), is best exemplified in the following century in the chapel in Bristol (17), designed for the Catholic Apostolic Church although never used by them and an early and surprising choice for that denomination; Bedford Street Chapel, Stroud (139), of 1835–7, also in this style, has an unusual and imaginative circular stair-tower to give access to the principal floor.

The general availability of good building stone throughout the Cotswold parts of the county has ensured that many of even the smaller and plainer chapels have an intrinsic merit and blend well with their surroundings. Little early brickwork was noted, the earliest being at Barton Street, Gloucester (75), of 1699. Roofs covered with small stone slates remain in a few places but their replacement by pantiles, blue slate or more recent materials has been widespread.

ALKINGTON

(1) CONGREGATIONAL, Newport (ST 698974). Built 1825 to replace a chapel of 1710. Rendered walls and patent tile roof gabled E and W; a small vestry with stone slate roof projects to the south. Original fittings include pulpit with bowed front supported by two columns and gallery around three sides with contemporary pews.

ASHCHURCH

(2) SEVENTH-DAY BAPTIST, Natton (SO 929326). A church which met here from the 18th century or before, divided in 1871 when seceders built a new chapel at Kinsham (see Worcestershire (6)). A small building on the site which may have been the former meeting-house was demolished c.1960–70. The burial-ground enclosed by brick walls has monuments dated 1761–1947. *Communion Table*: see Tewkesbury (145).

(3) WESLEYAN, Aston Cross (SO 942340). Three bays with hipped roof, 1845.

AVENING

(4) BAPTIST (ST 884979). Built on steeply sloping site, with coursed rubble walls and hipped stone slated roof; tablet between two round-arched windows in side wall inscribed 'This Place of Worship was Erected 1805, Enlarged 1821'.

AWRE

(5) BAPTIST, Blakeney (SO 671069). Built 1835, altered and refenestrated 1874.

(6) CONGREGATIONAL, Blakeney (SO 669070). Three-bay ashlar front with pyramidal finials. Built 1849 to replace a chapel at Blakeney Hill opened 1823. (URC)

Bright (1954) 17–18.

BERKELEY

(7) CONGREGATIONAL 'Union Chapel', Salter Street (ST 683993). Dated 1835; ashlar front with pedimental gable, two tall windows with four-centred arched heads and an open porch.

BISLEY-WITH-LYPIATT

(8) BAPTIST, Eastcombe (SO 890043). A large building of rubble with a slate roof, built in 1800–1, enlarged 1816 and greatly altered by heightening and refitting in 1860. The S front, largely of the late 19th century, is gabled and has a stone bell-cote with one bell above a clockface and two tiers of round-arched windows. Traces of earlier work in E wall include a blocked doorway with remains of windows above and to the left, with indications of an extension to the rear. The interior is divided by cast-iron arcades of five bays carrying galleries around three sides and a barrel vault over the central space.

Fittings – *Coffin Stools*: two, with enriched upper rails, early 18th-century. *Monuments*: in chapel (1) Rev. Thomas Williams, 1806, founder and first pastor, and Phebe his widow 1827; (2) Richard Faulkes, 1847, and Esther his wife 1845; (3) Henry Hook, 1833, *et al. Organ*: with Gothic case, *c*.1800, formerly at Bussage House, re-erected 1863.

The Free Churchman (Stroud District Free Church Council), June 1901–Jan. 1902.

BITTON   *Avon*

(9) CONGREGATIONAL, Upton Cheyney (ST 693701). Built 1834, much altered *c*.1900. End-entrance in semicircular porch between two round-arched windows. (URC)

Eayrs (1911) 175–7.

(10) Former WESLEYAN (ST 681697). Three-bay ashlar front with pediment, terminal pilasters, round-arched windows and obscured tablet above entrance formerly dated 1834.

BLOCKLEY

(11) Former BAPTIST (SP 16303483), now village hall. Built in 1792 for a church formed by Rev. Elisha Smith (1754–1819) and superseded by a new chapel (see below) in 1835. The walls are of coursed rubble and the roof is hipped and covered with slates. The front wall has a central doorway with moulded architrave and a tripartite lunette above with a small square tablet dated 1792 above the entrance. Two windows in the rear wall which flank the site of the pulpit have round-arched heads with keystones. The side walls are blank. The interior (26½ft by 18½ft) has a small gallery next to the entrance.

(12) BAPTIST, High Street (SP 16283480). Chapel dated 1835, replacing the foregoing, stands at the rear of a large burial-ground. The walls are of rubble with an ashlar front and the roof

is slated. The pedimented front wall is of three bays with Ionic pilasters next the corners, two plain round-arched windows and a central doorway with open pediment supported by columns and a tablet above bearing the name 'Ebenezer'. Two round-arched windows in each side wall; former British School at rear.

The interior has a plaster ceiling with moulded cornice and circular ceiling rose. A gallery above the entrance, supported by two cast-iron columns of quatrefoil section, has a front with partly open cast-iron traceried panels. The pulpit and lower seating were renewed in the late 19th century, original cast-iron gates and piers next to the street were removed *c*.1960–70. (Internal subdivision proposed 1971; reported disused 1982)

Lindley (1969), pl. 7.

BOURTON-ON-THE-WATER

(13) BAPTIST, Station Road (SP 169207). Built 1876 superseding an earlier meeting-house on another site; the front is gabled and has a large wheel window above the entrance. *Monuments*: in chapel (1) Rev. Benjamin Beddome, 1795, 50 years pastor, and Elizabeth his wife, 1784, signed Lewis, Gloster; (2) Hannah, daughter of William and Mary Palmer, 1787; (3) Rev. Thomas Coles A.M., 1840, signed H. Roff, Stow and Gardner, Cheltenham; (4) Letitia, widow of Rev. William Wilkins,

1844. Also in rear room (5) _____, 'eldest surviving daughter of Benjamin Seward of Bengworth, Worcs', late 18th-century tripartite monument with columns flanking central panel, partly concealed by inserted ceiling.

The *former meeting-house*, 400 yards E (SP 172207), built 1701, rebuilt 1765, for a church in existence by 1655, has been demolished; the surrounding burial-ground adjacent to the public cemetery is enclosed by a stone wall. *Monuments*: (1) Hannah Coller, 1713, small headstone with scrolled top and hour-glass; (2) Sarah Coller, 1713, comparable design to last, with book; (3) Mary Hartwell, 1819, and later panel above to William Hartwell, 1852 and Sarah his wife, 1850, cast-iron, signed Hartwell, Bourton; (4) Sarah (Kyte) wife of John Hall, 1803, with oval inscription panel; (5) Thomas Coles A.M., 1810, who 'preached in the adjoining place of worship for nearly forty years', Elizabeth his widow, 1836, *et al.*, capstone from table-tomb; (6) William Wood, 1794, Sarah his wife, 1776, and three children, rectangular box-tomb with pilasters, cornice, and moulded capping; (7) Benjamin Beddome, 1795, 50 years pastor, headstone erected late 19th century, probably on site of vault in chapel; (8) John Nicholas, 1703, and Joshua Head, 1739.

Oliver (1968) 114–15.

BRISTOL   *Avon*

(14) BAPTIST, 'Broadmead', Union Street (ST 59007335). The chapel was replaced in 1969 by a new development of shops and offices incorporating a meeting-house on the upper floors. The site N of Broadmead has been occupied since the late 17th-century by a church which originated about 1640 as an Independent society, becoming Baptist in 1653. For a few years after 1660 meetings were held in the Friars, then in Whitson Court, and in 1671 'we tooke the Meeting house at the lower end of Broadmead (where the heretics called Quakers had formerly used to meet)'. The meeting-house was desecrated in 1681 and until 1687 the congregation met in various places before returning 'to their old Meeting-place' in that year. A new meeting-house (40ft by 50ft) was built in 1695 which was subjected to a series of alterations and enlargements principally in 1764–5, 1871–2 and 1875, leaving a building ultimately 92ft by 50ft of which less than half of the E wall only may have formed part of the original structure. The W wall was rebuilt or refaced in 1876–7 to designs by Alfred Harford when the adjacent Lower Union Street was laid out.

BRSP XXVII (1974) 'The Records of a Church of Christ in Bristol, 1640–1687': Child, R.L. & Shipley C.E., *Broadmead Origins* (1940): Hewell, W., MS history in Bristol Record Office: Ivimey II (1814) 523–30; IV (1830) 262–83: Oliver (1968) 94–7.

(15) BAPTIST, Old King Street (ST 592734). The church which originated *c*. 1650, met first at the Friars, and in 1679 purchased land in Red Cross Street, jointly with the Broadmead church, for a burial ground. About 1699 a 'sope house' at the Pithay was converted to a meeting-house. The chapel dated 1815, demolished in 1957 after the congregation had removed to Cairns Road, had an ashlar front of three bays with a pediment and two tiers of round-arched windows.

Ivimey II (1814) 541–4; IV (1830) 283–9: Oliver (1968) 97–8.

(16) BAPTIST, 'Buckingham Chapel', Queens Road (ST 574732). Stone and slate, built 1842 to designs by R.S. Pope in French Gothic style of the late 13th century.

(17) Former CATHOLIC APOSTOLIC, Colston Avenue (ST 586731), on the W side of the former quay, was built 1839–43 to the designs of R.S. Pope. Financial difficulties amongst the promoters forced the sale of the building before completion to

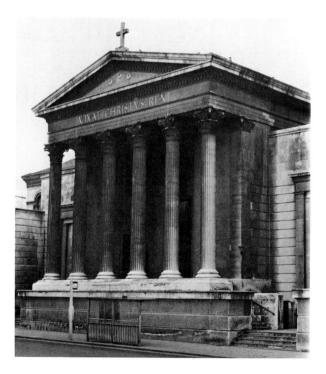

the Roman Catholics who continue to use it as the 'Church of St Mary on the Quay'. The front, of ashlar, has a central portico of six Corinthian columns supporting a pediment and two similar columns *in antis* behind. The interior has an elaborately detailed sanctuary at the W end with four columns of the same order flanking the chancel, N and S transepts, and a nave of five bays with an E gallery.

Little (1966) 75.

(18) THE TABERNACLE, Penn Street (ST 593734), demolished in 1958, was built for a Methodist society formed in 1739 which continued to support George Whitefield after his break with the Wesleys. The society met until 1753 in Smith's Hall, latterly 'Cutlers' Hall'; on 13 July in that year Whitefield laid the foundation stone of the Tabernacle which was opened on 25 November. The Calvinistic Methodist society became Congregational in the 19th century.

(A second Calvinistic Methodist society was commenced by the Countess of Huntingdon in 1775, meeting in an assembly room in St Augustine's Place; a new chapel built in Trenchard Street (ST 585731) in 1831 was demolished before 1970 after a long period in commercial use.)

Photograph © R. Winstone.

The Tabernacle appears to have been of five bays in length divided into nave and aisles by tall Tuscan columns of stone, with a coved ceiling to the nave, central octagonal lantern, and galleries around three sides. The roof was gabled to front and back, hipped down to the lantern, and with separate roofs above the side galleries. The W front of three bays with a pediment had two tiers of segmental-arched windows. The interior was partly refitted in the late 19th century but the *pulpit* (reported to be now in The Whitfield Memorial Tabernacle, Horfield, Bristol) was original and had a square base with Ionic columns at the corners, a pedimented back panel and pair of staircases. Immediately S of the chapel stood the Sunday-school of 1834 with Whitefield's house, subsequently vestries, behind.

Belden [*c*.1930] 197–8: Caston (1860) 118–27: Photographs in NMR.

(19) HOPE CHAPEL, Clifton (ST 56907265). When in 1785 Lady Glenorchy and Lady Henrietta Hope visited the Hotwells for medical treatment they determined to build a chapel for Calvinistic evangelical worship. Lady Hope died in January 1786 and Lady Glenorchy 'procured a plan for a neat place of worship, plain but elegant, and which will be a suitable monument for my dear friend Lady Henrietta, and which I mean to call Hope Chapel'. On the death of Lady Glenorchy in July 1786 the completion of the building was left to her executrix Lady Maxwell and this was achieved by the end of August 1788. Until 1820 it was a proprietary chapel with, for most of that period, liturgical services; in that year an Independent Church was formed. The establishment in 1866 of a new congregation in Oakfield Road (closed 1929) at Pembroke Chapel caused a serious decline in the support for Hope Chapel. By 1971 services were being held in a back room.

The chapel, built in 1786–8, was partly rebuilt and enlarged to the rear in 1838 at a cost of about £2,000. The present fenestration and some of the fittings are of the latter date but the seating was all renewed in the late 19th century. The original building was described by the first regular minister, William Jay, as 'a plain structure with small doors, small windows and plastered walls', the pulpit 'small and high up' and at its sides 'pews for invalids with curtains which could be drawn if need be'.

The walls are of rubble with stone dressings and the roof is hipped and slated. The S front is of four bays with panelled corner pilasters, moulded cornice, and parapet with raised centre. The side walls, originally of four bays, extended to the N by one bay, have tall windows with two-centred arched heads, divided by stone panels at gallery level; the E wall has been

rebuilt but a joint in the W wall marks the original extent of the building. At the N end is a two-storied vestry wing of 1838. The interior (now 68½ft by 48½ft; originally 48½ft square) has a gallery around four sides approached by staircases in the SE and SW corners, and an organ recess at the N end at gallery level. The roof is supported by five queen-post trusses all probably dating from 1838.

Fittings – *Monuments*: in chapel (1) S. Gell, 1848, late of Liverpool; (2) Henrietta Buchan, 1823, and Helen her sister, 1815; (3) Adamina Buchan, 1825; (4) William Hope Weir, 1811, of Craigie Hall and Blackwood in North Britain, signed Hy. Wood, Bristol; (5) Rev. W.H. Guy, 1830, ten years minister; (6) Joseph Lawrence, 1841; (7) Lady Henrietta Hope, 1786, daughter of James, Earl of Hopetown, oval tablet on grey marble backing surmounted by a plain urn; (8) Sarah, daughter of William and Rebecca Friend, 1791; (9) Mary Ann, wife of Joseph Lawrence, 1848; (10) Rev. William Gregory, 1853, 21 years pastor; (11) Henry Foster, 1819, 'sometime one of the managers of this chapel'; (12) Charles Hope Weir, 1797; (13) Catherine Henrietta Hope Weir, 1802; (14) Elizabeth Lamplow Burder, daughter of Rev. George and Sarah Burder, 1801; in vestibule, two monuments removed 1933 from Pembroke Chapel, (15) Rev. Samuel Luke, 1868, first pastor; (16) Jemima wife of Rev. Samuel Luke, 1906, authoress of 'I think when I read that sweet story of old . . .'. Also numerous monuments in burial-ground around chapel.

Organ: given 1840, reputedly from Bath Abbey. Case of three bays divided by stepped buttresses with crocketed pinnacles and cusped arch with finial over each bay; *c*.1840. Brass plate 'W.C. Vowles, Bristol, 1886'. *Pulpit, Communion Table, and Chairs*: matching set in wood with Gothic enrichment in plaster and cast iron, *c*.1838. The pulpit, octagonal on open square base with crocketed pinnacles at corners and pair of curved stairs; table, small box with white marble top; chairs, three, one with arms.

Caston (1860) 140–53: Thompson (1967) 56–61: Wicks (1910) 134–7.

(20) ZION CHAPEL, Coronation Road (ST 589720), was built 1829–30 by John Hare, a manufacturer of 'Indian matting floor cloth' and placed in trust for Independents. The walls are of rubble with stone dressings and the roof is slated. The front wall has an open loggia of five bays with four cast-iron Greek Doric

columns between end bays, a central entrance replacing two former doorways, and round-arched upper windows with a pediment above. Original galleries around three sides are supported by fluted Ionic columns; an organ-gallery was added and the seating renewed in 1878–80. There is a schoolroom below the chapel.

Caston (1860) 161–71: Cozens H.B., *The Church of the Vow* (1930).

(21) BRUNSWICK CHAPEL, Brunswick Square (ST 59257370), was built in 1834–5 for a section of the oldest Independent church in the city which then met in a chapel, rebuilt in 1815, at Castle Green (now at Green Bank Road, Easton); the secession was caused by disagreement over a ministerial appointment. After meeting for a short period in the former Pithay Chapel the seceders built Brunswick Chapel to the designs of William Armstrong. The rendered walls have two tiers of windows, the upper ones with round-arched heads, and a continuous moulded cornice and parapet. The front of three bays has a central portico with two pairs of giant Ionic columns. Prior to its closure *c*.1950 and conversion to Masonic and later to commercial use the interior had galleries around three sides with contemporary seating and a pulpit centrally against the back wall.

Caston (1860) 183–99.

(22) HIGHBURY CHAPEL, St Michael's Hill (ST 582739), built in 1842–3 for a newly-formed Independent congregation, is believed to be the earliest work of William Butterfield who later expressed his regret at having assisted in the erection of 'a schism shop'. The chapel of stone and slate in the Perpendicular Gothic style comprises an aisled nave of five bays with a polygonal chancel at the E end. A tower by E.W. Godwin was added against the S wall in 1863, the lower stages forming a transept with gallery. The N and S arcades have four-centred arches supported by octagonal piers and a dwarf clerestory with grouped quatrefoil lights. (Sold to the established church *c*.1975)

Ayres W.F., *The Highbury Story* (1963): Caston (1860) 209–18.

(23) ARLEY CHAPEL, Cheltenham Road (ST 590743), built 1854–5 by Foster and Wood for a Congregational church, has been used since 1968 by a Polish Roman Catholic congregation.

Rubble with ashlar dressings in an Italianate style having a pedimented S front with semicircular portico and clock-tower. Unaisled nave with band of clerestory lights in timber roof, transepts and apse.

Caston (1860) 225–33: *CYB* (1857) 241–2.

(24) Former FRIENDS, Quakers Friars (ST 593733). The first meeting-house on this site was built in 1670 superseding a building 'at the lower end of Broadmead' which then passed into the hands of the Baptists. In 1681, together with the meeting-houses of other denominations, the building was despoiled but later repaired and registered as a place of worship 12 August 1689. An illustration on James Millerd's Plan of Bristol (1673) shows a building of three bays and two tiers of windows at the S end, perhaps square on plan, with a hipped roof surmounted by a lantern. It apparently faced W and from 1701 had a burial-ground to the east. The present meeting-house, sold in 1956 and now serving as a Registry office, was built in 1747–9 on the earlier foundations to designs by George Tully, a member of the society, but with additional details attributed to Thomas Paty. A separate smaller meeting-house was added alongside in 1759.

The principal meeting-house, dated 1747, has rendered walls and a flat lead roof with hipped slated roofs surrounding a central lantern; the walls have a low plinth and plain platband and rise without a cornice to a parapet with simply moulded coping which sweeps up slightly at each corner of the building. The windows, which are in two tiers, have moulded stone architraves with segmental-arched heads and keystones. The broad E front of three bays has a central doorway with pediment and triple keystone. The N and S walls have each three principal bays

of windows and a fourth eastern bay with an external doorway, now closed, and a window above to light the gallery stairs. The W wall is blank and partly covered by earlier buildings.

The interior (46ft by 60½ft) has galleries around the N, S and E sides with fielded panelled fronts and stairs in the NE and SE corners (the former now removed). The square central space in front of the galleries is bounded on three sides by tall Roman Doric columns of stone with high plinths, two columns on each side being free-standing with half-columns against the W wall and grouped columns in the opposite corners. Centrally in the ceiling is a square lantern with one window in each face and a balustraded opening (now closed at ceiling level). The fittings were mostly removed on conversion but some seating remains in the gallery. The stand with three tiers of seating was against the W wall with two ranks of seating facing towards it which were originally described as comprising eight seats each side of a central aisle, the two pairs of seats at the front being narrower than the rest and having each 'a sliding seat to draw out 14in.'.

A *burial-ground* in Redcliff Way, 'Redcliff Pit' (ST 590724), used by this society 1665–1923 was converted in 1950 to a public garden; the front boundary wall and flat rectangular marker-stones were then removed. In the natural rock face on the E side is a mediaeval stone arch.

Architectural Review, April 1946: *BRSP* XXVI (1971); XXVII (1973); XXX (1977): Lidbetter (1961) 73: Wicks (1910) 59.

(25) Former FRIENDS, Kings Weston Road (ST 549782). A small meeting in existence by 1670 was reported in 1710 to be in need of larger premises. The erection of a new meeting-house was notified to Yearly Meeting in 1713 although the present building, which is dated 1718 above the entrance, was not conveyed to trustees until April 1718. Meetings ceased in 1893 and the property was sold in 1924.

The former meeting-house (22¾ft by 36¼ft externally), now divided between two houses adjoining N and W, 'Quakers Rest' and 'Ferns Hill', has rendered rubble walls and a hipped roof covered with patent tiles. The S front, of three bays, has a central entrance and flanking windows with moulded stone architraves; a fanlight was inserted above the doorway in the early 19th century.

Mounting Steps: E of meeting-house, 18th-century.

A *burial-ground* in Kings Weston Lane (ST 540780) given to the society in 1690 is a rectangular walled enclosure with 18th-century gateway at the SW end.

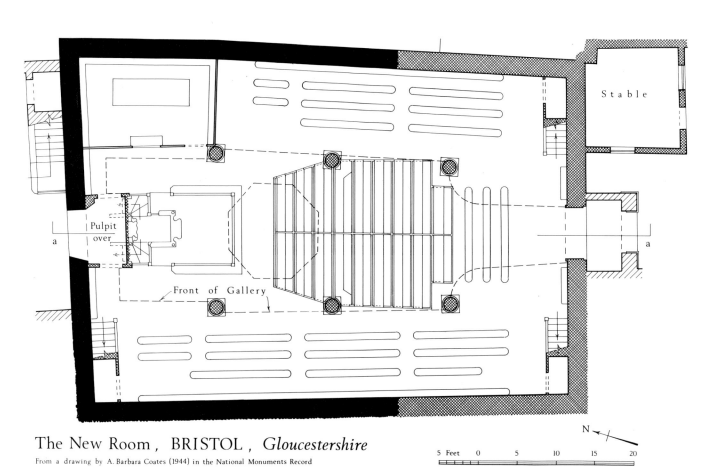

Pulpit over

Front of Gallery

Stable

a —————— a

The New Room , BRISTOL , *Gloucestershire*

From a drawing by A. Barbara Coates (1944) in the National Monuments Record

N

5 Feet 0 5 10 15 20

N front.

Interior from S.
(26) BRISTOL. The New Room, Broadmead and The Horsefair.

(26) THE NEW ROOM, Broadmead and The Horsefair (ST 59107338), was first built in 1739 to accommodate certain religious societies formerly meeting in Nicholas St and Baldwin St. These societies had been fostered by George Whitefield, but on his departure for America their oversight passed to John Wesley. Wesley records the laying of the first stone on 12 May 1739. The building, which became a principal centre for Methodist activity, was greatly enlarged and much rebuilt in 1748 although parts of the N and E walls probably remain from the earlier structure. The society at the New Room was weakened in 1792 by the opening of Portland Chapel, where Wesley's rigid policy over ministerial qualifications for the administration of communion was not accepted, and in 1794 a major division occurred over this issue resulting in the erection of Old King Street Chapel. In 1808 the New Room was sold to Welsh Calvinistic Methodists who retained possession until 1929; it was then repurchased by Wesleyan Methodists and restored under the guidance of Sir George Oatley.

The building, which has rendered walls and hipped pantiled roofs, stands on a site formerly concealed by surrounding buildings; it comprises a galleried chapel and a series of small rooms on a floor above which served the needs of John and Charles Wesley and their assistants. The original entrance from the Horsefair was by a narrow alley at the NE corner of the building opening to a small court against the N wall. The principal entrance was removed to the opposite end when the building was extended to the S in 1748. The external walls make little attempt at architectural pretension. A segmental-arched doorway at the centre of the N wall with a similarly-arched window above may be part of the original design; an attenuated window in the E wall may also relate to the earlier building. At the S end is a central entrance with round-arched window above and domestic windows to the upper floor.

The interior, of irregular plan, (approx. 63ft by 42ft) with separate E and W galleries and six tall Tuscan columns of stone supporting the upper floor, has a pulpit centrally at the N end and an octagonal lantern in the ceiling which rises through the upper storey. A small vestry or 'Conference Room' in which many of Wesley's early conferences were held occupies the NE corner of the lower floor. The upper rooms are ranged around three sides of a central common room which is lit by two windows in the S wall and by the central lantern.

Fittings – *Clock*: on front of W gallery, with shaped case and circular dial, early 18th-century. *Inscription*: on stone, externally in N wall near NE corner, 'THE REV: Mr. J : WESLEY AM : LD : THS STONE AD1739' (surname and degree altered). *Organ*: in gallery, small chamber organ by John Snetzler, 1761, from Little Plumstead Church, Norfolk, given 1930. *Poor-box*: on outer face of N door, brass plate with slot inscribed with texts from Mark x.21 and Prov. xiv.21 and date 1755. *Pulpit*: two desks with panelled front and balustraded staircases, approached from gallery only; lower desk 18th-century, upper desk a replica of c. 1930 to replace one removed when an organ was sited here in the 19th century. *Seating*: box-pews to lower floor, early 19th-century, also plain benches some of 18th-century date. *Miscellaneous*: many items of general Methodist interest are exhibited in the upper rooms.

Dolbey (1964) 41–3: Edwards M., *The New Room* (1972).

(27) PORTLAND CHAPEL (ST 585738) was built 1791–2 to serve Methodists living in the new residential districts N of the city centre and to relieve the pressure on the 'New Room'. One of the principal supporters of the new cause was Captain Thomas Webb who was earlier notable for his part in introducing Methodism to America and who is buried in the chapel.

The walls are of rubble and brick with a rendered surface and the roof is slated. Prior to 1871–2, when the building was extended by one bay to the W, the original entrances closed and a polygonal organ-chamber erected against the N wall, the N and S walls were symmetrical. These were of five bays with a slightly projecting pedimented centre of three bays with an entrance in the middle bay and round-arched windows with keystones and impost blocks. The N pediment has been removed but that to the S remains and has within it a circular panel. At the E end is a lower vestry wing with hipped lean-to roof, and at the W end, extended in a similar style, an original octagonal wooden bell-cote with weather-vane dated 1792 has been reset above the later gable.

The interior (originally 55½ft by 39ft) has a plaster ceiling with a wide cove along the principal sides. At the E end is a small apse with arched opening to the chapel and an upper arch

Portland Chapel, BRISTOL
Gloucestershire

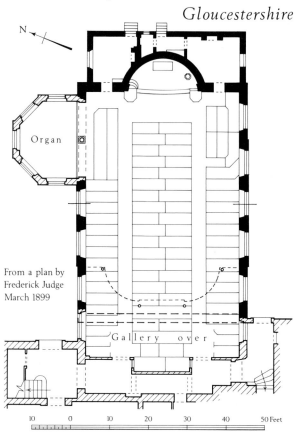

Organ

From a plan by
Frederick Judge
March 1899

Gallery over

10 0 10 20 30 40 50 Feet

S wall.

Interior from W.
(27) BRISTOL. Portland Chapel.

springing from the line of the cornice at the base of the ceiling. A gallery at the W end with concave panelled front was re-sited one bay W of its former position when the chapel was extended. The seating, of panelled box-pews in three ranks, was altered in 1864, prior to which it comprised two principal ranks with a centre aisle. The pulpit and reading desk, formerly combined as a central feature with a communion table behind them in the apse, were re-sited further E in 1864 when the table was brought forward; they were subsequently divided and placed N and S of the apse.

The original decorative scheme at the E end, now entirely obliterated, is reported to have comprised within the apse 'a scene of tropical vegetation, the centre foreground being occupied by a tomb or sepulchre surmounted by an urn' with 'three winged cherubs' heads' in the clouds above. On the wall around the arched opening, presumably below the upper arch, 'were painted crimson curtains draped back'. The latter were painted out in 1913 but the former, in spite of a proposal in 1872 to substitute the traditional tables of Lord's prayer, creed and decalogue, remained, although possibly retouched, until more recent years. The painting has been ascribed to Edward Bird R.A.

Other fittings include – *Bell*: in bell-cote, reported to be dated 1698, formerly at St Ewen's Church, Broad St., Bristol. *Font*: stone or composition octagonal pillar with tapered panelled stem, moulded base and bowl, late 18th-century. *Monuments*: in chapel, on N wall (1) Thomas Foster junior B.A., architect, 1846, and Sophia his widow, 1874; (2) Mary (Stoakes) Coleman, 1795, recording a bequest of £100; in E wall (3) Lieut. (Captain) Thomas Webb, 1796, 'the principal instrument in erecting this chapel'; (4) Rev. James Wood, 1840, 67 years Wesleyan minister, and Mary his wife, 1832; on S wall (5) John Hall, gent., 1798, preacher; (6) Rev. Joseph Collier, 1842, and Sarah his widow, 1851; on W wall (7) Rev. Thomas Roberts A.M., 1832; (8) Rev. John Sugden Smith, 1825; on S wall of vestry, externally (9) Thomas Westell, 1794; also many monuments in burial-ground to S and east. Burial-vaults below chapel include, below apse, 'Captain Webb's Vault, 1796'. (Chapel closed 1970–1 and since demolished. Bell removed to Victoria Chapel, Whiteladies Road, Bristol. Remains of Captain Webb and his wife reburied at New Room 1972; his monument (3) removed to John Street Chapel, New York, U.S.A., 1973)

Lambert, A.J., *The Chapel on the Hill* (1929): *WHSP* XXXVIII (Aug. 1972) 127–30; XXXIX (Oct. 1973) 57–60.

(28) EBENEZER CHAPEL, Old King Street (ST 591734) on the W side of the street (now 'Merchant Street'), 80 yards N of the New Room, was built in 1794–5 for a Wesleyan society formed by secession from the New Room. This followed the refusal of the trustees to allow preaching by a minister without episcopal ordination who had assisted in administering the Lord's Supper at Portland Chapel. The chapel had a front of five bays with a pediment, shaped parapet and two tiers of round-arched windows. The interior, partly refitted in 1859, had a gallery around four sides, rounded at the back. (Closed and demolished 1954)

Lambert, *op. cit.*, 23–5: *WHSP* XXIX (1954) 124–30: Williams T.M., *A Short History of Old King Street (Ebenezer) Methodist Church, Bristol* (1954).

(29) WESLEYAN, British Road (ST 582714). Late 19th-century; formerly with four giant columns supporting a pediment between staircase wings, now entirely transformed by partial demolition and refitting. The former 'Ebenezer Chapel' of 1836 alongside (derelict 1977) has rendered walls and a slate roof hipped to the front. The front wall is of three bays with a pedimented centre bay and a simplified Venetian window above the central round-arched entrance.

(30) ZION CHAPEL, Two Mile Hill Road (ST 644739). Free Methodist, dated 1854.

(31) MORAVIAN, Upper Maudlin Street (ST 587734). Land on the E side of the street was bought in 1756 by a recently formed congregation and a chapel built which was opened in 1757; a burial-ground behind the chapel was surrounded by related buildings including, on the N side, a minister's house, a sisters' house and girls' school, and on the E the cooperage house (rebuilt 1863–4 as day and Sunday-schools) and the brethren's house. About 1827 the roof and ceiling of the chapel were rebuilt and in 1854 it was reseated and the pulpit 'exchanged for one of a chaster and more modern style'. In 1871 the street was widened and its level raised, involving the removal of some buildings which had stood partly in front of the chapel, notably a manse built in 1853 which was then replaced by another alongside the first minister's house N of the chapel. Some further alterations to the chapel were made in 1875 but in 1896 a more drastic change was made involving substantial rebuilding to provide a new chapel at the street level with a hall below.

The chapel, of which the lower part of the walls dates from 1756–7, has rendered walls with a brick superstructure and tiled roof. The original building had rusticated quoins and tall segmental-arched windows with rusticated surrounds, of four bays to E and W; these features remain but the windows have been reduced in height. At the N end is a small doorway with keystone which gave access from the minister's house. The upper chapel (54½ft by 30ft) has at the S end a re-used gallery of c.1757 with bowed centre supported by two Tuscan columns; in the gallery is an early 19th-century organ. The pulpit of 1854 is semi-octagonal with an arched back-board, dentil cornice to the upper stage and a low reading desk in front: *Glass*: in circular window above pulpit, includes symbol of Lamb and Flag (now in St Nicholas Church Museum). *Monuments*: in burial-ground, many rectangular marker-stones, re-sited 1955, (1) Elizabeth Skrine, 1763; (2) Mary Moor, 1777; (3) Sarah Bell, 1780; the latest stone visible, to Bishop George Macleary, is dated 1963. (Site sold for redevelopment 1971)

England II (1887) 2–4, pls. XIV, IV.

(32) LEWIN'S MEAD MEETING-HOUSE (ST 58687332). A Presbyterian congregation was in existence in Bristol by 1672 in which year John Weeks, ejected Vicar of Buckland Newton, Dorset, was licensed as a 'teacher' and 'a room or rooms in the house of John Lloyd, lying on St James's Back' was allowed as a

S front.

Interior from S.
(32) BRISTOL. Lewin's Mead Meeting-house.

meeting place. This place remained in use until December 1681 when the contents were destroyed and the congregation forced to meet elsewhere. A permanent meeting-house was next obtained in 1686 by the conversion of a theatre in Tucker Street, S of Bristol bridge, but a rapid growth in the society appears to have necessitated the provision of a second place of worship in the N part of the town in 1693–4. The two congregations formed a single society at least until the death of Weeks in 1698 but had divided by the early 18th century when the former is credited with 500 and the latter with 1,600 hearers. The Tucker Street society, which built a new chapel in Bridge Street in 1786, remained largely orthodox, becoming Congregational before 1868 when it removed to Clifton Down. The society at Lewin's Mead which supported the contrary position became generally regarded as Unitarian by the early 19th century.

The meeting-house built in 1693–4 on the NW side of Lewin's Mead was demolished in 1787 and the present building erected on the same site was registered 1 September 1791. It then included stables and coach-house to which were added in 1818 a lecture-room above the stables and in 1826 two large school-rooms, a committee room, kitchen and a 'small tenement' for the master and mistress of the infant school and the mistress of the girls' day school.

The chapel, designed by William Blackburn of London, has walls of rendered rubble with ashlar dressings and ashlar facing to the front wall above a rusticated lower stage; the principal roof is hipped and covered with slates. The body of the chapel is a broad rectangle with a projecting pedimented centrepiece to the S having an open semicircular porch with paired Ionic columns and, above it, a large tripartite window with arched head which is repeated centrally at the E and W ends of the building and as a row of three on the N side. The re-entrant corners at the front are occupied by staircase wings which rise in two stages to the level of the springing of the arches of the principal windows.

The interior (45ft by 70ft excluding front bay), although superficially redecorated in the late 19th century, retains most of its original fittings. The ceiling is divided into panels and ornamented by six large ceiling roses. Galleries at the E and W ends are approached independently by semicircular stone stair-cases, linked by a third gallery to the S which is occupied by the organ and singers' seats; the galleries have plain fronts with late 19th-century ornament and are supported by cast-iron columns.

The *pulpit*, centrally against the N wall is of mahogany with a square panelled desk with chamfered corners rising from a flared base, a panelled back-board and semicircular canopy surmounted by an urn; to the W is a desk for the chapel clerk and in front is a segmental communion-rail with turned balusters; the contemporary communion table is now in the vestry. Inside the principal S entrance is a semicircular lobby, formerly smaller with an inner passage between it and the tall ends of the adjacent pews; these have now been conflated and the pew ends raised to full height. The seating to the lower floor comprises a full set of box-pews, with seats for doorkeepers directly accessible from the staircase lobbies; in the E and W galleries are box-pews with some open benches in the latter and in the S gallery.

Other fittings include – *Boundary Stones*: below W window of S wall, two, marking boundary between parishes of St James and

St Michael. *Collecting Shovels*: mahogany, with oval box and single handle. *Monuments*: in chapel on N wall (1) Lant Carpenter D.D., pastor, 1840; (2) Mary Carpenter, 1877. *Paintings*: oil portraits of three ministers, including Rev. William Richards, minister 1731–68, and Rev. William James, minister 1842–76. *Plate*: includes four two-handled cups and four plates of 1727; also two (formerly six) bottles of dark green Bristol glass which served in place of flagons.

Burial-Ground, Brunswick Square (ST 59287375), is entered on the N side of the square through an arch flanked by Doric columns between a pair of lodges. In the centre of the ground is a small square mortuary chapel with rendered walls and gabled roof. *Monuments*: in the chapel (1) Rev. John Prior Estlin, 1817, and Susanna (Bishop) his widow, 1842; (2) Ann, widow of Rev. Thomas Wright, 1814, and Daniel their son, 1810; (3) Rev. Thomas Wright, 1797; (4) Anne Shurmer, 1789, *et al.*, (5) William Lloyd, 1842, and Betty Elizabeth his wife, 1837; in burial-ground (6) John Latimer, author of *Annals of Bristol History*, 1904, *et al.*; (7) Elizabeth, wife of William Bonner, 1787; (8) Rev. James Davis, 'late Pastor of the Congregation of Protestant Dissenters in Bridge Street', 1797, and Mary his widow, 1814; (9) Amy Perry, 1785, monument with weeping infant and urn in bas relief.

BRSP XXVII, 74–5: Caston (1860) 80–9: Evans (1897) 35–6: Murch (1835) 99–135: *UHST* IV (1927–30) 287–9; VI (1935–8) 116–29.

CAM

(33) CONGREGATIONAL, Upper Cam (ST 757992). Built *c*.1702 on a newly acquired site for a congregation originally regarded as Presbyterian; it was much altered in 1818. The walls are of rubble and the roof which is half-hipped is covered with patent

tiles. The broad N front formerly had doorways in the end bays, one is now altered to a window. The S wall, which now has windows arranged as at the front, retains traces of two earlier windows which flanked a central pulpit, and of a blocked door-way to a vestry built in 1790 but since removed. Two bays of windows in the end walls have been partly covered at the E end by Sunday-schools added in 1895.

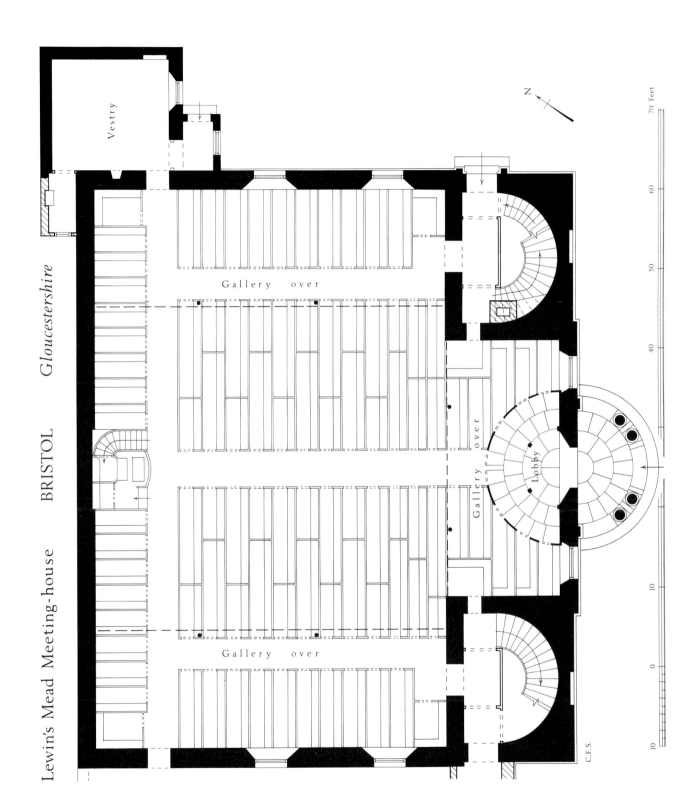

Lewin's Mead Meeting-house   BRISTOL   Gloucestershire

Vestry

Gallery over

Gallery over

Gallery over

Lobby

N

C.F.S.

10   0   10   20   30   40   50   60   70 Feet

The interior (30¼ft by 45ft) was refitted in 1818 and the pulpit re-sited at the E end. The seating was renewed in the late 19th century. The ceiling has a coved plaster cornice. Galleries around three sides, rounded to the W, were added in 1818 and are supported by cast-iron columns.

Fittings – *Clock*: on front of W gallery, with shaped face, repainted, early 18th-century. *Monuments*: in chapel (1) Alexander Baine of Dursley, mercer, 1749, and Alice his wife, 1740, marble tablet in stone surround with swan-neck pediment and egg-and-dart enrichment; (2) Rev. Joseph Twemlow, first minister, 1740, recording that the meeting-house at Water Street, Dursley, was erected at his sole expense jointly for the use of the minister of Cam meeting and for the education of forty poor children; (3) Rev. Thomas Griffith, 21 years minister, 1855, and Ann (Ballinger) his wife, 1823; (4) Rev. John Thomas, 40 years pastor, 1816, and Mary his widow, 1840; (5) Samuel White, 1816, Eleanor his wife, 1795, *et al.*; (6) Charles Whittard, 1830, Elizabeth his wife, 1802, and three children; in burial-ground N of chapel (7) William Harding of Lower Mill, 1793, Dorothy his widow, 1800, *et al.*, pedestal-tomb with oval inscription panels on each face; also six brass tablets on ledger-stones, including (8) George Minett, 1728, and George his son, 1722. *Pulpit*: reeded and panelled with bowed front above trumpet-shaped stem, *c*.1818. *Plate*: includes a pewter plate with overall decoration and the name Lydia Purnel and date 1673.

Davis, R.A., *The Up-to-Date History of Cam Meeting Congregational Church* (1962).

(34) WESLEYAN, Chapel Street, Lower Cam (SO 751003). Three-bay front with two tiers of large round-arched windows. Dated 1825; tablet at rear inscribed 'ENLARGED 1838'.

CHALFORD

(35) BAPTIST, Coppice Hill (SO 901027). The Tabernacle, by J. Tait of Leicester, was built in 1873. The former meeting-house which remains at the lower end of the burial-ground was built *c*.1740 when the church was formed but has been much altered by enlargement to the front *c*.1810 and by the addition at one end of a long Sunday-school wing.

The original building has rubble walls and a hipped roof covered with patent tiles. The rear wall retains traces of two tall windows which flanked the pulpit, now replaced by other windows at two levels; the lower ones occupy in part the sites of the earlier openings. The SE end wall has the remains of two three-light mullioned windows at ground and gallery level and the outline of the base of a double gable below the present eaves. In *c*.1810 this wall was extended at an angle and a round-arched upper window inserted centrally to the enlarged end. The front, of the early 19th century, is of three bays with two tiers of round-arched windows with Y-tracery and a central doorway altered in the late 19th century to form a carriage or stable entrance. The interior (formerly about 16ft by 31½ft) has no original features. The Sunday-school wing, of slightly later date than the enlarged chapel, has three similar upper windows and an oval tablet inscribed 'CHALFORD TABERNACLE SUNDAY SCHOOL ROOM.'

Monuments: In front of former chapel (1) Rev. James Deane, 50 years pastor, 1857, and Elizabeth his wife, 1840, with brass inscription plate; at rear (2) Daniel M . . ., minister, ?1760, headstone.

(36) CONGREGATIONAL, France Lynch (SO 898030). A 'new erected house at Chalford' was registered in 1695 for Presbyterians and a meeting existed in the early 18th century at Chalford Bottoms with Theodore Westmacott as minister. The present chapel, inscribed 'FRANCE MEETING REBUILT 1819', is a large and prominent building of stone with a hipped tiled roof (formerly stone). The S front has a wide round-arched central doorway with a small blind-glazed Venetian window above and two tiers of round-arched windows in the end bays which are repeated, in four bays, in the side walls. A lower Sunday-school wing was built against the E side in 1854.

The interior has a gallery around three sides. The seating was renewed in the late 19th century but the pulpit, apart from the staircase, is of *c*.1819.

Fittings – *Brass*: refixed to front of pulpit, small tablet inscribed 'V.D.M./Theodorus Westmacote/Obijt 31mo Aug.^{ti} 1728.' *Monuments*: in chapel (1) John Innell, clothier, 1806, Mary his widow 1813, and three children, double monument with shields; (2) Henry Ballinger, clothier, 1785, *et al.*, double monument with shields below. Also, in burial-ground, monuments of early 19th century and later, some with brass inscription plates.

(37) PRIMITIVE METHODIST, Chalford Hill (SO 897031). Greatly altered; large tablet inscribed with two verses of a hymn and 'BUILT AD 1823 REBUILT AD 1824'.

Kendall (1905) II, 296.

CHEDWORTH

(38) Former CONGREGATIONAL, Pancakehill (SP 069111). Built 1804 to replace a meeting-house of 1752. Square building with rubble walls and a pyramidal slate roof. The SE front has a central porch, added in the mid 19th century. Two paired lancet windows at rear flank the pulpit. There is a single gallery at the

Interior before alteration.

entrance, other fittings date from the late 19th century.

Monuments: in burial-ground against SW wall, two table-tombs with brass inscription tablets (1) Rev. Stephen Philipps, 36 years pastor 'in whose time and by whose exertions principally the adjoining place of worship was erected...', 1836, and Mary his widow 1839; (2) Mary, (first) wife of Rev. S. Philipps, 1829; also several late 18th-century headstones with border enrichment. (Converted to domestic use and monuments removed *c*.1980)

CHELTENHAM

(39) Former BAPTIST, Knapp Road (SO 94572260). 'Bethel Chapel', facing St James's Square, was built in 1820 for a section of the Tewkesbury church which became autonomous in 1753 having met from 1690 in a former malthouse and from 1703 in a small meeting-house probably on the present site. The church, weakened by secessions in 1835 and 1866, closed the chapel in 1951 which has since been used by Mormons and Christadelphians.

The chapel has brick walls with an ashlar front and slate roof. Pedimented front of three bays with two tiers of windows enclosed in round-arched recesses.

Oliver (1968) 103–6.

(40) BAPTIST, Clarence Parade (SO 94782242). 'Salem Chapel' was built in 1844 for the 1835 seceders from 'Bethel Chapel' who first met in a picture gallery in Clarence Street and subsequently converted an existing building in Regent Street which they named 'Salem'. The chapel has a gabled front of ashlar with giant pointed-arched entrances flanking a large traceried window with crocketed label. Terminal buttresses were formerly surmounted by pinnacles. The interior has a gallery around four sides with arcaded panelled front supported by iron columns and a carved stone pulpit. The gallery, now rendered unusable by an inserted ceiling, retains its original box-pews.

The *former Chapel* in Regent Street (SO 94902225) stands behind other buildings on the E side of the street. It was built in the early 19th century as Barrett's Riding School and opened as a chapel on 1 January 1836. It is now a warehouse. Brick and slate

with the principal S front facing Ormond Place, having a narrow doorway off-centre to the right replacing a wider entrance; when the building was converted a three-centred arched window with intersecting glazing bars was inserted at this end and three pointed-arched windows at the N end replaced earlier openings.

Blake (1979) 24: Oliver (1968) 105–6.

(41) BAPTIST, Cambray Place (SO 95032224), by H. Dangerfield the borough surveyor. Built in 1853–5 for a section of the Salem church which seceded in 1843 and met temporarily in 'The Tabernacle', Clare Street (43) and 'Ebenezer Chapel', King Street (48). The chapel has a pedimented ashlar front of three principal bays with sub-pediments to the side bays and two tiers of grouped round-arched windows. The side walls are of brickwork.

Oliver (1968) 105–6.

(42) GAS GREEN CHAPEL, Russell Street (SO 94252318), was built c.1836 to replace a chapel on a site required for the erection of the gas-works; it has been used by various denominations including Primitive Methodists, Independents from c.1848, and latterly by Baptists. The walls are rendered and the front of three bays has a low gable and two tiers of windows separated by a platband; the upper front windows have round-arched heads with keystones.

A History of Gas Green Chapel, Cheltenham, 1849–1949 [1949]: Blake (1979) 25.

(43) Former CHAPEL, Clare Street (SO 94762122), latterly in commercial use, was built in the early 19th century as 'The Tabernacle' and briefly used in 1843 by Baptist seceders from 'Salem Chapel'. Brick with rendered pedimented front and two large round-arched windows flanking altered entrance. (Demolished since 1971).

Blake (1979) 24–5: Oliver (1968) 105–6.

(44) Former CALVINISTIC METHODIST, High Street (SO 94682263). 'Cheltenham Chapel', designed by Edward Smith, was built in 1808–9 for services 'conducted on the plan of Lady Huntingdon's chapels'. The cause was weakened by the formation of other societies and in spite of re-organization in 1851 as a Congregational church the chapel was closed in 1857. It was re-opened in the following year for a congregation of the Presbyterian Church in England (now URC) which removed in 1886 to Fauconberg Road (52) and has since been used as a hall by the Salvation Army (which bought it in 1894), as a furniture store, and latterly as a wine store.

The former chapel, on the S side E of Ambrose Street, has brick walls rendered at the N end and a hipped slate roof. The N front has rusticated quoins and a platband which continues around the building; the central entrance is tall with a round-arched head and is flanked by arched recesses enclosing two tiers

of windows. The side wall to the W is of four bays with similar fenestration. A low Sunday-school wing is attached to S end. The interior, although altered by the insertion of a floor, retains the original gallery structure around three sides supported by reeded cast-iron columns with acanthus capitals. There is a coved plaster ceiling. A small burial-ground to the E contains some 19th-century headstones.

Hart, W., *A History of St Andrew's Presbyterian Church, Cheltenham* (1966): Seymour (1839) I, 440.

(45) PORTLAND CHAPEL, North Place (SO 951227), was built in 1816 by Robert Capper, previously a supporter of 'Cheltenham Chapel', who appointed Thomas Snow, a former Anglican, as minister. After Snow adopted Strict Baptist views, Capper resumed control of the chapel, giving it to the Countess of Huntingdon's trustees who re-opened it 27 June 1819. The

walls are of ashlar and the roof is hipped and slated. The front has a pointed-arched doorway and a porch, added 1865, with paired Roman Doric columns; two tiers of windows in pointed-arched recesses with basement windows below continue around the side walls.

Blake (1979) 9: Seymour (1839) I, 440.

(46) Former CHAPEL, Grosvenor Street (SO 95232223), was built in 1817–18 for the Rev. Thomas Snow after his removal from 'Portland Chapel' and used for Strict Baptist services until 1822 when Snow reverted to the Church of England and handed the building over to Anglican trustees. In 1827 it was sold to Congregationalists who re-opened it as 'Highbury Chapel', named after the London residence of Thomas Wilson the denominational benefactor. With the opening of a new chapel in Winchcombe Street in 1852 (superseded 1934 by the present chapel in Priory Walk) it became a Sunday-school and latterly a youth club.

The walls are of brick and the E front is rendered in stucco. Five bays with three-bay centre having a raised pediment above blind panels and swept parapets above the recessed wings. Round-arched upper windows above altered lower openings. The interior has a segmental barrel-vault with traces of a circular cupola at the centre; galleries around three sides with mid 19th-century cast-iron fronts.

Blake (1979) 9–10: *CYB* (1853) 255–6.

(47) Former FRIENDS, Clarence Street (SO 947225). A meeting-house built in 1836 on the S side of the then Manchester Walk was superseded in 1902–3 by the present meeting-house in Portland Street and is now part of St Paul's College Adult Education Centre. An earlier meeting-house of 1702 which stood on an adjoining site to the W was subsequently used by Unitarians,

Baptists and Primitive Methodists; It was demolished in the late 19th century.

The surviving building of 1836 has brick walls faced to the N with ashlar. Prior to *c*.1902, when an upper floor was added, it was of a single storey with a front of five bays the three centre-bays slightly recessed and fronted by a lower porch, and a secondary entrance at the W end.

Blake (1979) 3–4, 24.

(48) Former WESLEYAN 'Ebenezer Chapel', King Street (SO 94462284). Methodist meetings commenced in 1764 when a chapel in Albion Street, built in 1723 by a Presbyterian, Mr Millet, was re-opened for their use. This was later abandoned from decay and another meeting-house of *c*.1730, also reputedly Presbyterian, in Meaking's Passage off High Street, was taken instead. The chapel in King Street, was built for this congregation in 1812–13 and after being superseded in 1840 by that in St George's Street (49) was used by Baptists and from 1859–1934 by Primitive Methodists; it is now in commercial use.

The chapel has rendered brick walls with stone dressings. The S front has a narrow pedimented centre bay between wide wings

with swept parapets and short rusticated quoins at the corners. A large tablet below the pediment carries the chapel name with the denomination erased, and the date 1812. A small Doric porch has been removed.

Blake (1979) 4, 8–9: Judge G.H. Bancroft, *The Origin . . . of Wesleyan Methodism in Cheltenham* (1912): *WHSP* XII (1919–20) 180–91.

(49) WESLEYAN, St George's Street (SO 94752279). The successor to 'Ebenezer Chapel' was built in 1839–40. It is a large building of brick, partly rendered, with an ashlar front and hipped slate roof. The W front is of five bays with plinth, platband and entablature. The three middle bays project slightly and have round-arched upper windows and an inscription in raised lettering on the frieze above with the date 1839 and name 'WESLEY CHAPEL'. A portico of four Roman Doric columns

has been removed and the entrances drastically altered *c*.1960. The flanking bays have two tiers of round-arched recesses. The side walls, divided horizontally by brick platbands, have two tiers of round-arched windows in five bays above a range of windows to a basement storey. At the E end is a gabled projection with wide lunette at the upper level incorporating a circular traceried panel perhaps from the former communion window.

The interior ($61\frac{3}{4}$ ft by $49\frac{1}{4}$ ft) has a flat plaster ceiling with a moulded cornice and a barrel-vault above the organ loft. The E end has been altered and formerly had a communion recess behind the pulpit lit by a circular window filled with painted glass, and a separate choir gallery above. A gallery around three sides of the chapel with altered front is rounded at the W end and is supported by cast-iron columns. SE of the chapel is a schoolroom built in 1901 and in the NE angle is a multi-storey wing with additional classrooms also of a relatively late date. The basement is occupied by small rooms for class meetings and Sunday-school use.

Fittings – *Font*: painted wood, octagonal with panelled stem, flared base and top, incorporating blue and white pottery bowl decorated with Classical scenes and having maker's initials TT in a Staffordshire knot; early 19th-century. *Monuments*: in chapel on E wall, all by Wingate of Gloucester, (1) Robert Middleton, 1856, and Hannah his wife, 1845; (2) Mary daughter of Richard Taylor, 1856, her sister Helen Elizabeth Wheeler, 1866, and brother John, 1872; (3) Frances Maria wife of Rev. Samuel Walker, 1857. *Pulpits*: (1) at E end, rostrum incorporating parts of original octagonal pulpit; (2) loose in chapel, octagonal, early 19th-century. *Seating*: late 19th-century pews to lower floor; later theatre-type seats in gallery. (Chapel closed 1971, now in commercial use)

(50) WESLEYAN, Great Norwood Street (SO 94552135). Brick with ashlar front and slate roof, built 1845–6, replacing a smaller chapel which stood to the south. Gabled front of three bays with windows in recessed panels between stepped corner buttresses

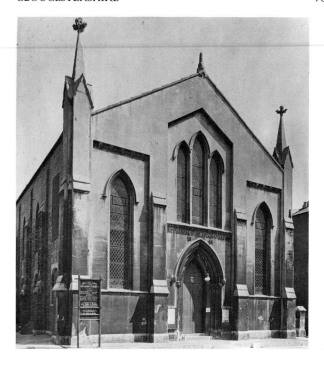

with gabled pinnacles. Pinnacles altered and inscription above entrance 'BETHESDA WESLEYAN CHAPEL' now removed.

Blake (1979) 26.

(51) Former WESLEYAN METHODIST ASSOCIATION, Regent Street (SO 950224). Built *c*.1840 as 'Bethany Chapel' and superseded in 1865 by the 'Royal Well Chapel'. Plain low building with rendered W front, blank except for a round-arched doorway with fanlight near the S end, and slate roof pierced by a roof-light on the E slope. Now used by the Brethren and renamed 'Regent Chapel'.

Blake (1979) 25.

(52) PRESBYTERIAN, St Andrew's, Fauconberg Road (SO 951218). Built 1885–6 for the congregation from 'Cheltenham Chapel' (44): rock-faced stone with corner tower and spire in Gothic style by Thomas Arnold. (URC)

(53) BAYSHILL CHAPEL, Chapel Walk (SO 94622224), was built in 1842–4 for a Unitarian congregation formed in 1832 by Thomas Faber of Bath. Brick with ashlar front and slate roof, in Romanesque style by H.R. Abraham of London. Gabled front with four graduated round-arched upper windows, central entrance and flanking pilaster buttresses which formerly rose to a panelled upper stage with pyramidal finials but now reduced in height and gable cross removed.

Blake (1979) 25–6: *CF* (1871) 136–9: Evans (1897) 43–4.

CHIPPING CAMPDEN

(54) BAPTIST, High Street (SP 150392). Ashlar front and stone slate roof, built 1872. Entrance below gabled turret, windows with angular heads and stop-chamfered jambs.

(55) FRIENDS, Broad Campden (SP 15853795). When purchased by Quakers in 1664 this site was occupied by an orchard and a

building of two bays. The latter, which was used as a meeting-house, was enlarged to the S or possibly rebuilt in 1677 in which year Quarterly Meeting minutes of 29 March refer to assistance given to Friends at Campden 'in building their Meeting House'. Regular meetings ceased in 1874 and the building, which had been occasionally used by other denominations, was sold in 1931; it was repurchased in 1960 and has since been restored to its original use.

The meeting-house has stone walls and the roof is covered with local stone slates. The W front facing Meeting-house Lane has two windows of four lights with straight-chamfered mullions and moulded labels; to the S the round-arched doorway of late 18th-century character has plain imposts, keystone, and blind tympanum. The N and S ends are gabled and have stone copings and finials; in the S gable is a mullioned window of three lights with a moulded label, renewed or inserted in 1960. The E wall, of rough rubble, has two windows matching those in the opposite wall and to the S a plain doorway with timber lintel and 19th-century dormer window above.

The interior is of irregular shape (approx. $39\frac{3}{4}$ft by 16ft) and comprises a single large room and a wide passage to the S with gallery over having a panelled front with shutters above and below. Some 17th-century panelling remains at the N end behind the site of the stand. The roof is supported by three king-post trusses of the late 18th century; inside the N gable is the outline of an earlier coved plaster ceiling.

Gorman M.R., *Broad Campden Quakers* (1971): Sturge (1895) 15.

(56) Former WESLEYAN (SP 148390). Stone with ashlar E front and slate roof; built as a house in early 19th century, converted to a chapel *c*.1840 when the doorway was re-sited. Remains of defaced denominational inscription on N wall. (Restored to domestic use *c*.1975)

Cox, B.G., *Chapels and Meeting Houses in the Vale of Evesham* (1982) 10.

CHURCHAM

(57) WESLEYAN, Birdwood (SO 742187). Built *c*.1800 reputedly for the Countess of Huntingdon's Connexion and later sold for Methodist use. Brick and tile with broad N front of three bays with two tiers of wide round-arched windows, central entrance now altered and flush ashlar quoins at each end. Plain gabled end

walls with porch at E end added in late 19th century. School-room of similar date built against S side and early 19th-century cottage of two stories adjacent to west. Interior with E gallery, refitted in late 19th century.

CINDERFORD

(58) WESLEYAN (SO 658140). Stone and slate with gabled ashlar front having sharply stepped octagonal corner buttresses surmounted by tall thin pinnacles and an elaborate cross finial to the

gable. Central porch with shield-shaped tablet and decayed inscription 'WESLEY CHAPEL 1849'; five-light traceried window above.

CIRENCESTER

(59) GOSDITCH STREET CHAPEL (SP 022021). The origins of the Presbyterian society, in existence by the late 17th century, are obscure and although the curate, Alexander Gregory, was ejected

in 1662 there is no direct evidence that he formed a separate society. A licence for Presbyterian worship was applied for in 1672 and by 1690 John Beeby or Beebee, ejected vicar of Tideswell, Derbys., was pastor. The society, which by the 19th century had adopted Unitarian doctrines, was disbanded in 1980.

The site of the meeting-house behind other property on the SW side of the street appears to have been in use by the late 17th century and the building is of that period, although much altered internally in 1891. The walls are of rubble with a later rendering and the roof is hipped and tiled around a central valley. The SE wall has a wide round-arched doorway with a keystone bearing the false date 1648 and two mullioned windows of two lights all beneath a moulded cornice possibly of the early 19th century; to the left is a similar window with hinge-pins for external shutters, and five upper windows one of which has been inserted. The NW wall has four bays of windows to the lower stage, partly altered, and gallery windows at each end. In the SW wall are two former gallery windows of two lights and in the opposite wall is a small blocked doorway near one corner.

The interior (25¾ft by 46ft) has an original gallery at the NE end now altered to form an upper room, with a front of six bolection-moulded panels; a corresponding SW gallery was removed, the pulpit formerly against the NW wall re-sited at the SW end and the seating renewed in 1891.

Fittings – *Chair*: spirally turned legs and tall back with carved upper rail above two cane panels, 17th-century. *Clock*: on front of gallery, with shaped face and Chinese scene on pendulum case, signed John Cannon, with false date '1648', early 18th-century. *Communion Table*: oak, square, with turned legs and grooved rails, late 17th-century. *Monuments*: in burial-ground at rear, several table-tombs of mid 18th century and later. *Plate*: includes a two-handled cup of 1732.

Evans (1897) 50–1: Murch (1835) 25–34: *UHST* V (1931–4) 262–87, 329–30.

(60) BAPTIST, Coxwell Street (SP 02150215). Built 1856–7 for a church formed in the mid 17th century; gabled ashlar front with round-arched windows grouped over entrance.

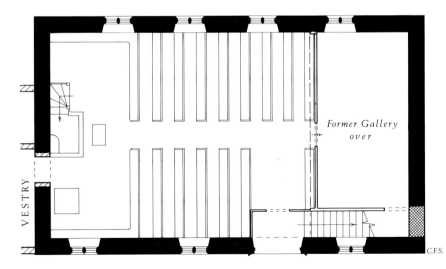

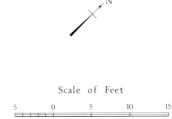

Gosditch Street Chapel
CIRENCESTER
Gloucestershire

VESTRY

Former Gallery over

N

Scale of Feet

5   0   5   10   15

C.F.S.

(61) Former STRICT BAPTIST, Park Street (SP 021021). Built 1854 for seceders from the earlier Baptist church, led by Joseph Tanner; closed *c*.1930. Pedimented ashlar front with two wide round-arched windows, now shortened and entrance between replaced by garage doors.

Oliver (1968) 113–14.

(62) FRIENDS, Thomas Street (SP 021022). Meetings were being held in or about Cirencester by 1660 in which year land at Siddington was acquired for a burial ground. In 1673 a lease of the present site was obtained and the earliest part of the existing structure is of this date. Some alterations were made to the building in 1726 and in 1809–11 a second meeting-house was built at the SW end. A porch with minor rooms was added against the NW wall in 1865. Regular meetings ceased in 1922 but were resumed in 1949.

The meeting-house stands on the SE side of the street; it has rubble walls and the roof is covered with stone slates. The NW front is partly obscured by a house and by the late 19th-century porch which has a round-arched doorway and windows below a boldly inscribed parapet. The SE side is of two distinct periods with dates 1673 and 1810 above the doorways, the earlier having a steeper roof-pitch; both parts have round-arched windows with hung sashes and intersecting glazing bars of the early 19th century.

SE side.

The interior (originally about 36ft by 27ft) is now largely of the early 19th century with a wide passage flanked by shutters formed out of one end of the original meeting-room separating the two parts of the building. The larger room to the NE has a stand with panelled front and back and two entrances with balustraded handrails; the ceiling is supported by four slender Doric columns inserted to strengthen the floor of an attic room which is approached from the adjacent house. The smaller meeting-room has a gallery at the SW end formerly balanced by another on the opposite wall.

Books: small library of early 18th-century Quaker books.

Stephens, L., *Cirencester Quakers, 1655-1973* (1973).

(63) Former WESLEYAN, Gloucester Street (SP 021024). Stone and slate with pedimental front gable and three round-arched windows above later porch. Built 1808, oval tablet removed; now Barton Hall Youth Centre.

COLEFORD

(64) BAPTIST (SO 574106). Built in 1858 by C.G. Searle for a church founded in 1799. Rubble with ashlar dressings and slate roofs.

(65) Former COUNTESS OF HUNTINGDON'S CONNEXION (SO 574106). Rendered rubble and hipped roof, greatly altered on conversion to a house 'Huntingdon House'. Built *c*.1788–90, closed *c*.1819, subsequently used by Wesleyans and as infants' school. Three-bay front formerly with rusticated quoins.

Bright (1954) 37–46.

(66) CONGREGATIONAL (SO 575109). Rendered walls and hipped slate roof, three-bay front with two tiers of round-arched windows with later frames and moulded cornice with name INDEPENDENT CHAPEL above projecting centre bay and date 1842 above central Doric-columned porch. Galleries added *c*.1854-5.

COWLEY

(67) Former STRICT BAPTIST, Birdlip (SO 927142). 'Moriah Chapel' of stone with gabled three-bay front is dated 1841 above the original entrance. Round-arched windows with later frames. Closed *c*.1954.

Oliver (1968) 112–13.

DEERHURST

(68) Former MORAVIAN, Apperley (SO 859276). Built in 1750 together with a small cottage alongside which served as the minister's house. In the early 19th century the property was leased and in 1845 sold to Wesleyans who in 1901 built a new chapel nearby and rebuilt the cottage. The former chapel (20ft by 30¼ft externally), now used for storage has brick walls and a tiled roof. The broad front is of three bays with a brick dentil eaves

cornice, flat-arched doorway and two segmental-arched windows; there are two similar windows in the rear wall.

Fittings – *Chair*: in present vestry, with panelled back and turned supports to arms, 17th-century. *Monuments*: include fragments of six late 18th-century Moravian tablets, five of which England records in a more complete state, (1) Elizabeth Heath, 1770; (2) Esther Hope [S.S.], 1771; (3) Timothy Watts, M.B., 1769; (4) William Dovey, M.B., 1768; (5) ——— ———, W., 1778; (6) small fragment of taller stone, possibly James Garne, 1780.

England I (1886) 5 and pl.7.

DRYBROOK

(69) BAPTIST, Ruardean Hill (SO 638168). Gabled front with simple Venetian window; mid 19th-century.

DURSLEY

(70) CONGREGATIONAL, Parsonage Street (ST 754982). Meetings of Presbyterians or Independents were commenced about 1702 by the Rev. Joseph Twemlow of Cam Meeting and a meeting-house was built in Water Street *c*.1718. Preaching by George Whitefield in the mid 18th century resulted in the formation of a separate Calvinistic Methodist society in Dursley for which the first 'Tabernacle' was erected *c*.1760. The new cause flourished at the expense of the older meeting which eventually ceased and the meeting-house was for a time used as a school. The Presbyterian meeting-house on the W side of Water Street (ST 758981) is now a roofless shell with rubble walls partly

rendered at the front and traces of a blocked doorway to the left of the remaining round-arched entrance.

The present 'Tabernacle' (now URC) was built on a new site in 1808. The walls are of coursed stone with ashlar dressings. The SE end wall, which resembles Uley (154), has a pediment with inscribed trefoil panel above two pointed-arched windows; the lower stage is covered by a later porch. The SW side, of three bays with two tiers of similar windows with stone Y-tracery, has a pedimented centre bay in which was the original entrance. The interior was entirely refitted *c*.1880 and the entrance re-sited in the end wall.

Monuments: in chapel (1) John Dando 'hattmaker', 1775, and Susanna his widow, 1791; (2) Hannah Rudder, 1808, signed Daw; (3) John Trotman 'Card Board maker', 1839, and Ann his wife, 1836; (4) Rev. William Bennett, 1830; (5) William Smith, 1829; (6) Richard Trotman 'baker', 1810; (7) Isaac Danford, 1788, and Rachael his widow, 1802; (8) William King, 1803, signed J. Green and son, Gloucester.

Evans, D.E., *As Mad as a Hatter: Puritans and Whitfieldites in the History of Dursley and Cam* (1982): Montgomery, E.C., *Milestones . . .* (1958).

FAIRFORD

(71) Former BAPTIST, Milton Street (SP 149009). A Baptist church originated *c*.1700 at Meysey Hampton moving to Fairford in 1724, when a 'New built House lately erected in Fairford' was registered for worship. The meeting-house was much altered and refronted in 1853. An Independent church also

existed in the early 18th century, building a new meeting-house in 1744 which was replaced in 1862 by a small Gothic chapel, 'Croft Chapel', designed by T. Rogers Smith (demolished 1965). In 1919 the two societies formed a united church meeting in the Baptist chapel.

The chapel has stone walls and a hipped slate roof. The NW front of three bays has thin terminal pilasters, a moulded cornice and parapet with anthemion ornament at the corners, and the date MDCCCLIII on raised block at the centre. The SE wall retains traces of two lower windows and one above, all of early 18th-century date. The rear wall has two round-arched windows flanking the pulpit. A mid 19th-century Sunday-school adjoins to the north-west.

The interior (35ft by 30ft) was entirely refitted in the 19th century and has a single gallery opposite the pulpit. Some fielded panelling from former pews has been re-used as a dado around the walls.

Monuments: in chapel (1) Rev. Daniel Williams, 1841, 45 years pastor; (2) Rev. Thomas Davis, 1784, 40 years pastor, wooden tablet; in burial-ground in front of chapel, several large monuments and headstones of 18th century and later, including (3) William Thomson, 1779, with brass inscription plate.

CYB (1863) 344.

FALFIELD   *Avon*

(72) CONGREGATIONAL, Mount Pleasant (ST 682926). Built 1813, rebuilt 1843. Schoolroom to S, 1848.

FRAMPTON COTTERELL   *Avon*

(73) CONGREGATIONAL, Upper Chapel Lane (ST 672812). North of the present 'Zion Chapel' of 1873 (now URC and Methodist) is the former chapel built *c.*1800, a plain building with rendered walls and pantiled roof, much altered *c.*1840 and in recent years. *Monuments* in burial-ground include several table-tombs of the early 19th century.

FRAMPTON ON SEVERN

(74) CONGREGATIONAL (SO 747088). The chapel, standing on a concealed site behind buildings on the NW side of the green, is said to have been built in 1760; a lower Sunday-school wing was added alongside in 1849. The walls of the older portion are of brickwork above a plinth formed of dark blocks of copper slag; the roof is tiled and has a double ridge with central valley at collar level. The wing is of brick and slate. The double-gabled SW front has a central entrance with pointed-arched window above and a low annexe alongside incorporating a later gallery staircase. Two wider windows with wooden tracery in pointed-arched heads occupy the side walls, blocked against the school, and two windows at the NE end flank the pulpit.

The interior (33ft by 27ft) was partly refitted in the early 19th century and has a SW gallery of that period with a panelled and balustraded front supported by two cast-iron columns.

Fittings – *Monuments*: in chapel (1) Rev. William Richardson, 1847, and Elizabeth his wife, 1843, signed Felix Morgan, Frampton; (2) William Barnard, 1802, Elizabeth his widow, 1825, and William their son, 1783, signed Pearce; (3) Thomas King, 1783, and Sarah his widow, 1793, sarcophagus-shaped tablet above two draped urns, signed J. Pearce, Frampton; (4) John son of Thomas and Jane Wiles, 1786, oval tablet surmounted by standing figure, signed J. Pearce, Frampton; (5) Daniel Hewlett, builder, 1822, and his three wives Elizabeth, 1786, Ann, 1794, and Lydia, 1843; (6) George Barnard, 1815, Elizabeth his wife, 1809, and three children, signed E. Morgan, Frampton. *Seating*: box-pews with arched end panels, *c.*1840, and plain side benches with shaped supports and later backs.

GLOUCESTER

(75) BARTON STREET CHAPEL (SO 834184) was built in 1699 for a society of Presbyterians and Independents of which James Forbes, formerly lecturer in the Cathedral, was pastor. In 1715, three years after Forbes' death, the congregation divided, the Independents forming a separate church while the Presbyterians retained possession of the chapel to which they called ministers of

Barton Street Chapel, GLOUCESTER
Gloucestershire

N

VESTRY

original site of pulpit

Gallery over

C.F.S.

5   0   5   10   15   20   25 Feet

increasingly unorthodox views; by 1815 the society was commonly regarded as Unitarian.

The chapel is set back on the N side of the street behind the

Exterior from E.

Interior from SW before 1893, from a water-colour drawing in Gloucester Public Library.
(75) GLOUCESTER. Barton Street Chapel.

Floor slab to James Forbes, 1712.

line of other buildings and concealed by an extension of 1844. In 1893 the N end was rebuilt to provide an organ-chamber and vestry and the interior was refitted. In 1968 the building was derelict and the congregation met privately. (Since demolished)

The original building has brick walls and a hipped roof now covered with slate. Prior to 1844 the S front, concealed from the street by a brick boundary wall, had a central doorway and two upper and two lower windows which remain internally; the N wall was similarly fenestrated. The E wall has two wide segmental-arched windows which formerly flanked the pulpit. The W wall has three windows with original wood frames. The S front of 1844 is of ashlar with a pediment above two tiers of windows in three bays; a central entrance leads to a passage between minor rooms with a schoolroom above.

Before 1893 the interior of the chapel (27½ft by 49ft) had galleries at the N and S ends and a cross gallery to the W which was probably an addition; a central aisle between box-pews led to a doorway in the N wall giving access to a small burial-ground at the back. The pulpit was central against the E wall with a canopy over. In the refitting a small gallery was built at the S end and a short chancel for the choir with organ-chamber behind was added to the north. The original roof structure remains with three king-post trusses and radiating struts.

Fittings – *Communion Table*: Murch (1835) refers to 'a handsome communion table with a marble slab'; unlocated. *Library*: a considerable library left to the congregation by the Rev. James Forbes in 1712 was removed in 1715 by the Independents (see below).

Monuments and *Floorslabs*. *Monuments*: in chapel (1) John Dobbins, 1844; (2) William Tupsley Washbourne, 1842, timber merchant; (3) Lucy Ann Sharp, 1836; (4) Richard Chandler, 1810; (5) William Price, 1815; (6) Rev. Henry Davies Ll.D.,

1848, 12 years pastor; (7) William Washbourn, 1816 (monuments 2, 4, 6 are by Cooke, monument 1 is by W. Russell and 3 by George Sharpe, all of Gloucester). *Floorslabs*: (1) James Forbes A.M., 1712, with shield-of-arms, worn Latin inscription and later brass tablet, reset on W wall from vault in front of former pulpit; (2) Thomas Steel, 1752, Sarah his widow, 1775, and Elizabeth their daughter, 1782; (3) Elizabeth, wife of Nathaniel Washbourne, 1839.

Evans (1897) 94–5; Lloyd, W., *A Brief Account...of the Protestant Dissenting Meeting-house in Barton Street, Gloucester* (1899): Murch (1835) 4–18: *UHST* VI (1935–8) 383–4.

(76) CONGREGATIONAL, Southgate (SO 829183). A section of the Barton Street congregation seceded *c*.1715, retaining in their possession the library and communion plate (sold 1966 and 1923 respectively) of the parent society. A meeting-house was built in 1730 on the site of the parish church of St Owen, enlarged in 1830 and replaced by the present building in 1849–51. This is of stone with a slate roof, in the Decorated style with a gabled front having a tall five-light traceried window above the entrance; the sides are of five bays with aisles and cusped clerestory windows. (URC)

CHST X (1927–9) 100–4: Lander, T.J., *The History of Southgate Congregational Church, Gloucester, 1660–1972* (1972).

(77) FRIENDS, Greyfriars (SO 831183). The meeting-house of 1834–5 by Samuel Whitfield Dawkes, is of brick with stone dressings and a slate roof. The N front, formerly with a three-bay centre, now covered by a large entrance wing, has end bays with tall round-arched windows in arched recesses. The interior is divided into two rooms by a screen with hung shutters, the larger room to the E has an unusually high stand at the E end; that to the W has a raised seat against the S wall. At the entrance from the road is a *gatehouse* with segmental archway and blind panels above and at the sides; heightened and windows inserted.

GOTHERINGTON

(78) COUNTESS OF HUNTINGDON'S CONNEXION (SO 965296). Built 1833 on land given by the Hon. Henry Augustus Berkeley Craven.

GUITING POWER

(79) BAPTIST (SP 093249). Rubble and slate, gabled W front dated 1835. Original W gallery.

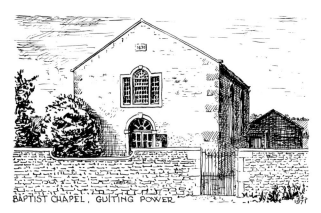

BAPTIST CHAPEL, GUITING POWER

HAMFALLOW

(80) WESLEYAN, Halmore (SO 699023). Brick with pointed-arched windows and wooden Y-tracery. Dated 1829

HAWKESBURY   *Avon*

(81) BAPTIST, Hillesley (ST 771897). The church formed about 1730 and reorganized in 1812 on Calvinistic principles, originally included both Particular and General Baptists. In 1732 the General Baptist Assembly sent a letter to encourage the church 'in their faithful ministry and good intentions of building a Meeting House' and this was registered in 1734. A link with the Seventh-day Baptists is also apparent in the appointment of William Hitchman of Natton as pastor in 1761 and in a donation received in 1766 for 'Sabbatarian Ministers' from the Mill Yard church in London. A vestry was added in 1770–1 and the chapel was rebuilt in 1823.

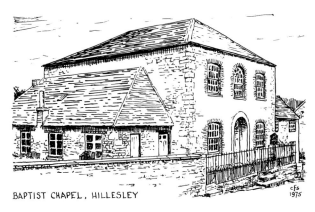

BAPTIST CHAPEL, HILLESLEY

The present building has rubble walls and a hipped slate roof. The S front is of three bays with two tiers of windows all with brick surrounds and segmental-arched heads except that above the central doorway which has a semicircular arch matching the entrance. Two windows in the N wall have round-arched heads of brick; the side walls are blank. A large vestry against the W side has a lean-to roof covered with stone slates.

The interior has an original gallery around three sides, now separated from the lower floor by an inserted ceiling, with contemporary box-pews and benches, some incorporating re-used 18th-century panelling. The lower seating and pulpit have been renewed.

Fittings – *Benefaction Board*: below W gallery, wood painted in imitation of marble, in moulded frame, recording bequests in 1794 and 1815 and a later inscription of 1846. *Monuments*: in chapel, a notable series of 18th-century wall monuments reset from the former meeting-house (1) Samuel Hook, 1768, and Margery his widow, 1775; (2) Joseph Bartlett, 1795, *et al.*; (3) Arthur Venn, 1768, and Arthur his son, 1794, with elaborate rococo cartouche and frame; (4) Mary (Venn) wife of John Taylor of Bristol, 1748, and William their son; (5–6) Edmund Dadge, 1768, and Hester his wife 1758, pair with swan-necked pediments and shaped cheeks; (7) Rev. Joseph Rodway, 1799, eight years assistant minister; (8) John Boulton of Killcott, 1795, reputedly a highwayman, with several cautionary texts, concluding 'All that's ever got by Thieveing Turns to Sorrow,

Shame, and Pain. Dr. Watts'; (9) William Rugg, 1794, and Thomas Davis, 1795; (10) Samuel Chappel, 1766, 'who died by the overturning of the Stage Coach at Faringdon, Berks.', and Ann his second wife, 1747.

Chappell K., *Hillesley Baptist Church, 1730–1980* [1980].

(82) CONGREGATIONAL, Hawkesbury Upton (ST 781869). 1844.

(83) PRIMITIVE METHODIST, Inglestone Common (ST 760884). 1836.

HAWLING

(84) WESLEYAN (SP 067231). Stone with hipped slate roof. Tablet dated 1837.

HEWELSFIELD

(85) Former CONGREGATIONAL (SO 567022). Opened 1822; derelict 1973.

(86) MORAVIAN, Brockweir (SO 540011). A new society was formed under Rev. Lewis West and the chapel built 1832–3 at the cost of the Bristol congregation. The chapel has rendered walls and a tiled roof with a bell-cote at the N end containing one bell; entrance in small porch at S and four lancet windows in each side wall. *Sunday-school* to E, of brick, by Foster and La Trobe of Bristol, late 19th-century.

Monuments: in burial-ground to W, flat marker-stones, also dwarf obelisk to Ann West, 1834, Zinzendorf Lewis West, 1839, and Louis Montgomery West, 1876.

England II (1887) 5.

KING'S STANLEY

(87) BAPTIST, Middleyard (SO 820032). Stone and tile, built 1824 for a church claiming to have originated in 1640. Gabled front with ball finials, two tiers of round-arched windows and later two-storied porch; blocked lunette in main gable. *Monuments*: in burial-ground, early 19th-century stones with brass inscription plates include (1) Rev. James Williams, 1818, signed Richard Dean, K[ing's] S[tanley], Engraver (plate 17in. by 12in.) (See p. 106).

(88) Former PRIMITIVE METHODIST, Selsley Road (SO 813034). Brick front with defaced tablet formerly dated 1861.

KINGSWOOD (near Bristol)   *Avon*

(89) BAPTIST, High Street, Hanham (ST 646722). A chapel built *c*.1721 for a church formed in 1714 and described as of stone with a parapet and round-headed windows has been demolished since 1965. Its successor of 1907 to the W, Gothic by La Trobe and Weston, has been drastically altered. *Monuments*: reset in vestibule of church hall, Charles Whittuck, 1788; in burial-ground, several headstones of late 18th century and after, some with winged cherub's heads, reset against E boundary.

Eayrs (1911) 149–153: Pevsner (1970) II, 260.

(90) WHITEFIELD'S TABERNACLE, Park Road (ST 649739). The spiritual needs of the colliers of Kingswood were an early concern of the Methodist preachers and a school-chapel was built in 1739 to which John Cennick was appointed as one of the two masters. In February 1741 after he had embraced Calvinistic

sentiments Cennick left with about fifty supporters and organized a separate society. In June of that year George Whitefield, who had encouraged the commencement of the former building but who had also subsequently revised his beliefs, wrote to Cennick from London with instructions to 'lay the foundations immediately' of the new Society Room at Kingswood, but to 'take care of building too large or too handsome'. The building was also used as a school-chapel, and in the disputes over its occupancy which followed Cennick's transfer of allegiance to the Moravians, in December 1745, it is referred to as 'Kingswood School'. It appears from the minutes of the English Calvinistic Methodist Association that Cennick and his supporters had retained possession of the building and that until the return of George Whitefield to London in 1748 the Calvinistic Methodists experienced difficulty in maintaining their rights. No further certain references to the building are known until after Whitefield's death in 1770, the first deed quoted being dated 1775 and followed by a trust deed of 1802. In the latter year a Sunday-school was commenced, meeting in the Tabernacle, and in 1830 further accommodation for this was provided alongside. In 1851 a new chapel was built nearby and placed in trust for Congregationalists to which denomination

the church by then adhered. (Now URC)

The *Tabernacle* stands behind other buildings on the N side of Regent Street, W of Park Road (formerly Tabernacle Lane). The walls are of rubble mostly covered by later rendering, and the roofs, in three sections parallel to the front, are hipped and covered with pantiles. The building dates from the mid 18th century and may incorporate parts of the Tabernacle of 1741. (Belden (p. 196) gives a date 1752 suggestive of a rebuilding comparable with that at the Moorfields Tabernacle in London, but no documentary support for this date has yet been found.)

The N front closely follows the design of the colliers' school-chapel of 1739 and is thus most likely to be part of the original structure. In the prototype the front was of five bays with a wide central doorway, wheel window above, flanking round-arched windows and minor entrances in the end bays with smaller windows over. At the Tabernacle the central doorway has been blocked and the upper window lengthened to match those in the adjacent bays, although the head remains higher. The minor entrances in the end bays have been moved nearer to the ends of the wall but small segmental-arched windows remain above the sites of the former doorways. The front corners of the wall have quoins of large blocks of cast purple slag, visible below the

Whitefield's Tabernacle, KINGSWOOD   *Gloucestershire*

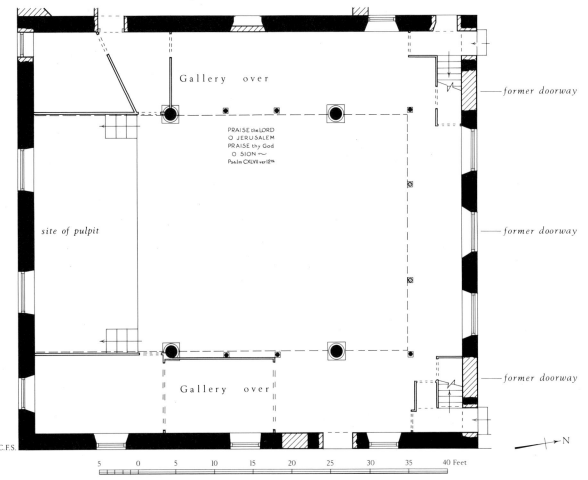

Gallery over

PRAISE the LORD
O JERUSALEM
PRAISE thy God
O SION ~
Psalm CXLVII ver 12th

site of pulpit

Gallery over

former doorway

former doorway

former doorway

N

C.F.S.

5   0   5   10   15   20   25   30   35   40 Feet

E side.

rendering at the NE corner; other pieces of this material are found elsewhere in the walling.

The S wall has a round-arched window each side of the pulpit and segmental-arched upper windows at the ends of the galleries. One original window remains below the E gallery but no trace of a corresponding window is visible; a modern opening has been made to the west. The E wall has three segmental-arched upper windows and three plain sash windows below; one doorway has been inserted and to the S is the site of another. The W wall, mostly covered by the 1830 Sunday-school block, was similar to the foregoing.

The interior (55ft by 50¼ft) is considerably larger than was the 1739 school-chapel, reputedly about 30ft by 60ft. There is a flat plaster ceiling without a cornice and the two principal valley-beams of the roof are supported by pairs of tall stone columns having attic bases on high square plinths and simple bell capitals with a single band of acanthus-leaf ornament. A gallery with fielded panelled front, perhaps dating at least in part from 1802, is carried around three sides supported by the principal columns and by slender intermediate shafts; the N gallery cuts across the line of the front windows. The gallery staircases in the NE and NW corners have been rebuilt and re-sited. The middle panel of the W gallery front is of stone, cut and painted to resemble the adjacent panels, and inscribed with a text from *Psalm* cxlvii.12. When the building was converted to Sunday-school use *c*.1851 a low platform was built at the S end to replace the pulpit and any original seating has also been removed.

The present *Chapel*, W of the former, was built in 1851 to the designs of Henry Masters of Bristol 'in the early English style'. The walls are of rubble with ashlar dressings and the roof is slate covered. The flanking towers of the S front were originally uniform; one has been reduced in height and a central tower has been removed. The interior comprises a nave and aisles of five bays with pointed-arched arcades on octagonal piers. At the N end is a polygonal apse for the organ and choir and at the opposite end is a small gallery for children which has external entrances and staircases in the front towers. The communion table, of wood in the form of a length of Gothic arcading, which formerly stood in front of a platform has been divided; this superseded the original intention of an open stone pulpit which would serve both purposes. The seating comprises open pews, with plain benches in the aisles to which backs have been added.

A large burial-ground between and to the N of the two buildings contains monuments of the 19th century and later.

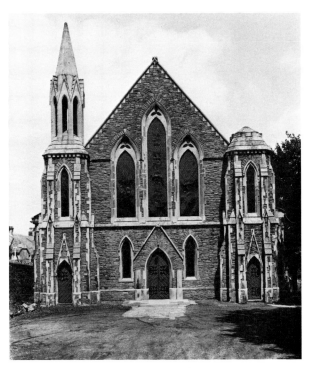

Other fittings include – *Baptismal Basin*: white pottery bowl with grey marbled decoration, inscribed on two faces '*WHIT-FIELDS/TABERNACLE*', early 19th-century. *Sunday-school Banners*: two, with illustrations of the Tabernacle and its successor. (Demolition of 1851 chapel proposed 1981)

Belden [*c*.1930] 196–7: *Bristol Congregational Monthly* (May 1928): *CYB* (1851) 259: Eayrs (1911) 161–5, and *passim*: England I (1886) 11: *LRSP* XI (1975) 28–9, 38.

(91) WESLEYAN, Blackhorse Road (ST 645738). The colliers' school-chapel of 1739 (see above) continued to serve as a place of Methodist worship until 1843. It originally comprised a central room about 30ft square used for services and other purposes, and, at each end, two rooms to the ground floor and two above

which at first included some living accommodation, but in 1803 about when the colliers' school was discontinued the upper rooms were incorporated into the chapel and the lower rooms were combined. From 1748, when the Kingswood (Methodist) School was established, it was used additionally as the school chapel. After the removal of the boarding school to Bath the building was repaired in 1897 for use by a Reformatory school. It was demolished c.1917.

The present chapel, about ¼ mile NE of the former, was built in 1843 'largely by the efforts of Samuel Budgett' to serve the Wesleyan society, with seats reserved for the school. This has rendered walls and a slate roof. The N front has an open pediment, three conjoined round-arched windows above a central porch, and two side entrances. The side walls, of four bays, have tall arched upper windows and smaller openings below. The interior has an original gallery around three sides. The S end has been altered. Mid 19th-century box-pews remain throughout most of the chapel with some open-backed benches in the gallery.

Glass: in all windows, obscured plain glass with a narrow intermediate band following the outline of the opening.
Monuments: in chapel (1) Samuel Budgett, 1851; (2) Edwin, son of Samuel and Ann Budgett, 1849.

Former 'Wesleyan School' of 1850 to S in similar style. (Congregation united with and removed to 'Zion Chapel', Two Mile Hill Road, Bristol (30), 1978; demolition of 1850 school proposed 1979)

Eayrs (1911) 49–59, 119–23, 183–4.

(92) FREE METHODIST, Chapel Road, Hanham (ST 643724). 'Founded 1851, enlarged 1903', with mid 19th-century pedi-

mented front of ashlar; apparently designed by D. Whitchurch. (Entirely refronted before 1981)

Eayrs (1911) 193.

(93) MORAVIAN, Regent Street (ST 649738). When John Cennick and his adherents were dispossessed of the Tabernacle c.1748 they removed to temporary premises, building a new chapel in 1756–7. This was a plain building with two round-arched windows and a gabled porch at one side and a two-storied minister's house attached to one end. The present chapel, of 1856–7, comprises a nave, transepts and a S apse. In the burial-ground are rectangular marker-stones of varied design dating from the 18th century.

Eayrs (1911) 178–81: England I (1886) 11.

KINGSWOOD (near Wotton-under-Edge)

(94) CONGREGATIONAL (ST 748920). 'A new built house at Kingswood', then a detached part of Wiltshire, was registered for use as a meeting-house in April 1702. This probably served the present church which was formed in the late 17th century apparently as a Presbyterian society. The chapel, 50 yards NE of the parish church, dates from the early 19th century and has walls of coursed stone rubble and a hipped roof now covered in patent tiles; a vestry along the N end has a lean-to roof of slate. The S front is of alternating deep and narrow stone courses. Two round-arched windows at the N end flank the pulpit. The roof is surmounted by a wooden bell-cote with one bell, a clock-face to

CONGREGATIONAL CHAPEL, KINGSWOOD, Nr Wotton

the W and a weather-cock above. Early 19th-century gallery around three sides with fielded panelled front; otherwise refitted.

Monuments: in burial-ground (1) Rev. Charles Daniell, [1832], 26 years pastor; (2) Rev. James Griffiths of Wotton-under-Edge, 1868; (3) Rev. William Davies, 18[?]7, 49 years minister; (4) Rev. William Coleman Woon, 1854, and William Harris his son, 1855.

LECHLADE

(95) BAPTIST, Sherborne Street (SU 214997). Built 1817. Pedimented front gable with lunette, round-arched doorway and two tiers of plain sash windows.

Before alteration.

LEONARD STANLEY

(96) WESLEYAN, The Street (SO 802035). Three-bay front with two tiers of sash windows. Opened 1809.

LITTLEDEAN

(97) CONGREGATIONAL, Broad Street (SO 670134). Built in 1820 for a congregation gathered about 1795 which from 1813 had met in a converted house. Rendered walls and hipped slate roof; segmental-arched doorway and shaped canopy between round-arched windows. Small burial-ground in front with early 19th-century monuments.

Bright (1954) 16–19.

(98) CONGREGATIONAL, Popes Hill (SO 687143). Dated 1844, much altered.

LONGNEY

(99) CONGREGATIONAL (SO 762127). Brick front; oval tablet dated 1839.

MANGOTSFIELD URBAN   *Avon*

(100) BAPTIST, Salisbury Road, Downend (ST 651765). The church, formed in 1814, owes its origin to Dr Caleb Evans, founder of the Bristol Education Society and pastor of the Broadmead church in Bristol, who in 1786 gathered a congregation and erected the chapel. After a period of neglect *c.*1873–93 the chapel was repaired and re-opened and the church re-formed; in 1903 the chapel was refitted and new vestries built. The adjacent Sunday-school was built in 1862.

The chapel is a tall building with rendered walls and a hipped roof. The front wall has a high parapet, stone quoins and rusticated surrounds to two round-arched upper windows; a later porch in a matching style has been rebuilt since 1974.

The interior (46ft by 30ft) has been much altered and a rear gallery removed. The original roof structure comprises four trusses each with a king-post, queen-posts and cross-bracing springing from the king-post at mid-height; on one of the queen-posts is the painted inscription 'Built 1786'.

Monuments: in chapel (1) Rev. Caleb Evans D.D., 1791, and Sarah (Hazle) his widow, 1817, grey and white marble with urn and swag in low relief; (2) Rev. John Foster, 1843, the essayist, pastor 1800–4 and 1817, erected 1896; (3) Rev. Joseph Mitchell, 1860 (*sic* but see below), 30 years pastor, and Ann his widow 1861; in burial-ground (4) John Foster, 1843, John his son, 1826, Sophia his daughter, 1868, and Elizabeth Peglar, 1877; (5) Rev. John Vernon, 1817, 'first pastor'; (6) Rev. Joseph Mitchell, 1859, *et al.*; (7) Rev. William Evans, 1892, 30 years pastor, *et al.*; (8) Thomas Nelmes, 1877, deacon, *et al.*, obelisk.

Eayrs (1911) 153–9.

MARSHFIELD   *Avon*

(101) THE OLD MEETING-HOUSE, High Street (ST 777737), was built in 1752 for a society of Independents and Presbyterians formed in the late 17th century; in 1672 John Fox, ejected vicar of Pucklechurch, was licensed here and in 1680 George Seal from Glamorgan is named as minister. An earlier meeting-house which appears to have been registered in 1699 stood on another site. In its later years the society favoured an heterodox ministry and the cause died out in the mid 19th century. The building is now used for social purposes.

The meeting-house has walls of ashlar and a hipped roof covered with stone slates except at the front where it has been re-covered in patent tiles (remainder of roof tiled 1982). The walls

THE OLD MEETING-HOUSE, MARSHFIELD

have a stone plinth and a continuous platband linking the windows at impost height. The N front has rusticated quoins, a central segmental-arched doorway with rusticated surround and two round-arched windows with keystones; in the S wall are two similar windows, and in the E and W walls are gallery windows at a higher level. A tablet on the front wall is dated 1752.

The interior (25ft by 36¼ft) has a flat plaster ceiling with coved moulded cornice and an original central ceiling-rose. E and W galleries have fielded panelled fronts without intermediate supports. The N wall and the end walls at gallery level are divided into three bays by arcading. The lower walls have a dado of two tiers of reset fielded panelling from former pews and the site of the pulpit against the S wall is marked by an iron hand which served to support a canopy. In front of the meeting-house is a small forecourt and stone gate-piers.

Monument: in burial-ground to the S, 18th-century table-tomb with panelled sides and shaped corners. Reset as paving are fragments of other monuments. (Murch records monuments in the meeting-house to Rev. Evan Thomas, 1762, and Rev. David Evans, 1817, also a foundation stone of 16 October 1752 with a lengthy oecumenical inscription.) *Sundial*: on S wall, with Roman numerals and iron gnomon.

Murch (1835) 36–46.

MINCHINHAMPTON

(102) WESLEYAN, Littleworth (SO 849016). Built 1790 but much altered and refitted 1887. Rubble walls and hipped slate roof. Three-bay front with two tiers of round-arched windows and later entablature; four-bay sides with two rows of lancet windows except where later building adjoins. The interior (34½ft by 32½ft) has a gallery around three sides, refronted and repewed in 1887.

MITCHELDEAN

(103) CONGREGATIONAL (SO 664182). The church originated in the late 17th century, rebuilding its meeting-house in 1735 and 1798 and replacing it by the present chapel in 1822. The walls are

of rendered rubble and the roof is hipped and slated. The front entrance, inside an altered porch, has a round-arched head with keystone and above it is a simple Venetian window; two slightly pointed-arched windows in each side wall have intersecting glazing bars. The interior, largely refitted, has a back gallery. In the small burial-ground is a monument to Hester Partridge, 1784, daughter of Thomas and Mary Partridge, and Samuel their son, 1799.

Bright (1954) 2, 14–15.

MORETON-IN-MARSH

(104) CONGREGATIONAL, Oxford Street (SP 205325). Built 1860–1 in 'the Italian style' by Poulton and Woodman of

Reading, for a church formed in 1801. Stone and slate, with grouped round-arched windows. *Pitch-pipe*: early 19th-century.
CYB (1861) 281–4.

NAILSWORTH

(105) BAPTIST (ST 847995). Seceders from Forest Green Chapel *c*.1705 built a meeting-house at Shortwood in 1714–15 which was rebuilt in 1837. 'Shortwood Chapel', built on a new site in 1881, has an ashlar front of three bays with pilasters and a pediment into which the centre bay rises as an arch.

Ivimey IV (1830) 469–80: Thompson-Smythe, F., *Chronicles of Shortwood* (1916).

(106) CONGREGATIONAL, Spring Hill (ST 847999). The Independent meeting at Forest Green originated in the late 17th century, one of the first promotors being William Tray, ejected rector of Oddington. A meeting-house built *c*.1687 was enlarged to the front in the early 18th century, a large vestry added 1745, and a plaster ceiling constructed in the chapel in 1761. In 1821 a majority of the church erected the present 'Forest Green Chapel' on a new site. This has stone walls and a slate roof. The front of three bays with a wide round-arched doorway and two tiers of windows all with round-arched heads has a pedimented gable, rebuilt at the apex, with a large lunette inscribed with the date of erection. The interior which has a gallery around three sides was refitted *c*.1880 and later.

Russell, C., *A Brief History of the Independent Church at Forest Green, Nailsworth* (1912).

(107) FRIENDS, Chestnut Hill (ST 848995). Considerable support for Quaker teaching is known to have existed by 1655 and the present building may have been in use before 1689 when it was registered as a meeting-house. Some external repairs were carried out in 1794–5 and alterations were made to the interior in 1807 and 1819. The building, which stands at right angles to a slightly earlier house facing a courtyard, dates in part from the

(107) NAILSWORTH. Friends' meeting-house.

mid 17th century; the walls are of coursed rubble and the roof which is double with a central valley is covered with stone slates.

The W front has a wide round-arched doorway with keystone and imposts below a square label with diamond stops; to the right is a window formerly of four lights with a transome, now altered, and to the left is a smaller window of two lights and another above; the lower windows have moulded labels. The S end has two gables: below that to the E is a mullioned window of three lights with a moulded label, reduced in width and with a hung sash inserted in the early 19th century, and an upper window of two lights; below the other gable is the blocking of a lower window with timber lintel. The N wall, partly covered by the house, has windows below the E gable corresponding to those at the opposite end but variously altered.

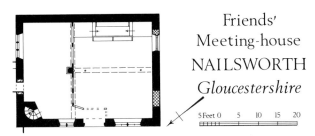

Friends' Meeting-house NAILSWORTH *Gloucestershire*

5 Feet 0   5   10   15   20

The interior (24¼ft by 33¼ft) is unevenly divided into two rooms by an early 19th-century screen with shutters incorporating a substantial earlier post which supports one end of the valley beam above the principal room. The S room, much altered in the early 19th century, has a panelled dado and stand at the E end; the upper window in the S wall, formerly lighting an attic, has been altered to serve the room below. The N room has a stone spiral staircase in one corner leading to an upper room at this end.

Inscriptions: scratched on window cill of upper room, initials and dates including 1683, 1684. *Seating*: in upper room, crude open-backed benches with shaped oversailing ends and thin splayed legs, possibly 17th-century with backs added; in meeting-room, early 19th-century benches. The burial-ground for this meeting is at Shortwood.

NAUNTON

(108) BAPTIST (SP 114234). Built 1850. Stone and slate, gabled W end with porch between staircase wings; four-bay sides with pointed windows and stone Y-tracery. *Gates*: contemporary cast-iron gates next to road. *Monument*: in chapel, Robert Rowlands, 1851, and Hannah his widow, 1874, 'the only members who assisted in building the old chapel about the year 1798 that lived to see the new one opened for public worship in 1850'.

NEWENT

(109) CONGREGATIONAL, Broad Street (SO 721259). Built *c*.1844. Ashlar front with red brick sides and slate roof. Gabled front with traceried windows and ogee labels; cast-iron window frames. (URC)

NEWNHAM

(110) Former CONGREGATIONAL, Littledean Road (SO 690118). Rendered front of three bays with two tiers of round-arched windows. Built 1826; new chapel built nearby after 1859.

(109) NEWENT. Congregational chapel.

NORTHLEACH WITH EASTINGTON

(111) CONGREGATIONAL, Northleach (SP 113147). By T. Roger Smith, 1860. Gabled front with bell-cote. The open single-span

roof incorporates clerestory lighting to overcome the absence of side windows on a restricted site. (Closed before 1981)
CYB (1859) 256; (1861) 280, 282.

NORTON

(112) Former WESLEYAN, Bishop's Norton (SO 850245). Brick with hipped slate roof, triple-arched front with later porch and tablet dated 1841.

OLDBURY-UPON-SEVERN *Avon*

(113) WESLEYAN (ST 610925). Opened 1835; pantiled roof.

OLDLAND *Avon*

(114) Former WESLEYAN, Longwell Green (ST 659711). Three-bay gabled front with later porch. Opened 1823; transferred to Free Methodists *c*.1870.

(115) Former FREE METHODIST, Longwell Green (ST 659710). Three-bay front with worn tablet dated ?1853. Used as Sunday-school after *c*.1870.

   Eayrs (1911) 193, 235.

(116) WESLEYAN, Warmley Tower (ST 669725). Rendered front with two tiers of windows. Dated 1833.

OLVESTON *Avon*

(117) Former FRIENDS, The Green (ST 601868). A meeting in Olveston was settled by *c*.1655 with Walter Clement as a principal supporter. The present building of 17th-century date was given to the society in 1696; in 1779 it was reported to be 'in a ruinous condition' and it was repaired in 1782 at a cost of £189 6s. 11d. The meeting-house was closed in 1872 and has since been converted to a private house.

   The walls are of rubble and the roofs are pantiled. The W front has a wide doorway with ovolo-moulded frame between two windows of four lights with oak mullions; two gables have recently been added. The roof over the E half is in two parallel sections with half-hips to the rear and formerly with a lower roof between. The interior (35½ft by 32½ft) is divided by partitions with shutters into a single meeting-room to the E with stand at the S end and two smaller rooms to the W with a room above which has two sashes opening to the principal room.

   To the N is a former stable, square with hipped roof, in similar materials.

(118) WESLEYAN (ST 601872). Oval tablet dated 1820 in shaped gable.

PAINSWICK

(119) Former BAPTIST, Jack's Green, Sheepscombe (SO 889099). Broad three-bay front with pointed-arched windows. Built 1820 and sold to Primitive Methodists 1831 on removal to (123).

(120) CONGREGATIONAL, Gloucester Street (SO 867099). Independents, believed to have been active here from the mid 17th century, were supported in 1672 by Francis Harris, ejected curate of Deerhurst. In 1689 the Town Hall was registered for meetings, possibly by this society, and in 1705 a meeting-house was built which was recorded as Presbyterian. The present chapel was erected in 1803 largely through the efforts of the pastor the Rev. Cornelius Winter and drastically altered in 1892 to the designs of J. Fletcher Trew when it was named 'The Cornelius Winter Memorial Chapel'. (now URC)

This is a square stone building with hipped roof having two tiers of windows and a platband; two tall round-arched windows in the NE wall mark the former site of the pulpit. In 1892 a moulded cornice and parapet were added, many of the windows were altered or embellished and a porch built against the SW front. The interior, which had a gallery around three sides, was divided to provide an entrance lobby with staircase and vestry and an upper room at the front and a smaller chapel behind in which the pulpit was re-sited at the SE end facing a single gallery. SE of the chapel is a separate schoolroom dated 1844.

   Glass: In SE window above pulpit, two angels with harps and vine-scroll border, by William Morris & Co., 1897–8. *Monuments*: in chapel (1) William Cox, 1866, clothier, and Henrietta (Wane) his wife, 1849, signed J. Wall, Stroud; (2) John Haynes, 1856, surgeon, and Harriet (Wane) his widow, signed C. Lewis, Cheltenham; (3) William Fowles, 1832, Elizabeth his widow, 1848, and Eliza their daughter, 1830; (4) Rev. Cornelius Winter, 1808, nearly twenty years pastor 'by whose Benevolence and exertions this Edifice was erected', and Miriam his widow, 1817; (5) Elizabeth Shepherd, 1805 and Martha Tyler, 1818, signed J. Pearce, Frampton; in vestibule (6) William West, 1792, 'Clerk of this Chapel'; (7) Sarah Thomas, 1839, and Joseph Beavins her son, 1861. Also, in chapel, a series of small late 19th-century memorials to 18th- and 19th-century pastors.

   CYB (1893) 194–5.

(121) CONGREGATIONAL, Edge (SO 851097). Three-bay ashlar front with pediment and pilasters; built 1856 for a society formed by Cornelius Winter. Inside are open-backed benches and two box-pews flanking the entrance. The original pulpit (now removed) came from the church of St Mary le Crypt, Gloucester, where George Whitefield preached his first sermon. *Inscription*: slate tablet, loose outside, inscribed 'CONGREGATIONAL CHURCH TRUST 1856'. (Disused)

   CYB (1857) 235.

(122) FRIENDS, Vicarage Street (SO 870097). Built in 1705–6 for an existing meeting which since 1658 had the use of a burial-ground at Dell Farm, the gift of Thomas Loveday. Major repairs

or alterations were made to the meeting-house in 1793–4; it was closed in 1894 and re-opened by Friends 1952. The walls are of squared stone with chimney-stacks on the E and W gables; the roof has been re-covered with blue slates. The S front has a central doorway, now blocked, with cambered stone lintel dated

Friends'
Meeting-house
PAINSWICK
Gloucestershire

C.F.S.   5 Feet 0   5   10   15   20

1706; to each side is a tall window with later timber lintel and hung sashes. In the E wall is a similar doorway below a gabled hood supported by shaped wooden brackets and two windows high in the gable. The W wall has two similar gable windows and a blocked window below.

The interior ($29\frac{3}{4}$ft by $23\frac{1}{2}$ft) comprises a single room with stand at the W end and small lobby to the E with shutters to the main room and a staircase leading to the upper floor. The staircase dates from the late 18th century and the attic floor, which provided residential accommodation, was largely refitted at that period. *Seating*: early 19th-century open-backed benches; front of stand removed.

Burial-ground: (SO 876094) N of Dell Farm, stone boundary-walls and W entrance closed by re-used stone slab with cast-iron plate dated 1658. Eight ledger stones, two with coffin-shaped outline, one with brass indent, with decayed inscriptions of 17th and 18th century to Loveday family.

(123) Former WESLEYAN, New Street (SO 867097). Built 1806, sold to Baptists 1831. Gabled front of three bays with two tiers of windows. Two tablets in gable inscribed with dates of erection and transfer.

(124) Former PRIMITIVE METHODIST, Bisley Street (SO 868097). 'Ebenezer Chapel' was built 1854 for a society formerly meeting in Vicarage Street.

PRESTBURY

(125) CONGREGATIONAL (SO 970238). Polychrome brick, corner tower with pyramid roof, 1865.

RANDWICK

(126) WESLEYAN (SO 831067). 'Randwick Chapel, Built 1807, Rebuilt 1824' is a substantial building of stone with a slate roof. The S end has a pedimental gable with inscribed tablet and bell-cote with one bell; two windows of three lights have pointed-arched heads and intersecting stone tracery. Long side-walls each with two pointed windows, and Sunday-school at N end. Refitted in late 19th century.

RODBOROUGH

(127) PRIMITIVE METHODIST, Butter Row (SO 856041). 'Zion Chapel' dated 1856.

For Rodborough Tabernacle see (140).

RUARDEAN

(128) BIBLE CHRISTIAN, Crooked End (SO 628176). Opened 1855.

RUSPIDGE

(129) BIBLE CHRISTIAN, Ruspidge (SO 651116). Squared stone front and rubble sides, each with two windows.

(130) BIBLE CHRISTIAN, Upper Soudley (SO 661103). Three-centred arched entrance and two small round-arched gallery windows. Tablet over doorway inscribed 'ZION CHAPEL 1846'.

SISTON

(131) FREE METHODIST, Bridgeyate (ST 682733). 'Ebenezer Chapel' dated 1810. Broad three-bay front extended at end in two stories.

SLIMBRIDGE

(132) Former CONGREGATIONAL, Cambridge (SO 746033). 'Union Chapel', built 1807, extended to rear 1876.

SODBURY   Avon

(133) Former BAPTIST, Hounds Road, Chipping Sodbury (ST 728821). 'REBUILT 1819'. Interior subdivided and floored for Sunday-school 1971.

STOW-ON-THE-WOLD

(134) BAPTIST, Sheep Street (SP 192256). The church originated as part of that at Moreton-in-Marsh, in existence by 1655, which came to be described as meeting near Moreton and Stow. The first known meeting-house at Stow was referred to as 'lately erected' in a lease of 18 April 1700 where its size is given as 37ft by 21ft with a burial-ground on the S side 51ft by 25ft with access from Back Street (now Sheep Street).

The present chapel built in 1852 on the site of the former, stands behind houses on the S side of the street and is approached through an arched passage of that period. The walls are of coursed rubble with ashlar dressings and the roof is hipped at a low pitch and covered with slates; wide, boarded, eaves are supported by paired brackets. The interior, refitted in 1892, has a N gallery only.

Fittings – *Book*: Geneva Bible with Apocrypha, 'printed at London by the deputies of Christopher Barker', 1597.

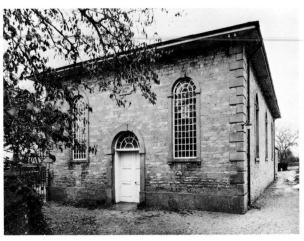

Bootscrapers: at N doorway, wrought-iron with scrolled standards, *c*.1852. *Inscription*: on stone reset in wall of outhouse, *TB 1732*. *Monuments*: in burial-ground (1) John Ellis, 1711; (2) Elizabeth Marsh, 1712; (3) John Marsh, 1700. *Plate*: includes two small tankards of 1709 given by Mrs Margaret Freeman of Guiting.

Blackaby, F.E., *Past and Present, History of the Baptist Church. Stow-on-the-Wold* (1892): Ivimey II (1814) 161–2: Oliver (1968) 115–16.

(135) Former FRIENDS (SP 193259). A meeting-house built in 1719 on a piece of land 47ft by 19ft, acquired in that year, stands in a lane behind the White Hart Hotel. The building, sold in 1887 and now used as a youth hostel, has rubble walls and a tiled roof. It has been much altered but blockings of former windows are visible in the end walls. The interior (26¼ft by 17½ft) has no old features.

Sturge (1895) 14.

(136) WESLEYAN, Sheep Street (SP 192257). Brick and stone with corner tower, built 1865; tablet dated 1814 reset from former chapel.

STROUD

(137) BAPTIST, John Street (SO 852051). Ashlar front of three bays with round-arched windows. Built 1824; much altered inside 1975.

(138) THE OLD CHAPEL, Chapel Street (SO 857051). The congregation formerly meeting here appears to have met in the late 17th century in Robert Viner's barn at Stroud Water which was registered in June 1689. The present site was acquired in 1704 and a meeting-house had been erected by 1711. Although the building was held in trust for Presbyterians, the church included Independents and by 1811, when John Burder was appointed pastor to revive the declining fortunes of the society, the cause had come to be regarded as Congregational. Burder's pastorate (1811–37) was marked by the first enlargement of the meeting-house to the S in 1813, and the flourishing condition in which he left the church was evinced by a further considerable alteration, heightening and refronting of the building in 1844; a detached

schoolroom was built to the N in 1854 and the chapel was largely refitted c.1881.

The walls are of rubble, rendered on the E side, and the roof is hipped and slated with a lead flat at the centre. The E and W walls of the early 18th-century structure remain and part of the N wall; the latter was pierced c.1844 when an organ chamber was added which has two round-arched windows on the N side. The W wall has two tiers of round-arched windows refashioned in 1844 but of which two to each level probably occupy the sites of the original openings; a ragged joint in the masonry marks the line of rebuilding to the south. The E wall is similarly fenestrated; the rendering was carried out prior to the heightening which is marked by a change in colour. The S front, added to

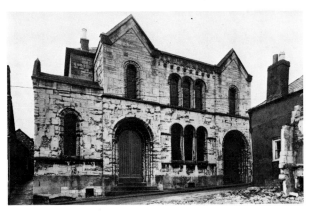

S front.

Exterior from NE.

provide a vestibule and staircases outside the former end of the building, is in the Romanesque style with two doorways and low staircase wings at the sides.

The interior (originally about 30ft by 40¼ft; enlarged to 45½ft by 40¼ft exclusive of the vestibule) has a plaster ceiling coved on all sides and a large semicircular arch at the N end opening to the organ chamber. The gallery, around three sides supported by wooden columns, was rebuilt or refronted in 1844. The S front, of 1813 and now internal, has a central entrance now blocked and replaced by two doorways.

Fittings – *Benefaction Boards*: in S vestibule, two, painted wood with shaped tops and leaf finials, recording eight benefactions, 1830–87, including a Communion service given 1830 by William and Ann Leach, and £1,300 given for renovation in 1881 by Mrs Franklin in whose memory a stained-glass window was erected on the E side of the chapel. *Monuments*: in vestibule (1) Henry Wyatt, 1847, Hannah his wife, 1826, and Priscilla his widow, 1865, double-arched Romanesque panel with shield-of-arms; (2) Elizabeth (Brownson) wife of John Grime, 1756; (3) Rev. John Burder M.A., 1867, 26 years pastor, with shield-of-arms; (4) Thomas Harmer, 1825, servant to Rev. John Burder, and Mary his widow, 1832; (5) Rev. William Harries, 1830, 28 years pastor; in chapel (6) Robert Morgan, 1740; (7) Richard Rawlin, 1725, Thomas Jenkins, 1749, and Samuel Ball, 1779, pastors, erected 1823; (8) Joseph Franklin, 1855, 'many years architect to the Corporation of Liverpool', Benjamin his brother, 1862, and Maria widow of the last, 1881, signed Hamlett, Stroud; (9) Mrs Susannah Davis, 1836, signed Hamlett; (10) John Okey, 1783, and Ann his widow, 1792; (11) Edward Okey, 1798, card-maker, Martha his widow, 1819, and three infants; (12) Anthony Paine, mercer, 1775, Sarah his widow, 1801, *et al.*; (13) Anthony Paine, clothier, 1735, Mary his widow, 1759, and Susannah their daughter 1760; (14) John Viner, 1723, and Sarah his sister, 1723; (15) Daniel Bloxsome, mercer, 1808, Sarah (Morley) his wife 1781, Ursula (Aldridge) his widow, 1828, and Sarah Aldridge her sister, 1811; externally, on E wall and adjacent are several reset 18th-century monuments, also brass tablets including (16) John Clissold, 1823, 'sexton of this Place 30 Years', *et al.*; further brass inscription plates on paving of E courtyard; in burial-ground N of chapel numerous monuments

---

In Memory of Henry Okey Clerk of yᵉ Church 41 Years, who died 3ᵈ Jan: 1765; Æ: 67.

---

of the 18th century and later including (17) Henry Okey, 1765, clerk, with inscription on brass tablet.

(Church united with Bedford Street 1970; chapel demolished 1977. The benefaction-boards and some of the monuments have been removed to Stroud Museum)

Fisher, P.H., *Notes and Recollections of Stroud, Gloucestershire* (1871) 319–28.

(139) CONGREGATIONAL, Bedford Street (SO 851052). A new congregation formed to relieve overcrowding at the Old Chapel built 'Bedford Street Chapel', originally named 'Union Chapel', in 1835–7. The names of Charles Barker and Dawkes (possibly Samuel Whitfield Dawkes) appear in the accounts against payments for plans. The chapel has walls of rubble faced at the front with ashlar. The front wall has a plain lower stage above which four fluted Ionic columns support a pediment; in the wide central bay is a Venetian window. The entrance is in a circular

stair tower to one side, in two stages surmounted by a dome and a (rebuilt) lantern. The body of the chapel has plain sides rounded to the rear with tall round-arched windows to the principal stage.

The interior of the chapel, which stands above Sunday-school rooms at ground level, is approached by a circular staircase. An original rear gallery was extended along the sides and around the apsidal end in 1851, and the three windows in the apse were blocked internally. The other windows were reglazed in 1889; alterations were made to the pews c.1919. The original pulpit, partly concealed by a platform, is circular and has a ring of Corinthian columns to the upper stage.

Fisher, op. cit., 319–28: Nott, R., The Bedford Street Congregational Church, Stroud (1937).

(140) RODBOROUGH TABERNACLE (SO 846040). A preaching-house built in 1750 for a group of Calvinistic Methodist societies in the neighbourhood of Rodborough forms the nucleus of the present chapel. These societies founded by George Whitefield, together with others more remote, later became known as the 'Rodborough Connexion' and eventually adopted Congregational practices. The building (now URC), which has stone walls and a hipped slate roof, was enlarged to the W and heightened in 1837 and subsequently extended to the E by the addition of a Sunday-school. The earliest part (40¼ft by 42½ft externally) faces N and is of three bays with a central segmental-arched doorway, now reduced in width, between two windows with segmental-arched heads and keystones. Three upper windows have had round arches added when the wall was heightened. The extensions to E and W are each of two bays with matching windows. The main entrance is now at the W end set between two late 19th-century staircase pavilions which front the end wall of 1837 in which is a plain Venetian window.

The interior (now 58¾ft by 38½ft) was refitted in 1837 when

the pulpit was resited at the E end and a gallery with fielded panelled front built around four sides. The seating and pulpit are of later date.

Fittings – Book: in locked case, The Great Bible or 'Treacle Bible', mid 16th-century. Chair: high-backed with arms and open round splat back, called 'Whitefield's chair', 18th-century. Monuments: in chapel (1) Henry Hodges 1838, Hester his wife, 1831, and Rebecca his sister, 1874; (2) Samuel Marling, 1777 (also a brass), Hester his widow, wife of John Figgins, 1801 (also a brass), William Marling, 1859, and Sarah his wife, 1856; (3) Edward Dicks, 1832, and Elizabeth his wife, 1815; (4) Thomas Adams, 1770, first pastor, Elizabeth his first wife, 1765, and Hannah his second wife, 1800; (5) Rev. Robert Heath, 1800, and Benjamin his son, 1797; (6) Rev. Orlando Augustus Jeary, 1817, Sarah his wife, 1806, and Elizabeth his widow, 1822; (7) Anne, wife of Rev. Eliezer Jones, 1837, and their two children Mary Jane, 1835, and Louisa Anne, 1837. Paintings: in vestry, oil portraits of John Cennick and various ministers including Thomas Adams and John Rees (pastor 1813–23). Miscellaneous: Walking stick of George Whitefield and cane of Thomas Adams.

(141) EBLEY CHAPEL (SO 827049), the successor to a chapel of 1797 built for an Independent congregation which was for a

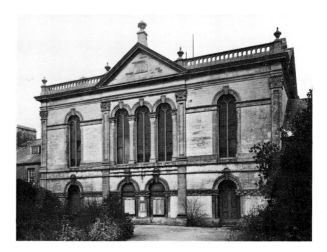

time associated with the Countess of Huntingdon's Connexion, was built in 1880–1 to designs of Rev. Thomas Thomas. It is a large building of stone having a wide S front with pedimented centre and wings with balustraded parapets and urn finials. The back is polygonal externally with a semicircular gallery facing the pulpit which is set between the front entrances. The manse adjacent to the W was built in 1798 with a room added in 1845; a cottage to the E is also of the late 18th century. (Demolished *c*.1972)

Criddle, L., *The Story of Ebley Chapel* [*c*.1947].

(142) Former METHODIST, Acre Street (SO 85450515). A society which had earlier suffered from internal dissentions had sufficiently recovered by 1763 to build what is now the oldest surviving octagonal Methodist chapel; John Wesley preached 'in the new house' on 18 March 1765 to an overflowing congregation. The building was greatly enlarged in 1796 by extension to the NW and superseded a century later by a new Wesleyan

Former Methodist Preaching-house, Acre Street STROUD *Gloucestershire*

Front of Gallery

N

5 0 5 10 15 20 25 Feet

C.F.S.

chapel in Castle Street, in the Classical style by James Tait of Leicester, opened 27 October 1876, closed 1981. The octagon is now used as the Salvation Army Citadel.

The former preaching-house has stone walls and a hipped slate roof. It was originally a regular octagon, the extension being accomplished by doubling the length of the sides and rebuilding one end. The original walls have a stone plinth, a flat-arched window to the lower stage and a smaller window above which terminated level with the eaves. The front doorway has a flat wooden canopy supported by shaped brackets. The walls of the extension are similarly fenestrated but with two large round-arched windows in the NW wall which formerly flanked the pulpit. A two-storied wing to the N may be contemporary with the enlargement. Alterations of 19th-century date included the erection of a short buttressing wing to the SW with wide flank walls enclosing raking timber shores and a narrow additional staircase between to the gallery. Pointed-arched heads in dormers were also added to the upper windows of the original building, the window over the entrance was blocked and a tall rendered parapet constructed at the front. The external character has also been much affected by the substitution of window frames with large panes in place of the original sashes. The interior (61ft by 40ft) has a gallery around five sides supported by timber columns with Roman Doric capitals. A large stepped platform has been constructed at the NW end with small rooms below and the principal windows at this end have been blocked. The roof was reconstructed after a fire in the early 20th century and the ceiling rebuilt at a slightly higher level.

(143) Former PRIMITIVE METHODIST, Parliament Street (SO 857052). Dated 1836. Now the Playhouse.

TETBURY

(144) BAPTIST, Church Street (ST 890931). A Particular Baptist church which claims to have been formed in 1721 appears to have occupied this site since 1764 if not earlier, a conveyance of 1719 refers to a building called The Red Lion which also appears in later documents and an inn called The Three Cups. A 'new built house in Tetbury' was registered for Baptist use in 1725. Two confronting buildings now stand within the boundary of the property: the present chapel and an earlier building which is supposed to have been its predecessor.

The earlier building, of rubble with a stone slate roof, has two gables to the front in each of which is a small attic window. Larger windows have been inserted below with round-arched heads of brick and keystones and a doorway of similar date and style between. Above the entrance a small window has been blocked and there are further signs of alterations elsewhere in the building. The interior which is narrow has been altered, probably by the removal of a floor, and now has a single end gallery with attics above.

The present chapel, of stone with a hipped stone slate roof, may be as late as *c*.1800. The front has two doorways and three upper windows all with round-arched stone heads with keystones. The interior, partly refitted, has an L-shaped gallery.

TEWKESBURY

(145) THE OLD BAPTIST CHAPEL, Church Street (SO 890325). A
Particular Baptist church was in existence in Tewkesbury by
1655 in which year it was represented at the first meetings of an
association of Midland Baptist churches. Although the first deed
of the property in Old Chapel Court (formerly Millington's
Alley and previously Merrie Cheaps or Millicheape's Alley) is
dated 1620, being a conveyance from Edward Millicheape to
Thomas Harris, carpenter, no specific reference to a meeting-
house appears until 1711. No licences for Baptist meetings were
issued under the 1672 Indulgence and the earliest monuments in
the burial-ground date from c.1680. A reference in the parochial
burial register (Matthews (1924) 214) to Paul Frewen, ejected
vicar of Kempley, Glos., later Baptist minister at Trowbridge
and Warwick, as 'speaker in ye Diss Bur Place' at Tewkesbury
could indicate that some meetings were being held in the open.
As a deed of 1686 mentions only a 'messuage divided into several
tenements in Millington's Alley' the formal conversion of part
or all of the property to a meeting-house may have been delayed
until after Toleration in 1689. Further alterations to the building
seem to have occurred in the late 18th century, but the need for a

more convenient place of worship was eventually felt: the church
books record 'Our meeting house being very old and much out
of repair and not sufficient to accommodate the Congregation a
purchase of ground was made in Barton Street and a new Meeting House commenced Sept. 1804 and opened 21 June 1805'.
The former building was then reduced in size by partial conversion to cottages leaving the central section only intact; by
1968 it had fallen into serious disrepair but it has since (1976–9)
been rehabilitated and restored to its original size.

The chapel, which stands on the E side of a narrow alley
behind no. 63 Church Street, 200 yards N of the Abbey Church,
is a timber-framed building with a tiled roof. The structure
originated about 1500 as a hall-house of three bays, the hall in the
centre rising through two storeys with a smoke louvre in the
roof and two-storied bays to N and south. The framing of the
front wall, until recently covered by plaster, has been exposed
and many missing or decayed timbers replaced; it comprises a
series of large panels with an intermediate rail and two lower
braces only between the cill and principal posts. The rear wall is
very plain with evidence only for one upper window in the
middle bay, of three lights, now blocked. The windows in the

South-West Elevation

Section aa

The Old Baptist Chapel
TEWKESBURY
Gloucestershire

(Before restoration)

Scale of Feet

5   0   5   10   15   20

Exterior before restoration.

Exterior after restoration.

Interior before restoration.

W front date from the 18th century or later, the central part being lit by two pairs of tall windows separated by the intermediate posts of the framing but cutting through the horizontal rail; a doorway was inserted below the southernmost window *c*.1805 but the window has now been restored to its former length; two upper windows and one below at each end have modern frames; the two remaining doorways which gave access to the early 19th-century cottages appear to have served as the entrances to the chapel.

The interior (reduced to 18ft square in 1805, now 18ft by 48ft) has an 18th-century segmental plaster barrel-vault above a moulded cornice which extends from the S end of the range to an upper vestry at the north. An earlier plaster ceiling just above this vault remains at collar level. Above a stairwell in the NE corner is a smaller vaulted ceiling. The pulpit is centrally placed against the W wall. Galleries around three sides have plain panelled fronts and moulded cornices, supported on the E by two turned oak posts with moulded capitals and tall bases; a further post incorporated in the staircase of the S cottage has been re-used. Walls were built in 1805 on the line of the N and S galleries but the fronts remained intact and the lower parts of the walls received a dado of two tiers of panelling. An upper vestry at the N end has a shuttered opening towards the chapel on the S side with late 18th-century boxing but renewed shutters.

Fittings – *Baptistery*: centrally in floor with steps at N end, brick-lined with narrow channel to W perhaps for filling and drain in SW corner, late 18th-century. *Chandeliers*: two, one of brass with six branches, 18th-century, one with turned wood body and formerly four metal arms, perhaps later. *Communion Tables*: two, one of oak with turned legs and altered top, late 17th-century, one with shaped legs, from Seventh-day Baptist chapel at Natton (see Ashchurch (2) above), 18th-century. *Inscriptions and Scratchings*: on wall plaster outside vestry next to NE stair, 'Hy Jenks', 'R. Yarnal 1795', 'I.E. 1797', and a figure of a cockerel. *Monuments*: in burial-ground N of chapel, many headstones and some table-tombs, (1) John Cowell, 1680 or 1681; (2) Mary wife of John Cowell, 16[?79]; (3) Margaret Millington 'twice widdow', 1684; (4) Richard Field, 1689; (5) Anne Attkinson, 1706; (6) William Steven, 1706; (7) Isaac Straford, 1792, 'many years deacon', Ann his widow, 1793, and Joseph their son, 1813. (Ivimey also records a monument to Eleazer Herring V.D.M., 1694, Mary his wife, 1690, Eleazer their son, 1695, and Anna Flower their daughter, 1760.) *Pulpit*: polygonal with panelled front and moulded dentil cornice, panelled back-board with shaped top and short cornice, *c*.1760, stairs later. *Seating*: before 1976 some fragments of fixed pews remained in the E gallery and open-backed benches, wall benches and stools below; stepped seating formerly in N gallery may be inferred from height of remaining *hat pegs* above vestry shutters.

Arnold (1960) 103–4, figs 9, 15: Ivimey II (1814) 167–8: VCH *Gloucestershire* VIII (1968) 163: White I (1971) 18 sqq.

(146) BAPTIST, Barton Street (SO 894326). Brick with hipped slate roof, built 1804–5 to supersede the foregoing ('plan by Rev. William Bradby') and schoolrooms added behind in 1839–40. It stands concealed behind other buildings on the S side of the street; the plain front has a brick dentil eaves cornice and two round-arched windows formerly with doorways below but altered in the mid 19th century and a central doorway inserted re-using an original canopy on shaped brackets. The sides have round-arched windows divided into two tiers in 1852. Gallery around three sides supported by cast-iron columns of six-foil section. Pulpit and seating renewed *c*.1892.

Benefaction Table: painted 1845 on wall plaster of rear room, recording items from 1749. *Monument*: in chapel, Rev. Daniel Trotman, 1850, 40 years pastor, and Rev. Jesse Hewett, 1843, six years co-pastor.

Ivimey IV (1830) 481–2.

(147) CONGREGATIONAL, Barton Street (SO 895327). Three licences for Congregational preachers were issued in 1672 including one for William Davison, ejected rector of Notgrove, Glos., but the society which had developed by the early 18th century, perhaps from these origins, was Presbyterian and continued to be so described until the later years of that century. By 1819, when Henry Welsford became minister of what was by then an Independent church, the cause is said to have been 'in a very low state', but during his ministry the meeting-house was much altered and enlarged, possibly amounting to a rebuilding in 1828 which is approximately the date of the present building. The chapel, of brick with a hipped slate roof, has a broad front of three bays with a low parapet, round-arched upper windows with shorter windows below and a central porch.

VCH *Gloucestershire* VIII (1968) 164.

(148) Former FRIENDS, Barton Street (SO 89423263). The Friends' *burial-ground* in St Mary's Lane, 50 yards NE of the Old Baptist Chapel (SO 890325), now a public garden, is reputed to have been in use from 1660. A conveyance of 1670 of 'three messuages in St Mary Street, Tewkesbury, with a parcel of ground where a barn formerly stood, now made use of by Quakers for a burial-ground on the West side, and the tenements of William Clarke the Younger on the East side' is followed by a further deed of 1677 in which the three messuages are described as in use as a Quaker meeting-place. Two timber-framed cottages on the E side of the burial-ground, although no longer exhibiting evidence of former use, may thus be identified as a former meeting-house.

The erection of a new meeting-house in Tewkesbury was proposed in 1794, but the site in Barton Street was not acquired until 1804; the building appears to have been erected in 1805 although the trust deed was not completed until 1810. By 1850 the new premises had proved to be too large and were let, meetings being held in private rooms. In 1861 the meeting-house, which had been in use as 'The Music Hall' or 'Philharmonic Hall', was sold to the nearby Baptist church which used it until 1880 for Sunday-school purposes. It was converted for its present use as a public hall (The 'George Watson Memorial Hall') in 1909. This has brick walls and a hipped slate roof. The front wall, partly obscured by later work, has a brick cornice and parapet and one blind semicircular arched recess with rubbed brick voussoirs. The interior was entirely altered in 1962.

THORNBURY   *Avon*

(149) BAPTIST, Gillingstool (ST 640900). Three-bay front with pointed-arched windows. Built 1828.

(150) CONGREGATIONAL, Chapel Street (ST 637899). Generally similar to the last but with round-arched windows. Dated 1826. (URC)

(151) Former FRIENDS, St John Street (ST 638901). A meeting was established by the late 17th century and a new meeting-house was erected in 1702. In 1792 Friends proposed to demolish two ruined tenements adjacent to this and to use the site for a new building; this was accomplished in 1794 and the present structure was registered in 1795. The meeting-house was closed in 1847 on union with Olveston and in the next year consideration was given to its lease for use as a school; it was sold in 1934.

The former meeting-house, now used as a builders' warehouse, has rubble walls rendered to N and E, and a hipped roof

covered at the back with pantiles. The plan is rectangular (38ft by 24ft) with a narrower wing projecting to the south. The E front, which includes the side wall of the wing, has a wide segmental-arched doorway with a pedimented canopy supported by shaped brackets, now fallen away, and a small tablet above dated 1794; each side of the entrance is a tall segmental-arched sash window. Two windows of a similar size occupy each of the N and S walls, those to the S having segmental heads with brick arches. The S end of the wing is gabled and has a projecting chimney-breast.

The principal meeting-room ($25\frac{1}{2}$ft by 24ft) at the W end has a boarded dado and segmental vaulted ceiling; an entrance passage to the E has a small room to the N and a women's meeting-room to the S with hinged shutters (now removed) on its W side. (Demolition of S wing proposed 1983)

THRUPP

(152) WESLEYAN, Brimscombe (SO 868022). Gabled front of three bays with two tiers of round-arched windows. Opened 1804.

ULEY

(153) Former BAPTIST (ST 790983). 'Betheseda Chapel' built 1821, coursed stone walls with polygonal front and large tablet

above entrance. Gallery around five sides with fielded panelled front supported by iron columns. (Closed before 1971, now in secular use)

(154) Former CONGREGATIONAL (ST 784981). 'Union Chapel', built in 1790 for a church which claimed to have been formed in 1735. The pedimented front having a cusped lunette in the typanum with a shield-shaped tablet bearing the date of erection, closely resembles Dursley Tabernacle (70) of 1808 for which it may have formed a model.

The interior ($40\frac{1}{2}$ft by $30\frac{1}{2}$ft) has a plaster ceiling with a coved cornice. A gallery around three sides is supported by iron columns of quatrefoil section; the gallery front, pulpit and ceiling were renewed in the late 19th century.

Fittings – *Chair*: in back room, panelled back with pointed-arched top and turned supports to arms, late 18th-century.

Monuments: in chapel (1) Thomas Tilley, 1814, 'of this Village, Artist, whose abilities promis'd An high degree of future fame...', also John Tilley, 1842, Martha his wife, 1824, Sarah their daughter, 1821, and Isaac Ford her husband, 1858; (2) Daniel Neale, 1844, yeoman, and Sarah his widow, 1849, signed Jackson, Uley; (3) Timothy Jackson, 1803; (4) Nathaniel Lloyd, 1808, and Elizabeth his wife, 1807; (5) James Harris, 1801, and Mary his widow, 1814, signed Cooke, Gloster. *Plate*: includes two cups of 1792 given by James Uley Harris. (Closed *c*.1972 and now in secular use)

WESTON SUBEDGE

(155) Former WESLEYAN (SP 125409), now 'Vale Cottage'. Built 1836.

WHITESHILL

(156) CONGREGATIONAL, Ruscombe (SO 838075). Stone and slate with two tiers of round-arched windows, built 1856 to replace Zion Chapel of 1825 which was then used for school purposes. New school built 1934 incorporates date-tablet from former chapel. (URC)
    CYB (1935) 257.

WICK AND ABSON   *Avon*

(157) CONGREGATIONAL, Wick (ST 707726). Three-bay gabled front inscribed 'WICK TABERNACLE 1837'. (URC)

WICKWAR   *Avon*

(158) CONGREGATIONAL, High Street (ST 724884). Gabled front with ball finials, later tablet 'BUILT 1817 RESTORED 1919'. The original back gallery and pulpit with reeded angle-panels survive from the 1919 refitting. *Monuments*: in chapel (1) Moses son of Moses and Elizabeth Amos, 1834; (2) Rev. William Summers, 1825, first pastor, B... his wife, 1818, and Mrs Ann Dartnall, their daughter, 1821.

WINCHCOMBE

(159) Former BAPTIST, High Street (SP 025283). Behind a 17th-century range on the N side of the street and approached through

a passage with semicircular arch at the S end inscribed 'BAPTIST CHAPEL JAN 1 1811'; this last marks the date of formation of the church and the approximate year of erection of the chapel. The church appears to have united with Congregationalists about 1878 when Union Chapel was built although a separate Baptist congregation may have resulted from the merger and continued to meet here; the chapel is now used for social purposes.

The walls are of coursed stone with an ashlar front and hipped slate roof. The S front has a low plinth and a platband at mid height. A central doorway from which a small gabled porch has been removed replaced a window in the late 19th century, the two original entrances being in the adjacent bays; three upper windows with stone lintels have had their frames replaced by sheet glass. Two tall side windows have timber lintels. There is a gallery at the S end.

WINSTONE

(160) BAPTIST (SO 959095). Rubble with half-hipped roof; built *c*.1822, two-storied N wing added. *Monument*: Richard Shipway, 1844, and Sarah his wife, 1844, slab with brass plate.

WINTERBOURNE   *Avon*

(161) FRENCHAY CHAPEL (ST 640776), at the N side of Frenchay Common was built in the early 18th century. Although the deeds of the site commence in 1692 there is little trace of Presbyterian activity until early in the following century when in 1704 a house at Frenchay was registered for their use. A further

certificate was issued in January 1724 for a house in Winterbourne and in June of that year the house of Robert Abbotts in the tything of Hambrooke was similarly recorded. Accounts of expenditure do not commence until 1755 but the provision of a bell in 1752, cited when it was recast in 1836, could imply the completion of the tower somewhat later than the body of the chapel. A major refitting was carried out in 1800–1 at a reported cost of £335 5s. 8½d. which probably included alterations to the windows and gallery; further repairs continued throughout the 19th century. The chapel was closed by the then Unitarian congregation *c*.1964 but reopened in 1980 after protracted repairs.

The chapel has rubble walls and a hipped tiled roof in two parallel ranges. The front is symmetrical about a central porch, which rises to form a small tower of four stages divided by stepped string-courses and having a moulded stone cornice and pyramidal roof surmounted by a ball finial and weather-vane. In the lower stage the outer S doorway has a flat-arched head and is flanked by pilasters, now much decayed; on the W side a smaller doorway has been blocked. The second stage has a circular window to the S below the segmental-arched head of an earlier window of different form; on the E side a segmental-arched upper doorway has been blocked. At the top of the third stage, on the S side is a small stone block cut out with a circular architrave and keystones, the centre is painted to resemble a circular window but splayed reveals internally appear to allow for an opening in this position. The top stage has large segmental-arched belfry openings on three faces and a narrow slit to the north.

The E and W walls of the chapel originally had pairs of

(161) WINTERBOURNE. Frenchay Chapel from SW. *Photograph* © *R. Winstone.*

South Elevation

West Elevation

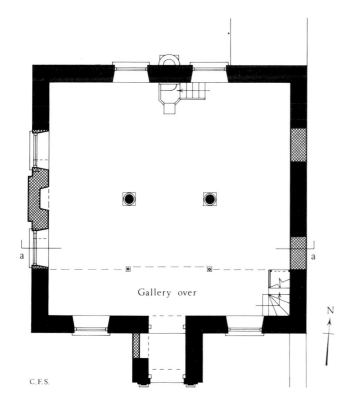

Gallery over

N

C.F.S.

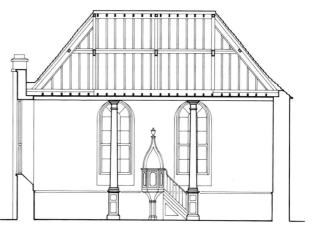

Section aa

Frenchay Chapel, WINTERBOURNE

Gloucestershire

Scale of Feet

5   0   5   10   15   20   25   30

(162) WINTERBOURNE. Friends' meeting-house. W wall.

windows at gallery level and below; in the alterations of 1800–1 the E windows were blocked and those to the W replaced by windows matching those in the front wall; a chimney-breast was also added against the W wall and a parapet replaced eaves around three sides of the building. The N wall has two round-arched windows flanking the pulpit.

The interior (29½ft by 30¾ft) has two timber columns with Tuscan capitals and high bases supporting the principal E–W beam of the roof. An early 19th-century gallery along the S side with panelled front on two columns may supersede end galleries which were allowed for in the fenestration. *Pulpit* against the N wall, contemporary with the refitting, flared base, panelled front with applied mouldings and a tall ogee back-board with urn finial. Many fragments of box-pews and other seating mostly of *c*.1800 which remained in 1971 have not been reinstated. Other fittings include – *Bell*: one, formerly in tower, given 1752 by R. Allbright, recast 1836 (stolen *c*.1970). *Monuments*: in burial-ground, near porch (1) small slab inscribed 'A S 1701'; against N wall, (2) Robert Bruce 1838, merchant of Bristol, Mary (Dye) his wife, 1809, Robert their son, 1874, and Isabella his widow, 1880, gradrooned urn on pedestal against pointed-arched backing. Also several table-tombs, small headstones and other fragments laid flat, early 18th-century and later. *Weather-vane*: on tower, representation of a comet (possibly Halley's, which appeared 1759), 18th century. *Plate*: includes a two-handled cup of 1728 given by E. Garlick, 1755.

Evans (1897) 89–90: Murch (1835) 48–52: *UHST* VI (1935–8) 260–1.

(162) FRIENDS, Frenchay (ST 641779). Meetings were held in the vicinity of Frenchay from *c*.1654 and a meeting-house believed to have been built *c*.1670–3 was registered in 1689. This was replaced in 1808–9 by the present building which has a stable wing at the front above which a women's meeting-house was built in 1815.

The meeting-house has walls of rubble and hipped roofs covered with patent tiles. The E front which had two arched windows is now largely concealed by two wings with a narrow gap between, the N wing being a cottage of two stories and the larger S wing having to the lower level a stable with passage to the left and the women's meeting-house above with two round-arched windows with external shutters facing the road. The W wall also has two arched windows above a covered walk and near the N end a small two-storied wing with two rooms intended for the use of travelling ministers.

The principal meeting-house has a through-passage at the S end giving access to the burial-ground at the rear and a central entrance; the room has a coved plaster ceiling, a S gallery closed above and below with vertically sliding shutters, and a stand at the N end with an arched window behind. *Book*: Bible, in two volumes, translated by Anthony Purver, (1702–77, schoolmaster at Frenchay and Clerk of the Meeting), published 1764.

Vintner, D., *The Friends Meeting House, Frenchay* (1970).

(163) CONGREGATIONAL, Whiteshill (ST 645793). Half-hipped roof behind swept parapet; three-bay front with round-arched windows, tablet dated 1816. 'Whiteshill Day School' behind.

(164) WESLEYAN, Watleys End (ST 658811). 'Salem Chapel', opened 1790, has rubble walls and a slate roof. The broad W front has three round-arched windows with altered glazing and a late 19th-century gabled porch; two similar windows in rear wall, one upper window at N end. Two-storied Sunday-school adjacent to south. Interior (41¼ft by 25¾ft) has an early 19th-century N gallery, otherwise refitted in late 19th century. *Monuments* in burial-ground to W date from *c*.1830.

(165) FREE METHODIST, Watleys End (ST 659 814). The chapel, no longer in regular use by 1974, has walls of coursed rubble with Bath stone dressings and a patent-tiled roof. The gabled front has a tablet inscribed 'Ebenezer Chapel 1868' above a later porch.

WOODCHESTER

(166) BAPTIST, Atcombe Road (SO 839020). Gabled front with tall finial and round-arched windows; dated 1825.

WOODMANCOTE

(167) COUNTESS OF HUNTINGDON'S CONNEXION, Stockwell Lane (SO 974273). Gabled S front dated 1854 with stone bell-cote containing one bell and shield-of-arms of the Countess of Huntingdon below.

WOTTON-UNDER-EDGE

(168) OLD TOWN MEETING-HOUSE (ST 758934). A Presbyterian society which originated in the late 17th century registered the present building as 'newly erected' in January 1702. The society (now URC) became Congregational by the 19th century and between 1898–1904 drastically remodelled the building. The walls (externally 48ft by 26¼ft) are of rubble and the roof is covered with stone slates; the windows are entirely altered but a bracketed eaves cornice at the side next to the road may be of the 18th century and a round-arched window over the end entrance could also antedate the alterations.

(169) THE TABERNACLE (ST 756936) was built in 1852 on the site of the original Tabernacle erected for a congregation formed *c*.1771 by the Rev. Rowland Hill and which eventually became Congregational. The building (sold in 1973 for secular use) was designed by Henry Masters of Bristol in a 13th-century Gothic style. The S front is flanked by small staircase towers intended to rise to open octagonal turrets, only one of which was completed.

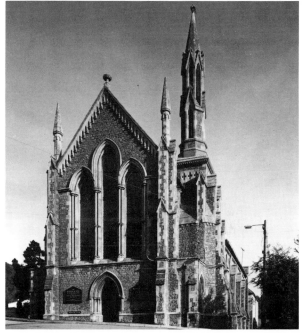

The interior has a gallery around three sides, a pulpit at the N end and a staircase behind leading up from the adjacent Tabernacle House.

Tabernacle House, of brick with stone dressings and a hipped roof, dates from the late 18th century. The N front of three bays has Venetian windows at each end of the two principal floors and a round-arched window above the doorway.

Fittings in chapel – *Bell*: loose in vestibule, small, with painted inscription recording its provenance in the former Tabernacle. *Inscription*: on tablet in vestibule 'ERECTED A.D. 1852 ON THE SITE OF THE TABERNACLE BUILT BY REVd. ROWLAND HILL A.D. 1771 HENRY MASTERS ARCHITECT'. *Monuments*: (1) Rev. Rowland Hill A.M., 1833, founder and minister, with bust in low relief; (2) Rev. Theophilus Jones, 1833.

CYB (1853) 259–60.

(170) Former WESLEYAN, Haw Street (ST 755933). Brick with round-arched windows, gabled front with tablet 'EBENEZER CHAPEL 1805'. Superseded 1896.

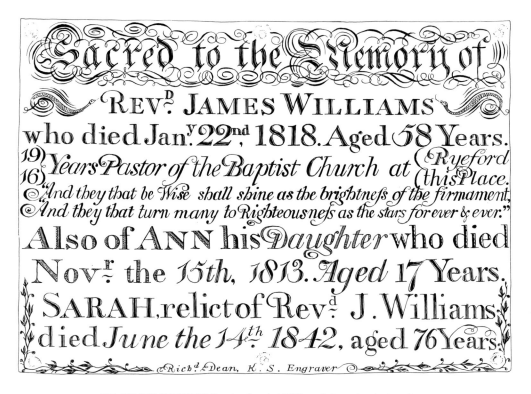

(87) KING'S STANLEY. Baptist chapel, Middleyard. Brass inscription plate.

HEREFORDSHIRE
Hereford and Worcester

Herefordshire is a small pastoral county behind whose calm exterior the waters of dissent run deep and where, in the western valleys bordering Wales, the name of the 15th-century Lollard martyr Sir John Oldcastle is not yet forgotten. Although the early history of the Baptist cause in the Olchon Valley is lost in legend (34), that of the same denomination in Leominster (29) can be traced back to the mid 17th century while the origin of the Quakers in Ross (41) is equally ancient. The Friends' meeting-house at Almeley Wooton (2), the only timber-framed building recorded here, is one of the oldest in the country whilst that in Bromyard (7), of 1722, illustrates the early use of brickwork in the north-east quarter of the county where the poor quality of the available stone is evident in the Congregational chapel in the same town (6). This last, erected in 1701, is of interest as the sole remaining representative of orthodox Presbyterian dissent, other congregations of similar derivation having rebuilt their chapels in the 19th century (13, 25, 40). Early Methodist history is epitomized by the surviving monuments in Kington (23) while the parallel but less successful expansion of the Moravian Church has left the late 18th-century chapel in

Leominster (31) as its best and almost only representative in this part of the country. The pair of early 19th-century Calvinistic Methodist chapels at Brilley Green (4) and Clifford (8) show a marked affinity with chapels of this period in the Principality, where the original seat of this denomination was at Trevecka (SO 144322) in the adjacent county of Brecknockshire; the third, Lady Southampton's Chapel at Kenchester (18), is in name more redolent of the aristocratic appearance of the English branch of Calvinistic Methodism, the Countess of Huntingdon's Connexion. Ruxton Chapel (36) and the former preaching room at Llangrove (32) are notable examples of evangelical patronage and Goff's school at Huntington (17) is a further instance of philanthropic provision for the needs of a rural community; this last is one of several schools established by Edward Goff with a master whose duties included Sunday preaching. The former Congregational chapel in Ledbury (25), of 1852, is an exceptionally sophisticated design but apart from chapels in Hereford (12), (13) and Ross (40) the later monuments are of little importance.

ALCONBURY

(1) PRIMITIVE METHODIST, Little Birch (SO 506325). Built 1834, rebuilt 1858.

ALMELEY

(2) FRIENDS, Almeley Wooton (SO 333524). A cottage built *c.*1672 and immediately converted for use as a meeting-house, was given to the Society by Roger and Mary Prichard under a deed of gift dated 11 July 1675 where it is described as 'all that new dwelling-house lately erected and built with the garden and plot of ground thereunto adjoining . . .'. Although perhaps never used exclusively for a dwelling, part of the building seems to have been occupied as a cottage as lately as 1858 when its occasional use by Primitive Methodists was sanctioned excluding '. . . that part of the house now inhabited'. Extensive repairs were carried out in 1956.

The building has walls of exposed timber-framing in square panels and a tiled roof with half hips at the NE and SW ends. The entrance inside a porch on the NW side has an inner doorway with chamfered frame and shaped board in the head, and an original door with strap hinges. The interior (approx. 26½ft by 17ft), now undivided, has a gallery at the NE end covering half

the floor area approached by a staircase with square newel and polygonal finial and flat shaped balusters. In the SE wall below the gallery is a fireplace and bread oven.

Arnold (1960) 104–5, 109 (measured drawing): RCHM *Herefordshire* III (1934) 6, mon. 2.

(3) PRIMITIVE METHODIST, Almeley Wooton (SO 334525). Red brick with polychrome dressings, 1870.

BRILLEY

(4) THE TABERNACLE, Brilley Green (SO 269489). Calvinistic Methodist. W front with a pair of doorways, one blocked, and tablet between windows inscribed 'TABERNACLE/1828'.

THE TABERNACLE, BRILLEY GREEN

Monuments: in small front burial-ground (1) Ann, wife of James Evans, 1841, and Martha their daughter, infant, signed W.P.c; (2) Joseph Davies, 1831; (3) Ann, daughter of Thomas and Elizabeth Stokes, 1832, signed R. Davies.

BRIMFIELD

(5) PRIMITIVE METHODIST, Wyson (SO 520680). Enlarged 1845, two rear bays perhaps slightly earlier; window-heads and front gable rebuilt.

BROMYARD

(6) CONGREGATIONAL, Sherford Street (SO 656546). The formerly Presbyterian congregation originated in the late 17th century. According to the Thompson MSS (Stevens, *op. cit*) 'in 1701 a large and handsome Meeting House was built by the direction and mostly at ye expense of Grimbold Panneifort of Clutter Park Esq' (i.e. Grimbald Pauncefort of Clator Park). The chapel, built in 1701, has walls of squared stone and a hipped slated roof. The entrance, placed centrally on the W side, has a timber surround with a pair of Roman Doric columns supporting a full Doric entablature. A small window above the doorway has been blocked and two tall windows each side of the entrance were altered in 1869 as were similar pairs of windows in the N and S walls. Two doorways on the E side, one now internal, flank the pulpit, with blocked windows above.

The interior (34¼ft by 42¼ft) has a flat plaster ceiling with coved border. The fittings were much altered in 1892 but the pews incorporate fielded panelling of the 18th century. The backboard of the pulpit, with a swept gable between matching gablets, dates from the late 18th century. Other fittings include – *Gallery*: for singers, above internal lobby of W entrance, with panelled front and moulded cornice, 18th-century. *Monuments*: on E wall (1) Rev. Joel Banfield, 1820, Effe his first wife, 1808, and Harriet his second wife, 1815; against front wall (2) John Bray, 1801; (3) Rev. Lewis Hopkins, pastor, 1789, and Rebecca his daughter, 1844; (4) Mary, widow of Rev. Lewis Hopkins,

W front.

1831. *Weathervane*: on ridge of roof, metal cock, early 18th-century. (Chapel closed before 1981)

Stevens, A.J., *The Story of Congregationalism in Bromyard and Neighbourhood* (1930).

(7) Former FRIENDS (SO 655546). Behind a range of buildings on the S side of Broad Street at the rear of no. 16. It was built in 1722 and registered in the following year, superseding a meeting-house of 1677 which may have stood behind 37 High Street. The building was only used sporadically between 1852 and 1923 and it was sold in 1939. The walls are of brick on a rubble plinth and

Former FRIENDS' MEETING-HOUSE, BROMYARD

the roof is hipped and slated. The front faces W and has a central doorway with a hood supported by shaped wooden brackets; windows flanking the entrance have wooden frames and flat-arched heads of brick with a brick platband above. Windows centrally in the N and S walls are similarly treated.

The interior (28¼ft by 20¼ft) is undivided and retains some original seating at the S end including the seat of the stand and raised benches which return along the E and W walls. The roof is supported by a pair of E–W trusses with half trusses at the N

Interior from N.

and S ends; the main trusses have a pair of collar-beams together with hammer-beams and posts, with quadrant braces ascending from the latter to the lower collar and descending to wall-posts which rise from floor level. (Demolished *c*.1976)

CLIFFORD

(8) CALVINISTIC METHODIST (SO 257452). Rubble walls and half-hipped slated roof; broad S front with two round-arched windows between a pair of doorways with segmental-arched heads, that to left now blocked. Dated 1827.

EARDISLEY

(9) Former CALVINISTIC METHODIST, Great Oak (SO 300497). Stone and slate with two pointed-arched windows in front wall and slate tablet 'Tabernacle/1848'.

FOWNHOPE

(10) BAPTIST, Oldway (SO 596340). The former chapel, now the Sunday-school, was built *c*.1826 in which year the church was formed. The earlier building has walls of rubble with a brick front and tiled roof. The broad W front of three bays has a central doorway, now blocked, between two windows with segmental-arched heads and three lunettes above. A contemporary manse adjoins to the S; in the late 19th century the manse was enlarged, a new doorway was made at the N end of the chapel and the interiors altered. Present chapel built 1884.

GARWAY

(11) BAPTIST (SO 454225). Built *c*.1817 for a church formed in

that year. Stone walls with blocked doorway in former N front; entrance re-sited at W end and chapel refitted in late 19th century. *Monument*: Elizabeth, wife of John Sims, 1835.

HEREFORD

(12) BAPTIST, Commercial Road (SO 514402). Yellow brick Italianate front with minimal stone dressings; by John Johnson and G. C. Haddon, 1880.

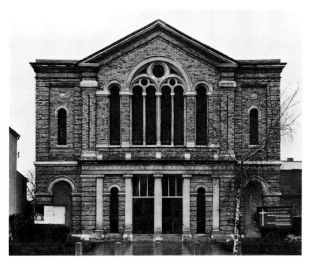

(13) CONGREGATIONAL, Eignbrook (SO 506401). The formerly Presbyterian church was founded in the late 17th century. The present Gothic chapel of yellow brick and stone with gabled S front and irregular SW tower, by Haddon Bros., 1873, replaces a building of 1829. (URC)

Lady Southampton's Chapel, KENCHESTER, *Herefordshire*

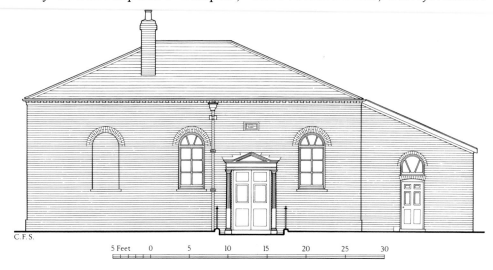

C.F.S.

5 Feet 0 5 10 15 20 25 30

(14) FRIENDS, King Street (SO 508398). The meeting-house, of red brick, standing behind buildings on the N side of the street, was erected in 1821–2 to replace an earlier building which was then sold; minor rooms were added *c*.1838.

The entrance at the S end of the E wall formerly had a semi-circular-arched head. The interior is divided into two principal rooms. The larger room to the N has two windows in the W wall and one in the N behind the site of the stand overlooking a small burial-ground; a gallery along the S and E sides, formerly approached by an external staircase, is supported by cast-iron columns and has an open iron balustrade. Fittings include plain open-backed benches with arm-rests, early 19th-century.

(15) Former WESLEYAN, Bridge Street (SO 509397). Opened 1829 by a society which met from 1804 in East Street; enlarged and refronted 1866.

(16) Former PRIMITIVE METHODIST, St Owen Street (SO 514397). Opened 1838 by a society formed in 1826. A new chapel was built 300 yards NW in 1880 in the Gothic style by T. Davies and the former became a Salvation Army citadel; it is now in commercial use.

The front wall, of three bays with pediment enclosing a date-tablet, originally had a central entrance with a small window above, flanked by two tall windows with round-arched heads.
Kendall (1905) II, 303–5.

HUNTINGTON

(17) CONGREGATIONAL (SO 248522). The society meeting here originated with the erection in the 18th century of a school-house, of two stories and attics with rubble walls and a slated roof, for a nonconformist day school established in 1791 by Edward Goff, coal merchant of Scotland Yard, London. The society was further regulated by an agreement dated 13 June 1804 in which regular Sunday services were directed to be held in the schoolroom. The chapel attached to the E side of the house is a later 19th-century extension of the original schoolroom. Fittings include a wall monument to Rev. Thomas Rees, 1858, 56 years pastor. In the burial-ground N of the chapel are head-stones of *c*.1830 and later. (URC)

KENCHESTER

(18) LADY SOUTHAMPTON'S CHAPEL (SO 438429). Built in 1830 for Calvinistic Methodists; walls of red brick and a hipped slated roof. Attached to the NW end is the contemporary manse and at the opposite end under a lean-to roof is a later Sunday-school room. The pulpit, opposite the entrance, and most of the other fittings have been renewed.

KINGSLAND

(19) Former PRIMITIVE METHODIST, Shirl Heath (SO 437596). 'Jubilee Chapel', dated 1861.

(20) WESLEYAN, West Town (SO 439619). Built 1857. Gabled front with ball finial.

KING'S PYON

(21) Former PRIMITIVE METHODIST, Ledgemoor (SO 415504). 'Zion Chapel', dated 1856.

KINGTON URBAN

(22) BAPTIST, Bridge Street, Kington (SO 599566). Built 1868. Brick with stone dressings, three-bay pedimented front with pilasters.

(23) Former WESLEYAN, Harp Yard, Kington (SO 297566). The Methodist society in Kington originated in the mid 18th century. John Wesley preached in the town in 1746 and the 'Old Gospel House' in Harp Yard (immediately S of mon. 22 in RCHM *Herefordshire* III (1934) plan, 93) is associated with early Methodist preaching. The first chapel, a small house converted in 1801, was superseded in 1829 by a new chapel still standing at one corner of Harp Yard. In 1902 the society removed to a new chapel in Park Avenue since when the penultimate chapel has been occupied as a warehouse. This is a large building with rubble walls and a hipped roof having a storage basement with external access and two tiers of round-arched windows above. The principal, W, front of three bays with a slightly projecting centrepiece has a central entrance. The interior has a flat plaster ceiling with moulded cornice; a floor has been inserted at gallery level.

LEDBURY TOWN

(24) BAPTIST, Homend, Ledbury (SO 709381). Built *c*.1836 for a newly-formed church. Three-bay brick front with two tall windows in arched recesses. Pediment rebuilt and interior refitted. *Baptistery*: in floor in front of pulpit, lead-lined tank supported above basement rooms. *Monument*: in front of chapel, Matilda Edwards, wife of James Dando Trehern, 1838.

(25) Former CONGREGATIONAL, High Street, Ledbury (SO 712377). The congregation, originally Presbyterian, developed in the late 17th century, one of the ministers being John Barston, ejected rector of Aylton. The chapel, which stands on the site of its predecessor behind other buildings E of the Market Hall, was

CONGREGATIONAL CHAPEL, LEDBURY

rebuilt in 1852 and closed *c*.1970. The W front, of brick with stone dressings in three bays, is of unusually high quality for its situation. The main cornice rising segmentally above a central Venetian window is capped by urn finials; blocking course inscribed 'REBUILT ANNO DOMINI MDCCCLII'.

(26) WESLEYAN, Homend, Ledbury (SO 710380). Built *c*.1849, refronted 1884.

LEINTWARDINE

(27) CONGREGATIONAL, Tipton's Lane (SO 404743). Rubble

with yellow and blue brick dressings, polygonal apse to W and small turret to E, 1869–70 by Habershon and Brock. Sunday-school added 1881. (URC)

　　CYB (1871) 414.

(28) PRIMITIVE METHODIST (SO 404740). Opened 1841. Concealed behind a cottage and later Sunday-school S of the parish church. Rubble walls and slate roof, entrance at the W end and rostrum pulpit opposite. *Monuments*: Moses Langford, 1849; Edward Langford, 1855.

LEOMINISTER BOROUGH

(29) BAPTIST, Etnam Street, Leominster (SO 499589). Prior to the erection of the present chapel in 1771 the Particular Baptist church, founded in 1656, met in a timber-framed house to the N, adjacent to the street, which had been converted into a meeting-house and manse and was given to the church in 1696 by John Davis of Eardisland. This building (see RCHM *Herefordshire* III (1934), 124, mon. 130) was demolished *c*.1966. The new chapel and the adjacent manse and almshouses were built at the expense of Mary Marlow, daughter and grand-daughter of the London goldsmiths Isaac and John Marlow.

The chapel has brick walls and a hipped tiled roof. The N front has a brick dentil cornice and pediment. The central entrance with a fanlight and timber surround with Roman Doric columns supporting an open pediment is flanked by a pair of round-arched windows and surmounted by a circular window inscribed on the upper keystone with the date of erection. The interior (40ft by 30ft), largely refitted *c*.1883, has an original gallery at the N end with two fluted Roman Doric columns carrying a triglyph frieze and moulded cornice below a later

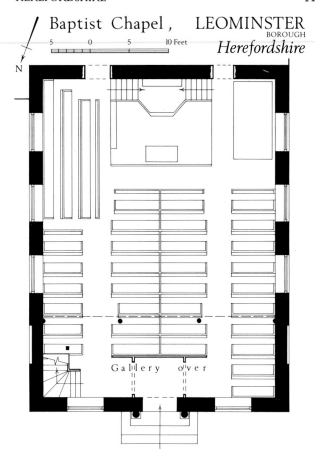

Baptist Chapel, LEOMINSTER
BOROUGH
Herefordshire

5   0   5   10 Feet

N

Gallery over

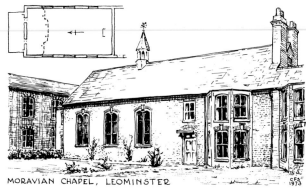

MORAVIAN CHAPEL, LEOMINSTER

The W front of the chapel has a moulded stone cornice; the entrance, originally central between two segmental-arched and keystoned windows, was removed to the N end in 1875 and a third window substituted. The E wall, similarly altered, also had a central doorway. The interior ($22\frac{3}{4}$ft by $42\frac{1}{4}$ft) formerly had the pulpit at the E side and galleries to N, S and, probably, also to the west. In 1875 the fittings, apart from the N gallery, were renewed, the other galleries removed, and the interior realigned with the pulpit at the S end. The *burial-ground* E of the chapel has late 19th-century monuments including many flat rectangular tablets of cast-iron.

England I (1886) 6 and pl.6.

LLANGARRON

(32) Former PREACHING-ROOM, Llangrove (SO 524193), was built *c*.1840 adjacent to Llangrove Cottage, a house dated 1824 which was acquired as a residence by the Rev. John Jones, minister and proprietor of Ruxton Chapel (see Marstow (36) below). The room was used as a Congregational chapel until *c*.1960.

The room has coursed stone walls and a hipped slate roof with

cast-iron front; the staircase has a latticed balustrade and pineapple finial to the bottom newel. Other original fittings include – *Clock*: on E wall. *Pews*: in gallery, with shaped ends. *Tablet*: on W wall, 'Erected by Mrs Mary Marlow 1771'.

Cole, J., *A Souvenir of the Two Hundred and Fiftieth Anniversary of the Baptist Church at Leominster* (1906): Ivimey II (1814) 207–9.

(30) Former FRIENDS, South Street, Leominster (SO 497588). The meeting-house, built in 1834 and superseding one of 1687, was enlarged in 1869; since 1977 it has been used by the Jehovah's Witnesses. The walls are of brick and the roof is hipped and slated. The earliest work at the S end has two sash windows in the E wall facing the former burial-ground at the rear. In 1869 it was extended to the N with two matching windows in the E wall and arched doorway between; additional vestibules were also built along the W side and a new entrance constructed. The interior is divided into two rooms by a moveable partition; the panelled dado behind the former stand remains at the S end.

(31) MORAVIAN, South Street, Leominster (SO 496587). Preaching commenced by John Cennick in 1749 resulted in the formation in 1759 of a regular Moravian congregation and in the erection of the present chapel opened 17 January 1761. A sisters' house N of the chapel was inaugurated in 1780 but rebuilt for other purposes in 1872. The chapel and manse adjacent to the S form one continuous range with brick walls and a slated roof.

moulded cornice below the eaves. At the N end is a central entrance covered by an open verandah with a swept metal roof supported by four thin columns. In the W wall are two tall sash windows. The interior, which resembles a drawing-room of the period, has folding shutters to the windows and a plaster ceiling with small central dome and elaborate cornice. The pulpit was at the S end.

(33) WESLEYAN, Llancloudy (SO 497210). 'Providence Chapel erected by Joseph Meadmore 1840'.

LLANVEYNOE

(34) Former BAPTIST, Olchon Valley (SO 285327). The church which formerly met here claimed to have originated in 1630 and to have earlier links with the 15th-century Lollard Sir John Oldcastle, but prior to the 19th century its existence appears to have been very tenuous and until the erection of 'Salem Chapel' in 1883 it met only in private houses. The chapel, which has rubble walls, has been heightened and converted to a cottage.

Howells, J., *The History of the Old Baptist Church at Olchon* (1887).

LLANWARNE

(35) Former PRIMITIVE METHODIST, Sandyway (SO 496261). Red brick with polychrome dressings. Built *c*.1860 on narrow roadside encroachment.

MARSTOW

(36) RUXTON CHAPEL, Ruxton Green (SO 542193), now converted to private use and renamed 'Ruxton House', was built *c*.1800 by the Rev. Thomas Jones, an Anglican clergyman of independent means who was much influenced by the evangelical preaching of the Rev. William George of Ross-on-Wye, and completed by his son the Rev. John Jones. The latter, educated at Rotherham Academy, conducted the morning services at Ruxton and later opened a room next to his house at Llangrove (see Llangarron (32) above) for evening worship. In 1852 shortly before his death the two congregations, previously without denominational attachment, were formed into a Congregational church and in 1880 united with the church at Doward Chapel (see Whitchurch (44) below). Services at Ruxton appear to have ceased about 1935.

The former chapel has rubble walls and a slate roof with gabled ends; a small cottage of one storey and attics is attached to the north-west. The broad SW front, although refenestrated, has at the centre an open porch with two Iopic columns *in antis* below a moulded entablature; this was added by John Jones to the original building and is described in the Church Book as 'a noble portico having antique columns and pilasters which being of freestone greatly adds to its respectability and is a lasting monument to his taste and munificence'. Each side of the main entrance were two tall windows and to the left a minor doorway with flat stone canopy supported by shaped brackets.

Monuments: in former burial-ground (1) Sarah wife of Isaac Skinner 'minister of Ruxton Chapel', 1824; (2) Thomas Jones, 1847, Mary his wife, 1845, and Ann their daughter, 1855; (3) James Hills, 1837, and Sarah his wife, 1852; (4) Rev. John Bulmer, 1857, and Martha his wife, 1856.

NEWTON

(37) PRIMITIVE METHODIST (SO 344322). 'Zion Chapel', of rubble and slate dated 1832.

(36) MARSTOW. Ruxton House, formerly Ruxton Chapel.

PEMBRIDGE

(38) INDEPENDENT (SO 366548). Three-bay front inscribed 'Independent Chapel & School House founded Oct. 24. 1844'.

ROSS URBAN

(39) BAPTIST, Broad Street, Ross-on-Wye (SO 600242). Yellow brick, Italianate, 1861, by G.C. Haddon.

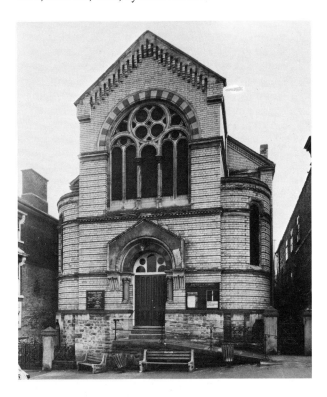

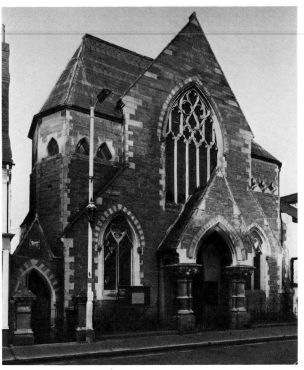

(40) ROSS URBAN. Congregational chapel. (URC)

(40) CONGREGATIONAL, Gloucester Road, Ross-on-Wye (SO 601241). The formerly Presbyterian congregation founded in the late 17th century met until 1868 in a chapel in Kyrle Street removing thence to the present building, of stone, by Benjamin Lawrence of Newport, Mon. The interior has galleries around three sides supported by cast-iron columns. *Monument*: Rev. Anthony Collier, ejected minister, and his successors, erected 1839, from former chapel. *Offertory Boxes*: two stone pillars attached to ends of pews near entrance, incorporating boxes for donations and inscribed with appropriate texts. (URC)

CYB (1868) 345–6: *EM* (1840) 448: Towers, L.T., *A Short History of the Congregational Church ... Ross-on-Wye* (1962).

(41) FRIENDS, Brampton Street, Ross-on-Wye (SO 601245). The meeting-house, dated 1804, replaced a building of 1676 on a site first given to Friends in 1675, twenty years after the commencement of meetings. The front, facing Brampton Street (formerly Brookend Street), is concealed by a high wall with two round-arched doorways, one of which is blind. The building has stone walls and a hipped slated roof. The entrance, in a lean-to porch incorporating the gallery stair, is on the E side; windows in the other three walls have flat-arched heads and hung sashes.

The interior (34ft by 30ft) has a moulded cornice. The walls are lined with a dado of vertical panelling. Along each side is a raised bench interrupted on the W by the stand opposite which is a gallery with fielded panelled front. A smaller meeting-house adjoins at the NE corner and a burial-ground lies to the west. Fittings – *Coffin Stools*: two, with turned legs, 18th-century. *Seating*: open-backed benches, some with shaped ends. *Stand*: entered at ends, front of fielded panelling.

Whiting, E.S. and Parker, W.H., The Story of the Quakers in Ross (1960), typescript. Copy per Clerk of Meeting.

WEOBLEY

(42) PRIMITIVE METHODIST (SO 404513). Red brick with stone dressings and slate roof; erected 1861.

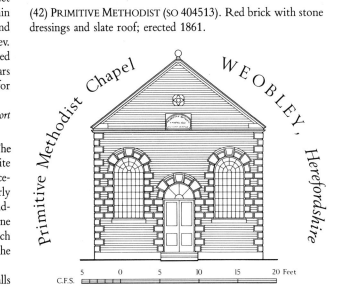

Primitive Methodist Chapel WEOBLEY, Herefordshire

C.F.S.

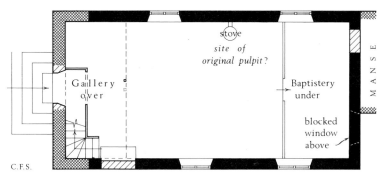

Former Baptist Meeting-house,
Ryeford,
WESTON UNDER PENYARD
Herefordshire

WESTON UNDER PENYARD

(43) BAPTIST, Ryeford (SO 640227). The former meeting-house standing behind the late 19th-century chapel dates from the early 18th century and may possibly be identified with a 'house in Weston under Penyard' registered for Anabaptists April 1723. It is a plain rectangular building (36ft by 17ft) with rendered rubble walls and a gabled slated roof. The original entrance, now blocked, was the SE wall, with two windows to its right and two in the wall opposite, all with wooden cross-frames now altered. The gallery at the SW end has a front of re-used timber

and is supported by a chamfered post. Some loose seating of the 18th century remains in the gallery. The present SW doorway, altered since 1929, had a fielded panelled door and flat canopy when the above photograph was taken.

RCHM *Herefordshire* II (1932) 211, mon. 3.

WHITCHURCH

(44) CONGREGATIONAL, Doward Hill (SO 551172). The chapel, standing high above the valley, was built *c*.1816 and a church formed in 1819 which was joined in 1880 by that at Ruxton and Llangrove. It has rendered walls and a slate roof. In the gabled front are two round-arched upper windows with leaded glazing in original wood frames and two blank window recesses below. In front is a lean-to porch in which is a staircase to

the gallery entrance immediately above the principal doorway. At the opposite end is a lunette above a later rostrum. The chapel was repaired and partly refitted in 1899 and 1908, and a Sunday-school room was built at the rear in 1906. (URC)

WIGMORE

(45) Former CHAPEL (SO 41356905). Altered on conversion to a cottage. Possibly the Independent Chapel built 1848.

(46) PRIMITIVE METHODIST (SO 414689). Red brick and stone dressings. Dated 1863.

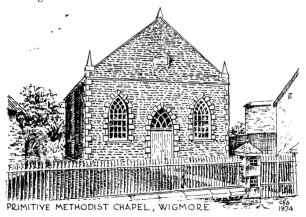

PRIMITIVE METHODIST CHAPEL, WIGMORE

WITHINGTON

(47) STRICT BAPTIST, White Stone (SO 564428). Stone and slate, dated 1821, the former manse adjoins to the north. Interior refitted in late 19th century. *Monuments*: behind pulpit (1) Rev. Joseph Davis, 1856, 23 years pastor 'brother of Rev. Reece Davis by whose labors and influence this chapel was built' and Susan his wife, 1850; against S wall (2) Mary Hughes, 1822, signed J. T. Green; (3) Daniel Edward Hinley, 1846, clerk at St Katharine's Docks, London.

Monument to Mary Hughes, 1822, by J. T. Green.

Some of the most respected names in nonconformity are associated with Leicestershire as their native county, although the principal monuments of their work lie further afield. Of these the first is George Fox, the Quaker, born in 1624 at Fenny Drayton, whose 'great persecutor' Nathaniel Stephens remained in the county to encourage the formation of the Presbyterian society in Hinckley (29) but whose own societies are here only minimally represented (16). The Hinckley Great Meeting is also associated with the early years of Philip Doddridge and in the same town the origins of the Strict Baptist preacher and hymn-writer William Gadsby may still be recalled (31). From the Particular Baptists at Arnesby (2) came Robert Hall, the son of the manse and a notable figure in the more liberal wing of that denomination, while the noble protagonist and supporter of Calvinistic Methodist preaching, the Countess of Huntingdon, was born at Staunton Harold, where the private chapel of 1653, although not included here, has from its date a peculiar claim to be regarded as nonconformist; the principal seat of her husband was also in the county, at Donington Park.

Two notable meeting-houses of the early 18th century remain in Hinckley (29) and Leicester (44) but each has suffered from considerable alteration in the 19th century both externally and in the renewal of fittings. Other meetings of comparable antiquity but which, unlike these last, remained loyal to religious orthodoxy now occupy buildings of more recent date. Of these Wigston (88) had the use of a former parish church for fifty years before being obliged to erect a building of their own, in 1732, which no longer remains. Kibworth Harcourt (43), also associated with Philip Doddridge, was rebuilt on a new site in 1761 and has since suffered enlargement, and Lutterworth (58), rebuilt in 1777, although the least altered has lost some of its character from the attentions of successive generations. The tiny meeting-house at Freeby (25), also much altered, has some historical links with Dr Isaac Watts.

The most outstanding feature of the county is in the number of General Baptist churches, most of which spring from the society formed independently at Barton in the Beans (72). The earliest remaining meeting-house at Diseworth (52), of 1752, retains the long and low proportions which, before enlargement, were adopted at Quorndon

(64), in 1770, and possibly also at Wymeswold (91) in 1781. The other wing of this denomination is principally represented by the Particular Baptist meeting-house in Arnesby (2), of 1798–9; the chapel at Sutton in the Elms (12) although dating in part from the late 18th century has been greatly enlarged.

Methodist chapels are equally though less unusually prominent, the earliest being at Hinckley (34), of 1783, but of greatest interest are those of the early 19th century: the Wesleyan chapel in Bishop Street, Leicester (50), of 1815, is a good example of a large town chapel, and at Wymeswold (92) the successive chapels of 1801 and 1845 illustrate the heightened standards demanded by a growing society. A group of three chapels dating from 1843–9 in the vicinity of Melton Mowbray (66, 70, 86) with broad fronts of three bays may all be the work of one builder. The most remarkable chapel of this period is undoubtedly the Baptist 'pork pie chapel' in Leicester (45), the only nonconformist work by the Roman Catholic architect Joseph Hansom, but the Congregational chapel in Market Harborough (60), of 1844, built in a grand Classical style by an equally competent, if unnamed, designer, and the smaller 'Hephzibah' chapel in Newton Burgoland (79), of 1807, are also notable. Calvinistic Independency is represented by a former chapel in Leicester (47) but particular mention should be made of Evington Chapel (48) in the same locality, where Independency under benevolent patronage produced a singularly successful essay in the Gothic style, other examples of which are rare although at Saddington (69) the cast-iron window frames impart something of the same spirit.

Many burial-grounds in the county have headstones and other monuments of slate for which the carvers of Swithland and district were famous. The most numerous examples occur at the Great Meeting, Leicester (44), and the General Baptist chapel at Quorndon (64). Roofing slates from the same locality still remain on a few buildings but these have mostly been superseded by Welsh slate; relatively few tiled roofs were noted and only one complete roof of pantiles in the NE corner of the county (24). Brick is used almost exclusively for walling except in the last-mentioned building, at Freeby (25) in the same district, where rubble was available, and at Rothley (68) in which slate rubble was used.

APPLEBY MAGNA

(1) BAPTIST, Brook End (SK 316093). Brick and slate, three bays with two tiers of round-arched windows, later cottage attached at end. Possibly the Particular Baptist chapel built *c*.1820–30 by William Hear. Interior generally refitted but with some open-backed benches. *Monument*: in burial-ground, to Joseph Radford, 1827, Mary his widow, 1842, and George their son, 1834, slate headstone. (Chapel disused 1974, now a house)
   Chambers (1963) 80.

ARNESBY

(2) BAPTIST (SP 618925). Brick with a hipped roof covered with small stone slates; built 1798–9 for a Particular Baptist church which had been formed *c*.1667 at Kilby, 2 miles north-east. About 1701 the minister, Benjamin Winckles, built himself a house at Arnesby and in 1702 erected a meeting-house adjacent to it which is now represented by a low outbuilding alongside the forecourt of the chapel: the end wall may contain some original brickwork but otherwise the building has been much altered and partly rebuilt in the later 18th century and after.

The present chapel has a W front of three bays with two round-arched doorways with fanlights and two tiers of segmental-arched windows. In the back wall two taller windows with pointed-arched heads flank the pulpit. The N and S walls are of three bays but the N wall is partly covered by a vestry of 1839 which was heightened to two stories in the mid 19th century.
   The interior, of 42¼ft by 36¼ft, has a plaster ceiling with moulded ribs and ceiling rose. The gallery around three sides has a fielded panelled front; the side galleries with lower fronts for use by children were added in 1816 and 1857. The pulpit and seating were renewed in the late 19th century.
   Fittings – *Communion Table*: in vestibule, long narrow top (1ft 9½in. by 8ft) with hinged flap on one side for convenience of the minister, Rev. R. Hall, 18th-century. *Monuments*: in chapel (1) Rev. George Hirst, 1813; (2) Rev. Benjamin Winckles, founder and pastor for 30 years, 1732, erected 1857; (3) Rev. Robert Hall senior, pastor 37 years, 1791, erected 1857; in burial-ground, many slate headstones have been removed and reset around the boundaries, including, on N side (4) Robert Hall Cotton, 1779; (5) Rev. Robert Hall, pastor, 1791, with oval inscription panel and weeper with urn in low relief; (6) Jane, wife of Rev. Robert Hall, 1776; (7) Sarah wife of John Waldren, 1804; (8) Elizabeth (Flude) wife of Charles Johnson, 1802, with representation of death as a skeleton and a crowned monument inscribed 'Tho' thou slay me, yet will I trust my GOD', signed Pollard, carver &c. Quorndon; (9) John Newell, 1737; (10) M.W. 1712; (11) Benjamin Winckles, 1732; (12) Benjamin Wright, 1729; on S side (13) Andrew Samuell, 1706. *Painting*: in vestry, oil portrait of Rev. R. Hall senior.
   Bassett, W., *History of the Baptist Church at Arnsby* (reprinted with memoir by Shem Evans 1862): Ivimey IV (1830) 603–9.

ASHBY DE LA ZOUCH

(3) CONGREGATIONAL, Kilwardby Street (SK 355167). Behind houses on N side of street. Built in 1825 for a church which originated in the late 17th century as a Presbyterian society; the first meeting-house on this site was erected in 1725. The walls are of brickwork rendered at front and rear. The front, of three bays with two tiers of round-arched windows, has a recessed porch with two Doric columns *in antis*. The interior was altered and refitted in 1867 by Bidlake and Tate of Leicester.
   CYB (1868) 347.

BARKBY

(4) Former WESLEYAN, School Lane (SK 638096). Opened 1823; entirely altered 1974 on conversion to house.

BARLESTONE

(5) GENERAL BAPTIST (SK 427057). Built 1865 replacing chapel of 1798. Polychrome brickwork.

(6) PRIMITIVE METHODIST (SK 428056). Dated 1833, grossly altered.

BELTON

(7) GENERAL BAPTIST (SK 445204). Dated 1813.

BILLESDON

(8) GENERAL BAPTIST (SK 721028). Built 1813. Three-bay front, segmental-arched windows. *Monuments*: in burial-ground; slate headstones (1) William Ellis, 1822; (2) Sarah Cumberland, 1839.

BOTTESFORD

(9) PRIMITIVE METHODIST, Devon Lane (SK 805392). Dated 1820. Brick with pantiled roof.

BREEDON ON THE HILL

(10) WESLEYAN, Wilson (SK 405247). Dated 1826.

BROUGHTON AND OLD DALBY

(11) WESLEYAN, Nether Broughton (SK 694257). Gabled front with acorn finial. Built 1839, enlarged to front and heightened *c*.1860–70, renovated 1889.

BROUGHTON ASTLEY

(12) BAPTIST, Sutton in the Elms (SP 521938). The church claims to have originated in the mid 17th century. The chapel, which

BURTON AND DALBY

(13) WESLEYAN, Great Dalby (SK 743143). Three-bay front with inscription dated 1846 above site of central entrance.

BURTON ON THE WOLDS

(14) WESLEYAN (SK 591213). Brick and slate. Small gallery to right of entrance, pulpit to left. Dated 1846.

dates from the late 18th century but has been greatly enlarged and altered, has brick walls and a hipped slate roof. The original building was widened along the NW side in the early 19th century and extended to the SW c.1912 when it was given a polygonal rear wall and a second vestry. The original NE front was symmetrical with a central entrance with pedimented door-case between a pair of flat-arched windows and two round-arched windows above; a second doorway and third upper window were added when the chapel was widened. The SE wall has two tall round-arched windows and a low vestry which has been extended and widened. The interior (originally about 34ft by 24ft) has an original NE gallery supported by two columns subsequently extended and a third column added.

Fittings – *Clocks*: on NW wall, Parliament clock with octagonal face and Chinese scene on pendulum case, 18th-century; on gallery front, circular face signed William Gray, Leicester, 19th-century. *Monuments*: in chapel (1) Rev. Cheney Burdett, 40 years pastor, 1852; in burial-ground, slate head-stones; (2) Rev. Clayton Mordaunt Cracherode, pastor, 1807, signed Langley; (3) Robert Gilbert, pastor, 1742; (4) Benjamin Moore, minister, 1739, and Mary his wife, 1729; (5) Rev. Isaac Woodman, above 26 years pastor, 1777; (6) Rev. Cheney Burdett, 1852, and his sons Samuel, 1834, and Edwin, 1853; (7) James Chapman, 1815; (8) Robert Chapman, 1818, and Ann his widow, 1820, signed Clay, Lester; (9) John Summerfield, 1807, and Mary his wife, 1807. *Seating*: in gallery, incorporating some 18th-century fielded panelling.

CASTLE DONINGTON

(15) GENERAL BAPTIST, High Street (SK 445274). This congregation which commenced about 1751 remained in connexion with the Kegworth branch of the church of Barton in the Beans until 1785 when it became a separate society. The chapel, built in 1774 and enlarged in 1807 and 1827, has brick walls rendered at the front and a slate roof. The E front is gabled and is four bays in width one of which is covered by a later building; the three exposed bays have two tiers of windows with rusticated lintels and keystones; the doorway, central to these

bays, has rusticated jambs and an open pediment above a fanlight. The S side which has a stone plinth and brick dentil cornice is partly covered by a later vestry wing, two upper windows with segmental heads have had round-arched windows substituted and the two upper windows in the W wall are of a like kind.

The interior (originally 32¾ft by 34¼ft) probably had the pulpit at the W end but *c*.1827 an enlargement to that end of 18ft appears to have included re-orientation of the fittings with the pulpit against the S wall, now with an organ chamber behind, and a gallery around three sides. The early 19th-century seating remains in the gallery.

Monuments: in chapel (1) Thomas Pickering, 1807, 20 years minister, signed Marples, Melbourne; E of chapel (2) railed enclosure with monuments to Bakewell including John Bakewell, 1825, and Ann his wife, 1822, with memorandum that 'in this corner there is 16 feet 6 inches long, and 10 feet wide of land reserved for a burial place for his descendants for ever', signed Bagnall; (3) Thomas Carr, 1819, John his brother, 1758, buried at Kegworth, and John son of Thomas Carr, 1787, signed Cartwright; (4) Elizabeth, wife of Thomas Carr, 1795, with oval inscription panel bordered by symbols of heaven and mortality, signed B. Pollard, Quorn; (5) Thomas son of Thomas and Elizabeth Carr, 1807, and Samuel his brother, 1814; (6) Susanna wife of James Pickering, 1841, signed Bagnall, Melbourne. Also in burial-ground to N many 19th-century slate headstones, some laid flat.

Taylor (1818) II, 24, 231, 343: Wood (1847) 191.

(16) Former FRIENDS, The Baroon (SK 451276). The meeting-house built 1828 for a meeting which had been in existence since 1697, was sold *c*.1959 and converted to a house. Brick walls with

hipped slate roof, broad front with large rebuilt central porch flanked by tall windows now divided into two stories; three windows in rear wall with flat-arched brick heads, altered.

CLAWSON AND HARBY

(17) GENERAL BAPTIST, Long Clawson (SK 725273). Dated 1845.

(18) WESLEYAN, Harby (SK 744310). Brick with hipped slate

roof, broad three-bay front with round-arched windows, dated 1847.

(19) WESLEYAN, Long Clawson (SK 724274). Rebuilt *c*.1956; tablet from 1840 chapel reset against rear boundary fence.

COALVILLE

(20) GENERAL BAPTIST, North Street, Whitwick (SK 434162). A chapel of 1823, originally a preaching station of Hugglescote, stands alongside a larger chapel of 1861; both buildings have brick walls and slate roofs with three-bay fronts to the road. The former chapel has a hipped roof, two tiers of round-arched windows and a large slate tablet above the entrance inscribed 'BAITH-THEPHILLAH / *ERECTED ANNO DOMINI* / MDCCCXXIII / Enter with Sacred Awe this house of Pray'r / Adore the God of Grace that's worshipped here / Come taste his Love and learn his pleasant way / Come – join in fervent pray'r and sound his praise / Ipsi sit gloria in Christo Jesu / Seculi secutorum Amen'; interior, entirely altered, was designed to have a gallery above the entrance.

Wood (1847) 192.

(21) Former WESLEYAN, North Street, Whitwick (SK 434163). Successive chapels of 1822 and 1879 stand adjacent.

COLEORTON

(22) PRIMITIVE METHODIST (SK 404176). Opened 1875; former chapel 50 yards N, dated 1839.

COUNTESTHORPE

(23) BAPTIST (SP 587955). Dated 1863. Pedimented front with three tall round-arched bays.

EATON

(24) WESLEYAN, Goadby Marwood (SK 781265). Small chapel of stone with pantiled roof, formerly a stable or outbuilding, fitted up for use after 1856. *Monument*: to G. H. Watson 'who was lost in California 1868, Aged 19'.

Gill (1909) 174–6.

FREEBY

(25) CONGREGATIONAL (SK 805201). A nonconformist meeting existed here in the late 17th century, apparently with the support

FREEBY CHAPEL   *Leicestershire*

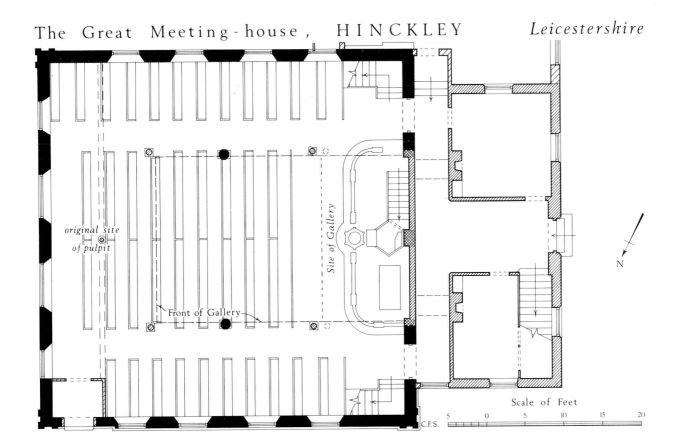

C.F.S.

former doorway   5 Feet 0   5   10   15

of Sir John Hartopp of Stoke Newington who possessed an estate at Freeby. Dr Isaac Watts, who was tutor to the Hartopp family from 1696, preached to the meeting in 1698. In the early 18th century the church shared a Presbyterian minister with Melton Mowbray.

The present chapel, a small building of stone with a tiled roof, was greatly altered in 1904 when the E and S walls appear to have been partly rebuilt, new windows inserted and the entrance moved to the W end. In the N wall, which may be of 18th-century date or earlier, is the blocking of a former central entrance. The interior (25½ft by 15¼ft) was entirely refitted in

1904. The pulpit incorporates earlier panelling. (URC)

Fountain, D., *Isaac Watts Remembered* (2nd ed., 1978) 36–8: LRCU (1962) 37.

GADDESBY

(26) WESLEYAN, Barsby (SK 699114). Rebuilt late 19th century; tablet from former chapel dated 1826.

GREAT GLEN

(27) WESLEYAN (SP 657979). Brick with hipped slate roof, two gallery windows above round-arched doorway and tablet dated 1827. Gabled Sunday-school alongside of 1879.

HALLATON

(28) CONGREGATIONAL, The Cross (SP 788966). Three-bay front with two tiers of windows, round-arched doorway with fanlight and date 1822 below later clock face.

HINCKLEY

(29) THE GREAT MEETING-HOUSE, Stockwell Head (SP 426941). The Presbyterian congregation originated in the late 17th century; Nathaniel Stephens, ejected minister of Fenny Drayton where as 'priest Stephens' he was George Fox's 'great persecutor', kept a conventicle here in 1669 and in 1672 the house of Samuel Ward was licensed for Presbyterians. In May 1722 John Jennings of Kibworth Beauchamp became minister bringing with him his academy at which Philip Doddridge was

The Great Meeting-house, HINCKLEY   *Leicestershire*

original site of pulpit

Front of Gallery

Site of Gallery

Scale of Feet

5   0   5   10   15   20

C.F.S.

Exterior from N.

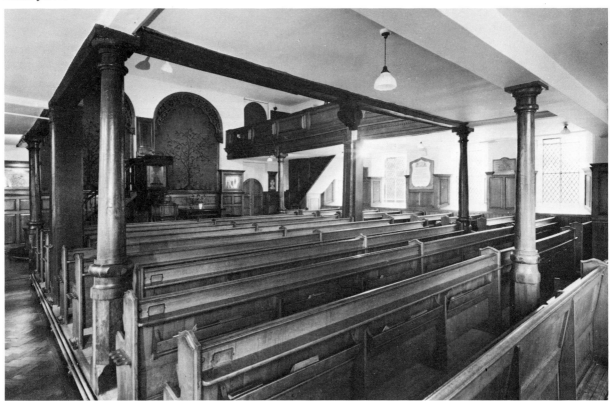

Interior from E.
(29) HINCKLEY. The Great Meeting-house, Stockwell Head.

then a pupil. Work on building a new meeting-house 'in our own yard' was already in progress by 22 July when Doddridge preached his first sermon in the earlier building, and the work was completed in November of the same year. About 1763 doctrinal disputes within the society resulted in a major secession after which the remaining members accepted an increasingly heterodox and ultimately Unitarian ministry.

The meeting-house stands on a concealed site behind industrial buildings and the front is further covered by a brick forebuilding of 1869 containing a vestibule between vestries with a school-room above, probably replacing an earlier addition serving similar uses. The original building has brick walls and a half-hipped tiled roof with a high central valley discharging to the rear. At each corner are narrow paired pilasters with moulded bases continuous with the plinth and capitals which extend as a moulded eaves cornice along the SE side; a similar cornice on the NW side may have been removed and an irregularity in the alignment of that wall could indicate that some more extensive alteration has occurred. Two round-arched doorways in the internal SW wall represent the original entrances. The NE wall facing the burial-ground has at the lower level two wide segmental-arched windows between two smaller windows with flat-arched heads of which that to the right was formerly a door-way, now re-sited in the adjacent wall; corresponding windows at an upper level all have segmental-arched heads of inferior quality. The side walls have each two tiers of windows in four bays: the upper windows have coursed brick heads, the lower windows on the SE side have flat-arched heads but on the opposite side the arches are segmental.

The interior (45ft by 44½ft) has a vaulted plaster ceiling rising from the front and side walls but arched at the NE end. Two principal posts, octagonal below and columnar above the gallery fronts, support the collar-beam of the central truss. The galleries with bolection moulded panels separated by panelled pilasters carried round three sides are said to have been added in 1727; supporting-columns near the SW end have been re-sited and it appears from this feature (together with the position of the gallery staircases, which contain some 18th-century material), the ceiling design and the fenestration of the rear wall, that the internal layout may have been reversed, perhaps in the late 18th century. The absence of documentary evidence for a major refitting does not invalidate this interpretation. The pulpit, now at the SW end, is flanked by two large arched recesses, now blocked, filled in 1902 with needlework panels, which opened to a former forebuilding providing gallery accommodation in an upper schoolroom.

Fittings – *Chairs*: pair, with arms, carved panelled backs and shaped tops, 17th-century. *Clock*: on gallery front, Parliament clock with square face, arched at top, and short pendulum case with oriental scene, signed 'John Sebire, London', 18th-century. *Monuments*: in chapel (1) Rev. Robert Dawson, 1751, brass reset from burial-vault 1939; (2) Hannah wife of Rev. Charles Case Nutter, 1837, signed Dare; (3) George Atkins, 1856, Elizabeth his widow, 1892, 'the last to be buried in the chapel graveyard', and George Beale Atkins their son, 1882; (4) Charles Noel, 1857,

and Mary Ann his wife, 1857. In burial-ground many slate head-stones have been laid flat including (5) William Hurst, 1793, and Jonathan his son, 1768, signed Hind; (6) Jonathan Hurst, gent., 1776, signed B. Pollard, Quorndon. *Pulpit*: hexagonal with moulded cornice and fielded panels, early 18th-century, reset lower on later base; staircase incorporates 18th-century balusters. *Seating*: in gallery, box-pews of 18th-century date, doors removed; lower seating, formerly box-pews with centre aisle, replaced by open pews 1912. *Tables of Decalogue*: in rear gallery, two, early 19th-century.

Bolam (1962) 23–6: Evans (1897) 103–4: *UHST* VII (1939) 65–6.

(30) GENERAL BAPTIST, Baptist Walk (SP 428942). The church, formerly united with Barton in the Beans, became autonomous in 1766. The chapel, built in 1806–7, is of red brick with three-bay sides; the front, drastically altered 1920–1, has three round-arched upper windows. The first meeting-house of 1768, now demolished, stood near the old *burial-ground* at the E end of Wood Street (SP 43059410) where a few slate headstones remain, including (1) Henry, son of Richard and Sarah Hulse, 1796, signed Pollard, Quorndon; (2) Sarah daughter of John and Ann Sutton, 1806, signed Pollard; (3) Rev. Joseph Freeston, 1819.

Godfrey (1891) *passim*: Osborne, S.C., *The Hinckley Baptist Church: the First Two Hundred Years* (1966): Taylor (1818) II, *passim*: Wood (1847) 182.

(31) Former STRICT BAPTIST, New Buildings (SP 42989418). 'Ebenezer Chapel', of brick with hipped slate roof, rendered front with one round-arched upper window and one pointed-arched lower window remaining, was built in 1803 for a small church formed in 1795, to which William Gadsby was then a preacher. The chapel passed to Primitive Methodists in 1846 and since c.1884 has formed part of an adjacent factory. The original congregation returned to a former meeting-house in Mansion Street, built Zion Chapel, Trinity Lane (SP 424938) in 1886 whence in 1974 they removed to Mount Road.

Chambers (1963) 51–4: *Grace*, Nov. 1974.

(32) CONGREGATIONAL, Regent Street (SP 425940). Orthodox seceders from the Great Meeting met first in a barn and from 1768 in a new meeting-house at Stockwell Head. The present chapel, on a new site in the Borough, was built in 1866–8 to the designs of F. Drake of Leicester. The walls are of red brick with an ashlar front and hipped slate roof. The front, of three bays with a gabled centre, has four columns with foliage capitals flanking the entrances. The untidy design of the front is the result in part of the attentions of Samuel Morley. (URC)

F[rancis], H.J., *The History of the Church of Christ…at Hinckley* (1918): Thomas, C.O., *The History of the First Noncon-formist Congregational Church in Hinckley* (1962).

(33) Former FRIENDS, Castle Street (SP 4293). A meeting-house built 1736 on land acquired in 1730 and superseding one of 1695, was closed in 1841. The building, which stood behind other property, is reported to have survived until 1958 but has since been demolished.

Arnold (1960) 132: Sturge (1895) 26.

(34) Former METHODIST, Stockwell Head (SP 428941). Brick with rendered front and hipped slate roof; probably the 'neat elegant preaching-house' referred to by John Wesley in his Journal, 27 April 1783. The building which dates from the late 18th century was enlarged to its present size (39¼ft by 50ft externally) c.1800; it was superseded by a new building in 1876–8 which has now been demolished. The N front, of five bays with two tiers of windows and doorways in the penultimate bays (partly altered since 1957), was originally of three bays and extended to the west. The S wall, which now has two tall round-arched windows with recent blocking, earlier had one upper and two lower windows.

(35) GENERAL BAPTIST, Earl Shilton (SP 472982), was built for a church which may have been in existence here since the mid 17th century, but the society was in a reduced state by the early 19th century when for a short period it was united to Hinckley and later with Thurlaston. The first meeting-house on this site, built in 1758–9, was replaced by the present building in 1844 and this was widened to the S, re-roofed and refitted, in 1890. The N wall is of three bays with two tiers of round-arched windows; the entrance is in a modern porch at the E end. *Monuments*: in the burial-ground include several slate headstones of the early 19th century.

Fursdon, H. W., *A History of the Baptist Church, Earl Shilton* (1931): Wood (1847) 212.

(36) CONGREGATIONAL, Earl Shilton (SP 468978), brick and tile, three-bay front with pedimental gable and tablet inscribed 'INDEPENDENT CHAPEL 1824'. Two tiers of round-arched windows to side walls with later wood frames, porch added at front in 1925. Burial-ground behind with many 19th-century slate headstones. (URC)

(37) STRICT BAPTIST, Stoke Golding (SP 398975). 'Zion Chapel', 1853 with parallel extension of 1874.

Chambers (1963) 58–9.

HOBY WITH ROTHERBY

(38) WESLEYAN, Hoby (SK 669175). Built 1834; three-bay front with later porch. Extended 1956.

Gill (1909) 142–6.

HUSBANDS BOSWORTH

(39) BAPTIST, Berridge's Lane (SP 642844). Built 1807. Brick with hipped slate roof. The front wall, originally with two doorways and a window centrally between at an upper level, was entirely altered in the late 19th century when a central doorway between two upper windows, all with round-arched heads, were substituted for the former arrangement. The side walls were also refenestrated and the interior refitted at that period. (Demolition proposed 1980)

IBSTOCK

(40) GENERAL BAPTIST, Chapel Street (SK 409104). Built 1856 superseding a chapel of 1814; Sunday-school added 1880.

Taylor (1818) II, 335.

KEGWORTH

(41) GENERAL BAPTIST, (SK 485268). The first meeting-house was built in 1755 and a society formed which remained a section of the church of Barton in the Beans until 1760 becoming a founder member of the New Connexion in 1770. The present chapel, built on a new site in 1815, was enlarged and partly rebuilt in 1865. The walls are of brick and the roof slated. Only the W wall is of recognizably early 19th-century date, the gabled S front, entirely of 1865, has bands of blue and red brick, a pair of round-arched doorways, and three windows. The interior, largely refitted in 1865, retains an original rear gallery. A Sunday-school was built to the N in 1880.

Monuments: in chapel (1) James Hardy, 1820, and Ann his widow, 1832; in burial-ground, slate headstones, (2) John Wilders, 1844, Baptist minister of Smalley, Derbys., signed W. Carrington, Loughborough; (3) Sarah wife of John Wilders; (4) William Pegg, 1840, and Elizabeth his widow, 1850; (5) Joseph Pegg, 1824; (6) James Hardy, 1820, and Ann his widow, 1832, signed White; (7) John Tarratt, 1817, minister 'upwards of forty years'; (8) William Felkin, 1824, 30 years minister; (9) Elizabeth (Crane) wife of William Felkin, 1818, and Sarah their daughter, signed Johnson, Woodhouse; (10) William son of Richard Crane, 1817, and Diana his sister, 1817; (11) Richard Crane, 1818, and Sarah his widow, 1846; (12) John Crane, 1804, and Sarah his widow, 1830, signed Wootton.

Godfrey (1891) 107: Taylor (1818) II, *passim*: Wood (1849) 181.

KIBWORTH BEAUCHAMP

(42) WESLEYAN, School Road (SP 681938). Dated 1846. Three-bay front with pedimental gable.

KIBWORTH HARCOURT

(43) CONGREGATIONAL (SP 679948). The congregation, variously described in its early years as Presbyterian or Independent, was formed by John Jennings, ejected rector of Hartley Wespall, Hants, who became chaplain to Mrs Pheasant at West Langton, the first meetings being held at Langton Hall. After c.1690 a meeting-house was provided behind the Crown Inn in Kibworth which was accidentally destroyed by fire in 1759.

Manse and chapel from S.

The present building, on a new site, was registered for use by Protestant dissenters on 13 January 1761. It was enlarged to the rear in the early 19th century, lengthened in the mid 19th century, and refitted in 1931. The walls are of brick and the roof is hipped and slated. The broad SW front was originally of three bays with a central doorway and two tiers of segmental-arched windows separated by a brick platband. A further bay was added at the SE end to provide a vestry and schoolroom above and the entrance has been twice re-sited. The NW wall, which has a similar platband and traces of former windows, has been extended to the rear. The former *manse*, a brick building of three storeys, at right angles to the NW end of the chapel, was built in 1793–4. (Demolition of manse proposed after 1973)

The interior of the chapel (originally about 22ft by 36ft) has been greatly altered and now has a mid 19th-century gallery at the SE end with a wide arch at the back with shutters opening to the schoolroom.

Fittings – *Chair*: in vestry, ladder-back chair of *c*.1700 associated with Philip Doddridge, minister 1723–9. *Cupboard*: in schoolroom, corner cupboard with shaped shelves, mid 18th-century. *Monuments*: in chapel (1) Philip Doddridge D. D., 1751, erected 1862; (2) Rev. Francis Islip, 1866; (3) Rev. Edward Chater, 1844, late 19th-century replacement of original monument now loose in burial-ground.

LRCU (1962) 18.

LEICESTER

(44) THE GREAT MEETING-HOUSE[1], East Bond Street (SK 586048). The 'Great Meeting' commenced in the late 17th century as two distinct congregations of Presbyterians and Independents meeting at first separately but by 1704 sharing the use of the Presbyterian meeting-house which is variously described as in Hangman's Lane, now Newarke Street, or near Infirmary Square. In 1716 the two parties came to a formal agreement over the allocation of seats in the meeting-house; separate pastorates though not necessarily separate services were maintained until 1730. An orthodox ministry appears to have continued until 1803 when, following the rise of other denominations, notably the Congregational church meeting in Bond Street, the meeting-house was left in the hands of a surviving Unitarian majority.

The meeting-house, built in 1708, is a nearly square building with brick walls and a hipped roof with central valley covered in Welsh slates which first replaced the original Charnwood slate in 1846. At each corner of the walls is a brick pilaster with moulded capital, the faces of the pilasters were rendered in 1838. The W

front, of four bays with two tiers of windows with moulded architraves and doorways in the end bays, was altered in 1866 by the addition of two porches joined by an open loggia having two Roman Doric columns *in antis*; the alterations, which included the addition of a chancel and minor rooms on the E side and a major internal refitting, were made under the direction of Shenton and Baker of Leicester. The N and S walls, also of four bays, have two tiers of windows with flat-arched heads, a moulded plinth, brick platband and a moulded eaves cornice which continues around the building. The E wall, which formerly had two tall windows flanking the pulpit, minor windows above and below the gallery ends, and the date 1708 in vitrified bricks, has been almost entirely covered by the 1866 additions.

The interior (41½ft by 47ft excluding the chancel) is almost entirely of 1866. The building did not have a gallery until after 1716 although it was designed to take one; the present gallery which continues around three sides may contain some of the 18th-century structure but has been refronted and cast-iron columns placed below. The plaster ceiling was constructed in its present form in 1786 replacing a ceiling which appears to have been generally similar in character. It comprises a truncated octagonal pyramid which rises to the level of the collar-beams of the roof trusses and has bands of applied ornament in low relief; ventilators were inserted into the lower corners in 1874.

Fittings – *Monuments*: in chapel (1) Mary widow of Matthew Reid, 1812; (2) Edward Alexander M.D., of Danett's Hall, near Leicester, 1822, buried in St Mary's Church; (3) Rev. John Hugh Worthington, 1827, sarcophagus-shaped tablet on claw feet; (4) John Worthington, 1824, signed S. Hull; (5) Rev. Hugh Worthington A.M., 1797, 56 years pastor; (6) William Rowlett, 1883, claiming his marriage to Elizabeth Sharpe, 26 July 1837, to be the first wedding (since the repeal of the Dissenters Marriage Act) in an English nonconformist chapel. In burial-ground and against the outer walls are many reset slate headstones, including (7) Milley (Billings) wife of Thomas Godwin, 1786; (8) Dolley Billings, 1784, with carved roundel; (9) Thomas Chapman, 1792, and Jane his wife, 1771; (10) Sarah wife of Benjamin Spencer, 1769; (11) Mary Spencer, 1765; (12) Samuel Matthews, 1757, and Philip his brother, 1760; (13) Thomas Scrivner, 1775; (14) Captain Nathaniel Spencer 'who died at Worksop on his march home', 1783, with military insignia; (15) Rev. Hugh Worthington A.M., 1797, 56 years pastor. *Plate*: includes a set of eight two-handled cups of 1786. (According to Thomas (1908) the original *pulpit* was removed after 1866 to the School building and a lead panel dated 1708 from a *rainwater head* was exhibited in the chapel library. A *royal arms*, probably original, was refurbished in 1760 to mark the accession of George III).

Bolam (1962) 29–33: Evans (1897) 129–30: Paget, A. H., *The Epitaphs in the Graveyard and Chapel of the Great Meeting, Leicester* (1912): Thomas, A.H., *A History of the Great Meeting, Leicester, and its Congregation* (1908).

[1]The name 'Great Meeting-House', while logically derived from that of the society, is not known with certainty to have been applied to this building.

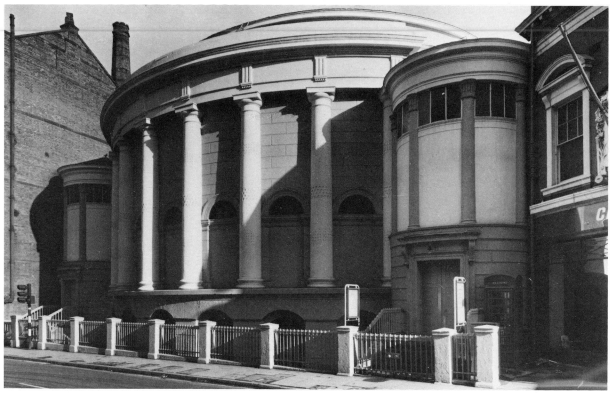

(45) LEICESTER. Former Baptist chapel.

(45) Former BAPTIST, Belvoir Street (SK 589042). A Particular Baptist church originated *c*.1750 by secession from the earlier General Baptist congregation meeting in Friar Lane Chapel (built *c*.1719, rebuilt 1785 and 1865, demolished *c*.1960–70). The new congregation first met in a chapel in Harvey Lane where William Carey was minister 1789–93. The chapel in Belvoir Street, to which the church removed in 1845, was designed by Joseph Hansom and known as 'pork pie chapel' from its outward appearance; it was closed *c*.1938–40 when the congregation united with that at Charles Street (46) and since 1946 has served as part of an Adult Education Centre.

The front, rendered in stucco, is terminated by circular pavilions (after the manner of the Choragic Monument of Lysicrates) which contain the two entrances and staircases. The interior is U-shaped in plan with a flat rear wall with two vestry doorways flanking the site of the pulpit. A gallery carried around the other sides above an entrance passage is supported by cast-iron columns and lit by a clerestory, with windows of three lights separated by Doric columns, which continues around the building but is set back from the front and side walls.

Illustrated London News 25 Oct. 1845: VCH *Leicestershire* IV (1958) 391–2.

(46) BAPTIST, Charles Street (SK 591043). Seceders from Harvey Lane built a new chapel for themselves in 1830; this has brick walls rendered at the front and a hipped slate roof. The front is of five bays with a slightly recessed centre of three bays incorporating an open porch with two fluted Greek Doric columns. The

upper windows are round-arched and separated by pilasters.

The interior has a continuous round-ended gallery with cantilevered front.

Fittings – *Chairs*: two, associated with Dr Robert Hall, minister at Harvey Lane, 1807–26. *Monuments*: in chapel (1) Rev. William Carey, pastor 1789–93, died at Serampore 1834, tablet removed from Harvey Lane; (2) Richard Harris 'one of the founders of this chapel', 1854, and Fanny his wife, 1842; (3) Rev. Thomas Lomas, 23 years minister, 1870, and Elizabeth his wife, *c*.1870; in burial-ground at rear (4) John Carryer, deacon, 1846; also several early 19th-century headstones. *Miscellaneous*: exhibits from Carey's cottage, Harvey Lane, demolished 1968.

(47) SALEM CHAPEL, Free School Lane (SK 585047) was built in 1817 for a Calvinistic Independent congregation gathered by Joseph Chamberlain who had become a follower of William Huntington in 1808 when in Grantham. It has long been used as a warehouse. The walls are of red brick with stone dressings and a hipped slate roof. The front and sides are of three bays with two tiers of round-arched windows; a stone panel above the centre bay at the front carries the chapel name and year of erection. (Derelict 1973)

Chambers (1963) 65.

(48) EVINGTON CHAPEL, Evington (SK 628030). An Independent congregation was formed in the village in 1811 when a small meeting-room was opened apparently in a stable loft. The present chapel was built 1837–8, together with a detached manse (rebuilt 1961), by Edward and Samuel Davenport and Thomas Bryan, who also endowed it. After the death of the first minister a Strict Baptist church was formed in 1883.

The chapel is a small building with rendered walls and slate roof in the Decorated Gothic style. A vestry projects to the rear. The interior has a small gallery above the front entrance – probably added in 1842. The pulpit at the opposite end rests on a corbel and is approached directly from the vestry through a two-centred arched doorway. The seating which is mostly contemporary comprises box-pews each side of the pulpit and open benches with shaped arms and inclined backs. The roof is supported by hammer-beam trusses. *Organ*: in gallery, reputed to have been built in 1838 by John Gray of London and installed in a royal palace; bought and erected here by Samuel Davenport, 1842.

Chambers (1963) 72–5.

(49) CONGREGATIONAL, London Road, Clarendon Park (SK 604027). Built 1885–6, by James Tate of Leicester. Polygonal masonry walls and tiled roof; broad rectangular tower at NE end with tall hipped roof and free use of late Gothic detail.

CYB (1887) 256–7.

(50) WESLEYAN, Bishop Street (SK 589043). The first regular Methodist preaching-house in Leicester was a barn in Millstone Lane, converted *c.*1755 and later rebuilt. The Bishop Street chapel which largely superseded it in the 19th century was built in 1815–6. It has brick walls with rendered dressings. The broad front to the street is of five main bays with a three-bay pedimented centre and two tiers of round-arched windows of two orders separated by a rendered platband and having conjoined cills in the centre bays. A pedimented doorway in the middle bay was inserted in 1883 and a weakly-detailed open pediment to the upper window may also be an alteration. Lower bays at the extremities of the front have original round-arched entrances and

narrow windows above in rendered recessed panels. The interior was altered in 1883 and considerably refitted in 1894. The organ is said to be the work of Father Smith.

Dolbey (1964) 138–9.

LITTLE STRETTON

(51) Former CONGREGATIONAL (SK 66850015). Small plain building of brick and slate; slate tablet, in the gable above the entrance, inscribed 'FREE CHAPEL . . . *Erected at the expense of* GEORGE HUDSON A.D. 1811'.

LONG WHATTON

(52) GENERAL BAPTIST, Diseworth (SK 454244). This society which has remained in association with the Kegworth branch of the church of Barton in the Beans, began about 1752, the first meetings being held in a weaver's shop; the present meeting-house was erected in that year. The walls are of brick with later rendering at the front and the roof is covered in part with small

stone slates but mostly replaced by blue Welsh slate. The broad W front is of three bays with a central doorway (blocked 1928) having a moulded architrave and keystone between two windows with plain stone surrounds, keystones and renewed frames. The E wall, which has a brick dentil eaves cornice, has two windows altered in the 19th century or later and an added central buttress which partly covers the site of a small upper window intended to light the pulpit. The N wall is gabled and has a two-course brick platband at eaves level; two lancets replace a pair of small square gallery windows. At the S end is a slightly lower extension of *c*.1790 in two stories.

The interior (18ft by 32½ft) was drastically altered and refitted in 1928 when a N gallery was removed and the pulpit re-sited at this end. The S extension has a lobby and vestry to the ground floor and schoolroom with lime ash floor above.

Monuments: in burial-ground to E, slate headstones (1) Ann, wife of John Jacques, 1787, signed Wootton; (2) John Jacques, 1792, signed Wootton; (3) John, son of John and Ann Tarratt, 1772; (4) Thomas, son of William and Sarah Hall, 1769.

Taylor (1818) II, 25, 228, 339: Wood (1847) 181.

(53) GENERAL BAPTIST, Long Whatton (SK 476236). The chapel, built in 1793 for a section of the Kegworth church which became autonomous in 1799, has walls of brickwork with later rendering and a slate roof. The front bay with two tiers of round-arched windows was added in 1838; the original building

behind (about 30½ft by 27ft externally) has two wide segmental-arched windows in each side wall and two narrower windows at the S end.

Taylor (1818) II, 227–8, 341: Wood (1847) 193.

LOUGHBOROUGH

(54) GENERAL BAPTIST, Woodgate (SK 538194). The first meeting-house on this site was built in 1792 for a congregation which originated about 1753 in association with the church at Barton in the Beans. The meeting-house was rebuilt in 1815 but in 1828 the church moved to Baxtergate (see below) and the premises came to be used by a separate church formed in 1846. A new chapel built on an adjacent site in 1881–2 to the designs of J. Wallace Chapman is of red brick with stone dressings and has a corner tower with pyramidal roof. The former chapel then used for a Sunday-school was rebuilt in 1904 but a two-storied brick wing of 1856 remains at the rear. (The church united with Baxtergate in 1973; chapel closed 1975, since demolished)

(55) GENERAL BAPTIST, Baxtergate (SK 537198). Built in 1828 for the church formerly meeting in Woodgate (see above), it is a

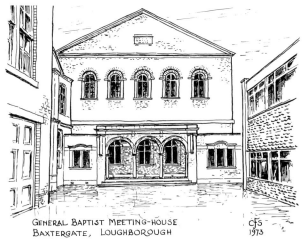

GENERAL BAPTIST MEETING-HOUSE
BAXTERGATE, LOUGHBOROUGH
CFS
1973

large building of brick with a wide pedimented front of five bays with two tiers of round-arched windows, the lower openings partly covered by a porch of *c*.1907, and a tablet above with the inscription 'GENERAL BAPTIST/MEETING-HOUSE/ MDCCCXXVIII'. A school building at the rear is dated 1846. The interior has a gallery around three sides supported by iron columns, a large rostrum pulpit of the late 19th century, and original straight-backed pews in the gallery but with doors removed. *Monument*: Rev. Thomas Stevenson, 31 years minister, 1841. (Porch rebuilt and major internal alterations carried out 1975)

Baptist Times, 12 June 1975: Brewer, J., *An Outline History of the General Baptist Congregation of Loughborough, 1760–1975* (1979): Taylor (1818) II, *passim*: Wood (1847) 181.

(56) Former CONGREGATIONAL, Derby Square, formerly Ashby Square (SK 534197). Built in 1828 for a society which originated in 1826 with meetings in an upper room in Mill Street. A new chapel was built in Frederick Street (SK 533195) in 1908 (now URC) and the former building used for a time by

Loughborough College is now a Masonic Hall. It has brick walls and a slate roof. The front, of four bays with two tiers of round-arched windows separated by a grooved platband, has a slightly projecting two-bay centre with pediment and date-tablet; the doorways have been altered.

CYB (1909) 151: LRCU (1962) 30–1.

LUTTERWORTH

(57) Former BAPTIST, Chapel Street (SP 54428455). Three-bay pedimented front. Gable tablet with painted inscription 'BAPTIST CHAPEL / ERECTED / 1839'. The Strict Baptist church formed in 1830 was disbanded *c*.1940.

Chambers (1963) 78–9.

(58) CONGREGATIONAL, George Street (SP 544846). The church (now URC) was formed in 1689 and the first meeting-house on this site was probably built at that time. A secession occurred in the early 18th century for which a new meeting-house was erected in Ely Lane, now Station Road, and registered in 1738. On the reunion of the two congregations *c*.1776 the present chapel was built. The walls are of brickwork and the roof is hipped and covered with local slates. Central entrance in W front, altered in the late 19th century and replacing a narrower pedimented doorway, has a small tablet in the wall above dated 1777. The flanking windows were apparently converted to doorways in the early 19th century but are now restored.

The interior (46¾ft by 35ft) has been partly refitted in the late 19th century but retains original galleries around three sides and an hexagonal pulpit with flared base and narrow stem. School-rooms were built on the S side of the chapel in 1818. *Monuments*: in chapel (1) Rev. Peter Dowley, 1731, and Rev. John Dowley, his son, 1774; (2) William Crisp, 1796, and Elizabeth his wife,

1778; (3) Rev. Thomas Grundy, 1827; in vestry (4) Elizabeth Halford, 1780, and Edward Halford, 1781, slate.

LRCU (1962) 32–3.

MARKET BOSWORTH

(59) Former GENERAL BAPTIST, Barton Road (SK 406033). Built 1848 as a preaching station for the church at Barton in the Beans, but used since 1949 by a distinct congregation.

Osborne, S.C., *The Hinckley Baptist Church; the First Two Hundred Years* (1966) 115: Wood (1847) 181.

MARKET HARBOROUGH

(60) CONGREGATIONAL, High Street (SP 733875). The congregation originated in the late 17th century largely through the efforts of Matthew Clark, ejected rector of Narborough, Leicestershire, who was licensed as a Presbyterian preacher here

(60) MARKET HARBOROUGH. Congregational chapel.

in 1672. An Independent church was formed and the church convenant signed in 1690. The original meeting-house, demolished after 1844, was a building of *c*.1690 which 'stood at the top of the lane leading for Great Bowden', it had brick walls and a hipped slate roof, the wide front wall had a platband, two tall windows flanking the pulpit, two doorways beyond and smaller windows below and above end-galleries. The roof structure was probably supported by freestanding columns.

The present chapel, on a new site, built in 1844, is in Classical style. It has walls of gault brick with stone dressings and a hipped slate roof. The five-bay front has a central open loggia. The parapet is inscribed 'INDEPENDENT CHAPEL'.

Coleman (1853) 119–45: Deacon (1980) 40.

MEASHAM

(61) GENERAL BAPTIST (SK 333123). Built 1841 to replace a chapel of 1811 for a section of the church in Austrey, Warwickshire, but from 1840 united with Netherseal. Lower openings of

GENERAL BAPTIST CHAPEL, MEASHAM

S front altered since 1972 when doorway was made central. Original gallery around three sides and later organ gallery behind pulpit. *Monuments*: in burial-ground, slate headstones now laid flat.

Taylor (1818) II, 337: Wood (1847) 231.

(62) WESLEYAN, Bosworth Road (SK 335122). Wide rendered front with four round-arched windows; opened 1854 (inscription defaced).

NEWBOLD VERDON

(63) GENERAL BAPTIST (SK 446038). Built in 1833 as a preaching station of Barton in the Beans; enlarged and greatly altered in 1928. Original inscribed tablet reset above porch in later end bay.

QUORNDON

(64) GENERAL BAPTIST, Meeting Street (SK 558162). Built in 1770 at a cost of £270 by a society formed a few years earlier, initially part of the Loughborough church. The meeting-house, of brick with a rubble plinth and a tiled roof of 1958–9 replacing local slates which remain on the adjacent buildings, has been greatly altered and enlarged. The original structure (23½ft by 36¼ft) was lower than at present with a wide central doorway between a pair of segmental-arched windows in the NW front, with gabled end walls having at the NE a segmental-arched

NW front.

window and probably another at the opposite end. In 1780 an extension of 12ft was made to the rear with a separate roof structure and end gables, two wide segmental-arched windows near the ends of the back wall and a small doorway next to the pulpit. In 1790 the walls were raised retaining two separate roof structures, the junction being marked internally by a pair of tall Roman Doric timber columns; three upper windows were placed in the front wall and three at the back of which the central one has a wide round-arched head; two doorways were substituted for the central entrance at this period. In 1819 a vestry and schoolrooms of three stories were built adjacent to the SW side and in 1897–8 a further schoolroom of a single storey was added. The interior of the chapel was partly refitted in 1930 and an obtrusive brick and glass porch erected in front *c*.1965–70.

The original date-tablet inscribed 'Ano Dom. 1770' is reset in the NE wall and a larger tablet was substituted in the front wall in 1856. The interior has a gallery of 1790 around three sides with a panelled front supported by timber columns; the NE gallery has been shortened to accommodate a large organ on the floor below. Most fittings are of the late 19th century or later.

Monuments: in chapel (1) Rev. Adam Smith, 10 years pastor, 1847, and later inscription to Sarah, his widow, 1881; (2) Rev. Benjamin Pollard, 38 years minister, 1818, and Catherine his widow, 1837. Externally on back wall (3) Rev. Thomas Owen, 24 years minister of the Unitarian congregations at Loughborough and Mountsorrel, 1824; (4) Joseph Thornell, 1782, and Dorothy, his widow, wife of John Johnson, 1808. In burial-ground an important series of slate headstones, all re-sited around boundary walls; (5) William Chapman, 1804, with oval panel with emblems of mortality, signed Pollard; (6) Children of Benjamin and Catherine Pollard, 1785–1796, with oval panel of bird resting on a death's head; (7) Amy wife of William Woodroffe, 1800, with figure of Hope, signed B.P.; (8) Benjamin Pollard, 1796, Ann, his wife, 1783, and Elizabeth their daughter, 1785; (9) Rev. Benjamin Pollard, 1818, panel from larger monument; (10) Ann Catharine, wife of Rev. Thomas Owen and daughter of Rev. Jeremiah Dethick, minister at Bardon and Ashby de la Zouch, 1804; (11) Edward Parkinson, 1803, with resurrection scene; (12) Thomas Trueman, minister, 1797, who died 'by a fatal accident as he was returning from an Evening Lecture held at Loughborough', and Mary, his widow, 1835, signed B. Pollard.

Mee, W. E., *Quorn Baptists* [*c*.1960]: Taylor (1818) II, 54, 159, 235, 348: Wood (1847) 206.

(65) Former WESLEYAN (SK 561165), behind the present Methodist chapel. Dated 1822.

REARSBY

(66) WESLEYAN, Melton Road (SK 652144). Broad three-bay front with tablet, 'HOUSE OF GOD / 1849 / WESLEYAN'.

ROTHLEY

(67) GENERAL BAPTIST, Woodgate (SK 584127). Built 1800 for a section of the Loughborough church which had met from 1785 in a converted barn. Drastically altered in the late 19th century and later. *Monuments*: early 19th-century slate headstones in burial-ground include (1) John Waters Goddard, minister, 1812; others are signed Bramley, Sileby, and Pollard, Swithland; also (2) Richard Ward, 1829, late warrener of Rothley Plain, and Sarah his wife, 1825, former wall monument.

Taylor (1818) II, 160–1, 237, 346: Wood (1847) 205.

(68) WESLEYAN, Howe Lane (SK 583126). Opened 1823 but extended to the S and greatly altered *c*.1900.

SADDINGTON

(69) BAPTIST (SP 659920). Built as a preaching station for the Arnesby church and apparently registered 10 December 1842.

SCALFORD

(70) WESLEYAN, New Street (SK 763240). Generally similar to Rearsby (66) but entrance removed to end wall *c*.1900. Lunette tablet with stone arch above former central entrance partly removed and converted to a window is inscribed 'WESLEYAN CHAPEL 1844'.

SEAGRAVE

(71) PRIMITIVE METHODIST, Green Lane (SK 616178). Three-bay gabled front with cast-iron tablet dated 1845.

SHACKERSTONE

(72) GENERAL BAPTIST, Barton in the Beans (SK 397064). The church meeting here, which occupies a pre-eminent position in the revival of the General Baptist interest in the 18th century, owes its origin to a combination of various evangelical forces active in the district in the early 1740s. John Taylor, a schoolmaster in one of the Countess of Huntingdon's schools, who commenced preaching in 1743, was followed by David Taylor, a former footman to Lady Margaret Hastings, with whom Moravian influences were strong; this led to the formation of a nominally 'Independent' society. The first meeting-house, built in 1745 at a cost of £170, was a small building (36ft by 22ft) with rooms above intended for the accommodation of single members after the fashion of a Moravian settlement. About 1753 after a slow process of change the members adopted Baptist practices while retaining an Arminian doctrine. In 1760 the society divided into five separate churches; Barton, Melbourne, Kegworth, Loughborough and Kirby Woodhouse, which similarly divided at later periods.

The present chapel, built in 1841, superseded the meeting-house of 1745 which had been enlarged in 1801 and 1809. The walls are of brickwork in Flemish bond with light-coloured headers above a red brick plinth and the roof is slated. The interior has a gallery around three sides and a further gallery behind the pulpit which is separated by shutters from a Sunday-school room at the back.

Monuments: in burial-ground, many slate headstones, against W wall (1) Robert Milligan, 1783, ruling elder, native of

Hollingwood near Dumfries, Scotland, and Mary his wife, 1804, sister of Francis Smith, General Baptist pastor at Melbourn, signed Pollard, Quorndon: S and W of chapel (2) Richard Hackett, 1798; (3) Thomas Orton, 1792, and Hannah his widow, 1816; (4) Thomas Alldridge, 1748, Sarah his widow, 1748, and two infants.

Cook, T., *Memoir of the late Mr Samuel Deacon* (1888): Godfrey (1891): Taylor (1818) II, *passim*: Wood (1847) 181 and *passim*.

(73) GENERAL BAPTIST, Congerstone (SK 369056). Built in 1821 as a preaching station of Barton in the Beans and closed *c*.1960. Narrow segmental-arched doorway with dated brick above.

GENERAL BAPTIST CHAPEL, CONGERSTONE · 1972

Two round-arched windows with cast-iron frames to each side wall and one window at rear above pulpit. (Derelict 1972)
Wood (1847) 181.

(74) Former WESLEYAN, Shackerstone (SK 373070). Brick with hipped slate roof, nearly square; round-arched doorway with blind fanlight between segmental-arched windows in N wall, pulpit between windows on E side and stepped seating opposite. Built *c*.1840–50.

SHARNFORD

(75) WESLEYAN, Chapel Lane (SP 482919). Brick with hipped slate roof; three-bay front with two tiers of round-arched windows and small tablet dated 1827. Two tall arched windows in each side wall. *Monument*: in front of chapel, Joseph Clarke, 1851, slate headstone laid flat, signed T. S. Lord, Burbage.

SHEPSHED

(76) BETHESDA CHAPEL, Loughborough Road (SK 483197), standing on a remote site behind a row of timber-framed cottages, was built in 1823 for a Strict Baptist church. The walls are of brick and the roof is covered with patent tiles. Gabled front with terminal pilasters rising to pyramidal finials, pointed-arched doorway with rusticated surround and blind window above. Original box-pews remain inside and a few early 19th-century monuments in the burial-ground.
Chambers (1963) 79–80.

SILEBY

(77) GENERAL BAPTIST, Cossington Road (SK 602149). Built in 1818 for a branch of the Rothley church; brick walls with later

rendering and a hipped roof covered with small local slates. Broad three-bay front with round-arched upper windows and later porch. *Monument*: re-sited in front yard, Elizabeth Thorman, 1823 and William her son, 1830, slate headstone engraved with urn on pedestal and symbols of mortality, signed Hack engraver, Loughborough.
Wood (1847) 205.

SPROXTON

(78) WESLEYAN, Stonesby (SK 822245). Opened 1885; former three-bay chapel of 1847 adjacent.

SWEPSTONE

(79) CONGREGATIONAL, Newton Burgoland (SK 371089). The

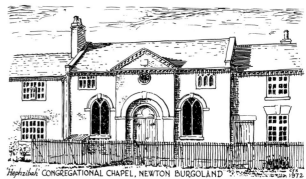

'Hephzibah' CONGREGATIONAL CHAPEL, NEWTON BURGOLAND · 1972

chapel is set in a terrace of two-storied cottages. The front, of the three bays, has a pedimented centre bay with a clock dial and a tablet inscribed 'Hephzibah Erected A.D. 1807'. Sunday-school behind dated 1840. *Gates and Railings*: in front of chapel and cottage, wrought-iron, early 19th-century.

(80) Former PRIMITIVE METHODIST, Newton Burgoland (SK 370090). Defaced tablet dated 1855; porch added 1895.

THEDDINGWORTH

(81) CONGREGATIONAL (SP 666856). Brick with hipped slate roof; built in 1833 and altered *c*.1860 when a S gallery was inserted, a porch and staircase built against the W wall, and land acquired to the W for a burial-ground. The original approach was behind houses S of the chapel and entrances centrally on the E and W sides. Two pointed-arched windows in N and S walls with wooden Y-tracery. Pulpit at N end, early 19th-century on later base.
LRCU (1962) 41–2.

TILTON

(82) WESLEYAN, Halstead (SK 746056). Opened 1837, enlarged to front 1863.

TUR LANGTON

(83) CONGREGATIONAL (SP 716946). Built 1846; refronted and original tablet reset *c*.1900.

TWYFORD AND THORPE

(84) WESLEYAN, Twyford (SK 729101). Brick with hipped slate roof, broad three-bay front with terminal buttresses rising to

finials, two pointed-arched windows with intersecting glazing bars, and circular tablet dated 1845 above site of central entrance.

ULLESTHORPE

(85) CONGREGATIONAL (SP 505875). Brick with hipped slate roof, three-bay front and sides with two tiers of round-arched windows. Built 1825, porch added and front windows altered 1883.

WALTHAM

(86) WESLEYAN, Waltham on the Wolds (SK 802252). Brick and slate, broad three-bay front with wide arched recesses enclosing windows, central entrance converted to window with original inscription on arch 'WESLEYAN CHAPEL 1843'. Two-storied early 19th-century cottage of brick with pantile roof adjoins end of chapel.

WIGSTON MAGNA

(87) STRICT BAPTIST, Frederick Street, Wigston (SP 608991). Small and austere chapel, built 1850.

Chambers (1963) 78.

(88) CONGREGATIONAL, Long Street, Wigston (SP 606989). The congregation, originally regarded as Presbyterian (now URC), commenced about 1666 under the guidance of Matthew Clark, ejected rector of Narborough, and was for a period united with the Great Meeting in Leicester. From c.1682 to 1731 they had the use of the old church of St Woolstan which was leased from the parish as a meeting-house. After the termination of the lease the first meeting-house on the present site was erected at a cost of £243 7s. 6d. and opened in 1732. The present chapel, built in 1841–2, has brick walls and a hipped slate roof. The interior has an original gallery around three sides with a fielded panelled front supported by fluted cast-iron columns. The seating was renewed and the building enlarged to the rear in the late 19th century.

Monuments: in chapel (1) John Phipps, 1846, 'Deacon and Clerk of this Place', and Mary his widow, 1847; (2) John son of Thomas and Jane Mays, 1838; (3) Sarah Jane, daughter of William and Elizabeth Pochin, 1834; (4) William Pochin, 1850; (5) George Edwin, son of William and Elizabeth Pochin, 1843, signed Matthews, sculptor; (6) Thomas Measures, 1837; (7) Rev. William Harrison, seven years co-pastor and minister, 1820; (8) Rev. Henry Davis, 43 years pastor, 1815, and Martha his wife; in front of chapel (9) William Pochin, 1850, signed Barfield, Lester. *Railings*: in front of chapel, cast-iron base and railings, with Greek anthemion ornament on gate piers, 1842.

Evangelical Magazine Dec. 1842, 603: LRCU (1962) 46–8.

(88) WIGSTON MAGNA. Congregational chapel. (URC)

WOODHOUSE

(89) GENERAL BAPTIST, Woodhouse Eaves (SK 530146). Built 1796–7 for a section of the Loughborough Church; largely, if not entirely, rebuilt in 1885. (Demolished 1980)

Monuments: slate headstones reset around sides of forecourt (1) John North, 1842, and Hannah his wife, 1832, signed Pollard, Swithland; (2) Elizabeth wife of Joseph Preston, 1797, and Catharine their daughter; (3) Sarah daughter of John and Sarah Pollard of Swithland, 1818, and Mary her sister, with figure of Hope; (4) Mary, daughter of Matthew and Mary Beston, 1802, and Joseph her brother; (5) William Johnson, 1833, slate merchant; (6) Edward Johnson, 1828, signed W. Johnson; (7) Thomas Wesley, 1825, minister, and Ann his widow, 1840, signed J. Pollard; (8) Thomas Storar, 1797, double panel with swag border, signed B.P; (9) Edward Johnson, 1807, 'who for many years gave the use of his dwelling-house for the Preaching of the Gospel, and as a more effectual Provision for perpetuating the cause he espoused gave this ground in which his remains are deposited and also by his last will and testament gave five pounds to the poor of this congregation', also Elizabeth his wife, 1799, signed B. Pollard.

Taylor (1818) II, 160, 234, 347: Wood (1847) 208.

WORTHINGTON

(90) WESLEYAN (SK 408204). Round-arched doorway with fanlight, small window above and partly defaced tablet dated 1820.

WYMESWOLD

(91) Former GENERAL BAPTIST (SK 604236). A church in existence here in 1651 was in membership with the General Baptist Association in the following century when it formed a joint society with Mountsorrel. Preaching by General Baptists of the New Connexion from East Leake, Nottinghamshire, resulted in the formation of a new cause and in the erection of the present building in 1781. The church was disbanded c.1960 and the chapel was converted for use as a house in 1964.

The chapel has brick walls and a slate roof. It was enlarged on the N side c.1815 and an annexe of two stories was built at the E end in 1847. The S front which now has three tall windows with pointed-arched heads of the late 19th century, originally had a central entrance between two windows; three windows formerly above these may have been added in the early 19th century when the wall appears to have been heightened. The N wall has three similar windows also formerly in two tiers.

The interior (originally 23ft by 36¼ft, almost identical in size with Quorndon) was enlarged to the N by 10ft, the former line of the back wall being marked by two tall octagonal posts with moulded capitals. There is a gallery at the E end with rooms below having hinged shutters opening to the chapel. A rostrum pulpit remains in the building and a baptistery centrally in the floor.

Inscription: on brick E of former S doorway, 'TB 1781'; on E wall, now internal '1781/1815 B-W'. *Monument*: external (1) Richard Thurman, pastor, 1823, and Sarah his wife, 1802, slate headstone signed Winfield.

Taylor (1818) I, 329; II, 161–2, 239, 349–50: Wood (1847) 184.

(92) WESLEYAN, The Green (SK 603234). Brick and slate with three-bay front in Flemish bond with light coloured headers and some vertical banding; tablet in gable dated 1845. *Former chapel* at rear, of similar materials with gabled front, two segmental-arched gallery windows, one moved, above entrance, and tablet dated 1801.

This county, which stretches from the Cotswolds to the Fens and has ready access to important quarries of freestone and deposits of brick earth, is notable for the high proportion of early meeting-houses which have survived, one in three of those recorded being of the 18th century or before. The strength of dissent in the early 18th century manifested itself not only in the larger Presbyterian and Independent meetings principally centred on the towns, but also in many small congregations of Baptists, few of whose contemporary buildings remain. The earliest Baptist buildings, at Irthlingborough (30), of *c*.1723, Roade (55), of 1736–7, and Burton Latimer (12), of 1744, have all suffered from alteration or enlargement in the 19th century, an unfortunate characteristic of all the chapels in the county. Somewhat later in the 18th century are the Baptist chapels at Walgrave (66), of 1786, and Thrapston (62), of 1787, in which the contemporary use of stone and brickwork may be compared in their unaltered fronts, although they have otherwise been much changed.

Most of the early chapels which survive were built by Congregational churches although the designation Presbyterian was occasionally applied. The earliest of these is at Castle Hill, Northampton (47) where the meeting-house of 1695, notable for the ministry of Dr Philip Doddridge, is still in part distinguishable though in a greatly enlarged building. The meeting-house at Daventry (20), of 1722, is more complete in spite of refitting and minor alterations. Of the later 18th-century chapels, Kilsby (33), of 1763, and Potterspury (54), of 1780, may be especially mentioned while the former Independent chapel in West Street, Wellingborough (73), of 1791, is also of interest in having passed into Methodist use.

Of the two 18th-century Methodist chapels recorded, that at Whittlebury (78) deserves particular attention for its early date, 1763, and its associations with John Wesley. Rather earlier is the former Moravian preaching-house at Eydon (26), in use from 1751, although this was a converted building superseded in 1818. The original Moravian chapel at Woodford Halse (83), of 1798–9, is likewise remarkable in spite of later alterations.

Only two Quaker meeting-houses are listed, both in the vicinity of Wellingborough: the former meeting-house at Finedon (75), of 1690, is the earliest nonconformist building remaining in the county, while that in Wellingborough (74), of 1819, is a good example of its period. The memory of a much different denomination, the Nonjurors, remains at King's Cliffe, the home of William Law, even though the date and purpose of his 'chapel' (34) may be questioned. Other nonconformist worthies whose names are particularly associated with Northamptonshire include the Baptists William Carey, founder of the Baptist Missionary Society, and Andrew Fuller whose rebuilt chapel in Kettering (31) now bears his name, a form of distinction also adopted by Kettering Congregationalists (32) to mark the lengthy ministry of the Tollers, father and son.

Comparatively few chapels remain of interest from the early 19th century, Bugbrooke (11), of 1808, being closer in design to work of the previous century, but the gabled fronts with round-arched windows at Yardley Gobion (86), of 1826, and Charlton (45), of 1827, are typical of this period. Some later chapels, which also merit attention include a minor Gothic work by W.F. Poulton at Oundle (52), of 1864, the extraordinarily grand Classical facade at College Street, Northampton (46), of 1863, and the outstandingly original plan of High Street, Wellingborough (71), of 1875.

ABTHORPE

(1) PRIMITIVE METHODIST (SP 649464). Rebuilt 1925; reset tablet in N wall dated 1839.

ADSTONE

(2) Former WESLEYAN (SP 596516). Stone and slate. Two round-arched windows with cast-iron frames and defaced tablet dated 1849.

BILLING

(3) WESLEYAN, Great Billing (SP 811627). Opened 1836. Brick walls with rounded corners and round-arched windows.

(2) ADSTONE. Former Wesleyan chapel.

BLISWORTH

(4) BAPTIST (SP 726537). Built 1825, much rebuilt and refronted in polychrome brickwork 1871.

BRACKLEY ST PETER

(5) CONGREGATIONAL, Banbury Road, Brackley (SP 582369). Coursed rubble and slate; built in 1836 for a newly formed congregation. The front is of three bays with pilasters of a lighter

coloured stone. In the central gable is a tablet inscribed 'INDEPENDENT CHAPEL 1836'. The interior was partly refitted in the late 19th century but the original pulpit remains in the schoolroom at the rear. There are no public galleries, but above the entrance-lobby is a *singers' gallery* with staircase, seating and precentor's rostrum of *c.*1836. (URC)

　Coleman (1853) 369–70.

(6) Former WESLEYAN, Brackley (SP 585371). Built 1816, superseded 1905. Coursed rubble and hipped slate roof. Gallery around three sides, rounded to rear. (Demolished *c.*1980)

BRAUNSTON

(7) WESLEYAN (SP 540661). Stone with brick dressings; gabled N front dated 1797, rendered 1875, with wide doorway, two tiers of sash windows and circular window in the gable.

　The side walls have each two lower windows and one between at a higher level. The interior ($32\frac{3}{4}$ft by $31\frac{1}{4}$ft) has an early 19th-century gallery around three sides with panelled front supported by timber columns and retaining contemporary box-pews; other seating is of the late 19th century. *Inscription*: on 19th-century stone tablet behind pulpit 'This chapel was erected by John and William Edmunds A.D. 1797 . . .'. *Monuments*: in chapel (1) Rev. William Breedon of Hathorn, Leics., 1837, 31 years a Wesleyan minister; in front of chapel (2) Harriet, wife of William Reeve, 1848, William their son, 1848, and Mary Ann their daughter, 1863.

BRIGSTOCK

(8) CONGREGATIONAL, School Lane (SP 946854). The congregation, which originated in the mid 18th century, was gathered into church order in 1778. Meetings were first held in a small rented building but in 1797 the church 'built a shell, the walls of stone, and covered with slate' followed by an appeal for assistance to finish the inside which was ready for use in 1798. A gallery was built *c.*1804 and in 1819 a large vestry with a school-room above was erected alongside the chapel, with shutters opening to the chapel, 'to accommodate the young and poor'. During the ministry of David Aitken (1876–85), the chapel was enlarged to the front, partly refenestrated and refitted. (URC)

　The chapel has stone walls and a slate roof with half-hip to the rear. The original building ($37\frac{3}{4}$ft by $28\frac{1}{4}$ft externally) has been extended to the SE ($19\frac{1}{2}$ft) and two tall round-arched windows in each side wall are of the date of enlargement, but the blocking of an upper window is distinguishable at the far end of the NE side. The front is gabled and has a window of three lights above the entrance. The vestry and schoolroom wing of 1819 stands against the SW side of the chapel and has a half-hipped roof. In the burial-ground to the SE are a few reset head-stones of the early 19th century and later, including some of slate. *Inscriptions*: on SW wall of chapel, square tablet with moulded cornice, inscribed in a lozenge 'Built 1797'; on SE front of schoolroom, similar tablet 'Built 1819'.

　Coleman (1853) 314–26: *CYB* (1899) 160.

BRINGTON

(9) BAPTIST, Little Brington (SP 662640). Built in the early 19th

BAPTIST CHAPEL, LITTLE BRINGTON

century for a church founded in 1825. The SE front has Flemish bond brickwork with light-coloured headers and cast-iron window frames. A Sunday-school was built alongside in 1887 and the chapel enlarged in 1890.

BRIXWORTH

(10) Former WESLEYAN, Church Street (SP 747711). Brick with some coursed rubble at W end and stone quoins to older walling in front; built 1811 but altered and walls raised in 1860. Three-bay N front, original pedimented doorcase with consoles to central entrance between two heightened round-arched windows; two similar windows in gabled W wall. A stone above the N doorway is dated 1811; a tablet at the apex of the W gable is inscribed 'ENLARGED 1860'.

BUGBROOKE

(11) BAPTIST, High Street (SP 677573). Coursed rubble with ashlar W front and hipped slate roof; dated 1808. A Sunday-school wing of 1885 adjoins to the S and an organ chamber of similar date projects to the east. The interior has an original W gallery only, with panelled front; the seating and pulpit are of the

late 19th century. *Monuments*: in chapel (1) John Atterbury, surgeon, 1846, died at sea; (2) Thomas Turland, 1819, and William Brown, 1820, 'the two first deacons of this church'; (3) John Wheeler, 30 years pastor, 1835, and Jane his wife, 1831; (4) Joseph Adams, 1866, Elizabeth (Oliver) his wife, 1831, and Joseph Oliver Adams, 1823; externally on W wall (5) James Daniel, 1848.

BURTON LATIMER

(12) BAPTIST, Meeting Lane (SP 902749). The chapel, erected in 1744 for a newly-formed congregation, was extended to the rear in 1832 and altered and refitted in 1878, 1889 and later. The walls are of coursed brown ironstone and the roof is covered with stone slates. The gabled S W front originally had two doorways and windows above, all with tripartite lintels. In 1878 the doorways were replaced by a central 'Tudor' style entrance with

square label; in the blocked former doorways were set recessed bootscrapers with double scraper bars; the windows were given stone mullioned and transomed inner frames, and a shield-shaped tablet was placed in the gable recording dates of erection and alteration. The side walls have moulded stone eaves cornices and two tiers of windows, the original building being of two bays with one bay added in 1832; this date appears on a tablet on the SE wall of the extension.

The interior (originally 32ft by $30\frac{1}{4}$ft, enlarged by 14ft) has a late 19th-century boarded ceiling rising above the tie-beams of the roof trusses; there is a gallery around four sides. *Chair*: in vestry, with panelled back and two arms, believed to have belonged to Andrew Fuller, 17th-century.

Burton Latimer Baptist Church Souvenir, 1744–1944 [1944].

CLIPSTON

(13) BAPTIST (SP 709819). Brick and slate, built 1803 to replace a chapel of 1777, but with rendered pedimented front added *c*.1864. Gallery around three sides, original date-tablet of 1803 reset at foot of stairs. *Monuments*: in burial-ground, several early 19th-century slate headstones, some signed Bonsor.

CORBY

(14) Former CONGREGATIONAL, Meeting Lane (SP 896890). Small chapel of rubble with a hipped slate roof, probably dating from the mid 18th century when 'an endowed Sabbath evening lecture was commenced'; soon after 1834 the walls were heightened, a gallery inserted and the interior refitted. A hall was built 50 yards S *c*.1930 with the intention of erecting a new chapel alongside, but the project was abandoned; the former meeting-house is now used by Jehovah's Witnesses. The W front has a blocked entrance near the S end with gallery window over and a doorway and larger window to the left. There is a blocked round-arched window at the N end. The interior ($42\frac{1}{4}$ft by $14\frac{3}{4}$ft) has no old features.

Coleman (1853) 332–4.

CRANFORD

(15) BAPTIST (SP 923769). Rubble with hipped roof; dated 1834.

CREATON

(16) CONGREGATIONAL, High Street (SP 707719). The congregation, originally regarded as Presbyterian, was formed in the late 17th century and a meeting-house seating 400 was erected

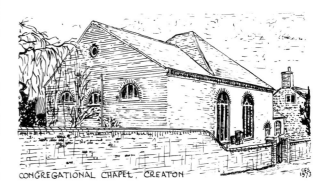

CONGREGATIONAL CHAPEL, CREATON

on a leasehold site *c*.1694. The present building, which superseded the former on the expiry of the lease, *c*.1794, has brick walls in Flemish bond with dark headers and a hipped slate roof. It was enlarged to the W in the early 19th century. The original S front had one tall round-arched window between two doorways, one of which to the W was replaced by a second window when the chapel was enlarged. The N wall has two similar windows in the older part flanking the former site of the pulpit. The gabled W wall of the extension has three upper lunettes and a single window below.

The interior (originally 35ft by 30ft, extended to W by 15ft) has a gallery in the W extension. The pulpit, re-sited on a later rostrum at the E end, is of the early 19th century; other fittings are later. *Monument*: in chapel, Rev. Joseph Whitehead, over 23 years pastor, 1816, 'such was his success as to render it necessary greatly to enlarge this place of worship'.

Coleman (1853) 179–85.

CRICK

(17) CONGREGATIONAL, Chapel Lane (SP 591724). A small chapel built soon after 1763 to replace a private room seems to have preceded the present building. The latter, of brick with a slate roof, has a gabled S front with round-arched doorway, two upper windows with wooden Y-traceried frames, all with round-arched heads, and a small tablet with moulded cornice and the date 1820. (URC)

Coleman (1823) 308–9, 313.

CULWORTH

(18) BAPTIST (SP 543470). Red brick with rendered SE front and hipped slate roof, built *c*.1842 for a church formed in that year; schoolroom wing at side added 1905. Two upper windows at front and later gabled porch. Interior refitted. (Demolished since 1971 and house built on site)

(19) Former MORAVIAN (SP 541471). The simple three-bay chapel of brick and slate with segmental-arched windows and small porch, opened 15 November 1809, has been entirely transmogrified.

England I (1886) 3, 5, pl.3.

DAVENTRY

(20) CONGREGATIONAL, Sheaf Street (SP 572624). The formerly Presbyterian congregation (now URC) which originated in the late 17th century bought a house on the NE side of Sheaf Street in 1722 and built the present meeting-house behind it which was placed in trust in July 1723. The houses, now facing the street, of three stories with brick walls and tiled roofs, were built *c*.1752; they have a three-centred arched opening leading to the rear over which a tablet placed in 1864 is inscribed 'Independent Chapel Erected A.D. 1722'. One house served as a residence for the minister, the other was used from 1752–89 by the dissenting academy formerly held in Northampton to which it subsequently returned; a tablet in the front wall records that Dr Joseph Priestley was a student here 1752–5.

The chapel has rubble walls and a hipped tiled roof originally with a central valley but altered since 1959, resulting in a raised

Exterior before late 19th-century alterations.

ridge at the front. The SW front wall, of six bays with two tiers of windows with renewed frames, was rendered in the late 19th century and the two doorways previously in the penultimate bays were re-sited in the adjacent centre bays. The rear wall, mostly covered by later buildings, had two windows flanking the pulpit, now blocked but with the timber lintels still in position, and upper windows at the ends of the galleries. The side walls are each of three bays with two tiers of windows.

The interior (41¼ft square) has two timber posts, supporting a valley-beam parallel to the front, of circular section with octagonal bases and small moulded capitals. The gallery around three sides was largely reconstructed in the late 19th century when a major refitting took place; a seating plan of 1775 indicates a single gallery at the SW end, side galleries being added *c*.1820.

Fittings – Clock: on front of SW gallery, octagonal face, early 18th-century. *Pulpit*: hexagonal with fielded panelled sides and staircase with twisted balusters, 18th-century, altered. *Rainwater-head*: centrally on front wall, lead, with monogram *GR* and date 1722.

Coleman (1853) 186–209: [Thornton, A.], *1672–1972. Daventry Congregational Church, Sheaf Street, Daventry* [1972].

(21) WESLEYAN, New Street (SP 575624). Stone with rendered three-bay front, rusticated surround to central entrance between thin pilasters, platband between terminal pilasters, round-arched upper windows and pedimental gable with altered tablet dated 1824.

DESBOROUGH

(22) Former BAPTIST (SP 801835). Built *c*.1848, extended to front 1855.

EARL BARTON

(23) BAPTIST (SP 851637) Earls Barton. Gothic with gabled front, 1874 by Edward Sharman, replacing a brick meeting-house of *c*.1795. Mid 19th-century Sunday-school adjacent. *Chair*: in pulpit, with carved square-panelled back and arms supported by enriched columns, reputed to have belonged to William Carey, *c*.1700.

Exterior before 1959 alterations.

Interior from E.
(20) DAVENTRY. Congregational chapel, Sheaf Street. (URC)

ECTON

(24) BAPTIST (SP 827635). Built *c*.1829, closed 1980. Three-bay rendered front with round-arched windows and later porch. Two round-arched windows flank pulpit, one altered to doorway in 1867 when schoolroom added behind. Refitted late 19th century.

EYDON

(25) Former FRIENDS (SP 54155030). Built *c*.1701 for a meeting which in 1691 registered the house of Thomas Smallbone. It was closed in 1868 but survived as a workshop until *c*.1960; it has since been demolished.

(26) MORAVIAN (SP 542503). Preaching began in the 1740s, and about 1751 a house was purchased for use as a meeting-house. This was superseded by the present chapel which was opened 30 September 1818. The former meeting-house, at the middle of a range of buildings at one side of the courtyard in front of the chapel, is a 17th-century building, of rubble, originally of one storey and attics with a thatched roof, but since altered; the entrance was to the right of the present glazed porch beyond which was a tall window inserted when the house was converted for religious use.

The chapel, of red brick with a hipped slate roof formerly surmounted by a wooden bell-turret and weather vane bearing the Moravian emblem, was refitted in the late 19th century. The

front wall of three bays with tall round-arched windows has above the entrance a gabled bell-cote with one bell, replacing that previously on the roof. There are two segmental-arched windows in the rear wall.

Fittings – *Chandelier*: brass, 12-branch, late 18th-century. *Clock*: loose in vestry, by J. Parker, Pudsey, 19th-century.

England I (1886) pl.4.

FLORE

(27) CONGREGATIONAL, Chapel Lane (SP 646600). The present chapel, erected in 1880, stands close by its predecessor, now the

Former CONGREGATIONAL CHAPEL, FLORE 1970

Sunday-school, built in 1810 as a preaching station for Weedon Bec with which the congregation at Flore had been associated since the late 17th century. The former chapel, of brick and slate, has a gabled W front with round-arched doorway, fanlight and semicircular canopy; two lunettes light the back of the gallery. The side and rear walls have each two tall round-arched windows. (URC)

Monuments: externally against W wall (1) Richard Clark Smith, 1822, and Mary Smith, 1843, slate headstone; (2) George Smith, 1834; other headstones of the early 19th-century stand in the burial-ground to S and west.

Coleman (1853) 266–7.

HIGHAM FERRERS

(28) WESLEYAN, High Street (SP 959683). Red brick with stone dressings, double-gabled front with elaborate pinnacles. Opened 1903.

HOLCOT

(29) WESLEYAN (SP 792698). Brick and slate, opened 1815. Two former entrances in side wall alternate with segmental-arched windows; present entrance in gable end.

IRTHLINGBOROUGH

(30) BAPTIST, Meeting Lane (SP 949708). The meeting-house was built in 1713 for a society which was reorganized as a Strict Baptist church in 1770. Galleries were added to the building in 1794. Further rooms were built at one end, the front windows were altered and the interior refitted *c*.1884 and other rooms

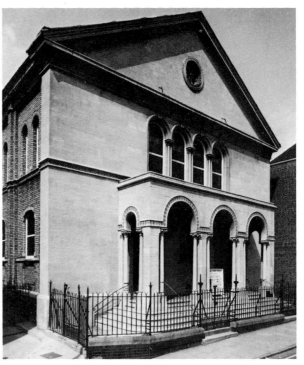

(31) KETTERING. Baptist chapel.

were added at the back in 1930 and 1941. The wide front has two doorways alternating with three windows, all with late 19th-century stone lintels, and three upper windows with altered round-arched heads. The rear wall has two tall round-arched pulpit windows and smaller windows at the gallery ends. The interior (28½ft by 37½ft) has a gallery around three sides; the pulpit was replaced by a rostrum *c*.1884.

Monuments: in chapel (1) Thomas Allen, pastor over 16 years, 1831, 'his mortal remains are deposited in the vestry'; (2) John Trimming, pastor 30 years, 1862.

Chambers (1963) 91–2.

KETTERING

(31) BAPTIST, Gold Street (SP 868789). The Baptist congregation originated in 1696 when some members separated from the Great Meeting; it is especially notable for the pastorate of Andrew Fuller (1783–1815) after whom the present chapel is named. The first meeting-house in Bayley's Yard was superseded about 1729 by the use of one in Goosepasture Lane (Meadow Road), built *c*.1715 for another group of Great Meeting seceders, and in 1768 by the conversion of a warehouse on the present site. The chapel was built in 1860–1 to designs by Edward Sherman of Wellingborough.

Barrett, G., *A Brief History of Fuller Church, Kettering* (1946): Chambers (1963) 88: Ivimey II (1814) 514; IV (1830) 526–34.

(32) CONGREGATIONAL, Gold Street (SP 867787). The Great Meeting was gathered in the late 17th century by John Maidwell, ejected rector of Kettering, who in 1672 took out a licence as a Congregational preacher at his own house. Meetings formerly held in a building in Allen's Yard were transferred to the present newly-erected meeting-house on Bakehouse Hill or

Newland in 1723 and the building was registered April 1724. The church experienced two notable ministries: of Thomas Northcote Toller (1777–1821), and his son Thomas Toller (1821–75), in honour of which the chapel was renamed. The meeting-house suffered from structural faults which occasioned repairs in 1728, 1741 and 1772. A major alteration and refitting was undertaken in 1849, the present front was added *c*.1875, and a further drastic refitting occurred in 1898–9, all of which has left little of the original structure intact.

The chapel (originally 55½ft by 48ft externally) has brown ironstone walls and a hipped slate roof; the later front is of red brick. The original side wall facing Meeting Lane, much altered but probably formerly of four bays, has two tiers of windows. The interior originally had two pillars to support the roof, replaced by four in 1741 and superseded by iron pillars in 1898–9. Among the fittings removed in 1849 was a 24-branch chandelier with dove and olive branch. A few *monuments* remain in the burial-ground at the rear, including: John Munn, 1763, slate headstone, signed G. Dawkins, Rowell. (URC)

Coleman (1853) 80–116: Goodman, F.C., *The Great Meeting* (1962).

KILSBY

(33) CONGREGATIONAL, Chapel Street (SP 562709). A dissenting congregation may have been in existence here from the late 17th century, encouraged by ejected ministers from Kilsby and Crick. In 1738 a house was fitted up for meetings and galleries added to it in 1750 and 1755. This was superseded in 1763 by the present building which has walls of squared stone and a tiled

CONGREGATIONAL CHAPEL, KILSBY

roof. The front has two doorways, windows with timber lintels and a tripartite lunette in the gable. The side walls have each two upper and two lower windows towards the back and in the rear wall are two windows, now blocked, flanking the pulpit. The interior (34ft square) has a single gallery opposite the pulpit with panelled front divided by narrow pilasters and supported by three oak columns with moulded capitals and high attic bases.

Fittings – *Monuments*: in chapel (1) Rev. Thomas Strange, 1784, pastor 1751–84, plain marble tablet inscribed ' . . . this House erected & this Congregation greatly improved, by the blessing of God on his wise & unwearied labours, are a much nobler Monument that any which the Sculptor's art could form.'; in front of chapel (2) John son of Abraham and Sarah Lee, 1837, brick table-tomb; (3) Samuel Bartlett, 1846; (4) Rev. Horatio Ault, 20 years pastor of the United churches at Repton and Barrow on Trent, Derbys., and 14 years of this church, 1871; (5) Peter, fourth son of Rev. Horatio Ault, 1862. *Pulpit*: desk remade lower but incorporating original pulpit front; narrow backboard with inlaid sunburst and octagonal canopy with moulded cornice and ogee top surmounted by acorn finial, *c*.1763. (URC)

Coleman (1853) 304–13.

KING'S CLIFFE

(34) DR LAW'S CHAPEL (TL 007971). A building of two stories with stone walls and hipped stone slated roof, 50 yards N of Hall Farm, home of the notable non-juror Dr William Law (1686–1761), is known as 'Dr Law's Chapel' although its use as a meeting-house for a non-juring congregation is open to question. The SW wall and parts of one side wall facing the house are of ashlar; the front, of three bays with pedimented centre and round-arched entrance between similarly arched windows, has a platband and a moulded cornice of late 18th-century character. The NW wall facing the road is of rubble with altered domestic windows. The plan is irregular but the principal S corner is square. A line of glass-houses contemporary with the ashlar walling formerly adjoined on the SE side. The memory of Dr Law is also preserved at 'Library House' (TL 011970) which carries the inscription 'Books of Piety are here lent to any Persons of this or the Neighbouring Towns'.

(35) WESLEYAN, Bridge Street (TL 007971). Coursed rubble with ashlar dressings and hipped stone slated roof. Narrow three-bay front with tablet dated 1823.

KING'S SUTTON

(36) BAPTIST (SP 497363). Rebuilt *c*.1863. Stone reset in front wall inscribed 'WT 1732/WK 1733'.

KISLINGBURY

(37) BAPTIST, Mill Road (SP 695594). Squared rubble and slate; gabled front with chamfered plinth, central entrance with flat canopy between two tiers of flat-arched sash windows, and tablet in gable with moulded cornice and date 1828. Gallery at front end only. Refitted 1875.

LONG BUCKBY

(38) BAPTIST, Market Place (SP 628675). Three-bay front of squared stone, dated 1846; large gable, two tiers of round-arched windows and two doorways all with semicircular moulded labels.

(39) CONGREGATIONAL, Brington Road (SP 629674). The chapel was built in 1771 for a congregation known to have been in existence by 1709 and to have previously occupied a small meeting-house near the present site. It was enlarged to the rear in

1819, altered internally in 1859 and the fittings further modified in 1899 and 1951. The walls are of squared stone and the roof is covered with slates. The N front, of three bays surmounted by a large lunette, has a tablet inscribed 'THIS CHAPEL ERECTED 1771 R D' (for Richard Denny, pastor 1763–95). The side walls, originally of three bays with one bay added, have two tiers of windows similar to those in the front wall. The rear wall is gabled with a moulded string-course at eaves level, two widely spaced pointed-arched windows with keystones, blocked segmental-arched recesses beneath and, in the gable, a round-arched access door to the roof space below a tablet inscribed 'ENLARGED 1819'.

The interior (originally 36ft by 34¼ft, extended 14ft to S) has a gallery around three sides and a pulpit of 1859 at the S end. The 1819 enlargement provided a further S gallery behind the former site of the pulpit which was removed in 1859 but the two substantial wooden columns which supported it at each end remain below the side galleries. *Monuments* in burial ground to S include several 19th-century slate head-stones; Coleman notes a head-stone to Rev. Thomas Cartwright, 1744. (URC)

Coleman (1853) 268–74: Ivory, L.S., *Long Buckby Congregational Church, 1707–1957* (1957).

MIDDLETON CHENEY

(40) BAPTIST (SP 498418). The chapel, built in 1806 for a Particular Baptist church formed in 1740, replacing a meeting-house of 1753 in Brewhouse Lane, is a large building of coursed

ironstone rubble with a slate roof. The S front has a central door-way which replaces a pair of entrances now altered to windows; in the gable is a small tablet inscribed within a lozenge 'L 1806 May 2'. Interior refitted 1875. *Monument*: in burial-ground, to Catharine Price, 1848, and Joseph Price, 9 years minister (date obscured by concrete resetting).

MILTON MALSOR

(41) BAPTIST (SP 734555). Wide three-bay front with central doorway and small upper windows; tablet below centre window dated 1827. Front gallery added *c*.1871 and reseated 1876 but still with box-pews; rebuilt pulpit incorporates original material.

MOULTON

(42) WESLEYAN (SP 783662). Tall gabled front dated 1835; windows with intersecting wooden tracery and marginal bars. Contemporary two-storied cottages flank the chapel (one demolished since 1967).

NASEBY

(43) WESLEYAN (SP 688779). Built 1825, entirely altered 1871, Sunday-school added alongside 1903.

NETHER HEYFORD

(44) BAPTIST (SP 659584). Built *c*.1826; two segmental-arched windows in front wall with former entrance off-centre between.

NEWBOTTLE

(45) CONGREGATIONAL, Charlton (SP 527359). Dated 1827. Gabled E front of three bays with platband between two tiers of round-arched windows. (URC)

NORTHAMPTON

(46) BAPTIST, College Street (SP 753605). The church formed in 1697 erected the first meeting-house on this site in 1714; this had stone walls and two tiers of windows in three bays with two intermediate doorways, it was twice enlarged during the notable pastorate of John Collet Ryland (1759–85). The present building designed by William Hull, erected in 1863, has walls of rubble with an ashlar front. The facade, which is wider than and architecturally unrelated to the chapel behind, is an elaborate Classical composition with rusticated lower storey and a raised pedimented portico with six Corinthian columns, paired at the ends, and flanking bays with terminal pilasters. *Monuments*: re-set gravestones in paving at front and side include one to Hannah Dadford, 1787, Thomas Dadford, 1837, and Sarah Dadford.

Ivimey IV (1830) 609–10: Payne, E.A., *College Street Chapel, Northampton, 1697–1947* (1947).

Front from SW.

Interior from SE.
(47) NORTHAMPTON. Castle Hill Meeting-house. (URC)

(47) CASTLE HILL MEETING-HOUSE (SP 750606). The church meeting in Quart Pot Lane or Doddridge Street was formed in the late 17th century and initially included both Presbyterian and Independent elements, although latterly Congregational (now URC); it is notable for the ministry of Dr Philip Doddridge (pastor 1730–51) who also maintained an important dissenting academy in the town. The original meeting-house, of 1695, much altered and enlarged to the N in 1862, forms the basis of the present building which has walls of coursed ironstone rubble and a hipped slated roof. The S front of three bays is partly covered by a large vestibule built in front in 1890 but three upper windows remain with altered lintels; the lower part formerly had two doorways and two windows between. The side walls, originally of three bays with two tiers of windows, have been extended by two bays to the north. A low gabled vestry of c.1695 projects on the W side.

Interior of original vestry.

The interior (originally 39¼ft by 52½ft, now greatly enlarged and refitted) has side and rear galleries of 1852, extended 1862, and contemporary box-pews. Prior to 1852, when the chapel was reroofed, the roof was supported by two massive wooden pillars 'one a little bandy', and the fittings included a 'clumsy white pulpit' at the N side approached by ten steps, and 'a mighty brass branched candlestick' on a chain. The W vestry is unaltered; it has a corner fireplace and wall benches and contains a small number of historical items including the former gallery *clock* with circular face and kidney-shaped pendulum case, of the early 18th century. *Monument*: in chapel, to Philip Doddridge D.D., 1751, 21 years pastor, oval tablet with elaborate rococo surround incorporating shield-of-arms, by John Hunt and Gilbert West. *Pulpit*: now in Congregational chapel, Middleton, Wirksworth, Derbyshire (146). *Sundial*: on S wall, dated 1695.

Arnold, T. & Cooper, J.J., *The History of the Church of Doddridge* (1895): Coleman (1853) 9–37: Deacon, M., *Philip Doddridge of Northampton* (1980): Godfrey, B.S., *Castle Hill Meeting*, (1947).

(48) Former CONGREGATIONAL, King Street (SP 752606). Seceders from Castle Hill meeting who left in 1775 after a disputed ministerial appointment built a chapel in King's Head Lane in 1777; the building was considerably enlarged in 1858 and greatly extended to the W and altered in 1880; the church removed to Abingdon Avenue in 1901 and the former chapel was further altered by a variety of users. The surviving parts of the original structure, at the E end and the E half of the S wall, are of stone, with two widely spaced pointed-arched windows in the E wall and a platband above. The interior (originally about 34ft by 20ft) latterly had the pulpit at the E end. Coleman records monuments to Rev. William Hextal, 1777, and Benjamin Lloyd Edwards, 1831, 45 years pastor. (Demolished 1967)

Coleman (1853) 37–42.

(49) BAPTIST, High Street, Kingsthorpe (SP 751633). Walls of squared ironstone and slated roof. Gabled front dated 1835 with wide porch added 1892 replacing two doorways with window between; two round-arched windows above former entrances and lunette ventilator in gable. Side walls of two bays extended to rear. *Monuments*: (1) Joseph Campion, 1850, 23 years deacon, and Charlotte his widow, 1868; (2) Rev. Joseph Roberts, 1847. (Demolition proposed c.1976)

(50) CONGREGATIONAL, Kingsthorpe Road (SP 753619). Built 1901–3, by Alexander Anderson of Northampton. Square rising

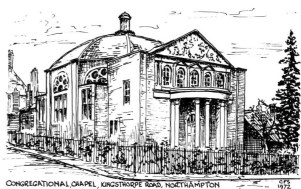

CONGREGATIONAL CHAPEL, KINGSTHORPE ROAD, NORTHAMPTON   CFS 1972

to octagon with low polygonal dome; front pediment carved in low relief.

CYB (1903) 158–9.

NORTON

(51) WESLEYAN (SP 601638). Rubble and slate, opened 1817, possibly the conversion of an existing cottage; further altered in mid 19th century.

OUNDLE

(52) CONGREGATIONAL, West Street (TL 039881). Rubble and slate, gabled front divided into three bays by buttresses rising to plain pinnacles, two gabled porches and tall pointed-arched window of four lights with cusped tracery. Built 1864, by W.F. Poulton of Reading, superseding a meeting-house of c.1724.

Coleman (1853) 250–61: *CYB* (1865) 297; (1872) 410.

(53) ZION CHAPEL, West Street (TL 038881). Built in 1852 for a Particular Baptist church formed in 1800, but was latterly in Roman Catholic use. (Disused 1979)

POTTERSPURY

(54) CONGREGATIONAL (SP 762434). The church (now URC) originated in the late 17th century. The chapel was built in 1780. A house for the minister was built alongside it in the same year and in 1846 Sunday-school rooms were added at the W end. The chapel has walls of brick in Flemish bond with blue headers at the front, rubble at the back and a tiled roof. The S front, which has a brick platband between two tiers of segmental-arched windows, originally had two entrances with two windows between and three above; one of the latter is dated 1780. The N wall has two round-arched windows flanking the site of the pulpit. The W extension of two stories and attics, in a similar style to the

Exterior from SW.

chapel, is dated 1846 on the keystone of the upper window in the S wall. The gabled W end has two bays of windows with lunettes to the attics.

Congregational Chapel, POTTERSPURY
Northamptonshire

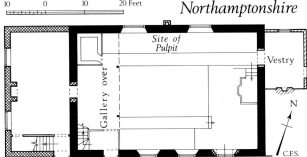

The interior of the chapel ($29\frac{1}{4}$ft by 46ft) was refitted in the mid 19th century and the pulpit re-sited at the E end. The W gallery is also of the later 19th century. Fittings – *Bootscrapers*: in wall recesses, pair, with cast-iron fronts and figures of storks and bridge, mid 19th-century. *Chair*: in pulpit, oak with panelled back carved in low relief, arms with turned supports, 17th-century. *Monument*: in chapel, to Rev. Isaac Gardner, 1821, 16 years pastor. *Organ*: front with seven bays of false pipes and Gothic ornament, mid-19th century. *Pulpit*: incorporates the late 18th-century pulpit front with fluted angle panels, moulded dentil cornice and shaped back-board.

Coleman (1853) 275–90.

ROADE

(55) BAPTIST, High Street (SP 759517). The chapel was built in 1736-7 for a church formed *c.*1688; some alterations were made in the late 18th century and in 1802 a major reconstruction seems to have taken place including heightening, re-roofing and renewal of the window heads. The walls are of coursed rubble with ashlar quoins and the roof is slated. The broad N front has two doorways with a sash window between and two 19th-century windows above. Two tall sash windows in the S wall flank the pulpit, with two lower windows at either side. A two-storied vestry and schoolroom wing of the early 19th century adjoins to the west.

The interior ($36\frac{1}{4}$ft by $44\frac{1}{4}$ft) has a N gallery only. The pulpit and seating date from the late 19th century. Fittings – *Baptistery*: in front of pulpit with steps at E and W ends, formerly filled by rainwater from pipe behind pulpit. *Clock*: with external face on front wall, late 19th-century. *Communion Table*: oak, with turned legs and moulded upper rails, early 18th-century. *Monuments*: in chapel (1) Mary widow of Samuel Deacon, 1796; (2) Samuel Deacon, 1779, pastor over 38 years, and Mary his daughter, 1773; (3) Rev. William Heighton, 1827, pastor nearly 40 years; (4) Rev. George Jayne, 1848, 20 years pastor.

Payne, E.A., *Roade Baptist Church, 1688–1938* (1938).

ROTHWELL

(56) CONGREGATIONAL (SP 814809) The church (now URC) was formed in 1655 and a covenant was signed by the members

in that year. The present chapel opened 9 November 1735 has been much altered and refitted, a vestry was added in 1762, in 1826 schoolrooms were built between the front entrances and in 1852 porches with gallery staircases were added, enlargements made to the rear and the roof replaced. Further works of alteration and embellishment were carried out in 1893. The walls are of coursed ironstone rubble and the roof, hipped over the original building, is covered with slates. The side walls to N and S have each three round-arched windows with keystones and three square windows above. The E front is entirely covered by the 19th-century additions which have round-arched outer doorways and paired round-arched upper windows, all of 1852; the elaborate cornice and parapet date from 1893.

The interior (40ft by 52ft) entirely refitted *c*.1852, has a gallery around three sides and box-pews. Prior to 1893, the projection behind the pulpit at the W end was filled with steeply raked choir seating and had a small organ against the E wall.

Congregational Chapel , ROTHWELL
Northamptonshire

10 Feet   0   10   20   30

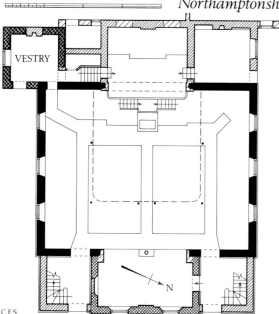

VESTRY

C.F.S.

Inscriptions: on stone reset in N wall, date 1676; on W wall of vestry, 1762; above E front 'Restored 1893/Enlarged 1852'; reset in S wall of former stables N of chapel 'Infant School 1830'. *Panelling*: in vestry, bolection-moulded panel with inlaid decoration, incorporated in front of cupboard, perhaps from early 18th-century pulpit.

Coleman (1853) 46–79: Glass, N., *The Early History of the Independent Church at Rothwell alias Rowell in Northamptonshire* (1871): Tibbutt (1972) 61–2.

RUSHDEN

(57) Former BAPTIST, Little Street (SP 960663). The Baptist congregation in Rushden, originally part of the church meeting at Stevington, Beds., became autonomous by 1723. The meeting-house was described in 1768 as a converted tenement and seems to have stood on the present site behind other buildings. The existing structure is a rebuilding of 1796 with rubble walls and a steeply pitched hipped and tiled roof; a schoolroom and vestries were added at the back in 1860 and in 1873–4 the chapel was enlarged to the S in yellow brick with a slate roof gabled to the front. In 1901 a new chapel was opened in Park Road and the Little Street building converted for use by the Sunday-school.

E side of chapel showing N and S extensions.

The side walls have two tiers of irregularly spaced windows. The S front before enlargement had two tall doorways incorporating windows, with a window between and one above, all with flat-arched heads with keystones; between the two windows was a tablet dated 1796 now reset in the E wall. The interior (about 42ft by 32ft) had galleries around three sides and round-arched windows each side of the pulpit.

Monuments: in burial-ground to N, headstones reset around boundary walls, (1) Rev. William Knowles, 1794, 42 years pastor, slate; (2) Rev. Joseph Belsher, 1797.

Bayes, G.E., *These Years Have Told: The Story of Park Road Baptist Church, Rushden* (1951).

SHUTLANGER

(58) WESLEYAN, Twitch Hill (SP 726499). Opened 1843, altered.

SILVERSTONE

(59) WESLEYAN, High Street (SP 669439). Rubble and slate, built 1811 and extended to front *c*.1840. The earlier work had a broad front, gabled sides and two large segmental-arched windows in the back wall. The present front has a wide gable with a

gabled porch, two tall windows with four-centred arched heads and a shorter one above the entrance; the original date-stone of 1811 is reset in the front wall. The interior, re-pewed in the late 19th century, has a gallery of *c*.1840 at the front. *Monument*: in chapel, to George Newman Robinson, 1859.

SLAPTON

(60) WESLEYAN, Chapel Lane (SP 640468). Rubble with red brick front and slate roof. Two pointed-arched windows in front wall and tablet between dated 1844; entrance in low wing against gabled end wall, the original doorway now internal has a segmental-arched head. Gallery next to entrance *c*.1844 with coved and panelled front and contemporary open-backed benches.

SULGRAVE

(61) BAPTIST, Little Street (SP 559454). Rubble with hipped

slate roof. N front with tall sash windows and central doorway, all with tripartite lintels. Tablet over entrance dated 1844. (Becoming derelict 1971)

THRAPSTON

(62) BAPTIST, Huntingdon Road (SP 999786). The chapel, which stands back on the N side of the street, has a brick front

and rubble sides. The low roof is concealed by a rebuilt parapet. The original building of 1787 (34ft by 36¼ft externally) was extended to the N in the early 19th century. The S front is of four principal bays with a fifth bay to the W covering a side-passage. A stone tablet in the parapet is inscribed 'This place of worship/was built by public Subscription/A.D. 1787/For the Promulgation of the/Gospel of/JESUS CHRIST'.

The interior, altered in 1884–5 and later, has a gallery around three sides, box-pews, and several *wall monuments* including: (1) Robert Bateman, 1852, 'the last survivor of the little band who in 1787 united in forming the Church meeting in this place . . .'; (2) Rev. Reynold Hogg, 1843, first pastor and first treasurer of the Baptist Missionary Society; (3) Mary, widow of Thomas Ekins, 1794. In the burial-ground to the N are several slate headstones.

TOWCESTER

(63) BAPTIST, Watling Street (SP 695485). Red brick with yellow brick dressings; pedimented front with three tall arched bays enclosing two tiers of windows and central doorway. Dated 1877.

(64) CONGREGATIONAL, Meeting Yard (SP 693486). Independents formerly meeting jointly with Baptists were obliged, after 1782, to provide a separate meeting-house. The present 'Independent Chapel' built in 1845 has walls of rubble and a slate roof. The two-bay front has a brick pediment and two pedimented doorways below windows. The front and side windows are set in wide round-arched recesses with brick infilling.

Coleman (1853) 357–60.

(65) WESLEYAN, Caldecote (SP 687510). Small chapel dated 1846; of pink brick with pointed-arched windows.

WALGRAVE

(66) BAPTIST (SP 802721). The church which originated *c*.1700 was meeting by 1763 in a converted barn. The present site was acquired in 1786 and the meeting-house erected in that year. The

chapel has rubble walls and a hipped slate roof. The S front has two entrances with a three-light transomed window between and three windows above; a square stone tablet with moulded cornice is dated 1786. The N wall has two round-arched windows flanking the pulpit; a similar window in the W wall replaces the earlier fenestration. A Sunday-school of 1899 adjoins to the east.

The interior (30ft by 36½ft), drastically refitted in 1886, has a S gallery; E and W galleries have been removed.

Monuments: in chapel (1) Rev. Alexander Payne, 1819, nearly 33 years pastor, and Mary his wife, 1814, white marble oval tablet; in yard S of chapel (2) William, son of Anthony and Elizabeth Barker, 1810; (3) Elizabeth wife of Anthony Barker, 1795.

(67) STRICT BAPTIST, Zion Lane (SP 803722). Tiny, brick and slate, with two round-arched windows. Dated 1853.

Chambers (1963) 85–6.

WEEDON BEC

(68) CONGREGATIONAL, Church Street (SP 631592). The church (now URC) originated in the late 17th century and by 1688 comprised a joint congregation at Flore and Weedon Bec. The former was described *c*.1715 as Independent, but the latter was regarded as Presbyterian in 1767, in which year John Wesley, when refused the use of the Parish Church, 'accepted the offer of the Presbyterian Meeting-house'.

The present chapel, built in 1792 and registered in the following year, has rubble walls with an ashlar front and a hipped slate roof with moulded eaves cornice. The E front, which has segmental-arched doorways with altered fanlights and high pedimented canopies, is dated 1792. The side walls of two bays have two tiers of segmental-arched windows. The rear wall has two

widely-spaced semicircular-arched windows and a low brick vestry or schoolroom of 1847 projecting to the north.

The interior (42ft by 30ft) has galleries around three sides, the E gallery being the earliest and the side galleries added in the early 19th century. The windows in the N and S walls have their original wooden frames with moulded centre mullions and rectangular leaded glazing.

Fittings – *Clock*: on front of E gallery, early 19th-century. *Monuments*: in chapel (1) Elizabeth, wife of Rev. James Pinkerton, 1824, signed Whiting, North-ton; (2) Rev. Joseph Gronow, 1817, over 21 years pastor, Mary Catharine his wife, 1816, and their children Joseph Whitehead Gronow, 1810, and William Hodgkinson Gronow, 1818, signed 'Whiting Sculp. North-ton'; (3) John Spencer, 1808, oval tablet; in front burial-ground, two slate headstones (4) James Barge, 1822, and Ann his wife, 1821; (5) Richard Smith, 1807, and Sarah his wife, 1804; also other early 19th-century monuments (monuments in rear burial-ground have been removed or re-sited). *Pulpit*: square with fielded panels, with original pedimented back-board, all reduced in height. *Seating*: in gallery, early 19th-century; box-pews of *c*.1850 below.

Coleman (1853) 262–7.

WELDON

(69) CONGREGATIONAL, Chapel Road (SP 924897). Meetings held from 1706 in the house of Edward Nutt were transferred

CONGREGATIONAL CHAPEL, WELDON

c.1736–8 to a small barn on the present site, which had been converted to a meeting-house. This was replaced in 1792 by the existing chapel which was enlarged in 1808 by the addition of a gallery.

The walls are of coursed and squared limestone and the roof which is gabled to N and S is covered with stone slates. The W front has a wide round-arched window with keystone between two doorways, that to the S now blocked. There is a single upper window in the E wall and two round-arched windows at the S end. The N wall, partly covered by a lower Sunday-school wing, has a stone chimney stack at the apex of the gable.

The interior (33¼ft by 20¼ft) has a plaster ceiling with coved sides. The single N gallery has a fielded panelled front and a wide-boarded floor; one original seat with shaped end remains next to the staircase. The pulpit and lower pews were renewed in the late 19th century.

Fittings – *Benefaction Board*: brass tablet recording the endowment in 1841 by Thomas Lash of Kettering, of a charity for distribution to the poor of Great and Little Weldon, irrespective of denomination, of 'good wheaten bread' and 'good wholesome meat' in the first weeks of November and March respectively. *Monuments*: in chapel (1) Rev. John Philip, 1837; in burial-ground (2) Rev. John Philip, 1837, Frances his widow, 1843, and Mercy their daughter 1857, table-tomb in railed enclosure; (3–5) group of three graves S of chapel, to children, including Ogden Coward, 1850, with uniform headstones, and short flat capstones covered by iron grilles.

Coleman (1853) 327–32.

WELFORD

(70) CONGREGATIONAL (SP 640803). The first permanent meeting-house for this congregation seems to have been built in 1700 on ground given by the Paynes of Sulby Hall. This was superseded in 1793 by the present chapel on a new site. The walls are

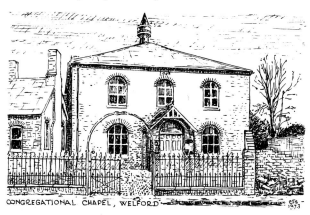

CONGREGATIONAL CHAPEL, WELFORD

of red brick and the roof is hipped and slate-covered. The NW front has a central porch replacing two doorways in the side bays; a tablet below the eaves is dated 1793. The side walls are each of two bays. Two large pointed-arched windows in the rear wall flank the pulpit. The interior (42ft by 37ft) was entirely refitted *c*.1891 and has a NW gallery of this period. *Monument*: in chapel, to Rev. Benjamin Hobson, 1848, minister 35 years.

Coleman (1853) 155–78.

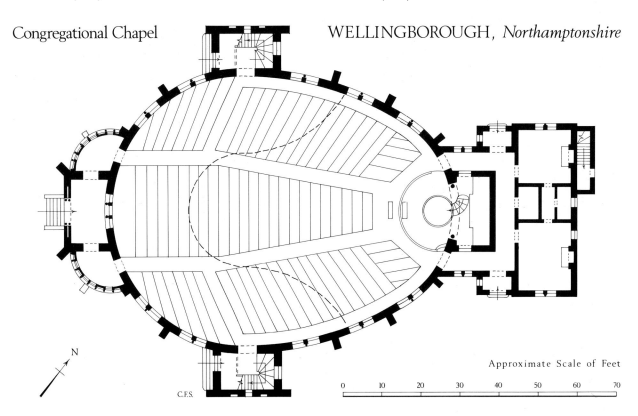

Congregational Chapel

WELLINGBOROUGH, *Northamptonshire*

N

C.F.S.

Approximate Scale of Feet

0   10   20   30   40   50   60   70

WELLINGBOROUGH

(71) CONGREGATIONAL, High Street (SP 890680). The church (now URC) originated in the late 17th century, following the ejection of the vicar, Thomas Andrews, in 1662. It was originally regarded as Presbyterian. The first meeting-house in

Silver Street was superseded in 1746 by a building in Cheese Lane. The present chapel was built in 1875 following the re-union in 1873 of the Cheese Lane church and that meeting at Salem Chapel (72) which had seceded from the main body in 1811.

The chapel, of coursed rubbled with a slate roof, is a notable

and unusual building designed initially by Caleb Archer, but completed under the direction of Edward Sharman of Wellingborough. The plan is ovoid with the pulpit at the narrower end and the principal entrance opposite in a gabled projection; further gabled wings at the sides accommodate the gallery staircases. The details are generally Gothic, with two tiers of windows at the sides and a window of three lights with cusped tracery above the main entrance.

Coleman (1853) 210–26: *CYB* (1876) 448–9: Drew, E.M., *Then and Now, a Brief History of the United Congregational Church, Wellingborough* (1925).

(72) Former CONGREGATIONAL, Salem Lane (SP 890681). 'Salem Chapel' was built in 1812 by seceders from Cheese Lane chapel, who objected to the introduction of an organ. After the reunion of the congregations, the chapel was converted for Sunday-school use. Brick walls and hipped slate roof; much altered and refenestrated in 1875, with paired round-arched windows to the upper floor.

Coleman (1853), 246–9: Drew, *op. cit., passim*.

(73) Former CONGREGATIONAL, West Street (SP 889678). An Independent congregation formed in the late 17th century and initially part of the Rothwell church became autonomous in 1691, in which year a meeting-house was opened in Crown Yard. This was replaced in 1734 by a meeting-house in West Street which was rebuilt in its present form in 1791. The church was disbanded in 1868 and the chapel was conveyed to the Primitive Methodists. It is still in Methodist use.

The meeting-house is a large brick structure with ironstone plinth and a hipped roof. The wide W front, of four bays with end entrances, has a tablet dated 1791 between the upper windows. The N wall of three bays has a similar tablet dated 1734 reset from the original building. The E wall has two round-arched windows flanking the site of the pulpit.

The interior ($40\frac{1}{2}$ft by $49\frac{1}{4}$ft) has been much altered. It formerly had a gallery around three sides, only the N gallery remains. Traces of the back-board and sounding-board of the pulpit are visible in the plaster of the E wall. A late 18th-century vestry at the S end has been enlarged.

Coleman (1853) 226–46: Drew, *op. cit., passim*.

(74) FRIENDS, St John Street (SP 889682). The meeting-house, built in 1819, has walls of squared ironstone and a hipped slated

roof. The N front has a small pedimented porch and square date-stone with moulded cornice. The interior is divided into two rooms by an entrance-passage between screens, the larger E room has a dado of reeded panelling, wall benches with shaped ends and a stand against the end wall. A stand in the W room has been removed. *Table*: in E room, dated 1667.

(75) Former FRIENDS, Church Street, Finedon (SP 919721). The meeting-house was built in 1690 on a piece of land, part of Townsend Close, which was acquired in that year. The building was much altered in the early 19th century; it was closed in 1912 and is now used as a funeral parlour. The walls are of coursed ironstone rubble and the roof, which is gabled to E and W, is slate covered. The wide S front of three bays with two segmental-arched windows and central entrance has traces of a former doorway below the W window. The N and S walls have been heightened and the outline of a steeper gable is visible at the W end.

WEST HADDON

(76) BAPTIST (SP 632719). Gabled front with two tiers of small round-arched windows. Built early 19th century for church formed 1821; refitted 1882.

WESTON AND WEEDON

(77) BAPTIST, Weston (SP 589470). The Baptist congregation in Weston existed in the early 18th century as part of a church embracing several other societies in the vicinity. The present chapel, registered July 1791 and described as 'newly erected', has walls of squared stone and a hipped slate roof. The NE front, of three bays, has a central doorway with segmental-arched bracketed canopy between tall sash windows; the windows were formerly much shorter and had segmental-arched heads. The walls appear to have been heightened in the early 19th century and a brick-fronted wing to the NW was added at that period. The interior (28ft by 22½ft), refitted in the early 19th century and later, has galleries around three sides with late 19th-century open iron fronts; the NE gallery is the earliest and has a vaulted

ceiling below. *Monuments*: in chapel (1) Thomas Kingston, 1810, and Hannah his widow, 1833, signed Cakebread, Bloxham; (2) Rev. John Law, 1805; (3) Isabel, wife of Rev. William Pain, 1807.

WHITTLEBURY

(78) METHODIST (SP 691438). On 23 June 1763 John Wesley 'preached at the side of the new preaching-house'; he visited Whittlebury on many subsequent occasions and in 1778 called it 'the flower of all our Societies in the circuit, both for zeal and simplicity'. The chapel has walls of coursed rubble and a slate

METHODIST CHAPEL, WHITTLEBURY

roof, gabled W front with central entrance and two upper windows with long timber lintels. The building of 1763 (about 25ft square externally) was enlarged to the E and the upper parts of the walls rebuilt in the early 19th century; the original thicker walling remains in the lower parts of the front and side walls and there are traces of two wide windows, now blocked, each side of the entrance.

WILBARSTON

(79) Former CONGREGATIONAL, Chapel Lane (SP 814883). An existing building fitted up for use as a meeting-house in 1793 had stone walls and a thatched roof. This was enlarged in 1820 and greatly altered in 1884 when the older part was entirely refenestrated and the roof re-covered in slates. Chapel use ceased *c*.1960. The original building (41½ft by 17ft) may have had an entrance on the W side replaced in 1884 by the present entrance in the gabled S end. An early 19th-century vestry projects at the N end of the W wall and a rendered wing on the E side may represent the work of 1820. The interior has been entirely refitted.

Monuments: in chapel (1) Rev. George Bullock, 1811, 'twenty years minister of Ashley and this place', slate tablet; (2) Frances, wife of Rev. George Bullock, 1799, elaborate slate tablet with oval inscription panel and roundel in shaped head above, with female figure and urn (see p. 154); in E wing (3) Ann, widow of Rev. George Bullock, 1826, and Ann their daughter; in burial-ground E of chapel, slate headstones including (4) Edward Ward, 1843, and Elizabeth his wife, 1823, with oval panel carved with urn and female weeper, signed 'John Bettoney, Oadby'.

Coleman (1853) 246–54.

WOLLASTON

(80) BAPTIST, Hinwick Road (SP 907626). Former chapel dated 1835. Later chapel of 1867 set back to west.

(81) Former CONGREGATIONAL, High Street (SP 908629). The chapel, standing behind houses on the E side of the street, has rubble walls heightened in brickwork. It was built in 1752 and a church was formed in 1788. The original building (30¾ft by 17¾ft) was lengthened to the S in the late 18th century incorporating a gallery and heightened in the mid 19th century. The wide W front is of three principal bays with round-arched doorway and windows and a lozenge-shaped tablet above the entrance dated 1752. The S extension has a second doorway and window above. Two windows in the N wall appear to have flanked a pulpit and a small doorway below one window leads to an early 19th-century vestry. The congregation ceased to meet in the early 20th century; the building has since been extensively damaged by fire.

Coleman (1853) 344–51.

(82) WESLEYAN, High Street (SP 907628). Coursed rubble and slate, three bay pedimented front with painted wood mouldings, tall narrow windows, central entrance with paired pilasters and entablature, and gable tablet dated 1840.

WOODFORD CUM MEMBRIS

(83) MORAVIAN, Parsons Street, Woodford Halse (SP 544526). A chapel built in 1798–9 by a newly established congregation, was altered internally and reorientated in 1828, further altered and the entrances removed to the NW end in 1875, and a new chapel built adjacent to that end in 1906.

erected. The gallery has a slightly projecting centre supported by two octagonal posts. The burial-ground behind the chapel has flat numbered tablets.

England I (1886) 4–6, pls.5–7.

WOODNEWTON

(84) WESLEYAN (TL 033944). Rubble and slate; three-bay N front with tall narrow altered windows and later porch. Tablet reset in front wall dated 1840.

WOOTTON

(85) WESLEYAN REFORM, High Street (SP 761567). Three bays with brick pilasters. Opened 1850, altered c.1900 and entrance re-sited.

YARDLEY GOBION

(86) CONGREGATIONAL (SP 766446). Rubble and slate; three-bay gabled front, two tiers of windows with semicircular brick-arched heads, lower windows partly blocked, wide arched entrance, and lunette-shaped tablet in gable inscribed 'Yardley Chapel 1826'.

Coleman (1853) 289.

YARDLEY HASTINGS

(87) CONGREGATIONAL (SP 865570). The chapel, built in 1813 to replace a meeting-house of 1718, has walls of rubble and a slate roof. The E front has an inscribed band below the pediment with

SW wall.

The original chapel has brick walls on a stone plinth and a slate roof; it incorporates a minister's house of two stories at the SE end. The SW side of the chapel originally had two doorways with small windows above and a taller window between, replaced in 1875 by three segmental-arched windows matching similar windows in the opposite wall. The interior (23ft by 35¾ft) originally had the pulpit against the NE wall; this was removed to the SE end in 1828 when the present NW gallery was

the name 'YARDLEY CHAPEL', and on a tablet between the upper windows the words 'Built 1718/Destroyed By Fire/March 1st 1813/Rebuilt and Enlarged/By Public Subscription 1813'. A late 18th-century manse adjoins to the S and a two-storied Sunday-school of the mid 19th century is against the N side.

The interior is square with the pulpit against the W wall between two round-arched windows. A gallery around three sides supported by cast-iron columns has early 19th-century pews to N and S; other seating is of the late 19th century. *Monuments*: in chapel (1) Rev. John Hoppus, 1837, 30 years pastor, and Rebekah his widow, 1843; on front wall (2) John Blower senior, son of Samuel and Mary Blower, 1832, signed 'Bunyan, Newport'. (URC)

Coleman (1853) 291–303.

YARWELL

(88) WESLEYAN (TL 069979). Built 1840, with cottage and Sunday-school added at S end. The chapel originally had two doorways in the W wall now altered to windows. The present S entrance is approached through a passage behind the cottage, in which is a separate doorway leading to a deep S gallery. The interior has been refitted.

YELVERTOFT

(89) CONGREGATIONAL (SP 598754). This congregation originated in the early 18th century when the minister from Welford registered a house for mid-week preaching. In 1758 a barn was fitted up for a meeting-house and the present chapel was erected in 1792; it was enlarged to the front in 1832 and schoolrooms built in the mid 19th century.

The chapel (originally 34½ft by 29½ft externally) has brick walls and a slated roof hipped to the rear. The gabled N front, of 1832, is of three bays with a later porch between round-arched windows and a circular window above between a pair of lunettes. In the W wall are two round-arched windows of 1792. *Monument*: N of chapel, to Jane, widow of Rev. Henry Knight, later wife of Thomas Broughton, 1847.

Coleman (1853) 335–42.

(79) WILBARSTON. Former Congregational chapel. Slate tablet.

NOTTINGHAMSHIRE

Nottinghamshire holds an important place in the early history of nonconformity as one of the counties from which came members of the expedition of the 'Pilgrim Fathers' in 1620; an Independent church formed at Scrooby at the beginning of the 17th century under the patronage of William Brewster emigrated to Amsterdam and Leyden where they joined with others in the historic enterprise. Later dissent in the county has been less spectacular although Mansfield played a significant part in the opening years of the Quaker movement and the same town served as a refuge for several of the ejected ministers in the difficult years following 1662. Nottingham, long notable for the breadth of its religious dissent, was the scene of some early Methodist activity and of one of the first and most serious divisions following the Kilhamite rebellion of 1797.

Surviving meeting-houses are disappointing, not one of the several which date from the 17th or 18th century has retained its original fittings and many have suffered greatly from 19th-century alterations. The Old Meeting-house in Mansfield (30), of 1702, is a classic example of the older type of chapel with two-column support for the roof into which a mediaeval church plan has been forced with unfortunate results. Perhaps the most interesting group comprises three General Baptist chapels, the earliest at Kirkby Woodhouse (23), of 1754, with sufficient evidence to visualize the original structure, the much rebuilt chapel at East Leake (9), of 1756, and the chapel at Upper Broughton (59), of 1795. The earliest Friends' meeting-house at Blyth (3) has been greatly altered, but that in Mansfield (31), of 1800, survived with little alteration. Early Methodist meeting-houses, of 1783 and 1787, remain in Nottingham (42) and Newark (34) but only in fragmentary or changed condition, and another in Mansfield (32), of 1791, survived until recent years; the effective loss in Nottingham of Wesley Chapel (43) and of the Baptist chapel in George Street (39) has left the city devoid of two important buildings and the uncertain future of the High Pavement Chapel (44) threatens the survival of a notable Gothic Revival interior of the later years of that century. The country chapels of the 19th century are mainly small, generally of brick, many having pantiled or slated roofs; of these the Primitive Methodist chapel at Wellow (61) may be mentioned for the felicity of its siting and the Wesleyan chapel at Cropwell Bishop (8) as a particularly complete example of its kind.

BEESTON AND STAPLEFORD

(1) Former WESLEYAN, Nottingham Road, Stapleford (SK 492375). Three-bay gabled front with tablet dated 1782–1848. Built 1848, Sunday-school at rear 1883. (Converted to study centre 1980)

BINGHAM

(2) WESLEYAN, Union Street (SK 704399). Opened 1818, much altered.

BLYTH

(3) Former FRIENDS (SK 624872). A subscription list dated 1701 for building a meeting-house in Blyth 'on that piece of ground upon the back of the hospitals endowed by Friend John Seaton unless a more convenient piece of land fall vacant', and a certificate issued 5 October 1702, appear to relate to this building. Accounts of 1702 include reference to the removal of seats from the old meeting-house. The meeting-house, closed *c*.1907 and sold in 1945, has been converted to cottages.

The walls are of brickwork covered with rendering and the roof is pantiled. The front wall facing NE has been entirely refenestrated and dormer windows added. In the SE gable are traces of a blocked window. The interior, now altered, formerly had a stand at the SE end and a gallery opposite.

Lomax, J., 'The Early Organization of the Quakers in Nottinghamshire', *Trans. Thoroton Soc.* XLVIII (1944): Quaker records (Q.2256), Nottingham City Library.

BRADMORE

(4) WESLEYAN, Farmer Street (SK 585312). Opened 1830. Brick with hipped slate roof; three round-arched windows at front.

CARLTON IN LINDRICK

(5) WESLEYAN (SK 592844). Brick and slate with stone dressings and pediment, dated 1861.

CLAYWORTH

(6) WESLEYAN (SK 728882). Brick and pantile. Built 1834, enlarged to front.

COLSTON BASSETT

(7) WESLEYAN (SK 701336). Opened 1838, porch added 1896.

CROPWELL BISHOP

(8) WESLEYAN (SK 683355). Dated 1842. Two round-arched windows in each wall.

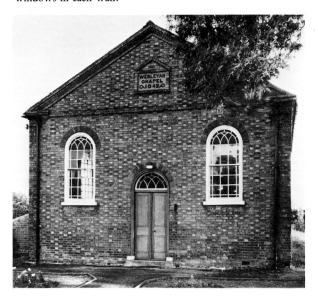

EAST LEAKE

(9) GENERAL BAPTIST (SK 559262). The church, formed in 1756 as a branch of the Loughborough church, became a separate society in 1782 in union with Wymeswold, Leices. (91) and Upper Broughton, Notts. (59) and joined the New Connexion in 1783. The meeting-house ($46\frac{1}{2}$ft by $33\frac{1}{4}$ft externally), built in 1756 and greatly altered and heightened in 1839, has brick walls and a slated roof. The original E wall remains largely intact and has two wide segmental-arched windows and a smaller window to the left with four small square windows in the heightening. The W wall is similarly fenestrated but the original brickwork

survives only in the lowest courses. The front N wall, also with a portion of older brickwork remaining, is mostly of 1839 which

date and the initials GBC (General Baptist Chapel) appear on a tablet in the gable; it has two doorways, one window between and two above, all with splayed lintels. A slightly lower Sunday-school wing of two stories, built *c.*1839, enlarged 1849, stands at the S end.

Monuments: in burial-ground, many slate headstones including against W wall, (1) Nathanael Bennett of Hoton, 1784, and Margaret his widow 1791, signed Winfield, former wall monument shaped at head and foot (for the sufferings of N. Bennett see Taylor II, 37–8); against S wall, (2) John Cross, 1838, signed Roworth; (3) Elizabeth wife of Joseph Barrow, 1776, signed W. Wootton.

Taylor (1818) II, 36–8, 161–2, 237–40, 350: Wood (1847) 184.

(10) Former WESLEYAN (SK 554263). Brick and slate, enlarged to front and original tablet dated 1827 reset in late 19th century. The present Gothic chapel opened 1862 stands opposite.

EDINGLEY

(11) WESLEYAN (SK 665560). Dated 1838.

EDWINSTOWE

(12) WESLEYAN, High Street (SK 626668). Opened 1848. Rendered front with rusticated lower storey and pedimental blocking course above central bay.

Ledger (1915) 36–7.

EGMANTON

(13) Fomer PRIMITIVE METHODIST (SK 733686). Brick and pantile; three bays. Tablet dated 1841.

EPPERSTONE

(14) WESLEYAN, Chapel Lane (SK 652488). Opened 1830; coursed rubble with hipped tiled roof. Entrance at W end covered by extension of 1891.

(15) Former PRIMITIVE METHODIST, Chapel Lane (SK 652486). Dated 1851.

FINNINGLEY   *South Yorkshire*

(16) WESLEYAN (SK 675994). Dated 1838.

FISKERTON CUM MORTON

(17) WESLEYAN, Gravelly Lane (SK 734510). Opened 1809.

FLINTHAM

(18) WESLEYAN, Spring Lane (SK 741459). Opened 1805; enlarged to front and heightened in later 19th century.

GRANBY

(19) WESLEYAN, Granby (SK 749363). Brick and slate, wide three-bay front with round-arched windows; opened 1807 but altered or rebuilt in mid 19th century.

(20) PRIMITIVE METHODIST, Sutton (SK 761375). Small three-bay chapel of brick with pantiled roof, inscribed 'INDEPENDENT/PRIMITIVE METHODIST CHAPEL/ A.D. 1860'. Pulpit between two windows in back wall faces entrance.

HAYTON

(21) WESLEYAN (SK 729844). Built 1823. Three-bay front with round-arched windows.

Biggs, B., *Hayton Methodist Chapel, 150 Years 1823-1973* [1973].

HICKLING

(22) WESLEYAN (SK 691290). Dated 1848. Pedimented front with later porch.

KIRKBY IN ASHFIELD

(23) GENERAL BAPTIST, Kirkby Woodhouse (SK 494544). The church originated about 1749 at first in association with that at Barton in the Beans, Leics. (72), becoming autonomous in 1760 and first appearing as a member of the New Connexion in 1773. The meeting-house, built in 1754, was enlarged in 1818 and much altered and heightened in 1865-6. It has brick walls now rendered to S and W and the roof is covered with slates. The original building had a pantiled roof and gables with low

Exterior before 1865. (Photograph courtesy G. Longdon)

parapets to E and west. The S front had two flat-arched doorways near the ends and a pair of round-arched windows between them. At the E end was a lower pantiled vestry with external S doorway. The 'enlargement' of 1818 appears to have been principally a re-arrangement of the interior with the blocking of the SW and vestry doorways and incorporating the vestry area to provide additional seating capacity. The present character of

the meeting-house results from the alterations of 1865-6 in which the remaining entrance was covered by a gabled porch, the arches of the principal S windows were replaced by lintels, the vestry raised to two stories and extended to the E to include a staircase to the upper room, and the whole structure was heightened and re-roofed.

Some original brickwork remains visible in the N wall which has a slight central projection with a three-centred arch, now blocked, in the main wall, possibly to accommodate a rostrum pulpit; original segmental-arched windows to right and left. The interior ($18\frac{1}{2}$ft by $33\frac{3}{4}$ft, extended to $47\frac{3}{4}$ft) has been entirely refitted in the late 19th century. The pulpit is at the W end with a small later vestry behind; at the E end a gallery above the former vestry serves also as a schoolroom and has the front closed by shutters.

Monuments: in chapel (1) George Hardstaff, 1842, fifty years pastor; (2) William Booth, 1836; in burial ground, slate headstones; (3) Elizabeth wife of Robert Booth, 1797; (4) Jacob, son of Robert and Elizabeth Booth, 1796 or 7; (5) Frances daughter of Robert and Elizabeth Booth, 1793.

Henstock, J., *Two Hundred Years of Baptist Witness; Bicentenary of Kirkby Woodhouse Baptist Church 1754-1954* (1954): Taylor (1818) II, 26, 54, 165, 251-4, 362: Wood (1847) 181.

LAMBLEY

(24) Former WESLEYAN, Chapel Lane (SK 630453). Brick and pantile with former round-arched entrance in gabled end; now a cottage. Initials T. C on stone tablet in gable, two bricks above

former doorway carved with masonic insignia, initials SS, IP, and numerals 5807 (?indicating date). The chapel does not appear on the plan of the Nottingham circuit until after 1828.

(25) PRIMITIVE METHODIST, Main Street (SK 632452), dated 1849.

LANEHAM

(26) WESLEYAN (SK 807764). Built 1834, refronted 1894.

LAXTON

(27) Former CONGREGATIONAL (SK 723670). Opened 1802, transferred to Primitive Methodists *c.*1910. Altered and partly rebuilt in late 19th century. *Monument*: loose outside chapel, to Ann Fairbanks, 1808.

LOWDHAM

(28) Former PRIMITIVE METHODIST, Main Street (SK 670464). Dated 1844; now Independent Methodist.

(29) WESLEYAN, Ton Lane (SK 665466). Opened 1826, much altered.

MANSFIELD

(30) THE OLD MEETING-HOUSE, Stockwell Gate (SK 536611). The town of Mansfield served as a refuge for several ejected ministers in the years following 1662. The Presbyterian society, which originated at that period and which has supported a Unitarian ministry since the late 18th century, first met in private houses including that of Robert Porter, former Vicar of Pentrich, Derbys., where it continued to assemble after Porter's death in 1690 until the opening of the present meeting-house in 1702. The building, which stands on a hitherto restricted site at the rear of the 'Old Parsonage', was registered 5 October 1702. It was drastically altered in 1870–1 when the entrances were removed from the E to the S side, a vestry added to the S and the interior entirely refitted and reorientated. In 1882 a chancel was added to the N and an organ-chamber was built to the NW, the former converted to a vestry and the S entrance remodelled. A new S porch was constructed in 1940.

The meeting-house has walls of rubble with ashlar quoins and dressings; the roof, now covered with slates, is hipped and has a central valley. The E and W walls have each four tall windows with square stone mullions and transoms and on the E side two former doorways with plain ashlar jambs and lintels. The S end has four tall narrow windows with transoms, partly covered by the modern porch, and four square windows above. The original N wall has been removed but prior to 1882 it had windows similar to those on the south.

The Old Meeting-house,
MANSFIELD, *Nottinghamshire*

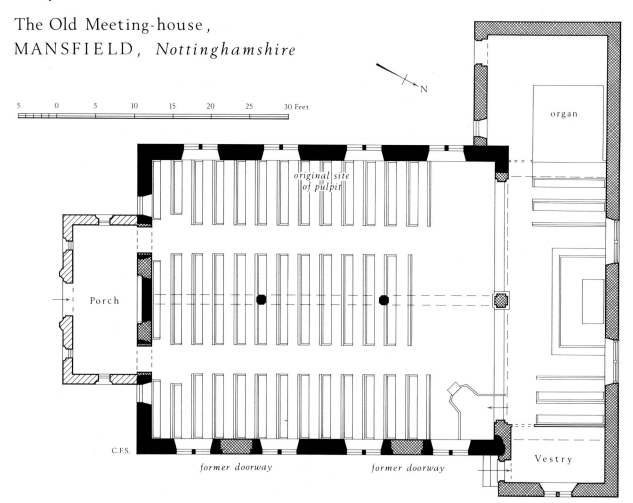

5   0   5   10   15   20   25   30 Feet

N

organ

original site of pulpit

Porch

C.F.S.

former doorway   *former doorway*

Vestry

The interior (originally 35ft by 44¼ft) has an arcade of three round-arched bays with two octagonal timber posts with moulded capitals supporting the main N–S valley-beam. The N wall is pierced by two semicircular arches opening to the 1882 chancel. The pulpit was originally against the W wall. Before 1870 a gallery for the singers is believed to have been sited between the E entrances and the upper N and S windows appear to have been intended to light corresponding galleries at these ends.

Fittings – *Clock*: on W wall, parliament clock signed 'Thomas Haley, Norwich', early 18th-century (see p. 166). *Monuments*: in chapel, on W wall (1) Rev. John Williams, 25 years pastor, 1835; on S wall (2) John Paulson, 1802, and Elizabeth his widow, 1803; (3) Joseph Paulson, 1807. *Pulpit*: incorporates early 18th-century front with two tiers of fielded panels.

Bolam (1962) 44–9: Evans (1897) 172–3: White, J.H., *The Story of the Old Meeting House, Mansfield* (1959).

(31) FRIENDS, Quaker Lane (SK 537610). The meeting-house, built in 1800 to allow increased accommodation for Quarterly Meetings, replaced one of 1690 the seats from which were sold to Friends in Derby in 1799 for five guineas. The building (58½ft by 30ft externally) which stands on the S side of Quaker lane has walls of coursed sandstone and a hipped slate roof. The principal wall faces S and has a central pedimented porch partly covered by a later building and two windows to the right set in arched

recesses; opposite these in the N wall are two lunette windows and two similar windows at the W end light an upper room. The interior is divided into two parts, a larger meeting-room to the E with stand at the E end and a smaller room to the W with loft above approached by a staircase in the porch. The date 'ANNO 1800' is carved on the S face of the lintel of the entrance from Quaker Lane. *Burial-ground* to S with uniform headstones mainly late 19th-century and after. (Demolished *c*.1975)

(32) Former METHODIST, Stockwell Gate (SK 635610). The chapel was built in 1791 for a society which originated in 1788 but joined the Methodist New Connexion *c*.1797; in 1815 it was sold to a Baptist church which joined the General Baptist New

Connexion in 1819. The chapel was enlarged in 1841. The walls are of rubble with ashlar dressings except the W side which is of brick; the roof is hipped and slated. The interior has a gallery around three sides with panelled front of the early 19th century. (Demolished *c*.1974)

Alcock, J.E. *Notes on the Progress of Wesleyan Methodism in the Mansfield Circuit* (1900): Wood (1847) 211.

NEWARK

(33) Former CONGREGATIONAL, Lombard Street, Newark on Trent (SK 797538). The chapel, built in 1822–3 to the designs of

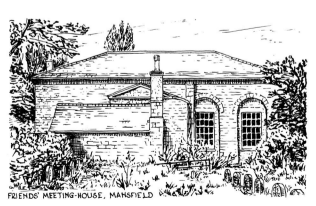

FRIENDS' MEETING-HOUSE, MANSFIELD

W. Wallen of London, was closed in 1932 and is now in industrial use. It has brick walls and a pedimented front divided by giant pilasters.

Peters, G.H., *New Light on an Old Town* (1951) 28–40.

(34) Former METHODIST, Millgate, Newark on Trent (SK 794536). A preaching-house built in 1776 for a society formed about 1747, remained in use until 1787 when it was superseded by the chapel in Guildhall Street; it was subsequently converted to a cottage. The walls are of brickwork and the roof is covered

Former METHODIST PREACHING-HOUSE, Millgate, NEWARK-ON-TRENT

with pantiles. The W front to the street is gabled, of two stories with segmental-arched upper windows and a large circular recess in the gable; the lower openings, now altered, are believed to have included two doorways. Some windows in the S wall have been blocked. The E end which is narrower than the front may have served as a house for the preachers.

(35) Former METHODIST, Guildhall Street, Newark on Trent (SK 801537). The chapel, opened by John Wesley, 11 February 1787, and described in his Journal as 'a lightsome, cheerful building', was much enlarged in 1815 by extension to the rear; in 1846 it was superseded by the chapel in Barnby Gate and was

then converted to a school in which use it continued until c.1980. The walls are of brickwork and the roof is hipped and covered with pantiles. The SW front approached from Balderton Gate, originally of four bays with two tiers of windows and two round-arched doorways to the centre bays, now has five windows to the lower stage. In the SE side facing Guildhall Street is a round-arched doorway and window with intersecting glazing bars. (Demolition proposed 1981)

(36) WESLEYAN, Barnby Gate, Newark on Trent (SK 800539). Brick with stone dressings, front of four bays with two tiers of windows, open porches to end bays with Tuscan columns *in antis* and double pilasters above carrying a stone entablature. By James Simpson of Leeds, opened 1846.

NORMANTON-ON-THE-WOLDS

(37) Former WESLEYAN (SK 622331). Brick with rendered front and hipped pantiled roof. The chapel was built in 1797 for a society formerly meeting in a cottage at Plumtree. It was heightened and extended to the front in the early 19th century and some of the window frames were later renewed in cast-iron. The front has two tiers of round-arched windows and a barrel-vaulted porch of the late 19th century; an oval tablet dated 1797 has been removed.

The interior (22ft, enlarged to 30ft, by $16\frac{1}{2}$ft) has a flat plaster ceiling and a deep gallery at the W end. The gallery front has three pairs of panels divided by pilasters and supported by two turned columns of the early 19th century. At the opposite end the pulpit, of later date, stands between two round-arched windows on a platform fronted by early 19th-century reset panelling.

Swift, R.C., *Lively People: Methodism in Nottingham 1740–1979* (1982) 25, 30.

NORTH COLLINGHAM

(38) BAPTIST (SK 829618). The church, which originated in the late 17th century as General Baptist but adopted Calvinistic sentiments a century later, has occupied a meeting-house on this site since 1705. The first building, which seems to have been a

(36) NEWARK. Wesleyan chapel, Barnby Gate.

(38) *Former chapel. (Photograph M. W. Barley, 1948)*

converted grain store, was rebuilt in 1762. This chapel, of brick with a hipped pantiled roof, was demolished in 1955 having been superseded at the beginning of the century by the conversion of an adjoining school building erected 1865. Several 18th-century headstones remain in the burial-ground.

Harrison, F.M.W., *The Story of Collingham Baptist Church* (1970).

NOTTINGHAM

(39) Former BAPTIST, George Street (SK 576400). The church formerly meeting here originated in the 17th century and occupied a chapel in Friar Lane until removing to George Street in 1815. The Friar Lane chapel, notable as the scene of William Carey's sermon in 1792 which led to the formation of the Baptist Missionary Society, subsequently passed to a society of Scotch Baptists and in 1862 to commercial use; it has since been demolished but its site is recorded on a plaque below Maid Marian Way (SU 570397). George Street Chapel, which continued in use until 1948, has been much altered on conversion to a theatre. The walls are of brick, now rendered, with stone dressings. The former Sunday-school behind, of three storeys, '. . . erected by voluntary contributions for the Instruction of Poor Children on the Sabbath day' is dated 1819. *Plate*: now in Castle Museum, includes four two-handled cups of 1773 (two), 1792 and 1815.

Godfrey, J.T., & Ward J., *The History of Friar Lane Baptist Church, Nottingham* (1903).

(40) Former GENERAL BAPTIST, Plumptre Place (SK 578398). The church originated *c*.1775 when William Fox, formerly of Kirkby Woodhouse, began to hold services in his own house. In 1779 a room was hired in Jack Knutter's Lane and in 1783 the Methodist Octagon Chapel was acquired. The present building, which stands in a large court off the E side of Stoney Street, was built in 1799 and enlarged in 1834. Meetings ceased *c*.1888 and the building was converted for use as a parochial school. It is now in commercial use.

The walls are of brickwork rendered at the front and the roof

Former GENERAL BAPTIST CHAPEL, Plumptre Place, NOTTINGHAM CFS. 1977

is slated. The wide W front, now of nine bays but perhaps originally shorter, with moulded dentil cornice, quoins, platband and two tiers of sash windows, has a round-arched entrance at the centre with pedimented surround partly if not entirely of the late 19th century. The gabled N and S end walls have been altered or rebuilt. The chapel has been enlarged to the rear; the E wall

(39) NOTTINGHAM. Baptist chapel, before conversion (left) and after (right).

has two tiers of windows mostly round-arched but of various shapes and sizes. The building is said to have been originally 'about 15 yards square with galleries on three sides'. The interior now has a narrow central area rising through two stories with a gallery around closed above by glazed shutters; most of the details are of the late 19th century.

Monuments: the former burial-ground to the E has been cleared but fragments of five stones remain at the NE corner of the building including (1) Joseph son of Robert and Susannah Moore, 1808, and five other children, slate headstone; (2) John Wells, 1791.

General Baptist Repository II no. viii [n.d., *c*.1806] 55: Taylor (1818) II, 173–7, 248–51, 360: Wood (1847) 183, 185–6.

(41) CONGREGATIONAL, Castle Gate (SK 573397). The Independent church formed in 1655 built its first meeting-house in Castle Gate in 1689; it was described as a low tiled building with two pillars supporting the roof. Side galleries were added in 1727 and the building enlarged in 1738. The present chapel, by R.C. Sutton erected in 1863–4 as a bicentenary memorial of the 1662 ejection, is of red brick with yellow brick and stone dressings in a 'free Venetian style' with central pediment and elaborately detailed cornices. (Chapel closed *c*.1975; under conversion to Congregational Federation headquarters 1981)

Fittings – *Monuments*: in chapel (1) Rev. Richard Plumb, nearly 19 years pastor, 1791; (2) Rev. Richard Alliott, nearly 46 years pastor, 1840; reset against E wall, slate headstones, (3) William Turner, 1775. *Plate*: includes a pair of two-handled cups of 1759.

Henderson, A.R., *History of Castle Gate Congregational Church, Nottingham, 1655–1905* (1905).

(42) Former METHODIST, Goose Gate, Hockley (SK 579399). Methodist meetings which commenced in 1740 were held for many years in private houses and in a hired room at the top of Bottle Lane. The first regular preaching-house, an octagon called the Tabernacle costing £128 2s. 7d. 'standing near the Glasshouse, St Mary's parish, and near a street called Boot Lane' (Milton St.) was registered 11 October 1764. This was succeeded in 1783 by the present building in Hockley. In 1797 a major division in the society left the chapel in the hands of the newly-established Methodist New Connexion, the Wesleyans building themselves a new meeting-house in Halifax Place in 1798 (rebuilt 1847, now demolished). The Wesleyan society recovered possession of Hockley Chapel in 1818 after legal action but on their removal to Broad Street (43) in 1839 it was sold to the Primitive Methodists. It is now in commercial use.

The building, of brick now rendered at the front, is of five bays originally with two tiers of windows; an upper storey and two-storied pedimented porch flanked by shops were added in the late 19th century and further alterations and heightening have since occurred. The interior (49ft by 49¼ft) has been entirely refitted.

Dolbey (1964) 95, 110: Harwood, G.H., *The History of Wesleyan Methodism in Nottingham and its Vicinity* (1872): Kendall (1905) I, 250; II, 468.

(43) Former WESLEYAN, Broad Street (SK 576400). 'Wesley Chapel' by S.S. Rawlinson, built in 1839 to replace Hockley Chapel (42), has been drastically altered since 1950 by conversion to secular use. The interior (97¾ft by 64ft) with a seating capacity of 1,927 had a continuous round-ended gallery.

Harwood (1872) 170.

© *Notts. County Library.*

(43) NOTTINGHAM. Wesleyan chapel.
Before conversion.

After conversion.

(44) NOTTINGHAM. High Pavement Chapel.

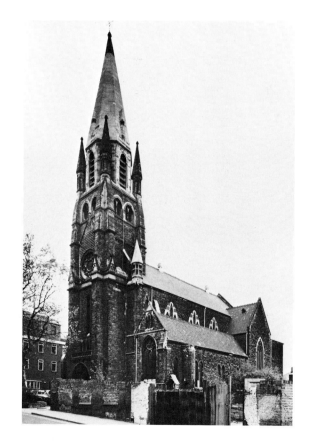

(44) HIGH PAVEMENT CHAPEL (SK 575396). The Presbyterian society, latterly Unitarian, originated in the late 17th century and built the first meeting-house in the High Pavement in 1690 or 1691. It was replaced 1804–5 by a plain building four bays wide and five in length with an unusual tulip-shaped pulpit directly accessible from the vestry, and a gallery around three sides. The present building by Stuart Colman of Bristol, occupying a larger area and extending further to the NE, was built 1874–6. It is of stone in the Gothic style with a one-bay chancel to the SW, transepts, nave and aisles of four bays, and a tower and spire centrally at the NE end.

Fittings – *Collecting Plates*: two, pewter, part of larger set, numbered on edge II, III, early 19th-century. *Glass*: in principal window of chancel, seven lights with central figure of Christ and three tiers of figures representing Truth, Light, Faith, Love, Hope, Joy, Peace, Justice, Courage, Reverence, Mercy, Purity, Humility, Science, Literature, Theology, Labour, Philanthropy, Art, Philosophy, and memorial inscription to Peter William Clayden, 1902, by Morris and Co. to design by Burne-Jones. *Monuments*: (1) Rev. James Taylor, 1831; (2) Rev. Henry Turner, 1822; (3) Rev. Benjamin Carpenter, 37 years pastor, 1860. *Paintings*: in Congregational Hall, miscellaneous collection of prints etc. including several oil portraits of ministers and others. *Plate*: includes a two-handled cup of 1726, given 1737, and a two-handled gadrooned cup of 1752.

Bolam (1962) 50–5: Carpenter, B., *Some Account of the Original Introduction of Presbyterianism into Nottingham and the Neighbourhood* (1862): Evans (1897) 191–2.

(45) Former PRESBYTERIAN, Halifax Place (SK 575397). The minister of High Pavement Chapel, the Rev. Dr Samuel Eaton, seceded from that congregation in 1760 following a dispute with his assistant minister and built a new meeting-house, registered 17 July 1760, where his supporters remained until 1775 when they reunited with the parent society. The building was then leased to other groups of dissenters and in 1804 was sold to the Wesleyans for use as a Sunday-school in connexion with their chapel built 1798 on the E side of Halifax Place.

The meeting-house, of 1760, variously altered and refronted in the 19th century and greatly altered internally in 1971 on conversion to 'The Lace Market Theatre', stands on the W side of the street. The walls (about 48ft by 27ft externally) are of brickwork with a rendered E front and the roof is covered with patent tiles. In the rear gable are traces of two flat-arched upper windows and in the N side two segmental-arched windows and a small doorway have been blocked. The original roof structure has king-post trusses and wind-braces to the lower purlins.

Carpenter (1862) 156–61.

ORSTON

(46) WESLEYAN, Chapel Street (SK 769409). Three-bay front with pointed-arched windows and intersecting glazing bars. Tablet in NE gable dated 1848. Vestry added to SW with slate tablet recording benefaction by Christopher Staveley, 1869.

OXTON

(47) WESLEYAN, Chapel Lane (SK 630517). Dated 1839. Three-bay front with blind upper windows and round-arched entrance covered by later porch.

SCARRINGTON

(48) WESLEYAN (SK 732416). Built 1818. Brick with hipped slate roof, narrow three-bay front with segmental-arched windows and later porch.

SCROOBY

(49) WESLEYAN (SK 652908). Rendered three-bay front. 1830.

SELSTON

(50) CONGREGATIONAL, Dove Green (SK 462528). The church, originally Presbyterian, appears to have been in existence from the late 17th century. The present chapel, with rendered walls and hipped tiled roof, dates from *c*.1800; it has been considerably altered and extended at one side.

SOUTH LEVERTON

(51) WESLEYAN, Church Street (SK 783809). Brick with hipped slate roof. The front wall, dated 1847, has two entrances, one to the left inscribed 'WESLEYAN CHAPEL', the other 'SCHOOL ROOM'.

SOUTHWELL

(52) BAPTIST, Nottingham Road (SK 700535). 'Park Street' church, founded 1811, has occupied the present chapel since 1839. The building, erected *c*.1800 as a work-house, has

rendered walls and a hipped slate roof. A semicircular projection at the centre which formed the original entrance is repeated at the rear and is flanked by wings of three storeys; the N wing which became the manse is unaltered but the S wing was converted to a chapel in 1839 by the removal of floors and substitution of round-arched windows through the two upper stories and a new entrance and porch were made at the S end. The interior was refitted in the late 19th century.

(53) WESLEYAN, Prebend Passage (SK 703539). The chapel, built in 1839 for a society formed *c*.1800, stands on a confined site and extends at the W end across a cartway leading to cottages in Prebend Yard. An open loggia at the front has a pedimented upper stage and tablet inscribed 'WESLEY CHAPEL 1839'. There are schoolrooms below the chapel.

STYRRUP WITH OLDCOTES

(54) WESLEYAN, Oldcotes (SK 591886). Rendered three-bay front dated 1840.

(55) WESLEYAN, Styrrup (SK 610906). Brick with polygonal end; small tablet inscribed 'Wesleyan Methodist/Chapel Built/182[?5]'.

SUTTON IN ASHFIELD

(56) WESLEYAN, Skegby (SK 498609). Dated 1844, front windows altered.

TRESWELL

(57) Former WESLEYAN (SK 787793). Brick and pantile, rendered three-bay front with four-centred arched openings, early 19th-century. (Disused 1972)

TUXFORD

(58) WESLEYAN (SK 736709). Dated 1841. Brick and slate with lancet windows.

UPPER BROUGHTON

(59) GENERAL BAPTIST (SK 684262). The congregation was formed in the late 18th century by preachers from East Leake (9) with which the society remained united until becoming autonomous in 1801. It joined the New Connexion in 1802. The meeting-house built in 1795 has brick walls now covered with

rendering and a slated roof. The broad E front has a porch of *c*.1900 concealing the two original round-arched entrances between which is a wide similarly-arched window; above the entrances are two smaller windows and a date-tablet between. Two large segmental-arched windows in the W wall flank the original site of the pulpit and have two tiers of windows to right and left. The interior (24¾ft by 31¾ft) has been greatly altered and refitted, N and S galleries removed and the pulpit placed at

the S end: an arched recess in the W wall marks its former site.

Fittings – *Monuments*: in chapel, on W wall (1) Elizabeth, widow of Rev. William Severn, Unitarian minister, 1819, oval marble tablet signed Hull & Pollard, Le'ster; on N wall (2) William Rouse of Hose, 1801, and Ann his widow, 1835, slate tablet signed Glenn, Hose; in burial-ground, several slate headstones, including (3) Elizabeth (Tuckwood), wife of William Hatton 'G.B. Minister', 1831; (4) William Hatton, 1855.

Taylor (1818) II, 162, 237, 350–1: Wood (1847) 205.

UPTON

(60) Former WESLEYAN (SK 735542). Dated 1831; now Pentecostalist.

WELLOW

(61) PRIMITIVE METHODIST (SK 670662), at N end of village green, behind maypole. Brick and slate with tablet above front entrance dated 1840, recut as 1847.

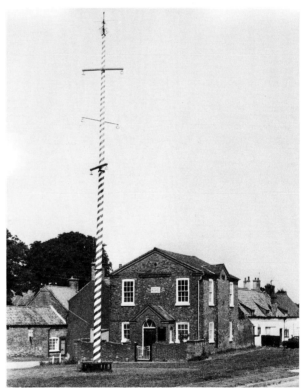

WEST DRAYTON

(62) Former WESLEYAN, Rockley (SK 716748). Brick with hipped pantiled roof; altered on conversion to garage but side walls retain original round-arched windows set in wide three-centred arched recesses. Tablet in S wall dated 1826. Present chapel 100 yards W is dated 1875.

WOODBOROUGH

(63) BAPTIST, Shelt Hill (SK 636479). Brick and slate with vestry wing at right-angles to front with stone tablet 'BAPTIST CHAPEL 1831'.

(30) MANSFIELD. The Old Meeting-house. Early 18th-century clock.

Early nonconformity in Oxfordshire is more apparent in the development of congregations of Baptists and Quakers than in those of the Presbyterians and Independents. Friends' meeting-houses were particularly numerous and of those that survive West Adderbury (106), of 1675, is especially notable and is one of the oldest in the country. A very similar building of 1692 exists at South Newington (94) and another at a smaller scale in Burford (23), of 1709. The larger meeting-house at Banbury (11), of 1751, has been greatly altered but that at Charlbury (26), of 1779, remains with little appearance of change. The late 19th-century Friends' meeting-house at Sibford Gower (92) is of interest as one of the few rebuilt to a larger size at a time when the society generally was suffering from a period of decline.

The Baptist chapel at Cote (6), of c.1739, may be claimed to be the most picturesquely sited of all the buildings listed in the county and as such is relatively well known. Although refitted in 1859 the continued use of box-pews and the rare presence of a table pew add to its significance. The chapel at Hook Norton (57), rebuilt in 1787, is also of some interest, but other Baptist chapels are relatively small or late. The early 19th-century refronting of New Road, Oxford (76) is a not entirely successful attempt to introduce architectural embellishment and the simple detailing and good proportions of the village chapels at Chadlington (25) and Leafield (65) may generally be preferred.

Although Presbyterian congregations existed in the major towns in the early 18th century most suffered a decline prior to more or less drastic reformation as Congregational churches. Only at Banbury (8) did Unitarianism develop in any strength, and to a lesser degree in the shorter-lived village churches of Bloxham and Milton (18, 69) at the first of which the meeting-house still remains intact. The only surviving town meeting-houses of the early 18th century are at Bicester (15), where the original external appearance can still be distinguished though the interior has been greatly altered, and at Witney (111) where it has outlasted its successor, but neither building is now in use for worship.

The development of the Gothic style in chapels is evident in the early 19th century, the Congregational chapel at Witney (112), of 1828, being an outstanding example and its demolition a major loss to nonconformist architecture. The chapel of the same denomination at Binfield Heath (46), of 1835, is one of several in the vicinity of Reading incorporating a tower on a much reduced scale. Later 19th-century Gothic chapels are typified by the Baptist chapel at Chipping Norton (31), of 1863, and W.F. Poulton's Congregational chapel at Thame (102), of 1871, while the castellated architecture of the Salvation Army was ably represented by the Oxford citadel (80) of 1888.

Methodism, born in the Holy Club at Oxford, has left many small chapels of which Freeland (51), dated 1805, and Watlington (104), of 1812, may be cited as examples; few larger buildings were required outside Oxford itself where the progression from small preaching-house (78) to Classical temple and on to large Gothic chapel is still partly visible in the same street. The transformation of an early 18th-century mansion in Burford (24) is also remarkable for the outward respect paid to an important example of domestic architecture.

The presence of good building stone in the county and of stone slates, notably from the vicinity of Stonesfield, has resulted in a predominance of these materials. Brickwork appears in the early 18th century at Bicester (15) for the front wall of the meeting-house and, at the end of the century, at Goring (52), as well as in several small 19th-century chapels in districts where stone was less freely available. The incursion of slate and, less frequently, tile as a replacement for other roof coverings is general, but thatch still survives on former chapels at Bloxham (18), Dorchester (40) and Epwell (44).

ALVESCOT

(1) STRICT BAPTIST (SP 271046). Rubble and slate, built early 19th century for church formed 1833. Gabled ends; doorway in side wall with stone brackets and moulded hood. Rear gallery with original open-backed pews, other seating replaced.

Monument: in burial-ground, Charlot (*sic*), daughter of John and Levina Peyman, 1840, headstone with urn in low relief.

(2) Former PRIMITIVE METHODIST (SP 270047). Built 1850, converted to reading-room 1885, now used as scout hut.

ARNCOTT

(3) WESLEYAN, Green Lane (SP 610174). Rubble with hipped slate roof, two tiers of windows in front with timber lintels and slightly altered tablet between lower pair originally inscribed 'W.C./1834'. Interior refitted.

ASCOTT-UNDER-WYCHWOOD

(4) BAPTIST, Shipton Road (SP 300187), behind 'The Swan' p.h. Long low outbuilding of rubble, converted c.1816.

ASTON BAMPTON AND SHIFFORD

(5) BAPTIST, Aston (SP 340031). Coursed rubble walls and slate roof, three-bay front with pointed-arched openings with thin labels and tablet over entrance. 'BAPTIST/CHAPEL/1845'. Two pointed-arched windows in each gabled end wall.

(6) BAPTIST, Cote (SP 351031). The Baptist church now meeting at Cote was formed in 1656 by division from the Abingdon church and originally met at Longworth, Berks, 3½ miles southeast. The site of the present chapel was acquired 1703–4 and the first meeting-house registered 22 September 1704. From a mortgage dated 26 February 1739/40 it appears that the chapel was then enlarged or rebuilt to its present size, the capacity being increased in 1756 by the addition of a gallery. Drastic internal alterations were carried out in 1859 in which the pulpit was removed from the S to the W wall, the galleries altered or rebuilt against the other three walls and the seating renewed.

The chapel has stone walls and a double roof covered by stone slates. The E front has a truncated gable, formed by a screen wall across one end of the central valley, surmounted by a stone panel with scrolled ends, an alteration possibly dating from the early 19th century. Two entrances have fielded panelled doors and flat canopies with shaped timber brackets. The W wall also has a screen wall across the end of the valley, two round-arched upper windows and a central window, now blocked, below. Two tall windows in the S wall flank the former site of the pulpit. A vestry against the N wall has been enlarged.

The interior (34ft square) has galleries around three sides with staircases in the NE and SE corners, the former incorporating work of the mid 18th century. The seating, entirely of 1859, comprises box-pews with a central table-pew above the baptistery. Some earlier panelling is re-used against the W wall and as a screen in the vestry.

Fittings – *Monuments*: in chapel, on S wall (1) Mary widow of John Williams, 1837, signed Godfrey, Abingdon; (2) Martha and Mary, twin daughters of William Talbot and Abigail Wallis, 1835, and Elizabeth Stewart Wallis, 1848; on W wall (3) Rev. Thomas Sunscombe M.A., 26 years pastor, 1811; in burial-ground many 18th-century headstones with elaborate carving, including (4) Francis Taylor, 1713, cherub's head with scrolls and egg-and-dart border; and (5) Mary, wife of John Williams, 1774, scrolled border ornamented with roses and urn, background formerly coloured black. *Plate*: includes a two-handled cup of 1734, given by John Morse 1774.

Stanley [c.1935].

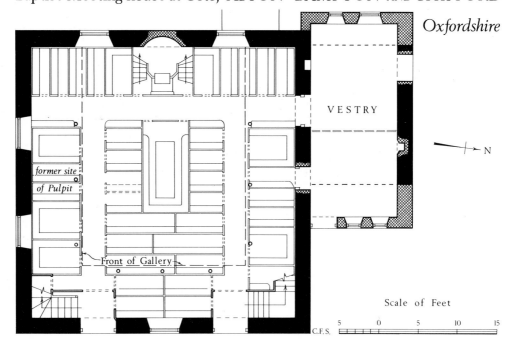

Baptist Meeting-house at Cote, ASTON BAMPTON AND SHIFFORD *Oxfordshire*

VESTRY

former site of Pulpit

Front of Gallery

Scale of Feet

C.F.S.

5   0   5   10   15

Exterior from SE.

Interior from SE.
(6) ASTON BAMPTON AND SHIFFORD. Baptist chapel, Cote.

BAMPTON

(7) BAPTIST (SP 316032). A Quarter Sessions certificate of October 1778 probably relates to this building which was erected for the use of the minister of Cote chapel. The walls are of coursed rubble and the roof is hipped and covered with stone slates. The E front of three bays has a segmental-arched doorway formerly with a pedimented canopy, a small window above and two plain round-arched windows each side; there are two similar windows in the S and W walls. The interior (32ft by 24ft) has an E gallery with panelled front and original seating; the lower pews have been renewed and the late 18th-century pulpit at the W end has been reset lower. (Lower pews reported 1981 to be replaced by chairs)

BANBURY

(8) Site of OLD MEETING-HOUSE, Horsefair (SP 453405). The site was acquired in 1716 by a Presbyterian, latterly Unitarian, congregation which converted an existing building into a meeting-house, altered or rebuilt it *c*.1742 and in 1850 replaced it by a Gothic chapel. This last was succeeded *c*.1965 by a Baptist chapel (see (9) below). Reset in boundary wall, foliated gable-cross from 1850 chapel.

Evans (1897) 9: *UHST* I (1917–19) 276–302.

(9) Former BAPTIST, Bridge Street (SP 458406). The chapel, built in 1841, was greatly altered in 1903 to designs by A.E. Allen; a more drastic change *c*.1975 on conversion to a supermarket followed the removal of the congregation to the Horsefair (8).

Front before conversion.

The original front was of two bays with a pediment supported by three pairs of Ionic columns and entrances in flanking wings. In 1903 the two middle columns were re-sited to support a narrower pediment slightly in advance of its predecessor and a central entrance was constructed. Only the columns and their superstructure now remain.

B. Hbk (1902) 346; (1905) 443–4: Potts, W., *Banbury Through a Hundred Years* (1942) 75.

(10) CONGREGATIONAL, South Bar Street (SP 454404). The congregation formed in 1787 built a meeting-house in 1790 in Church Passage which, after the erection of the present building in 1857, survived in other uses until after 1942 but has since been demolished. The present chapel, on a site partly concealed by earlier buildings, is by W.M. Eyles of London. It has stone walls with a front of three bays, the centre projects and has tall pilasters supporting a Doric entablature. The entrances, in flanking wings, have Doric columns *in antis* and windows over. (URC)

(11) FRIENDS, Horsefair (SP 454406). The site was acquired in 1664 and a meeting-house erected in 1664–5 which was largely rebuilt in 1748–51 although retaining parts of the N wall and one end wall. This was drastically reconstructed in 1861 and the present building retains little earlier work beyond the basic

structure of walls and roof. The walls are of stone and the roof hipped and covered with stone slates. The S front has been refenestrated and the entrance is now at the W end. The interior (43¾ft by 21¼ft) had galleries on E, S and W sides of which only the last remains. The stand now at the E end but perhaps formerly on the N wall has also been renewed.

(12) Former WESLEYAN, Church Lane (SP 456406). Pedimented front with paired pilasters. Built 1812, enlarged 1828, sold 1865 to Primitive Methodists, now in commercial use.

BARFORD ST JOHN AND ST MICHAEL

(13) Former BAPTIST, Barford St Michael (SP 436328). Dated 1838.

(14) WESLEYAN, Barford St Michael (SP 436325). Dated 1840, with initials 'W.N.' on keystone of front window. Kelly (1931) calls this 'Reformed Wesleyan'.

BICESTER

(15) CONGREGATIONAL, Chapel Street (SP 585223). The congregation, originally Presbyterian, was gathered after 1662 by John Troughton, fellow of St John's College, Oxford. In 1672 Troughton's house was registered as a meeting-place and in October 1691 a certificate was issued for the 'New house of Henry Cornish'. The latter was superseded in January 1728 by the present building, then described as in Water Lane adjoining the Swan Inn.

The walls are of rubble with a front of brick on a rubble plinth

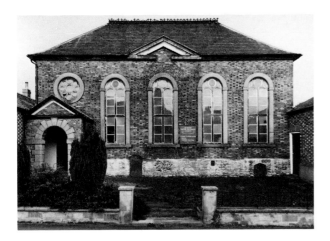

and the roof is hipped and slated with a central valley. The W front, of five bays, greatly altered about 1873, formerly had a central entrance above which was a circular window beneath a gablet, flanked by tall round-arched windows. Two similar windows in the E wall adjoin the original site of the pulpit.

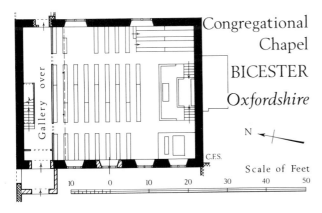

Congregational Chapel BICESTER Oxfordshire

The interior (33½ft by 44ft), also reconstructed, now has a rostrum pulpit at the S end and a single gallery opposite supported by two turned wood columns of the 18th century. The original roof structure survives and closely resembles that at Buckingham, Bucks. (16). (Chapel closed; under conversion to recreational use 1982)

Fittings – *Clock*: on E wall, Parliament clock with arched dial

and chinoiserie decoration on case, signed 'George Langford, London', early 18th-century. *Monuments*: in chapel on E wall (1) Thomas Sirrett, 1828, and his wives, Mary, 1797, and Sarah, 1827; (2) John son of Thomas and Sarah Sirrett, 1849; on S wall (3) Rev. Richard Fletcher, 36 years pastor, 1832, his wives Mary, 1810, and Ann, 1812, and his daughters Mary, 1815, and Hannah, 1820, signed Godfrey, Abingdon; (4) William Rolls, 1798, and Mary his widow, 1803, with later inscriptions to John, father of William Rolls, 1733, Elizabeth his wife, 1777, and Elizabeth wife of Thomas Harris, daughter of William and Mary Rolls, 1799, marble tablet with shaped apron and surmounted by urn in low relief against obelisk-shaped backing; on W wall (5) Samuel Sayer, Gent., 1778, and Benjamin Sayer, 1781, 'The Grandchildren of The Learned and Revd John Troughton M.A. & Fellow of St John's College Oxford from whence he was Ejected for Nonconformity 1662', grey marble tablet; (6) James Gurden, 50 years deacon, 1830, Susannah his wife, 1810, 'by whom he had 14 children', and Benjamin their youngest son, 1808; externally, E of chapel, loose (7) Ann, wife of Andrew Major, Apothecary and Surgeon, daughter of William and Elizabeth Wheeler, 1729.

(16) Former WESLEYAN, North Street (SP 584228). Built 1841, now the Masonic Hall. Rubble with rendered dressings; pedimented front concealed by extension over forecourt 1976.

BLACKTHORN

(17) CONGREGATIONAL (SP 621193). Coursed rubble and slate. Front resembles Launton (64) but with lintel to central entrance

CONGREGATIONAL CHAPEL, BLACKTHORN

and without parapet finials; seating of loose benches with panelled backs and shaped arm-rests also comparable. Said to have been built 1841 but stylistically slightly later. At rear is part of a late 18th-century building of two stories comprising a former cottage and minor rooms now used for church purposes. (URC)

BLOXHAM

(18) Former PRESBYTERIAN (SP 430357). The 'Court House' immediately S of the Parish Church, of stone with a thatched roof, incorporates part of a building of 1610 and some earlier details. The building largely dates from the late 17th century and

(24) BURFORD AND UPTON AND SIGNET. Wesleyan chapel, High Street, Burford.

was used until *c*.1842 as a Presbyterian meeting-house by a congregation which existed jointly with a society of slightly earlier origin meeting in Milton.

Evans (1899) 77–8: *UHST* II, pt2 (1920) 9–32.

BODICOTE

(19) WESLEYAN (SP 460377). N front gabled with terminal pilasters, dated 1845.

BOURTON

(20) WESLEYAN, Little Bourton (SP 458441). Brick and slate. Gabled front dated 1845.

BRIZE NORTON

(21) PRIMITIVE METHODIST (SP 299080). Although dated 1908, this chapel appears to be of *c*.1840 and may perhaps be the former Congregational chapel built in that year. The walls are of rubble and the roof slated. Gabled front with round-arched entrance.

BURFORD AND UPTON AND SIGNET

(22) BAPTIST, Witney Street, Burford (SP 254121). The congregation which originated *c*.1700 built the present meeting-house in 1804 on the site of its predecessor. It has stone walls and a slated roof. The gabled front has a central doorway with flat hood and shaped stone brackets, two round-arched windows to the lower stage and one above. Interior, much altered in 1886 and later, has a rear gallery with front incorporating re-used

fielded panels. *Monuments*: in chapel (1) Rev. John Smith, pastor, 1807; (2) John Waymouth of Exeter, who died in Burford 18 May 1768 'when on a journey to Bristol for the recovery of his health'. *Singers' Desk*, with splayed top, early 19th-century.

(23) FRIENDS, Pytts Lane, Burford (SP 252121). The meeting-house built in 1709 superseded one at Barrington, 2 miles west. It was closed in 1854, reopened for twenty years at the beginning of the 20th century and again reopened in 1955. The walls are of stone and the half-hipped roof is covered with stone slates. The N front is of three bays. A window in the E wall has been

Friends' Meeting-house, BURFORD & UPTON & SIGNET

5   0   5   10   15 Feet

Oxfordshire

Gallery over

site of stand

N

CHARLBURY

(26) Former FRIENDS, Market Street (SP 357196). A meeting-house of 1681 was superseded by the present building in 1779.

Coursed rubble with hipped slate roof. Broad S front with three round-arched windows with red brick surrounds and stone cills. Wide doorway left of centre and small stone tablet above with date of erection. Later lean-to extension to west. Interior (approx. 39ft by 20½ft) is divided into two rooms by an original screen. Now an architect's office.

(27) WESLEYAN, Fisher's Lane (SP 359194). Built 1823, Sunday-school adjacent 1844. Gabled front of three bays with two tiers of round-arched windows with intersecting glazing bars.

CHARLTON-ON-OTMOOR

(28) BAPTIST (SP 560156). Low rubble walls and hipped slate roof. Built *c.*1843 for a church formed in that year. *Pulpit:* elaborate Gothic backboard of five bays with crocketed ogee-headed side panels behind later rostrum pulpit.

CHINNOR

(29) CONGREGATIONAL (SP 756013). The chapel has walls of flint with brick dressings, rendered to the SW, and a hipped slated roof. It was built in 1805 but considerably enlarged in 1811; alterations of the late 19th century, in 1862–8 and 1888, included heightening and re-roofing and renewal of the pews. The original entrance is in the NE wall with two round-arched windows above, traces of a former gable and of a slight enlargement to each side. Two windows in the SE wall flank the pulpit, reset between them is a lozenge-shaped tablet 'erected 1805'. A new entrance was made on the SW side in the later 19th century.

The interior, which is nearly square, has a gallery of *c.*1811 around three sides with a blind balustraded front ornamented at the corners by flat obelisks. Some early 19th-century benches with shaped ends remain at the back of the NW and SW galleries. *Monument* in burial-ground to SW, 'The Venerable Father Mead', born 1747, died 1843, who in 1762 'was converted in this village under a sermon by the Revd. George Whitefield.'

Summers (1905) 225–8.

blocked; a corresponding window in the W wall comes at gallery level. The interior (26ft by 24ft) has a gallery along the S and W sides with signs of enlargement, and an attic room above lit by windows inserted in the end walls in the later 18th century. The lower walls are lined with a dado of horizontal boarding rising on the E side at the back of the former stand removed 1947.

(24) WESLEYAN, High Street, Burford (SP 252122). Large baroque mansion house of *c.*1715, former residence of the Chapman family, sold in 1848 and converted to a chapel in 1849 by removal of the upper floor and partitions. The elaborate ashlar front has a giant order of Corinthian pilasters with full entablature and balustraded parapet. Stone urns formerly on the parapet and flanking the stairs to the entrance were removed in 1849 to Cornbury Park, Oxfordshire.

Burford Methodist Church Centenary, 1849–1949 [1949].

CHADLINGTON

(25) BAPTIST (SP 330219). Dated 1840. Coursed rubble with ashlar dressings and hipped slate roof.

BAPTIST CHAPEL, CHADLINGTON

(30) Former INDEPENDENT (SP 756011). A brief secession from the Congregational chapel (29) resulted in the building of a second chapel opened 26 June 1826 and placed in trust 19 September 1826. The congregations reunited *c*.1828. The former chapel, now the Congregational manse, has rendered walls and a tiled roof, half-hipped at one end. Front of three bays with central entrance and added dormers.

CHIPPING NORTON

(31) BAPTIST, New Street (SP 312272). Built 1863, by Gibbs, Thomson and Colbourne, for church formed 1694. Drastic internal alteration 1980.

(32) Former FRIENDS, New Street (SP 311271). Stone with hipped slate roof, built 1804 superseding a building of 1695. Closed 1910; much altered 1975 on conversion to two cottages. Original round-arched entrances remain in N and E walls.

(33) Former WESLEYAN, Distons Lane (SP 312272). A chapel now converted to two houses, standing immediately behind the Baptist Chapel, was built in 1796 and superseded by the present chapel in West Street in 1868. Coursed rubble and slate with wide gabled S front with central doorway and two tiers of windows, all altered or inserted. Side walls originally of two bays partly covered on the W by a low annexe but with two upper windows remaining on this side and small square tablet between inscribed with the date of erection.

CLANFIELD

(34) Former PRIMITIVE METHODIST (SP 287021). Gabled front to N with outline of former pointed-arched doorway. Traces of flanking windows and defaced tablet above. Built 1844, much altered on conversion to cottage 'Greenfield'.

CLAYDON WITH CLATTERCOT

(35) Former PRIMITIVE METHODIST, Claydon (SP 456500). Brick and slate; built 1837, rebuilt 1861.

CROPREDY

(36) WESLEYAN (SP 469468). Dated 1881. A former chapel of 1822 stood behind, where a house of red brick may incorporate parts of the earlier building.

DEDDINGTON

(37) Former CONGREGATIONAL, The Tchure (SP 467316). A 'dissenting congregation of great antiquity' is reported to have decayed following the introduction of heterodox preaching and the meeting-house closed. A fresh attempt to commence services was made about 1819 under the auspices of the North Bucks. Association of Independent Churches and a Mr Harris converted a barn for their use which was opened in August 1820. The new cause developed into a Congregational Church, formed 1842, and continued to use the barn until the present chapel in New Street was built in 1881 to the designs of John Sulman.

The former barn stands on the S side of a lane opening from the E side of New Street and is now named the 'Foresters Hall'. It has coursed rubble walls and a slate roof. The N front has a small doorway remaining from its earlier use blocked and superseded in 1820 by end entrances with windows over and two windows between. The S side, presumably facing the former farmyard, has traces of a wider barn opening near the W end together with a later doorway and windows.

CYB (1879) 409: *NPAB* (1820) 17–9; (1821) 14–15.

(38) WESLEYAN REFORM, Chapel Square (SP 468316). Brick and slate with square rendered front, central round-arched doorway between pair of two-light windows and wider window of three lights above. Tablet over entrance dated 1851 and a gallery inside of this period but otherwise largely refitted in late 19th century.

Former Chapel at rear, facing Church Street, of coursed rubble with a hipped slate roof was built in the early 19th century but altered *c*.1851 when a gable with urn finials was added to the E front incorporating a tablet inscribed 'WESLEYAN SUNDAY SCHOOL 1822'. The front has a narrow doorway between a pair of windows, all with lintels and keystones. Two windows in the S wall have timber lintels. A round-arched recess remains internally at the W end marking the site of the pulpit; a fireplace in the N wall was probably added on conversion for Sunday-school use.

(39) Former CONGREGATIONAL, Hempton (SP 446318). Built *c*.1849. Now in farm use.

DORCHESTER

(40) Former BAPTIST, Watling Lane (SU 576943). Small cob and thatch building attached to and now forming part of an earlier timber-framed cottage 'Orchard House' was registered for worship in 1820. The Baptist church formed in 1849 which was in membership with the Berkshire Association was dissolved before 1882. The chapel, possibly a pre-existing structure, was slightly extended to the N in brickwork in the early 19th century and given an entrance in the N wall to which a small porch was later added.

(41) Former PRIMITIVE METHODIST, Bridge End (SU 579938). Low building with rendered walls. Built *c*.1839; later used by Salvation Army and now converted to a cottage.

EAST ADDERBURY

(42) Former WESLEYAN (SP 471356). Ironstone with two round-arched windows in N wall flanking site of pulpit. Roof lowered. Built 1810; superseded by present chapel 150 yards W in 1893.

ENSTONE

(43) WESLEYAN, Neat Enstone (SP 377244). Brick and slate with two wide round-arched windows in front and back walls. Lower extension at SW end. Opened 1811 incorporating some older masonry in rear wall.

EPWELL

(44) Former CHAPEL (SP 353405), immediately NE of the parish church. Coursed stone walls and a thatched roof, appears to have been registered in 1825 for a ' Revivalish', possibly Baptist, meeting. It soon after passed to (Primitive) Methodists who used

it until *c*.1970; it is now used for storage. The S front has two sash windows, possibly alterations, and an inserted doorway to the left. In the W end is a former doorway with window above, both now blocked.

EWELME

(45) Former WESLEYAN (SU 644916). Brick with three-bay gabled front and two tiers of windows; dated 1826. Now a post office.

EYE AND DUNSDEN

(46) CONGREGATIONAL, Binfield Heath (SU 744779). Diminutive Gothic chapel of ashlar with a slated roof, built 1835 under the influence of Rev. James Sherman of Reading. Narrow battle-

mented tower at NW end incorporating porch with arched entrance and ogee label with finial. Side walls of five bays with two-stage buttresses and lancets. Sunday-school to SE added 1836.

    Summers (1905) 189–90.

EYNSHAM

(47) BAPTIST (SP 431092). Rubble and slate, gabled front with parapet and small finial, three bays with four-centred arched doorway and square moulded labels. Tablet between windows 'erected A.D. 1818'. *Monuments*: in front of chapel (1) Nathaniel E. Adams, 1835; (2) Frances wife of Richard Buckingham, 1837.

FENCOTT AND MURCOTT

(48) PRIMITIVE METHODIST, Murcott (SP 589154). Gabled front with small circular window above a recent porch. Stone tablet at apex of gable dated 1847.

FILKINS AND BROUGHTON POGGS

(49) PRIMITIVE METHODIST, Filkins (SP 237042). Dated 1853. With wide pointed-arched windows.

FINSTOCK

(50) WESLEYAN (SP 361161). Built 1840, school extension in front 1902.

FREELAND

(51) WESLEYAN (SP 415127). Rubble with half-hipped roof covered with stone slates. Original front to SE has blocked

round-arched doorway between windows and small circular recess above which is a painted metal panel 'NOV 19th/ WESLEY'S/CHAPEL/1805'. Later doorway added at SW end.

GORING

(52) COUNTESS OF HUNTINGDON'S CONNEXION (SU 599807). An Independent church was formed in 1786, the members subscribing to a Confession of Faith 64 pages in length and divided into 33 chapters. The first meeting-house on the present site was built in 1793 and opened by Lady Ann Erskine, it was superseded in 1893 but survives in altered form as the Sunday-school. This has walls of brick with some flint at the sides and a hipped and tiled roof with a central flat or valley. The N front is of three bays with two tiers of windows and a central arched entrance all with late 19th-century dressings. The S wall has two original round-arched windows flanking the site of the pulpit. The interior (25¼ft by 27½ft) has a gallery around three sides with panelled front divided by fluted pilasters and supported by square wooden posts; some original seating remains in the gallery. (Entirely refitted c.1980)

Summers (1905) 107–10.

GREAT HASELEY

(53) Former CONGREGATIONAL (SP 641019). Built c.1841.

GREAT MILTON

(54) WESLEYAN (SP 629030). Rubble with brick dressings and tiled roof; three-bay gabled front with lancet windows, pointed-arched doorway in later porch, and tablet dated 1842.

HENLEY-ON-THAMES

(55) Former INDEPENDENT, New Street (SU 762829). Now 'Kenton Theatre', was built 1809 for a section of the older Congregational church which seceded in that year but ceased to meet after 1836. It stands behind other buildings on the N side of the street and has brick walls with two round-arched windows to each side.

Summers (1905) 120.

(56) FRIENDS, Northfield End (SU 759831). Part of an existing range of buildings was in use as a meeting-house from c. 1668 and purchased in 1672. This was demolished and the present meet-ing-house of brick and tile with terracotta dressings built on the site in 1894. An early 17th-century timber-framed cottage which formed the end bay of the range adjoins to the south-east.

HOOK NORTON

(57) BAPTIST, High Street (SP 354331). The chapel, built in 1787, replaces one of 1718. It has walls of ironstone and a hipped roof now re-covered in tiles. Two round-arched windows in the N wall with later cast-iron intersecting glazing bars are repeated on the S and E sides. The entrance is at the W end in a two-storied porch which incorporates the gallery staircase; there are four

small windows at two levels in the W wall. Between the N windows is a stone tablet reset from the previous chapel with the initials and date H/WA/1718 (see monument 3 below).

The interior (36¾ft by 26¼ft) has an original W gallery with fielded panelled front, and later galleries added along the N and S walls. The box-pews and pulpit, which date from a re-fitting of 1856, have stop-chamfered panelled sides. The roof is supported by two king-post trusses and butt-purlins.

Fittings – *Monuments* and *Floorslab*. *Monuments*: on N wall (1) James Walford, 1840, and Mary his widow, 1846, oval stone; (2) Ann Poole, 1817, oval stone; (3) William Harwood of Broad Marston, Glos., 1720/1, 'of his piety towards God & Benevolence to Mankind This Edifice for Divine Worship And other Donations at this Place of his Nativity are Perpetuated as a Memorial . . . ', also his niece Elizabeth Griffith, 1721, and his widow Anne, daughter of Thomas Edwards of Rhual, Flints., n.d., marble tablet with moulded base and capping; on E wall (4) James Wilmot, 1795, Ruth his wife, 1795, and James their son, 1799; (5) Charles Newberry, 1820, and Patience his widow, 1833; on S wall (6) George Westbury, late of Wigginton, 1728, recording that he added £40 to a gift of £20 from Amos Sansbury of Banbury 'to purchase a burying place at Hooknorton' and that he 'bought Bury Orchard for that Purpose, where he lieth interr'd', later inscription below 'This Meeting House Rebuilt 1787'; (7) Mary, wife of James Surridge, 'Citizen & Freeman of the Clock-makers Company, London', 1790, and two infant sons. *Floorslab*: re-used as threshold to W door, worn, with date 1765.

The burial-ground N of chapel contains many 18th-century headstones, some carved in high relief with cherubs heads and decorative cartouches.

Ivimey II (1814) 517–21.

(58) FRIENDS, Southrop (SP 357328). The meeting-house built in 1704 which stood SE of Southrop House was demolished in 1950. It had stone walls and a gabled roof covered with stone slates, two timber mullioned and transomed windows and a doorway in the SE side and a third window in the SW gable wall. The interior (28½ft by 16ft) had a stand at the SW end and a small gallery opposite. A rubble boundary wall remains around the site.

Drawings and photographs by H. Godwin Arnold in NMR.

HORLEY

(59) WESLEYAN (SP 418436). 'A building lately erected at Horley' registered in March 1802 was probaby the rear portion of the present chapel, built as an extension to a 17th-century cottage and enlarged to the front c.1840. The chapel has walls of ironstone rubble with a gabled front of three bays having a four-centred arched doorway and pointed-arched windows.

HORNTON

(60) Former PRIMITIVE METHODIST (SP 393451). Built 1836 behind cottage to left of 1884 chapel, latterly a youth club but now disused. Stone and slate with round-arched doorway and window above in gabled front; two windows in side wall with keystones to lintels and remains of leaded glazing in large panes.

KINGHAM

(61) WESLEYAN (SP 262241). Rubble and slate, with gabled ends, two round-arched windows in the side walls and one above the N entrance. Refitted c.1872 but probably built in the early 19th century.

LANGFORD

(62) CONGREGATIONAL (SP 247029). Services began c.1840 in a barn; the first chapel was built alongside in 1850 and rebuilt in 1884. The barn, which remains in use as a Sunday-school, was partly refaced c.1853 and has a stone gabled front with pointed-arched windows; it is linked to the chapel by a low range of building perhaps also converted from farm use.

Summers (1905) 239–41.

(63) PRIMITIVE METHODIST (SP 248027). Dated 1849, 'Ground Kindly Given by Mr J.K. Tombs'.

LAUNTON

(64) CONGREGATIONAL (SP 610225). Rubble with ashlar dressings and slate roof, front with pineapple finials and large tablet inscribed 'BETHEL/1850'. Original benches with panelled backs and shaped arm-rests.

LEAFIELD

(65) BAPTIST (SP 314153). Rubble with ashlar dressings and hipped slate roof. Three-bay front closely resembling (25) above. Perhaps built as a Congregational chapel, opened 1838.

Summers (1905) 299.

LEW

(66) Former CONGREGATIONAL (SP 321059). Built 1840. Pointed-arched entrance, quatrefoil tablet in gable above.

(64) LAUNTON. Congregational chapel.

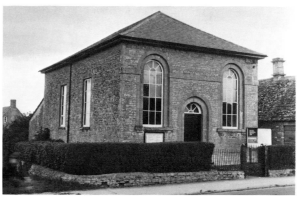
(65) LEAFIELD. Baptist chapel.

LITTLE TEW

(67) BAPTIST (SP 385284). Dated 1871. Cusped windows under square labels and unusual crow-stepped gable with finial.

LOWER HEYFORD

(68) Former WESLEYAN, Caulcott (SP 509243). Built 1841, closed 1955 and converted to garage.

MILTON

(69) Former PRESBYTERIAN (SP 449351). The house of Samuel Cox was licensed for Presbyterian use in 1672 and a meeting-house subsequently provided which is described in a trust deed of 1708 as standing 'in the Backside or Close belonging to a Messuage or tenement of the said Samuel Cox the elder' then occupied by his son Simon. The meeting-house, evidently in use for some years previously but perhaps erected for this purpose, was 'about Three Bayes' in length and had a thatched roof. After the demise of the then Unitarian congregation c.1842, which enjoyed a joint pastorate with Bloxham (q.v.), the meeting-

house was used *c*.1850–7 as a chapel-of-ease for Adderbury prior to the erection of the present parish church and subsequently as cottages. Amherst Tyssen writing in 1920 says that 'the building . . . was demolished a few years ago'. A fragment of rubble walling on the W side of Chapel Lane, just N of Chapel Cottage, has been identified as the remains of this building. This now forms part of a row of garages of which the N wall, bounded by larger quoins, survives for its entire length (23½ft externally) and portions of the E and W walls also remain. Some internal wall-plaster is still visible in the NW corner and the lower part of a blocked window with splayed and plastered jambs is to be seen internally on the W wall.

UHST II, pt 2 (1920) 9–32.

MILTON-UNDER-WYCHWOOD

(70) BAPTIST (SP 263180). A chapel opened in 1808 was reported in 1839 to be in a dangerous state. It was replaced in the same year by the present building at a reported cost of £372. 9s. 6½d. The front wall is of ashlar in three bays. The interior has a rear gallery; the pews were renewed in the late 19th century. *Monument*: in chapel, Rev. John 'Hiorns' or Hirons, first pastor, 1844, and Susannah his wife, 1844.

Davidson, G.W., *A Brief History of the Baptist Church, Milton, Oxfordshire* [*c*.1905].

(71) STRICT BAPTIST (SP 264182). 'Zoar Chapel' was built in 1841. The entrance is covered by a modern porch, a stone above is pierced with ventilating holes to form the date 1883, presumably that of a major refurbishing.

Oliver (1968) 116.

(72) Former WESLEYAN (SP 264181). The former 'Wesleyan Mission Room' is a low building of stone and slate built *c*.1860.

In the gable facing the road is a small niche carved below with the denominational name and containing a fragment of mediaeval carving in wood representing an ecclesiastic playing a flute, perhaps removed from the parish church when rebuilt in 1854 (see p. 186).

MINSTER LOVELL

(73) Former PRIMITIVE METHODIST, Charterville (SP 313101). Dated 1892 or 1898. Gate with scrolled supports and railings in front of chapel, wrought-iron, 18th-century, reset.

MOLLINGTON

(74) Former PRIMITIVE METHODIST (SP 440474). Built 1845 and refronted *c*.1860, closed 1947 and subsequently used by Brethren, now in secular occupation. Red brick and slate with two windows in E and W sides, the foremost windows heightened, and entrance at S end of W side: The S front, block-bonded to the sides, has dressings of dark brick with vitrified headers comprising terminal pilasters, entablature and raking cornices to the gable, and two windows with round-arched heads in glazed headers. Part of the structure of a S gallery remains.

NETTLEBED

(75) Former CONGREGATIONAL (SU 703869). Tablet in S gable 'Erected 1838'; altered after 1968 on conversion to house.

Summers (1905) 124–5.

OXFORD

(76) BAPTIST, New Road (SP 512062). A Baptist church was in existence by 1656 in which year it sent messengers to the Abingdon Association. The cause fell into decay in the early 18th cen-

(76) OXFORD. Baptist chapel.

tury and when, in 1715, the Baptist and Presbyterian meeting-houses were severely damaged by rioters the two societies united and built a new meeting-house in New Road *c*.1721. The church was reorganized in 1780 without restriction on baptismal beliefs, but a secession of paedobaptists in 1830 left the other party in the majority.

The present chapel dates from a rebuilding of 1798 of which only parts of the side walls now remain. This was a square building of rubble with a hipped roof surmounted by an octagonal lantern. The front had two doorways alternating with three circular windows and two larger circular or oval windows above. In 1819 the chapel was enlarged to the S and the present front built; this is of ashlar in three bays with a central pedimented porch, having paired Roman Doric columns, between small round-arched windows and rusticated corner pilasters; the upper stage has a central bay with Ionic columns and a wide stilted lunette window, round-arched niches to the side bays, and corner pilasters. The side walls were raised in brickwork and the building re-roofed and refitted *c*.1896. (Interior reported entirely altered 1980)

Fittings – *Monuments*: in chapel (1) Samuel Steane, 1832, and Emma his widow, 1840; (2) John Bartlett, 1822, Jane his widow, 1825, and their children; (3) Thomas Pasco, 1806; (4) Jesse Elliston, 1853; (5) Rev. James Hinton, 1823.

New Road Baptist Church, Oxford... Tercentenary Booklet (1953): Summers (1905) 246–50.

(77) Former BAPTIST, The Croft, Headington (SP 544074). The chapel, built *c*.1835 and superseded *c*.1900 by the present Baptist

chapel in Old High Street, may have been interdenominational in origin. It has walls of squared stone with a gabled S front of three bays. The windows are small and of two four-centred arched lights; the entrance is similarly arched and has a quatrefoil above. Under conversion to cottage, 1977.

(78) Former METHODIST, New Inn Hall Street (SP 51200625). Houses, nos. 32 and 34, were built or converted in the late 18th century for use as a Methodist preaching-house and a modern tablet records visits by John Wesley on 14 July 1783 and later. It was superseded by a new Wesleyan chapel, built in 1818 to designs by William Jenkins on a site further N on the opposite side of the road but now demolished, and again in 1878 by the present Gothic chapel in the same street, by Charles Bell.

The former preaching-house has rubble walls and a hipped tiled roof. The W front is of two stories with a wide doorway near the S end. (For mediaeval vaulting incorporated in N wall see RCHM *City of Oxford* (1939), mon. 124.)

Dolbey (1964) 173: Oxley, J.E., *A History of Wesley Memorial Church, Oxford, 1818–1968* (1967–8).

(79) Former WESLEYAN. Rose Hill, Cowley (SP 535039). Built 1835 by Henry Leake of Iffley but transferred to United Methodist Free Church in 1860. Widened, porch built and round arches added to windows in 20th century. *Monument*: in burial ground, John Leonard, 1846, *et al.*, headstone reset.

VCH *Oxfordshire* V (1957) 94.

(80) SALVATION ARMY, Castle Street (SP 511061). Red brick with S front in two stories, end bays treated as towers with

(80) OXFORD. Salvation Army Citadel.

battlements and tall roofs with iron cresting. Dated 1888, Com. Sherwood, architect. Windows have opaque glass with yellow bands and red squares at intersections. (Demolished since 1970)

PIDDINGTON

(81) CONGREGATIONAL (SP 641174). Built 1848. Three-bay gabled front; contemporary iron railings.

RAMSDEN

(82) Former WESLEYAN (SP 355152). Built 1832. Gabled front with round-arched doorway and two segmental-arched upper windows.

ROLLRIGHT

(83) EBENEZER CHAPEL (SP 323311), formerly Baptist but now in domestic use, is dated 1833. Coursed stone walls with two tall windows and doorway to left in front, all with flat-arched heads. Cottages adjoin at each end.

(84) BETHEL CHAPEL (SP 324311), built 1838, probably by seceders from 'Ebenezer' and of similar materials, has an entrance in the exposed gable wall, two windows at the front and one at the back. Now used for storage.

ROTHERFIELD PEPPARD

(85) CONGREGATIONAL (SU 708809). The chapel, now concealed by the manse and later buildings to E and W, was opened in 1796 and paid for by Peter French, one of the trustees of Castle Street Chapel, Reading. It has brick walls and a hipped tiled roof; the later roofs are slated. The entrance is at the E side but was perhaps formerly at the S before the erection of the manse. A window in the W wall at mid height has been blocked and replaced in the early 19th century by two windows to the south. There are two windows of two lights in the N wall. An aisle was added to the W in the early 19th century and a British school-room was built to the E in the late 19th century, possibly replacing a second aisle. The interior (originally 33¾ft by 19¾ft) has a gallery at the S end. Colonnades of three timber columns with moulded caps and bases divide the building. *Monument*: in W aisle, Rev. Joseph Walker, 1828, pastor upwards of 30 years, Elizabeth his wife, 1816, and their children Rev. Joseph Walker,

Independent pastor at Bracknell, 1811, William, 1807, Henry, 1805, and Mary Ann Saunders, 1849, signed Wheeler, Reading.
　Summers (1905) 152–6.

SALFORD

(86) WESLEYAN (SP 288280). Small square building of rubble and slate with later porch; opened 1848.

SHENINGTON

(87) Former CHAPEL (SP 376428). Built *c*.1817 by Independents but subsequently occupied by Primitive Methodists. Closed after 1962 and entirely altered on conversion to a house.

SHILTON

(88) BAPTIST (SP 266084). Originally a small barn with cart entrance in side wall facing lane. Church formed 1830; pointed-arched windows and pedimented doorway of later 19th century.

SHIPTON-ON-CHERWELL AND THRUPP

(89) Former BAPTIST, Thrupp (SP 483159). Rubble and slate, gabled to NW with porch and large blocked window with tablet in infilling dated 1876. Round-arched windows in side walls with traces of earlier openings. Early 19th-century with contemporary cottages to SE, original use uncertain. (Chapel derelict 1970)

SHUTFORD

(90) Former FRIENDS (SP 386404). Coursed stone walls and a tiled roof; built as a meeting-house in the late 17th century and converted to a cottage *c*.1840.

　The S front has at the centre a window with flat-arched head and wood frame of two lights, and a small later dormer above; the original doorway to the right has a flat-arched head and contemporary moulded oak frame and plank door; a cottage door-

Former Friends' Meeting-house SHUTFORD *Oxfordshire*

way at the opposite end of this wall replaces a window. The E and W walls are gabled and surmounted by small brick chimney-stacks of recent date; there is a single window centrally to ground and first floors at each end. The N wall is blank.

The interior (18¼ft by 33¼ft) was divided by two partitions with shutters to form narrow ground-floor rooms at the E and W ends, the E room having a segmental-arched fireplace in the NW corner and an original staircase with flat balusters and newel with ball finial in the SE corner giving access to a gallery of which the plain slatted balustraded front remains in an upper partition. A similar gallery appears to have existed at the W end; the area between was floored over in the 19th century.

(91) Former WESLEYAN (SP 385403). Opened 1837, much altered.

SIBFORD GOWER

(92) FRIENDS (SP 352378). A small meeting-house of 1678–81 was rebuilt in 1864 to meet an increased demand resulting from

the proximity of the Friends' school at Sibford Ferris. Stone and slate with gabled S front between lower cloak-room wings. Single meeting-room with lobby to S and stand against N wall. Blocked doorway in W wall and trace of partition at S end of room indicate minor alterations.

(93) WESLEYAN (SP 352379). Brick and slate, opened 1827. *Monuments*: in front of chapel (1) Thomas Bloxham, 1839; (2) Sarah, wife of William Matthews, 1848, and their children Mary Ann, and William; (3) John Woodfield, 1843, and Maria his wife, 1839.

SOUTH NEWINGTON

(94) Former FRIENDS (SP 407331). The meeting-house built in 1692, now used as a village hall, has walls of squared ironstone rubble, the roof is covered with stone slates. The S front has a central entrance covered by a porch built in 1927; a tablet above with the inscription 'DOMVS HÆC/QVÆ ÆDIFICERET/ANNO:DOM:/.1692:RC:*JB*'. A small dormer window near the W end lights one end of a gallery. The E and W walls are gabled and the latter has an ashlar chimney-stack at the apex. The interior (29¾ft by 18¼ft) has a W gallery, probably inserted in the later 18th century, and a fireplace below in the NW corner. The

Former FRIENDS' MEETING-HOUSE, SOUTH NEWINGTON

roof is supported by two arched-braced collar trusses. No original fittings remain.

SOUTH STOKE

(95) INDEPENDENT (SU 599834). The chapel, built in 1820 in association with the Countess of Huntingdon's congregation at Goring, has brick walls and a hipped tiled roof. Entrance at E end with gallery window over and two windows in S side. Date 1820 and initials EH on bricks at W end of S wall.
    Summers (1905) 110–11.

STANDLAKE

(96) BAPTIST, Brightampton (SP 387034). Rubble and slate with pointed-arched windows and three-bay gabled front; built 1832 for a section of the church at Cote. (Now closed.)
    Stanley [*c*.1935] 191–2.

STEEPLE BARTON

(97) Former WESLEYAN, Middle Barton (SP 435259), on E side of Worton Road. Rubble with half-hipped slate roof. Built *c*.1835, closed before 1939 and much altered to a cottage.

STOKE ROW

(98) INDEPENDENT (SU 684840). Brick on flint footings with hipped slate roof. Three-bay S front with later gabled porch; two windows in E and W sides. *Inscriptions*: on bricks in side walls, date of erection, 1815, and initials. *Monument*: in chapel on E wall, John Olding Alanson, 1831, 'Who in the hands of GOD was a willing and efficient Instrument in the erection of this Chapel'.

STONESFIELD

(99) Former WESLEYAN (SP 391171). Stone walls and half-hipped roof covered with Stonesfield slates; porch added 1907, tablet above inscribed 'WESLEYAN CHAPEL 1827'. Super-seded 1867 by present chapel 100 yards north-east.

TACKLEY

(100) WESLEYAN, Lower Hades Road (SP 478206). Dated 1853. Probably the conversion of a small early 19th-century barn.

THAME

(101) BAPTIST, Park Street (SP 710056). Dated 1865.
    Baines, A.H.J., *The Baptists of Thame* [*c*.1965].

(102) CONGREGATIONAL, High Street (SP 708057). Gabled front of rubble with brick sides, by W.F. Poulton of Reading, 1871. Organ in small rounded apse behind pulpit; schoolrooms below. (URC)

CYB (1872) 414.

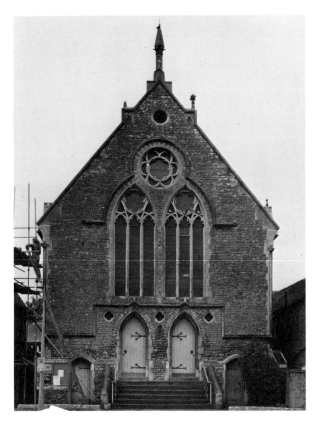

(103) WESLEYAN, High Street (SP 707058). Wesleyans met from 1778 to 1853 in the former Presbyterian meeting-house in Sun Yard, originally registered in 1728. The present chapel of 1876, replacing one of 1853 which was destroyed by fire, has a gabled stone front with three graduated lancet windows and octagonal

corner pinnacles. (Converted to secular use *c.*1977 and congregation united with (102) above)

WATLINGTON

(104) WESLEYAN (SU 691945). Dated 1812. W front in Flemish bond with glazed headers and cast-iron gable ornaments. Original gallery around three sides, seating later.

WEST ADDERBURY

(105) Former INDEPENDENT (SP 468355). Pedimented ashlar front with circular tablet dated 1829. Doorway widened on conversion to industrial use.

(106) Former FRIENDS (SP 465354). The meeting-house, now a store for adjacent public cemetery, was built in 1675 by Bray Doyley or D'Oyly of Adderbury, a prominent Quaker. It has walls of coursed rubble and the roof, formerly covered with stone slates, is now tiled. The S front has a wide central entrance

(106) WEST ADDERBURY. Former Friends' meeting-house. (Chimney stack dated 1675).

between two windows with wooden frames of three lights and leaded glazing. Above the entrance is a small gabled dormer. The E and W walls are gabled and have shaped kneelers and parapets; at the W end is an ashlar chimney-stack with a panel on the S face bearing the date 1675. There is a wide upper window of three lights in the W wall, a similar window to the lower floor at the E end, and a smaller window above. A window appears to have formerly existed centrally in the N wall.

The interior (19ft by 30¾ft) has deep galleries with plain balustraded fronts around the E, S and W sides, possibly the extension of a gallery or upper room at the W end only, where one roof truss remains closed above collar level. The stand against the N wall dates from the 18th century.

A smaller meeting-house, demolished c.1955, stood to the S and had rubble walls and a thatched roof; it was built in the early 18th century for women's meetings and later became a cottage.

The burial-ground to the E contains uniform headstones of 19th century and later, also, fixed to S boundary wall, four cast-iron monuments with pointed-arched heads, of 1855–79.

Arnold (1960) 101–3.

WESTON-ON-THE-GREEN

(107) WESLEYAN, North Lane (SP 532189). Dated 1838.

WHEATLEY

(108) BRETHREN (SP 594058). An early 19th-century granary with rubble walls lined in brickwork and gabled ends with shaped kneelers. Converted by partial removal of upper floor leaving a gallery at one end.

(109) CONGREGATIONAL (SP 598056). A late 18th-century barn or outbuilding associated with an adjacent tannery was con-

verted to a meeting-house about 1842 and the front wall rebuilt. The walls are of rubble and the roof is tiled. The gabled NE front has three lancet windows and a former central entrance now replaced by a gabled SE porch. Traces of an earlier wide cart-entrance with timber lintel remain in the NW wall. (URC)

Summers (1905) 265–8.

WIGGINGTON

(110) Former BAPTIST (SP 390331). Coursed ironstone walls, ashlar front, and roof re-covered in tiles; three-bay front with keystones to lintels and formerly external shutters to the windows. Built c.1835.

WITNEY

(111) Former PRESBYTERIAN, Meeting-house Lane (SP 355097). A Presbyterian society appears to have been in existence in Witney by 1672 in which year Francis Hubert (or Hubbard), ejected vicar of Winterbourne Monkton, licensed his house for meetings. The present building, erected in 1712 during the ministry of Samuel Mather, grandson of the Puritan divine Richard Mather of Toxteth Chapel, Liverpool, continued to serve the society until 1828 when a new chapel was built in High Street (see below). The congregation suffered from various divisions in the late 18th century due in part to the presence of a considerable Baptist element, but became more firmly established as a Congregational cause in the early 19th century. After 1828 the meeting-house was used for Sunday-school and other church purposes; it now serves as a Scout hall.

The meeting-house, said to have been paid for out of the private fortune of Samuel Mather's wife, a Townsend of Staple Hall, is a rectangular building with tall rubble walls and a tiled roof. The N and S ends are gabled, each having a tall upper window and at the S end next to the lane is a wide central doorway with an early 18th-century wood frame. The W wall, concealed from view by an adjoining late 19th-century brick building, faces towards the premises of the Batt School; it has a pair of windows set close together which formerly flanked a central pulpit and two windows towards the ends; that to the S is blocked, the others have timber lintels and original wooden cross-frames. The E wall has two similar windows more widely spaced.

Monuments: reported 1951 as internal were (1) Thomas Howell, 1780; (2) Richard Witts, 1755, Jane his widow, 1770, and Richard their son, 1828; (3) James Marriott, 1803. The last was (1969) loose in the 1828 chapel.

Summers (1905) 268–75.

(112) CONGREGATIONAL, High Street (SP 355098). Built in 1828 at the expense of William Townsend, of the same family as the wife of Samuel Mather whose money had paid for the earlier

building. The walls are of squared stone. The E front is of ashlar; the principal windows, of two lights with uncusped tracery, are set in projecting panels surmounted by false parapets. Above the entrance is a circular window with quatrefoil tracery and in the gable is a tablet with the inscription 'ERECTED/BY/WILLIAM TOWNSEND/OF/HOLBORN, LONDON/A.D. MDCCCXXVIII' with a small shield-of-arms below. The interior has a flat plaster ceiling with moulded cornice, central plaster ceiling-rose and four ventilating grilles with Gothic tracery. A gallery at the E end has a panelled front supported by cast-iron columns.

Fittings – *Bootscrapers*: pair, at front entrance, cast iron, 1828. *Monuments*: in chapel on N wall (1) Mary (Roffey) wife of Rev. Robert Tozer, 1837; on S wall (2) Rev. Robert Tozer, 18 years

minister, 1855. *Organ*: small, with wooden case, front of five panels with crocketed central arch, pinnacled corners and dummy pipes, mid 19th-century. *Pulpit*: original front of three panelled sides reduced in height and set on late 19th-century plat-

Congregational Chapel, WITNEY
Oxfordshire

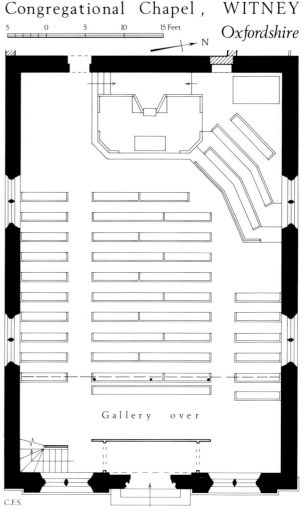

C.F.S.

form. *Railings*: in front of chapel, wrought-iron, rising in centre to double gates with tall standards and scrolled overthrow, 1828. (Chapel demolished *c*.1970–2 and replaced by a supermarket)

Summers (1905) 268–75.

(113) Former FRIENDS, Wood Green Hill (SP 360104). A meeting-house of 1676 was replaced in 1712 by the present building, but this was not registered until January 1745/6. It was enlarged to the NE in the late 18th century and a wing added to the NW a century later. The walls are of rubble and the roof is covered with stone slates. The original structure has been much altered. The SW wall is gabled and has one blocked lower window and another above with a large timber lintel surviving from a previous window. The SE wall, facing the burial-ground, has two segmental-arched windows of the late 18th century and

SE wall.

the remains of former openings including a wide doorway near the SW end and a window alongside with external timber lintel. The NE extension has at the front a segmental-arched doorway with rusticated brick arch and jambs and double doors and at the back a corresponding pair of doors with vertical panelling.

The interior (41ft by 18ft) has a narrow NE gallery with an original fireplace. The walls have a panelled dado which rises at the SW end behind the site of the stand; a false wall behind the stand and a flat canopy above probably date from *c*.1800. The NE extension comprises a wide stone-paved entrance-passage with minor rooms on the ground floor and a single room above; the staircase has a straight moulded string of the late 18th century and a ball finial to the lower newel. The roof is supported by two trusses with exposed tie-beams and two collars; the plaster ceiling has been inserted. (In use 1969 as a hall, converted to residential use *c*.1980)

Inscriptions: (1) inside SW gable, on plaster surface of original window lintel, 'Richard May'; (2) on glazing quarry in SW window of upper room at NE end 'Wm Mills glazier Witney 1786'.

(114) WESLEYAN, High Street (SP 357099). Rubble walls and slated roof, in Gothic style by J. Wilson of Bath, 1850, replacing a chapel of 1800. Narrow gabled entrance bay facing street with tall window of four lights and cusped tracery in a two-centred head. A decorative bell-cote and elaborate pinnacles have been removed. Five lancet windows in low side walls. Galleried interior. *Bootscrapers*: at entrance, pair, cast-iron, double arms bracketed to single standard.

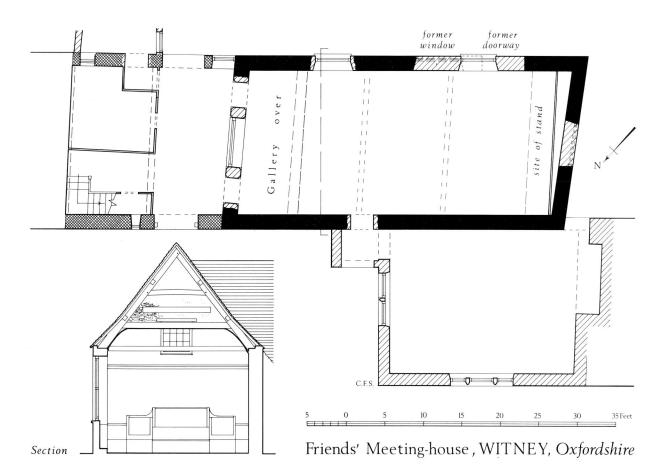

Section

Friends' Meeting-house, WITNEY, *Oxfordshire*

(115) WESLEYAN, Newland (SP 363101). Gabled front with upper window; concealed behind other buildings. Opened 1828.

WOODSTOCK

(116) BAPTIST, High Street (SP 445167). Rendered front of three bays with pediment, round-arched doorway and windows with marginal lights. Built early 19th century for a church formed c.1825–7.

WROXTON

(117) WESLEYAN, Balscote (SP 391419). Small chapel with walls of squared ironstone and slated roof; dated 1850.

(118) Former WESLEYAN, Wroxton (SP 413418), behind 'Sundial Farmhouse'. Built c.1820, with walls of squared stone and a slate roof. Two windows in W front with entrance near S end replaced by garage doors. Site of pulpit at N end with painted inscription on wall and traces of gallery opposite. Present chapel 250 yards W dated 1935.

(72) MILTON-UNDER-WYCHWOOD: Former Wesleyan Mission Room. Mediaeval carving.

RUTLAND

Leicestershire

The smallest historical county in England, although not figuring greatly in the history of dissent, nevertheless possesses in microcosm examples of the meeting-places of most of the principal denominations and was the native county of Robert Browne who, prior to his defection, laid the foundations of Independency and gave his name to a new religious party. The two surviving early 18th-century meeting-houses in Oakham present in marked contradistinction the traditional stone vernacular of the Friends' meeting-house (10) and the still simple but *avant garde* brickwork of the Presbyterians (8). Stone predominates throughout the 19th century, and the only early 19th-century brick chapels noted were in the south-west corner of the county. Although large and spectacular chapels are lacking, the simpler country meeting-houses such as Barrowden (1), of 1819, and Wing (15), of 1841, are worthy examples of their class, and the Congregational chapel at Oakham (9), of 1861, is representative of the great rebuilding in which Congregationalists particularly were indulging at that period.

BARROWDEN

(1) GENERAL BAPTIST (SK 948002). The church meeting here, long united with Morcott, claims to have been founded in 1710. Barrowden Chapel, built in 1819, has coursed rubble walls with ashlar dressings and a hipped slated roof. The S front has a round-arched doorway with fanlight and date-stone between gallery windows. The interior (30ft by 26ft) was refitted in the late 19th century but the original gallery seating remains. *Monuments*: on W wall (1) Thomas Wade, 1835; (2) John Arnold, 1816, Elizabeth his wife, 1827, and Elizabeth their daughter, 1788. There is a small *burial-ground* with early 19th-century headstones; entrance gates to E have decorative iron piers of *c.*1819.

Taylor (1818) II, 428–9: Wood (1847) 209.

BELTON

(2) BAPTIST, Loddington Lane (SK 817015). Built 1842.

BAPTIST CHAPEL, BELTON

KETTON

(3) CONGREGATIONAL, Chapel Lane (SK 981043). Built in 1829 for an Independent Church formed in 1827. The walls are of coursed rubble with ashlar dressings; the roof, hipped to the S, is covered with Collyweston slates. Two round-arched windows face the lane. At the N end is a later building with a date-tablet reset from the chapel. A gallery was erected *c.*1837.

CYB (1877) 364, obituary of Rev. T. Gammidge.

(4) WESLEYAN (SK 982046). Ashlar with Collyweston slate roof. Gabled NW front with three-light traceried window between gabled porches. Foundation stone laid 13 September 1864.

LANGHAM

(5) BAPTIST, Church Street (SK 843111). Brown stone walls and a slate roof; built in 1854 for a church formed in that year. The SE front is gabled with clasping pilaster buttresses at the corners surmounted by dwarf finials, a central doorway with shield-shaped date-tablet above, and two tiers of windows.

LYDDINGTON

(6) WESLEYAN (SP 875973). The chapel occupies part of the S wing of an L-shaped house of two stories and attic with stone walls and stone-slate roof. The house was built in 1674 and the S wing added or altered in the early 18th century. The S room of this wing was converted and extended to the E for Wesleyan use in 1849, the date inserted into the tympanum of the 18th-cen-

Photograph J. A. Gotch, 1902.

Photograph T. C. Legg, 1951.

tury round-arched doorway. To the right of the entrance were formerly two windows to the ground floor and one above, but these were replaced early in the 20th century by two tall windows with round-arched heads. The interior (31½ft by 19½ft) has been largely refitted. To the S of the chapel is a former cottage of two storeys, the lower room now used as a vestry and the upper floor abandoned.

OAKHAM

(7) BAPTIST, Melton Road (SK 858089). A Baptist church meeting in Oakham, Uppingham, Braunston and Empingham existed in the early 18th century. The present Particular Baptist cause was formed in 1770 and the original chapel, enlarged in

1851, was rebuilt in 1870. The latter has walls of brown stone with ashlar dressings and a slate roof. The gabled front wall has a central porch inscribed with the date of erection, two two-light windows with plate tracery, and a circular window with cusped border above the porch.

Chambers (1963) 113–15.

(8) Former PRESBYTERIAN, at Oakham School (SK 861086). A Presbyterian congregation existed in Oakham in 1672 when two houses were licensed with Benjamin King as teacher. The first regular meeting-house, a barn in Northgate Street, was superseded in 1727 by the present building which was opened by Dr Philip Doddridge and continued in use until 1861 when the church, by then Congregational, removed to a new building (see below). The old meeting-house was used for Sunday-school purposes until 1910 when it was sold to Oakham School; it is now divided for use as two classrooms.

N wall of former Presbyterian meeting-house.

The meeting-house stands N of the Congregational chapel, just inside the school grounds; the walls are of brickwork above a stone plinth, and the roof, gabled to E and W, is covered with Collyweston slates. The original entrance was at the E end with two small flat-arched windows above to light the rear of a gallery. The windows in the side walls have been altered. The interior (19¾ft by 45ft) has been entirely refitted but slight traces of the E gallery remain in the wall plaster.

Monuments: reset along the S wall of the former *burial-ground* to the SE are nine headstones dating from *c.*1811 to 1855 including (1) Rev. George Foster, 1849, and Sarah his wife; (2) Rev. Robert Chamberlain of Ravenstonedale, Westmorland, 1855, pastor for one month, slate headstone signed J.D. Barlow; (3) David Cooke Royce, 1841, and Mary his wife, 1843, slate headstone with inscriptions enclosed in foliage wreaths, and emblems of mortality (see p. 190).

LRCU (1962) 39–40: VCH *Rutland* II (1935) 26.

(9) CONGREGATIONAL, High Street (SK 861087). Built 1861 for the formerly Presbyterian congregation (see above). Walls of stone with slated roof, nave and aisles with timber arcades and clerestory. N front gabled with flanking spirelets and entrances at

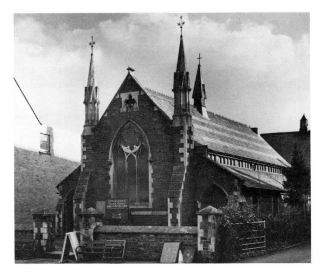

ends of aisles. Brick schoolroom, added at rear *c.*1910, has on external E wall the following *monuments* reset from the old meeting-house: (1) Rev. Robert Eakins, 1716; (2) Rev. Thomas Linnat, 1785; (3) illegible.

(10) FRIENDS, Gaol Lane (SK 859087). The meeting-house, built in 1719 at a cost of £166, and standing in an enclosure on the S

side of the lane bounded by a high stone wall, has walls of coursed ironstone ashlar and is roofed with Collyweston slates. The S wall is of three bays. A square stone tablet with moulded cornice in the gable wall is inscribed 'R.H. 1719'. The N and W walls are blank. The plan (18¾ft by 37ft average) is trapezoidal. The walls are lined with a dado of plain panelling and the roof is ceiled at collar level. The stand at the E end has been altered and the wall-benches widened. The meeting-house was closed in 1837 and later leased to the Primitive Methodists, but is now again in Quaker use.

Sturge (1895) 27.

PRESTON

(11) Former CONGREGATIONAL, Cross Lane (SK 872025). Built 1830 by a former owner of the Manor House, to which it stands adjacent. In the late 19th century it served as a mission station for the church at Uppingham but has long since become a workshop. The walls are of brickwork and the roof is covered with

FORMER CONGREGATIONAL CHAPEL, PRESTON

slates. The S front is separated from the road by a forecourt with iron railings. Two round-arched windows in the N wall flank the site of the pulpit. There are no original fittings. (Demolished *c.*1980)

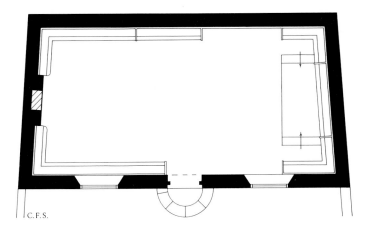

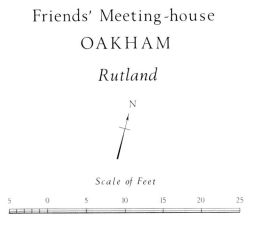

Friends' Meeting-house

OAKHAM

Rutland

N

Scale of Feet

C.F.S.

UPPINGHAM

(12) CONGREGATIONAL, Adderley Street (SP 869997). The church, founded about 1700, was originally Presbyterian and was in the early 18th century, as a joint congregation with Luffenham, the largest dissenting meeting in the county.

The original meeting-house (claimed in 1962 to be still standing near the present chapel) was described in 1869 as 'a thatched building of barn-like appearance'. The present chapel, erected in 1814, has walls of red brick and a hipped tiled roof. The W front has a wide porch, added in the late 19th century, covering the lower half of the wall; above it is a stone tablet with the inscription 'EBENEZER. HAEC DOMUS AD CULTUM DEI ÆDIFICATA AN. DOM. 1814. OBSECRO JEHOVA PROSPERA NUNC'. The side walls originally had two tiers of windows in three bays but now replaced by single round-headed lights. The interior, largely refitted in the late 19th century, has two arches in the E wall behind the pulpit which open on to an upper schoolroom. The walls are divided by pilasters. *Monument:* on N wall, to Rev. John Green, 1868, pastor 1808–58.

CYB (1869) 245–7: LRCU (1962) 43–4.

(13) WESLEYAN (SP 866998). A chapel described as having stone walls, a hipped slated roof and three-bay two-stage front with central doorway was replaced by the present building in 1872. Behind it is the Wesleyan School of 1887.

Gill (1909) 237–40, pl. opp. 224.

WHISSENDINE

(14) PRIMITIVE METHODIST, Ashwell Road (SK 834142). Red brick with yellow dressings, lancet windows, trefoiled tablet dated 1868.

WING

(15) WESLEYAN (SK 892031). Preaching began *c.*1819 and services were held in a room and subsequently in a barn. The chapel, built at a cost of £152 3s. 8d. and opened 24 June 1841, has grey stone walls and a hipped roof covered with slates.

Gill (1909) 242–4.

WESLEYAN CHAPEL, WING

(8) OAKHAM. Former Presbyterian chapel, slate headstone.

With the exception of the Baptist cause in Bridgnorth, and that of the Baptists and in some degree the Independents in Shrewsbury, the oldest surviving nonconformist congregations in the county are all of Presbyterian origin. Their varied fortunes are most clearly exemplified in the history of the High Street congregation in Shrewsbury (88), which was repeated at Wem (108) and at Whitchurch (113), all of which suffered the loss of a meeting-house in the riots of 1715 and were the scene of doctrinal divisions and secessions later in the same century; at Bridgnorth (6), however, in the southern half of the county, divisive influences are less apparent. The origins of the Independent congregation in Ludlow (49) about 1736 and of the Baptist church at Broseley (8) in 1741 are of interest as indicating the continued vitality of the older dissent immediately prior to the spread of Methodism. With this last the name of John Fletcher of Madeley will always be associated; although he remained vicar of Madeley from 1760 until his death in 1785, Fletcher's peripatetic and enthusiastic ministry (27, 28) laid the foundations of many of the Methodist societies in the industrial region east of Shrewsbury in which the parish of Dawley predominates. In the same area the Quaker meetings near Ironbridge (9, 18) received much support from the Darby family, ironmasters of Coalbrookdale.

The oldest surviving chapels in Shropshire are fragmentary or much altered and even those of the late 18th century are more remarkable for their age than their architecture; of these the former Congregational chapel in Market Drayton (51), of 1778, is externally the most complete. Some architectural pretention is found in the chapels of the early 19th century such as Newport (60), of 1832, and Ebenezer Chapel, Shrewsbury (95), built by the Methodist New Connexion in 1834, both in the Classical manner, and in the later part of the century in the Gothic designs of Bidlake of Wolverhampton (52, 89, 91) and Spaull of Oswestry (68, 70), while R. C. Bennett's Romanesque chapel in Shrewsbury (96), of 1870 is a natural sequel to his Congregational chapel in Gloucester Street, Weymouth, Dorset, of ten years earlier. Also notable, as an instance of private patronage, is the chapel built by Thomas Barnes at The Quinta (110). Many of the country chapels of the 19th century are small three-bay buildings of which Welshampton (105), of 1832, is an example of a type which continues into the later part of the century, e.g. (39), (55), (107), with some slight increase in the degree of elaboration.

Walling materials in the eastern parts of the county are generally brick but rubble occurs in the south and west while some use of impressively large blocks of sandstone is found in the north, e.g. (59), (75). Polychrome brickwork of the later 19th century is especially noticeable in the vicinity of Dawley; yellow, white, blue, red and brown brick being used in various contrasting combinations. Cast-iron window frames are particularly frequent in the county, including geometrically-patterned glazing bars in the later years, e.g. (30), (55), (107), and the same material is used at Broseley (6) for funerary monuments.

BASCHURCH

(1) PRIMITIVE METHODIST, Walford Heath (SJ 446200). Built 1841, extended at front and date-tablet reset.

BAYSTON HILL

(2) Former CONGREGATIONAL, Baystonhill (SJ 486088). Rendered walls and slate roof; three-bay front, gabled centre bay with tablet inscribed 'MOUNT PLEASANT 1834' above former arched entrance. Doorway re-sited at end in late 19th century. (URC)
   Elliot (1898) 247–8.

(3) Former CONGREGATIONAL, Lyth Hill (SJ 467067). Brick and slate, now rendered and converted to a house, formerly entered at the S end, no original features survive. Reputedly built c.1800, but possibly later.
   Elliot (1898) 175–6.

BERRINGTON

(4) PRIMITIVE METHODIST, Cross Houses (SJ 539075). Built 1836, transferred to Methodist New Connexion 1839 and renamed 'Ebenezer'.
   VCH Shropshire VIII (1968) 27.

BRIDGNORTH

(5) BAPTIST, West Castle Street (SO 716930). The chapel, rebuilt in 1842 by a congregation in existence since c.1700, has brick walls and a rendered front of three bays separated by paired pilasters with high panelled parapet above. The entrance, in the central bay, is surmounted by a rectangular window with eared architrave and similar but taller windows occupy the adjacent bays. The interior has an end gallery supported by two fluted cast-iron columns; other contemporary fittings include – communion table with end drawers; seating in gallery; gates and

gate piers of cast iron in front of chapel. *Monuments*: flanking pulpit (1) Rev. John Sing, 1753, and John Sing, Gent., his son, 1810; (2) John Sing, and Sophia his wife, both 1819; in front of chapel (3) John Macmichael, 1820, Hannah, his widow, 1850, *et al.*

(6) Former CONGREGATIONAL, Stoneway Steps (SO 718930). The church formerly meeting here but since 1966 in the Wesleyan chapel, Cartway, originated in the late 17th century as a Presbyterian cause following the ejection of Rev. Andrew Tristram from the Parish Church of St Leonard. A meeting-house erected on the present site 'on the North side of the Stoneway' in 1709 was a small building with two doorways below windows in the E wall, double gables at the N and S ends, and two pillars internally to support the roof. The existing chapel was built in 1829, schoolrooms were added in 1841–2 and the chapel reseated in 1888. The building, now occupied as a theatre, has brick walls with two round-arched windows at one end flanking the site of the pulpit. The original wide entrance remains with a wooden surround having pilasters with incised key ornament and a moulded cornice. At each side of the entrance are contemporary cast-iron railings and gate piers.

Elliot (1898) 70–86.

(7) WESLEYAN, Cartway (SO 718931). Dated 1853, designed by Thomas Powell. Three-bay pedimented front of blue brick with contrasting pilasters and round-arched iron-framed windows.

BROSELEY

(8) BROSELY OLD CHAPEL (SJ 671018). The Particular Baptist church meeting here was formed in 1741 and the present chapel opened 2 February 1742. A secession led to the erection in 1803 of the Strict Baptist 'Birch Meadow' chapel which has since been closed. The Old Chapel has brick walls and a tiled roof; it was originally of three bays with an entrance in the middle bay on the N side but was extended to the W in the mid 19th century and a new entrance constructed at the E end and cast-iron frames added to the round-arched windows. The vestry and former manse adjoining to the S are approximately contemporary with the original building.

Manse and chapel from SE.

BROSELEY OLD CHAPEL, *Shropshire*

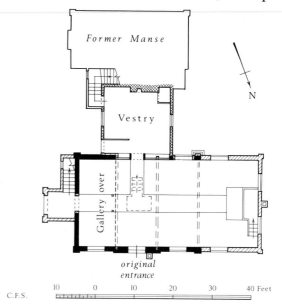

The interior of the chapel (22ft by 30ft enlarged to 46ft) has an early 19th-century gallery at the E end but has otherwise been refitted in the late 19th century. The roof of the older portion is supported by two collar-beam trusses with the feet of the principal rafters resting on posts embedded in the original brick-work of the walls and strengthened by curved braces at the junctions. The *vestry* wing, linking the chapel and manse, is of one storey with basement and attics. A wide outer doorway in the E wall and a wooden cross-framed window adjacent are of the mid 18th century. Two small attic rooms above the vestry, approached by a later staircase, are ceiled at collar level with bent principals below the collar. The *manse* is of two stories and attics with a three-bay elevation to the south.

Fittings – *Communion Table*: in vestry, oak with turned legs, early 18th-century. *Monuments*: in burial-ground N of chapel flanking original approach (1) John Guest, 1788, and Penelope his wife, 179[?3], brick table-tomb with stone cap, (2) Jeremiah Baker, draper, 1794, Eleanor his wife, 1804, *et al.*, double size table-tomb with cast-iron sides and stone cap, in railed enclosure, (3) George Brooks, 1777, Elizabeth his wife, 1777, *et al.*, stone table-tomb, railed, (4) Job Barker of Lightmore Iron Works, 1824, fragments of entirely cast-iron monument with pyramidal top, (5) William Roden, 1812, *et al.*, (6) Anna (Wyke) wife of Rowland Hill, 1775, *et al.*, brick table-tomb with stone cap in railed enclosure; E of vestry (7) Martha, wife of Charles Parker, 1837, brick table-tomb with cast-iron cap. *Plate*: includes a gadrooned two-handled cup of 1704, given by Dr J. W. Perrott, 1763.

(9) Former FRIENDS (SJ 67190223). A meeting-house built in 1769, superseding buildings of 1691 and 1742, was closed in 1778. From 1837 it was used as a preaching station by Independents until the erection of a chapel in 1841 when it became the

Sunday-school. Abraham Darby of Coalbrookdale was buried here, 1717. The site has now been cleared.

Elliot (1898) 251–8.

(10) WESLEYAN, Jackfield (SJ 682031). Brown brick with tiled roof. Three-bay gabled front dated 1825.

CAYNHAM

(11) WESLEYAN (SO 557735). Brick and slate with entrance in gabled end; two pointed-arched windows with wooden Y-tracery face the road. Segmental plaster ceiling. Opened 1836.

CHERRINGTON

(12) PRIMITIVE METHODIST, Tibberton (SJ 674203). Dated 1843, much altered.

CHESWARDINE

(13) WESLEYAN, Great Soudley (SJ 727288). Three-bay front with pointed-arched windows; circular tablet inscribed 'The Land graciously given by Mr John Butterton. Wesleyan Chapel Erected A.D.1837'.

CLIVE

(14) Former INDEPENDENT (SJ 517243). Yellow sandstone ashlar with a slated roof, built in 1844 replacing a chapel erected in 1830; now a workshop. Gabled to front and rear with copings and shaped kneelers. Hollow-chamfered round-arched windows at sides, altered three-bay front with date-tablet in gable.

Elliot (1898) 168–70.

(15) PRIMITIVE METHODIST (SJ 513242). Generally comparable with the foregoing but with lancet windows, 1859.

CLUNBURY

(16) PRIMITIVE METHODIST, Twitchen (SO 370793). Rubble and slate; SW front of three bays with blocked doorway between windows. Opened 1833.

CONDOVER

(17) Former CONGREGATIONAL, Dorrington (SJ 478030). Built in 1808 at the expense of Rev. William Whitfoot, Countess of Huntingdon's minister, a native of Dorrington. The chapel was pewed and a gallery added in 1822; it was enlarged at SE end in 1840 and later. Date-tablets of 1808 and 1908 in NW gable wall. *Monuments*: in burial-ground include one to Rev. John Jones Beynon, pastor, 1852, and Mary his wife, 1852, coped slab on two proto-Ionic supports. (Demolished 1973, monuments remain)

Elliot (1898) 171–6.

DAWLEY

(18) FRIENDS, Coalbrookdale (SJ 666050). Abraham Darby, who took over an existing ironworks in Coalbrookdale about 1709, gave considerable encouragement to Quaker meetings in the district and his son, also Abraham, built a meeting-house close to his works for the benefit of his workpeople, many of whom were of this persuasion. The meeting-house erected in 1745 was enlarged in 1763 and superseded by another in 1808. This was sold in 1954 and demolished *c*.1965 when a house and

shop were built on the site. The burial-ground, to the S on a steeply sloping site, is a long rectangular plot enclosed by a brick boundary wall in 1763. *Monuments*: many small rectangular stone tablets intended to lie flat but now upturned and loose against the surrounding walls, include (1) Mark Gilpin, 1799; (2) Abraham Darby, 1789; (3) Rebecca Darby, 1834; (4) Abraham Darby, 1763; (5) Abraham Darby, 1794; (6) George Titterton, 1798.

Raistrick, A., *Dynasty of Ironfounders*; *The Darbys and Coalbrookdale* (1970).

(19) WESLEYAN, High Street, Dawley (SJ 684075). Built 1860 by

Griffiths of Bridgnorth to replace a chapel of 1825. Blue brick with yellow brick dressings and slate roof. (Demolished 1977)

(20) PRIMITIVE METHODIST, Finger Road, Dawley (SJ 688069). Dated 1863. Red brick with blue brick dressings. (Demolished 1977)

(21) BAPTIST, Dawley Bank (SJ 684084). Front of blue brick with yellow brick dressings and elaborately shaped gable with

ball finials; two-storied porch added. Built 1860 on site of a chapel of 1846, date-tablet from former reset in rear wall.

(22) Former WESLEYAN, Dawley Bank (SJ 683084). Three-bay rendered front with pediment, formerly dated 1840. (Demolished 1977)

(23) WESLEYAN, Dawley Parva (SJ 683060). Three-bay front divided by pilasters, the centre bay rising through a pediment and terminating with a horizontal cornice. Dated 1837.

(24) BAPTIST, High Street, Madeley (SJ 698044). Yellow brick

and slate, three-bay front with arched centre-bay enclosing iron tablet with name ÆNON and roundel with date 1858 above.

(25) PRIMITIVE METHODIST, High Street, Madeley (SJ 700044). Yellow brick with bands of blue and dressings of blue, red and white brick. Gabled front with grouped windows and ogee hood-mould over entrance, name Mount Zion and date 1865 on gable tablet.

(26) WESLEYAN, Court Street, Madeley (SJ 696045). Dated 1841. Yellow brick with rendered dressings and slated roof.

Spacious interior with gallery around three sides supported by fluted cast-iron columns.

(27) 'ROCK CHAPEL', Madeley Wood (SJ 679034). Cottages, nos. 52 and 53 New Bridge Road, built as a single dwelling in the 17th century have been largely refaced in common brick, they were used between 1760 and 1785 by John Fletcher of Madeley as a preaching station.

(28) Former METHODIST, Madeley Wood (SJ 679035). Preaching-house erected 1777 by John Fletcher of Madeley for use as a day school and for evening worship; it was used for regular Sunday services until 1837 when superseded by a new chapel nearby (29). It has brick walls and a modern tiled roof. The gabled W front had a central round-arched doorway with small flanking windows, a tablet over without traces of inscription, and a lunette in the gable; in each side wall are three

round-arched windows with moulded stone arches, keystones and impost blocks. The interior (36ft and 24½ft) has a plaster barrel-vault of elliptical section with a moulded plaster cornice along the N and S walls; a W gallery has been removed.

(29) WESLEYAN, Madeley Wood (SJ 678036). The chapel, built in 1837 as successor to the foregoing, has walls of yellow brick; the centre bay rises through a pediment and terminates in a moulded cornice and parapet (cf (23) above).

(30) WESLEYAN, Old Park (SJ 692095). Built 1853, with lancet windows and patterned cast-iron frames; porch later. (Derelict 1980)

(31) Former PRIMITIVE METHODIST, Old Park (SJ 690096). Three-bay gabled front with two tiers of round-arched windows with iron frames; tablet with name 'Bethesda' and date 1857 above entrance. (Derelict 1973)

(32) WESLEYAN, Stirchley (SJ 694066). Low three-bay front with pediment and round-arched windows, brick surround to doorway partly covered by later porch. Built 1840–1, enlarged to rear and refitted in later 19th century.

EDGTON

(33) PRIMITIVE METHODIST (SO 387859). Rubble and slate with round-arched doorway on W side. Dated 1834; rostrum pulpit at N end.

(29) DAWLEY. Wesleyan chapel, Madeley Wood.

ELLESMERE RURAL

(34) WESLEYAN METHODIST ASSOCIATION, Dudleston Heath (SJ 365361). Brick with half-hipped slate roof, two tiers of plain pointed-arched windows in W wall and side-entry porch with tablet inscribed 'EBENE'ZER/CHAPEL.A.D.1835./STAND fast therefore in the *liberty* wherewith Christ hath/made us *free*, and be not/entangled again with the *yoke*/of *bondage*. Gal.V. & I.'. Brick bell-cote and weathervane at N end.

(35) CONGREGATIONAL, Frankton (SJ 366331). Rubble with brick dressings to round-arched windows. Built 1834, refitted 1877. (URC)
Elliot (1898) 238–9.

ERCALL MAGNA

(36) WESLEYAN, Ellerdine Heath (SJ 618219). Opened 1813.

FARLOW

(37) WESLEYAN (SO 644798). Rubble and slate, gabled front with a tablet inscribed 'MELVILLE/CHAPEL/EBENEZER PLACE/1833'.

GREAT NESS

(38) CONGREGATIONAL, Wilcott (SJ 374192). Built in 1834; walls of large blocks of sandstone rubble and a slated roof gabled

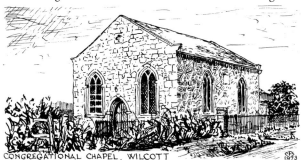

CONGREGATIONAL CHAPEL, WILCOTT

to N and S with shaped kneelers. The entrance is at the S end. *Monument*: Mary, widow of Richard Jones of Oswestry, 1852 and their daughters Elizabeth, 1857, 'more than 24 years nurse in the family of John Horatio Lloyd, Barrister at Law, London', and Susan, 1858, table-tomb. (URC)
Elliot (1898) 243–6.

HADNALL

(39) Former PRIMITIVE METHODIST (SJ 521197). Red brick with stone dressings and a tiled roof. E front of three bays, with

PRIMITIVE METHODIST CHAPEL, HADNALL

brick pilasters rising to simple stone pinnacles, gablet between centre pair with defaced date-tablet of 1862.

(40) Former PRIMITIVE METHODIST, Yorton Heath (SJ 504223). Dated 1859.

HINSTOCK

(41) WESLEYAN (SJ 692269). Opened 1831. Squared sandstone walls with trefoiled window over later N porch and three round-arched windows on E side.

HODNET

(42) CONGREGATIONAL, Wollerton (SJ 620304). Wheel window: 1867–8 by Thomas Huxley of Malpas. (URC)
CYB (1869) 323–4; Elliot (1898) 156–61.

(43) Former PRIMITIVE METHODIST, Kenstone (SJ 596287). Brick and tile with three-bay front and round-arched windows; mid 19th-century.

HOPESAY

(44) BAPTIST, Aston on Clun (SO 394818). Rubble and slate, three-bay gabled front with rectangular labels over windows and tablet inscribed 'BAPTIST/CHAPEL, 1844/PREPARE TO/ MEET THY GOD.' Pulpit opposite entrance has two turned wood candle-sticks on front corners.

(45) Former PRIMITIVE METHODIST, Aston on Clun (SO 395819). Dated 1862.

KINNERLEY

(46) BAPTIST, Maesbrook Green (SJ 304212). 'ÆNON CHAPEL', dated 1844, has red brick walls with stone dressings and a slated roof. Three-bay gabled front with shaped kneelers and lancet windows.

(47) PRIMITIVE METHODIST, Maesbrook (SJ 310214). The former chapel of 1844 stands at right angles to its successor built 1899. Brick and slate with pointed-arched windows.

LILLESHALL

(48) Former BAPTIST, Queens Road, Donnington Wood (SJ 710133). Tablet in gable 'BAPTIST CHAPEL/ESTABLISHED 1820/RESTORED 1906'. Now a builder's store.

LUDLOW

(49) Former CHAPEL, Corve Street (SO 511753). A former dissenters' meeting-house erected in 1736 behind houses on the W side of Corve Street was demolished c.1960. It was built, following disturbed meetings in a private house, by a congregation which appears to have had slender denominational attachments. About 1800 the church was re-formed as Independent, removing in 1830 to a new chapel in Old Street (see (50) below). Some use by other denominations, including Moravians, has also been claimed and in 1889 Congregational services were resumed.

The chapel (44¾ft by 17ft externally), of which only some foundations remain, had brick walls and a tiled roof. It was gabled to E and W with an entrance below the E window removed to the S side c.1876. The pulpit in front of the W window with its sounding-board and a complete set of box-pews were still in position in 1951.

Elliot (1898) 97–105: England (1886) I, 5, pl.8.

(50) Former CONGREGATIONAL, Old Street (SO 513746). The chapel, built in 1830 by a congregation which removed from Corve Street (see (49) above), was closed c.1968 and has since been converted to a house. It stands on a restricted site behind

houses on the W side of the street. The walls are of brick and the pedimented front has the date of erection displayed in large raised numerals below the apex. A single end-gallery of later date was approached by a staircase covering part of the frontage.

Plate: includes two gadrooned two-handled cups: of 1703, given by Mary Reed, 1744; of 1768, given by James Hockey, 1859.

Elliot (1898) 97–105.

MARKET DRAYTON

(51) Former CONGREGATIONAL, Church Lane (SJ 67553405). Although the vicar was amongst those ejected for non-conformity in 1662 no continuous thread of dissent can be established. Meetings of Independents commenced about 1768, a church was formed in 1776 and the meeting-house erected two years later, the builder being William Griffith. A gallery was added c.1841–7 and substantial additions were made to the rear in 1865–7. In 1895 the chapel was drastically altered internally by the insertion of a floor at gallery level and the conversion of the lower part to classrooms. The chapel was closed by 1949 and has since been used for a variety of purposes.

The walls are of red brick and the roof is hipped and covered with tiles. The broad SE front has a brick dentil eaves cornice and a central entrance from which a wooden doorcase has been

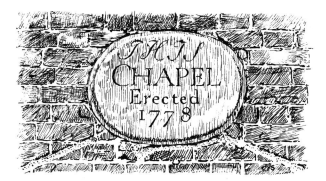

removed. Above the doorway is an oval tablet dated 1778. The late 19th-century enlargement to the rear has two tiers of round-arched windows and a triple gable to the north.

The interior (34ft by 44ft) has a flat plaster ceiling and original moulded cornice. Before subdivision the gallery stairs were in the front corners approached directly by doorways inserted in place of windows in the side walls. The basic structure of the mid 19th-century gallery remains, supported by cast-iron columns of quatrefoil section; short lengths of the panelled gallery-fronts also survive. In the late 19th century the NW wall was pierced at gallery level to provide an organ-chamber and choir gallery behind the pulpit, the walling above being supported by two cast-iron columns and half-columns with Corinthian capitals, by Barwell & Co., Northampton. When a floor was inserted at gallery level a new staircase was built opposite the front entrance and the former staircases removed.

The roof is supported by two main trusses with king-posts, queen-posts and diagonal struts; there is no ridge-piece. A half-

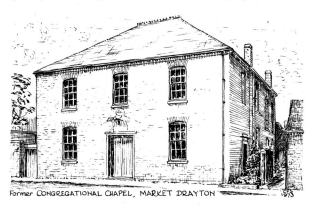

Former CONGREGATIONAL CHAPEL, MARKET DRAYTON

Former Congregational Chapel, Church Lane

MARKET
DRAYTON
Shropshire

N

5 Feet 0   5   10   15   20

truss on the principal axis supported a central chandelier for which a large stone counterweight remains.

Inscriptions: painted on roof timbers, 'Wm: Griffith 1778 Fecit'; 'Thomas Tuker 1778'; 'Isaac Griffith & Thos Corfield repaired this Ceiling Novr. 2 1832'. *Monument*: in yard SW of chapel, to William Griffith, 1822, 'he erected this Chapel in the year 1778 and filled the office of Deacon until his death', Elizabeth his wife, 1814, and John his brother, 1805, deacon.
Elliot (1898) 115–24.

(52) WESLEYAN, Shrewsbury Road (SJ 671340). Red brick with stone dressings, broach spire at corner carried by dwarf columns; by G. Bidlake, 1864.

(53) PRIMITIVE METHODIST, Frogmore Road (SJ 674341). Red brick with blue brick dressings and slate roof, round-arched windows, corner pilasters carried up to simple stone pinnacles (see (39) above). Tablet in front gable 'Ebenezer . . . 1867'.

MELVERLEY

(54) Former CONGREGATIONAL, Cross Lanes (SJ 331183). Built 1842–5. Converted to a cottage and refenestrated.
Elliot (1898) 265–7.

(55) PRIMITIVE METHODIST, Cross Lanes (SJ 329182). Dated 1865. Red brick with yellow brick dressings and slate roof.

MINSTERLEY

(56) CONGREGATIONAL (SJ 375050). Baptists and Independents commenced joint meetings in the late 18th century forming a

united church in 1805. In 1833 the two groups separated, the former building a chapel 'close to Snailbeach Mines' (see (116) below) and the latter erecting the present building. The chapel has brick walls, now rendered, and a slated roof, two tiers of round-arched windows with iron frames, a gabled front from which a parapet has been removed, and a gabled porch of two stories. Date 1833 in front wall.
Elliot (1898) 137–40.

MUCH WENLOCK

(57) Former WESLEYAN, Shineton Street (SJ 623001). The chapel, which stands well back on the W side of the street, was built *c*.1830; it is now in commercial use. Rubble walls with brick dressings and a hipped tiled roof. The E front, now rebuilt, had a small porch between pointed-arched windows; the side walls have brick dentil eaves cornices and original round-arched windows with iron frames.

(58) PRIMITIVE METHODIST, King Street (SO 622999). Brown brick with dressings of blue and white brick, gabled front dated 1862; 'Sabbath-school' in similar style adjacent to left, 1883.

MYDDLE

(59) Former INDEPENDENT, Harmer Hill (SJ 489226). The chapel, built 1833–4 as the result of successful preaching by Rev.

George Rogers of Bomere Heath (see (75) below), was transferred in 1920 to the Calvinistic Methodists (Presbyterian Church of Wales) who still use it. The walls are built of large squared blocks of red sandstone and the roof is hipped and slate covered. The S wall has a porch with two crude stone columns supporting a segmental-pointed arch; a tablet above the entrance is inscribed 'INDEPENDENT CHAPEL 1833'. The E and W walls originally had two windows but a third was added to each side when a minor room to the N was incorporated into the chapel. The manse adjacent to the N has been enlarged. *Monuments*: W of chapel, three mid 19th-century table-tombs, including one to Elizabeth Wilkinson Rogers, 1841.

Elliot (1898) 240–2.

NEWPORT

(60) CONGREGATIONAL, Wellington Road (SJ 746187). The chapel, built in 1832, has brick walls rendered at the front in

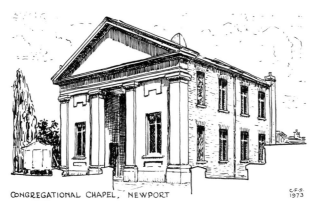

CONGREGATIONAL CHAPEL, NEWPORT

stucco. The front has an open bay at the centre to form a porch with doorways in the return walls. The interior was refurbished in the late 19th century but retains an original gallery supported by thin iron columns. *Fontlet*: pottery, Winchester type, with pyramidal cover. (URC)

Elliot (1898) 106–14.

(61) Former PRIMITIVE METHODIST, Wellington Road (SJ 746188). Red brick with yellow brick dressings and tiled roof. Three-bay gabled front with arched centre bay (*cf* (58) above) date-tablet of 1866, now defaced.

OAKENGATES

(62) CONGREGATIONAL, Lion Street (SJ 696109). Brown brick and slate. pedimented front; four-bay sides with fifth bay of two stories added at rear. Built 1847–8; side galleries inserted after 1857. (URC)

Elliot (1898) 275–8.

(63) UNITED METHODIST FREE CHURCHES, New Street (SJ 703110). Three-bay pedimented front; tablet inscribed 'METHODIST FREE CHURCH 1855'. (Derelict)

(64) WESLEYAN, Ketleybank (SJ 694103). Three-bay pedimented front with later porch. Dated 1823.

(65) PRIMITIVE METHODIST, Ketleybank (SJ 691103). Built 1859; enlarged and refronted 1907.

(62) OAKENGATES. Congregational chapel. (URC)

(66) PRIMITIVE METHODIST, Station Hill (SJ 699110). Brown brick with blue brick dressings and slate roof, 'erected 1847 rebuilt 1868'.

OSWESTRY

(67) Former CONGREGATIONAL, Arthur Street (SJ 28982978). The congregation, which for a period prior to *c*.1777 was regarded as Presbyterian, originated in the mid 17th century and is said to have met from 1651 at Sweeney (2 miles S) having a burial ground near Sweeney Hall, and to have built a meeting-house in Oswestry in 1659. The site in Arthur Street, described as 'a Building and Malt Mill, lying in Oswestry near the Castle Hill...', was acquired in 1748 and a new meeting-house erected thereon was opened in 1750; this was several times enlarged and in 1830 replaced by the present building which served the church until 1872 (see (68) below) being then converted for use as a Sunday-school. It is now in commercial occupation.

The chapel has brick walls with two tiers of round-arched windows, three-bay front with heightened and rebuilt gable, central doorway and porch with two fluted Doric columns *in antis*. *Burial-ground*: at side of chapel, now derelict.

Elliot (1898) 29–46.

(68) CONGREGATIONAL (SJ 290298). 'Christ Church', 50 yards NE of the foregoing, was built 1871–2 on the site of the Borough Gaol to designs in the Gothic style by W. H. Spaull of Oswestry. It has stone walls and a corner tower with broach spire. (URC)

CYB (1873) 428: Elliot (1898) 29–46.

OSWESTRY RURAL

(69) BAPTIST, Sweeney (SJ 284260). Rubble and slate, three windows and doorway in front wall all with two-centred arched heads, built *c*.1831 but woodwork renewed in late 19th century.

(70) CONGREGATIONAL, Maesbury Marsh (SJ 312252). Brick with stone dressings and slate roof, corner spire supported by dwarf columns (*cf* (52) above), 1868 by W. H. Spaull of

CONGREGATIONAL CHAPELS, MAESBURY MARSH.

Oswestry. Former chapel adjacent with two pointed-arched windows in brick gabled front dated 1855. (URC)

CYB (1870) 381: Elliot (1898) 47–50.

(71) CONGREGATIONAL, Trefonen (SJ 259269). Rubble walls and a modern tiled roof. The E wall has three pointed-arched windows and a stone tablet above the entrance apparently inscribed 'CARNEDAU INDEPENDENT CHAPEL . . .' but largely concealed by the roof of a later porch. Built 1834.

Elliot (1898) 50–4.

(72) PRIMITIVE METHODIST, Ball (SJ 306266). 'Bethesda Chapel', dated 1834, of rubble and slate. Windows have pointed-arched heads.

(73) PRIMITIVE METHODIST, Morton (SJ 290240). 'Bethel Chapel', dated 1838, of rubble and slate with later porch.

(74) PRIMITIVE METHODIST, Treflach Wood (SJ 260252). Dated 1833.

PIMHILL

(75) Former CONGREGATIONAL, Bomere Heath (SJ 474197). The chapel, built in 1827, has been used since c.1879 by Calvinistic Methodists. The walls are of red sandstone in large squared blocks and the roof is covered with small slates. The entrance at the E end of the N wall is covered by a later stone porch and has above it the mis-spelt tablet 'ZION'S HIIL 1827'. The windows have been much altered; two windows in the N wall formerly had stone lintels and external shutters, and a large

E window replaces a much smaller circular light. Two-storied vestry wing at W end. *Monuments*: in burial ground (1) Mrs Mary Ash, 1841 and Mrs Rachel Ash, 1844, (2) Elizabeth Hill, 1843, (3) Rev. George Rogers, minister of Bomere Heath and Harmer Hill, 1868, also Annie Hickson Rogers. (*cf* (59) above).

CYB (1869) 274: Elliot (1898) 208–12.

(76) WESLEYAN, Bomere Heath (SJ 473198). Alongside the red brick chapel of 1903 stands the smaller former chapel with walls of squared red sandstone blocks and a tiled roof. Although

inscribed '. . . erected 1836 rebuilt 1868' the building is of the former date and prior to drastic refitting had an entrance in the front gabled wall and three windows with round-arched heads at the sides.

PONTESBURY

(77) BAPTIST, Chapel Street (SJ 401060). Built c.1828 for a church founded in that year. Rendered walls and tiled roof; two round-arched windows in the front wall, entrance perhaps formerly between.

(78) PLEALEY CHAPEL (SJ 423070) was built in the early 19th century on the estate and at the expense of 'a gentleman who resided in the neighbourhood' who at first supported the Independents but later, c.1839, transferred his allegiance and the chapel to the Baptists and again, c.1858, to the Wesleyan Methodists who still use it. Brick walls and slate roof with small

PLEALEY CHAPEL, PONTESBURY

porch at one end. *Monument*: in yard at rear, to Richard France, 1829, Richard France, 1862, Hannah, his widow, 1866, *et al.*, table-tomb.

Elliot (1898) 140.

(79) CONGREGATIONAL (SJ 397062). Independents deprived of the use of Plealey Chapel (78) erected a new chapel in 1839. This has rendered walls and a slate roof. It forms part of a continuous range with the chapel at the centre, manse at the W and two-

storied Sunday-school to the east. Two tall round-arched windows in the S wall and two in the N light the chapel; a third window beyond the S porch is bisected by the upper floor of the Sunday-school. Interior refitted 1871.

Elliot (1898) 137–43.

(80) PRIMITIVE METHODIST, Asterley (SJ 375071). Dated 1834. Sandstone rubble with brick eaves-cornice and slate roof. Gabled front with two round-arched windows with iron frames and mean later porch. Interior has open-backed benches, rostrum pulpit, and rows of hat pegs.

(81) PRIMITIVE METHODIST, Pontesbury Hill Road (SJ 398058). Opened 1845. Rendered three-bay front. Original open-backed benches.

PREES

(82) WESLEYAN, Darliston (SJ 581335). The chapel, designed by William Smith of Whitchurch and built by John Powell of

Wesleyan Chapel, Darliston, PREES, *Shropshire*

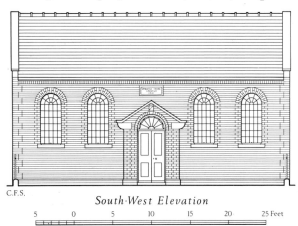

C.F.S.

South-West Elevation

5   0   5   10   15   20   25 Feet

Darliston, has walls of red brick with dressings of blue and yellow bricks used alternately in the eaves-cornice, the doorway and window surrounds, and as quoins at the ends of the front elevation; the roof is covered with slates. The windows have cast-iron frames, and above the porch is a tablet inscribed 'WESLEYAN CHAPEL/ERECTED/1861'.

RODINGTON

(83) PRIMITIVE METHODIST, Marsh Green (SJ 608142). Dated 1841.

(84) WESLEYAN, Rodington (SJ 582141). Dated 1834; enlarged to E in late 19th century.

RUYTON-XI-TOWNS

(85) CONGREGATIONAL (SJ 392228). The chapel, erected 1833, stands N of the village close to the S entrance to Ruyton Park. The builder was Nathanael Edwards of Ruyton. It has walls of yellow sandstone rubble with ashlar dressings and a slate roof,

pointed-arched windows and buttresses originally intended to terminate in pinnacles. (URC)

Elliot (1898) 227–37.

ST MARTIN'S

(86) PRIMITIVE METHODIST, St Martin's Moor (SJ 315358). Red brick with polychrome dressings, steeply-gabled porch with tablet inscribed '. . . built 1829 rebuilt 1870'.

SHAWBURY

(87) WESLEYAN, Moretonmill (SJ 577226). Alongside the red-brick chapel of 1875 stands its smaller predecessor, of brick and slate with tablet dated 1846 in the front gable and pointed-arched windows with intersecting glazing bars in the side walls.

SHREWSBURY

(88) HIGH STREET CHAPEL (SJ 492124). The Presbyterian congregation, in existence by 1673, traces its origins to the two ejected ministers Rev. Francis Tallents, vicar of St Mary's, and Rev. John Bryan, vicar of St Chad's. Prior to 1690 meetings were held in the house of Mrs Hunt, widow of one of the members of the Long Parliament, and afterwards in the house of Francis Tallents until the completion of the first meeting-house

on the present site, then known as Bakers Row, in October 1691. This survived until 6 July 1715 when it was destroyed by a mob and subsequently rebuilt at the public expense. On the appointment of Job Orton as minister in 1741 the congregation was joined by a large personal following of Independents to form a joint church which then preferred the designation 'Christian'; in 1766 a doctrinal dispute over the appointment of a minister resulted in the withdrawal of the orthodox members to re-form the Independent meeting which then gathered at Swan Hill (see (89) below); the remaining 'Presbyterian' members gradually adopted a liberal system of theology and now support a Unitarian ministry. In 1839–40 the meeting-house was almost entirely rebuilt in consequence of its poor structural condition and the requirement of part of the site for street improvement; an addition to the front of the chapel was made in 1885.

The chapel stands on a restricted site on the SW side of the street, in 1691 it measured 50ft 2in. deep and from 27ft 7in. to 29ft 2in. in width. The walls are of brick and the front is faced in ashlar. The front wall, of 1885, is of three bays with tall pilasters, central entrance and round-arched upper windows. The side walls, not visible externally, are each pierced at a high level by a rectangular window of three lights and by a smaller window at each end; the end wall is blank. Behind the forebuilding, which provides on the ground floor an entrance lobby, vestry and stair-case and a large meeting-room above, the chapel (56ft by 24½ft) is of irregular shape with a gallery at the NE end having a bolection-moulded panelled front of the early 18th century supported by two square fluted wooden posts; the pews were reconstructed in 1905.

Fittings – *Clock*: on gallery front, dated 1724. *Communion Table*: with turned baluster legs, 18th-century. *Glass*: in side windows, double-glazed *c*.1839. *Monuments* include one to Charles Darwin, 1882, a native of Shrewsbury, and a brass tablet to Samuel Coleridge who preached here in 1798 with a view to the pastorate (see William Hazlitt's essay 'My first acquaintance with Poets'). *Plate* includes a pair of tall cups of 1736 given by John Bryan. *Panelling*: on SW wall, early 18th-century. *Royal Arms*: on SW wall, Hanoverian 1714–1800, large framed panel. *Seating*: chairs, pair, with tall panelled backs, 18th-century.

Broadbent, A., *The Story of Unitarianism in Shrewsbury* (1962): Evans (1897) 223–5: Evans (1899) 181–93: Reavley (1925).

(89) SWAN HILL CHAPEL (SJ 489123). A society of Independents is believed to have met prior to 1662 in a house in the King's Head Shut or Peacock Shut. This united with the Presbyterian congregation in 1741 (see (88) above). In 1766, following the resignation of the minister, Job Orton, and on his advice, a separate Independent meeting was recommenced and a meeting-house erected on the present site in Swan Hill in the following year. This had brick walls and a hipped roof, with a two-stage front of three bays having round-arched doorways with pedimental surrounds in the end bays and three round-arched windows with triple keystones and imposts to the upper stage. In 1868 the chapel was rebuilt to a larger size by George Bidlake of Wolverhampton incorporating parts of the side walls of the former building; schoolrooms were added in 1880.

The lower part of the SW wall, dating from 1767, is of brick

having two blind windows with flat-arched heads and triple keystones; the upper part has been rebuilt. The NE wall is covered by later building. The present chapel, of brick with stone dressings, has a gabled front to the SE with a four-light window above the entrance with plate tracery in a two-centred head. The interior (38ft wide, being the maximum dimension of the former meeting-house) is divided into nave and aisles by arcades of four bays with cast-iron columns supporting two-centred arches with a clerestory over, and has a gallery around three sides.

Fittings – *Chair*: in front of pulpit, with round-arched back panel inscribed 'S 1611 P'. *Monuments*: pair in chapel to Rev. Thomas Weaver, 1852, and Mary his wife, 1838; in forecourt late 18th-century ledger-stones. *Paintings*: (1) Rev. Richard Heath, died *c*.1666; (2) Rev. James Owen, 1654–1706; (3) Rev. Francis Tallents, 1619–1708, dated 1704; (4) Rev. Job Orton, 1717–83; (5) Rev. Samuel Lucas, *c*.1748–99. *Plate* includes two cups of 1778.

CYB (1868) 335: Barker [*c*.1910] 18–24: Elliot (1898) 14–28.

(90) BAPTIST, Claremont (SJ 490125). The church seems to have originated in the late 17th century; a meeting-house was built 1735 in Stilliards Shutt whence the congregation removed to the

present site, then named Dog Lane, in 1780. The chapel, rebuilt 1877–8, is of brick with stone dressings, the centre bay having a pediment supported by paired Corinthian pilasters and with open balustrades with urns above the flanking bays. A few decayed grave-slabs of the early 19th century remain in the fore-court.

Barker [*c*.1910] 24–5.

(91) CONGREGATIONAL, Abbey Foregate (SJ 497124). Stone and slate, in geometrical Gothic style with corner tower and banded stone spire, by George Bidlake of Wolverhampton. Built for a newly-formed congregation in 1863 as a bicentenary memorial. (URC)

CYB (1864) 289: Elliot (1898) 294–302.

(92) THE TABERNACLE, Dogpole (SJ 493125). Three-bay Italianate front of ashlar; bicentenary memorial chapel built 1862, architect Rev. T. Thomas of Swansea, for a Welsh Inde-pendent church formerly meeting in a chapel on Pride Hill.

CYB (1862) 317: Elliot (1898) 259–64.

(93) Former FRIENDS, St John's Hill (SJ 48851240). The meeting-house, rebuilt *c*.1807, stands 50 yards E of St Chad's church behind 24 St John's Hill, a house of brick and tile with two stories and attics contemporary with the original building of 1746. After Friends use ceased prior to 1863 it was used by seceders from the Baptists in Claremont and subsequently as an office for the Board of Guardians; it is now used in part as a Kingdom Hall of the Jehovah's Witnesses. The entrance from the street is through a semicircular archway with triple keystone and imposts and double doors. The meeting-house has brick walls and a slate-covered roof, the E and W walls have pedimented gables and in the N and S walls are three flat-arched windows with hung sashes; traces of a former porch remain on the S side. The interior, formerly divided into two rooms, has an original moulded plaster ceiling cornice.

Barker [*c*.1910] 27.

(94) WESLEYAN, St John's Hill (SJ 489124). Methodist preaching commenced in 1761 with the visit of John Wesley. Twenty years later a preaching-house was erected in Hills Lane by John Appleton at his own expense and in 1804–5 a new chapel was built on the present site. The chapel, rebuilt in 1879, of red brick with stone dressings, has a front of five bays with a pediment, central entrance and round-arched windows.

Barker [*c*.1910] 33–49.

(95) Former METHODIST NEW CONNEXION, Town Walls (SJ 491122). 'Ebenezer Chapel', built in 1834 for a cause founded in the previous year, has walls of brick, rendered at the front and sides in stucco, and stands above basement rooms. The front is of five bays with Corinthian pilasters and porches with fluted Doric columns. (Under conversion to secular use 1983)

Barker [*c*.1910] fig. 54, 64.

(96) PRESBYTERIAN, Castle Street (SJ 494127). A congregation of the Presbyterian Church in England was formed in 1865 as a preaching station of the Lancashire Presbytery and first met in the Music Hall. The present building, which stands on the site of the mediaeval chapel of St Nicholas, was built in 1870 to designs

by Robert C. Bennett of Weymouth. It is a tall building in the Romanesque style with stone walls and a tiled roof. The SW front has a wide arched entrance of three orders flanked by pilaster buttresses and a circular staircase tower at the W corner. There are minor rooms on the ground floor below the chapel. (Closed 1975 and congregation united with (91))

Reavley (1925).

STANTON LACY

(97) WESLEYAN, Hayton's Bent (SO 518805). Rubble walls and tiled roof. Opened 1838.

(98) Former PRIMITIVE METHODIST, Upper Hayton (SO 518809). Rubble with polychrome brick dressings; tiled roof. Gabled S front with tablet dated 1877.

STOKE UPON TERN

(99) Former CONGREGATIONAL, Ollerton (SJ 650253). Built 1838. Walls of squared red sandstone blocks and hipped slated roof. Entrance at E end and external stone staircase to E gallery. Pointed-arched windows in N and S walls.

Elliot (1898) 180–2.

(100) CONGREGATIONAL, Wistanwick (SJ 668288). The chapel, built about 1805 by Rev. John Wilson of Market Drayton at his own expense, was put in trust in 1833, enlarged between 1859 and 1864 and a manse was added in 1873. The walls are of squared red sandstone blocks and the roofs are tiled. The S half of

CONGREGATIONAL CHAPEL, WISTANWICK

the chapel appears to date from c.1805, and has a gable to the E and traces of a former doorway in the S wall; when the chapel was enlarged to the N the fenestration was made uniform throughout with three round-arched windows to N and S and two entrances covered by low gabled porches were made in the extended double-gabled E wall. The manse, a small two-storied cottage, is attached to the west. (URC)

Elliot (1898) 177–80.

(101) PRIMITIVE METHODIST, Stoke Heath (SJ 647294). Built 1841; former three-bay front extended to left and heightened.

STOTTESDON

(102) WESLEYAN (SO 670829). Rendered rubble and slate. Gabled front dated 1849. Small rear gallery with plain balustraded front; open-backed benches with shaped ends.

TELFORD (For monuments within the boundaries of the new town see: DAWLEY, LILLESHALL, OAKENGATES, WELLINGTON RURAL, WELLINGTON URBAN)

WELLINGTON RURAL

(103) Former WESLEYAN REFORM, Ketley (SJ 680110). On N side of Watling Street. Brick and slate; pedimented S front with terminal pilasters; dated 1852.

WELLINGTON URBAN

(104) Former BAPTIST, King Street, Wellington (SJ 652119). Built in the early 19th century for a church formed in 1807. Square, with brick walls in three bays and two tiers of round-arched windows. (Derelict 1973)

WELSHAMPTON

(105) PRIMITIVE METHODIST, Breaden Heath (SJ 447364). Brick and slate, three-bay front dated 1832; contemporary cottage adjacent.

(106) PRIMITIVE METHODIST, Welshampton (SJ 438351). 1843.

WEM RURAL

(107) PRIMITIVE METHODIST, Northwood (SJ 466333). Brick and slate 'Jubilee Chapel' dated 1860, 'The land kindly given by W. Williams'. Front with patterned cast-iron window frames.

WEM URBAN

(108) Former PRESBYTERIAN, Noble Street, Wem (SJ 512289). A Presbyterian congregation met in a converted barn in Leek Lane (Chapel Street) in the late 17th century; the building was destroyed by a mob in 1715 and a new site, 'Sarah Thornhill's garden in Noble Street', was acquired and a meeting-house built there the following year. Between 1755 and 1817 heterodox preachers filled the pulpit but in the later 19th century the orthodox party appears to have prevailed and in 1874 when the chapel closed the remaining members joined the church meeting in Chapel Street (see (109) below). William Hazlitt, the father of the essayist, was minister here 1788–1813 and is commemorated by a modern tablet on the wall of the former manse, 17 Noble Street, adjacent to the chapel.

Former Presbyterian Chapel, WEM, *Shropshire*

N ←—|———

former doorway

5 0   10   20 Feet
C.F.S.

The former chapel of 1716, standing on the S side of the street at the back of the White Horse p.h. in High Street, has been drastically altered and reduced in height for use as a garage. It has walls of brown brick with dressings of yellow sandstone; the roof was formerly tiled. The walls rise from a moulded stone plinth and have rusticated quoins and a plain stone platband above mid-height. The original entrance at the N end, now blocked, has a stone lintel and jambs; traces of three upper windows are visible, one with a pointed-arched head. Two closely-set windows in the S wall flanking the site of the pulpit and three windows in the E wall, apparently repeated in the W wall but now altered by the insertion of garage doors, all have pointed-arched heads. The interior ($40\frac{1}{4}$ft by $20\frac{1}{2}$ft) retains no original features. Fittings now dispersed included two mid 18th-century communion cups and a large library presented in 1730. Elliot (1898) 60–6: Evans (1897) 252–3.

(109) INDEPENDENT, Chapel Street, Wem (SJ 513288). The congregation originated with meetings held at the house of John Henshaw who enlisted the assistance of students from Trevecka, built the chapel in 1775 at his own cost next to his house and placed it at the disposal of the Countess of Huntingdon's Connexion. The patronage was subsequently returned to the donor the cause becoming fully Independent about 1792 (now URC). In 1834 the chapel was drastically enlarged; it was further altered, refitted, and an organ chamber erected after 1873.

The chapel has brick walls faced at the front with yellow sandstone ashlar and the roof is covered with slates. The E front, probably of 1834, is of three bays with a pediment and terminal pilasters. Brickwork of 1775 remains visible in the side walls with a round-arched window with keystone at the former centre of the S wall; the chapel has been extended to the west. The interior (originally 26ft by $40\frac{3}{4}$ft, the former increased to $46\frac{1}{4}$ft in 1834) has an E gallery of the early 19th century now approached from the S by a staircase wing added post 1873; the walls are divided by pilasters carrying a Doric entablature with a semicircular organ-arch on the W side behind the rostrum.

Monuments: in chapel (1) John Henshaw Esq., attorney, 1801

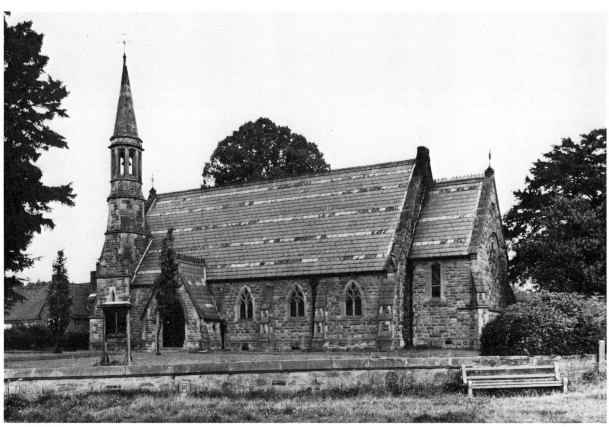

(110) WESTON RHYN. Congregational chapel, The Quinta. (URC)

(113) WHITCHURCH URBAN. Former Presbyterian meeting-house from W.

'. . . this edifice having been erected and endowed at his sole expence . . . ' and Jane (Tippet) his wife, 1800, marble tablet with wreath, signed Bacon, London, S. Manning Ft; in burial-ground on E side of road opposite chapel; (2) Rev. W. Jones, 1852, [Baptist] 'minister of the gospel in this town'.

Elliot (1898) 59, 66–9: Seymour II (1839) 39–40.

WESTON RHYN

(110) CONGREGATIONAL, The Quinta (SJ 281360). The chapel was built in 1858 by Thomas Barnes, Liberal M.P. for Bolton 1852–7 and 1861–8, who had recently acquired and rebuilt a house at the Quinta. A church (now URC) was formed in 1862. Stone and slate in the Gothic style comprising a short chancel, nave of six bays, S porch and SW turret. The E window of the chancel is circular, the N and S windows of the nave are of two lights with tracery in two-centred arched heads, and the S porch has a pointed-arched outer doorway with decorative wrought-iron grilles. The SW turret rises to an octagonal belfry with one bell and has a short spire.

Elliot (1898) 280–8.

(111) Former WESLEYAN, Weston Rhyn (SJ 287359). Dated 1849. Yellow sandstone rubble with segmental-arched doorway and two pointed-arched windows in side walls.

(112) PRIMITIVE METHODIST, Pontfaen (SJ 279369). Rubble and slate, three-bay front dated 1839.

WHITCHURCH URBAN

(113) Former PRESBYTERIAN, Dodington, Whitchurch (SJ 54254130). The congregation formerly meeting here is believed to have originated in the late 17th century partly through the ministrations of Philip Henry, father of the commentator Matthew Henry, who was ejected in 1662 from Worthenbury, Flintshire, and in 1672 licensed his house at Broad Oak in the

same county (3 miles W of Whitchurch). A meeting-house at Broad Oak was registered in 1689 and superseded by one in Whitchurch built in 1707; the latter was destroyed by a mob in 1715 and replaced in the following year by the present building, the former meeting-house at Broad Oak perhaps serving meanwhile as temporary accommodation (a baptism is recorded at Broad Oak, 3 September 1715 'the chappel at Whitchurch being demolished by ye mobb on July 15th, 16th, 18th and 19th, before'). The meeting suffered severely from an orthodox secession in 1798 (see (114) below) and the remnant who countenanced a more liberal theology disbanded in 1844. The building subsequently served as a British School, a dance hall, and is now a builder's store.

The meeting-house stands on a confined site behind buildings on the SW side of Dodington. It has brick walls and a hipped tiled roof with gablets to NW and SE. The front wall is rendered and has a moulded stone plinth and rusticated quoins, the doorway, left of centre, and two segmental-arched windows have been altered in the 19th century; two windows in the rear wall, formerly with round-arched heads, flank the probable site of the pulpit. The NW end wall has been much rebuilt and the SE wall was removed in the 19th century when the building was extended by 12ft at this end. The interior (originally $27\frac{3}{4}$ft by $40\frac{1}{2}$ft) has a plaster ceiling with a wide cove along each side. No traces of galleries or other fittings remain.

Brasses: a series of twenty-three memorial tablets was rediscovered by George Eyre Evans concealed behind wall panelling and removed in 1896 to the Church of the Saviour, Whitchurch, of which he was then minister. The tablets, now in the care of the Congregational (United Reformed) Church (items 5 and 15 missing), are fully described in Evans (1899), 241–5. (1) Samuel Benyon, 1791, and Lydia his widow, 1801, with shield-of-arms, signed W. Bowley, Engraver, Shrewsbury; (2) Mary Benyon, 1765; (3) Elizabeth, wife of Benjamin Benyon, 1797, with shield-of-arms; (4) Elizabeth, wife of S.Y. Benyon, 1802, with shield-of-arms; [(5) Samuel Yate Benyon K.C., 1822, Vice Chancellor of the Duchy of Lancaster, Attorney General and Recorder of Chester, with shield-of-arms]; (6) Constance Benyon, second wife of S.Y. Benyon, 1836, with shield-of-arms; (7) Lydia Collyer, 1744; (8) Edward Edwards, 1785, and Mary his widow, 1802; (9) John Edwards, 1825, and William his son, 1825; (10) John Edwards, 1827, and Margaret his widow, 1832; (11) Robert Gentleman, 1757, and his daughters Sarah and Martha (12) John Holt, 1781, and Ann his widow, 1782, with remains of earlier inscription on back to Thomas Keay, 17[80] (see (15) below); (13) Rev. 'Ebeneezer' Keay, 1779, 40 years minister of this place; (14) Hannah, wife of Rev. Ebenezer Keay, 1766; [(15) Thomas Keay, 1780, and Lydia his widow, 1785, with shield-of-arms] (16) Thomas Yate Keay, 1826, with shield-of-arms; (17) Thomas Yate, 1746, Elizabeth his wife, 1756, their sons Thomas and Collyer and daughters Susannah, and Anna, 1754, with cartouche-of-arms; (18) Samuel, son of Thomas Yate, 1729, and Abigail his daughter,

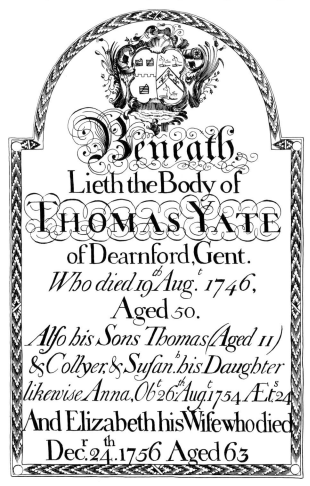

widow of Edward Ellis, 1746; (19) Benjamin Yate, 1756, with cartouche-of-arms; (20) Elizabeth Yate, 1767; (21) Thomas Yate, 1765, and Lydia his wife, 1757, with cartouche-of-arms; (22) John Yate, 1780, and Constance his widow, 1787, with shield-of-arms; (23) Constance Mary Yate, 1762, Anna Yate, 1762, and Margaret Yate, 1769, with cartouche-of-arms.

Elliot (1898) 88–90: Evans (1897) 255–7: Evans (1899) 240–8.

(114) CONGREGATIONAL, Dodington (SJ 543413). The church (now URC) originated in 1798 as a secession from the Presbyterian congregation, the seceders first meeting in a small building on the present site. The chapel was rebuilt in 1845–6 and has brick walls with a rusticated ashlar front and slated roof. The front, of yellow sandstone, is pedimented and has an open porch of three bays with two Roman Doric columns carrying an entablature inscribed 'Congregational Chapel 1846' and three round-arched windows above; the side walls of four bays have round-arched upper windows. The window frames, formerly hung sashes, were replaced c.1900 and the interior of the porch altered. Galleried interior with original seating.

Elliot (1898) 88–94: Tomalin, R. W., *Dodington Congregational Church, Whitchurch, Shropshire, 1798–1948* (1948).

(115) Former WESLEYAN, St Mary's Street, Whitchurch (SJ 542416). Rendered walls and hipped slate roof, front of three bays divided by pilasters with a pediment over the middle bay, plain Venetian window above central doorway, round-arched windows at sides, lower front windows altered for post-office use. Built 1810 and superseded 1879 by a Gothic chapel in St John's Street.

WORTHEN

(116) BAPTIST, Lordshill (SJ 380020). Baptists who had formerly been united with Independents at Minsterley (see (56) above) built a chapel here 'close to Snailbeach Mines' in 1833. The present chapel, which has rendered walls and a tiled roof, was built in 1873; it has a gabled front with round-arched windows. A cottage adjoins to the right. *Baptistery*: a flight of steps NW of the chapel leading down to a stream appears to indicate the first baptizing place; a later external baptistery lies SW of the chapel. *Monuments*: in burial-ground in front of chapel (1) Thomas Young, 1857, and Martha his wife, 1836; (2) Martha, 1838, and Anne, 1847, daughters of Edward and Mary Eveans.

Elliot (1898) 138.

(117) PRIMITIVE METHODIST, Aston Rogers (SJ 342064). Three-bay front; opened 1845.

(118) PRIMITIVE METHODIST, Snailbeach (SJ 372021). Rubble and slate, lancet Gothic with gabled front, 1876.

STAFFORDSHIRE

The county is notable for two major conurbations, centred on Wolverhampton, Walsall and West Bromwich in the south and on Stoke-on-Trent in the north. In both of these districts, the result of rapid industrial expansion in the 19th century, many chapels were erected; but whereas in the latter numerous examples, particularly of Methodist architecture, are to be found, the former has retained little of consequence. The Congregational chapel at Mayers Green, West Bromwich, of 1807, demolished in the course of road improvements, is one of the more recent losses, while mention must also be made of the former Presbyterian Chapel in John Street, Wolverhampton, of 1701, which figures in the historically important 'Wolverhampton Chapel Case' of 1817, in which the Unitarian trustees and congregation were dispossessed after a protracted and expensive legal battle.

The oldest remaining Presbyterian meeting-houses in the county, at Dudley (31) (until recently a detached portion of Worcestershire), Newcastle (68) and Stafford (79), suffered severely in the Sacheverell riots of 1715, the first two having to be entirely rebuilt. All, including Tamworth (96), of slightly later date, were greatly altered in the 19th century or later. The four Friends' meeting-houses (27), (58), (81), (102) are small buildings of which the latest, at Stafford, of 1730, is the most complete. Also in Stafford, the Brethren's meeting-room of 1839–40 (80), is noteworthy as one of the few buildings remaining from the opening years of the movement. The various branches of Methodism are well represented throughout the county and the early spread of Primitive Methodism from the site of the first camp meeting at Mow Cop on the borders of Cheshire is evidenced by the presence at Cloud (78) of perhaps the oldest chapel of that denomination still in use. Amongst the more prominent early 19th-century Methodist chapels are those in the pottery towns of Burslem (85), Hanley (89) and Stoke (93), and at Merrial Street, Newcastle (70) the Wesleyan chapel of 1857–8, by James Simpson, is a worthy representative of the later period. A few Congregational chapels of 1840–50 are of interest, including King Street, Dudley (32) in a stuccoed Classical style, and Burton (19) and Cheadle (22) where Gothic was preferred; of wider importance are the two patronage chapels at Armitage (7), of 1820, and Oakamoor (73), of 1878, the latter being a particularly successful design for its purpose.

Throughout the lowland areas of the county brick is used almost exclusively as a walling material, the earliest being at Stafford of 1689; the brown brick with brown glazed headers at the New Meeting-house, Tamworth, (96), of 1724, is a local characteristic, but in the later 19th century the use of polychromatic brickwork is little in evidence. Tiles predominate as a roofing material although slate spread rapidly throughout the country. In the higher regions to the north-east around Leek, at the southern tip of the Pennines, good building stone is found in use in many small and sometimes remote chapels, and the Friends' meeting-house in Leek (58) was, when erected in 1697, a typical example of the Pennine vernacular style.

ABBOTS BROMLEY

(1) CONGREGATIONAL (SK 080244). Brick and slate, built 1824. Two pointed-arched windows in W gable wall with blocked doorway between, similar windows in N wall, low porch at E end. Original pulpit. *Monument*: in burial-ground, to Sarah wife of Eustace Sammons, 1846, small terracotta headstone.

ALDRIDGE-BROWNHILLS   *West Midlands*

(2) CONGREGATIONAL, Brownhills (SK 042059). Brown brick and slate with three-bay gabled front dated 1858, superseding chapel of 1830 which was then converted to a day school. Sunday-school to right; red brick with blue bands, 1868. (Proposed conversion to warehouse 1982)
  CYB (1860) 256.

ALREWAS

(3) Former WESLEYAN, (SK 168150), SE of Kents Bridge. Brick with a hipped tiled roof, built in 1805 and extended to the N in 1846. In the late 19th century it was converted to a school-house and the interior entirely refitted. Traces of pointed-arched windows, now blocked, remain in the E and W walls and at the N end, with smaller windows at each end of a former N gallery. The roof has king-post trusses.

(4) Former PRIMITIVE METHODIST, William IV Road (SK 172151). Brick with round-arched windows. Built 1828.

ALSTONEFIELD

(5) PRIMITIVE METHODIST, Milldale (SK 139548). Small chapel of rendered stone, tiled roof. Dated 1835.

ALTON

(6) PRIMITIVE METHODIST (SK 072423). Red brick on ashlar plinth, tiled roof; date-tablet 1826.

ARMITAGE WITH HANDSACRE

(7) ARMITAGE CHAPEL (SK 078162). Congregational services commenced in 1811 in a private house and the present chapel was built in 1820 apparently by Thomas Birch of Armitage Lodge

ARMITAGE CHAPEL

rendered dressings and a tiled roof. It comprises, besides the body of the chapel, a N aisle, E vestry and W porch; a schoolroom was added to the NE in the later 19th century. The W front has a gabled porch of two stories with angle-buttresses, a four-centred arched doorway with square label and shield-shaped stops and traceried wheel window above. The principal W gable behind is crowstepped and flanked by gabled diagonal buttresses. The S

who placed it in trust for Congregationalists in 1831 (now URC). It is of particular interest as an example of patronage building in which the orientation and the diversity of building elements appear to indicate the advanced aspirations of the original proprietor, who in 1831 retained the right of burial in a private vault under the N aisle. The chapel has brick walls with

wall, of two principal bays, is divided by two-stage buttresses and has large rectangular windows with moulded labels. The E vestry has a S doorway with two-centred arched head and moulded label, and two pointed-arched windows in the E wall. The N aisle has a two-centred arched W doorway in a gabled projection.

Armitage Chapel
ARMITAGE WITH HANDSACRE
Staffordshire

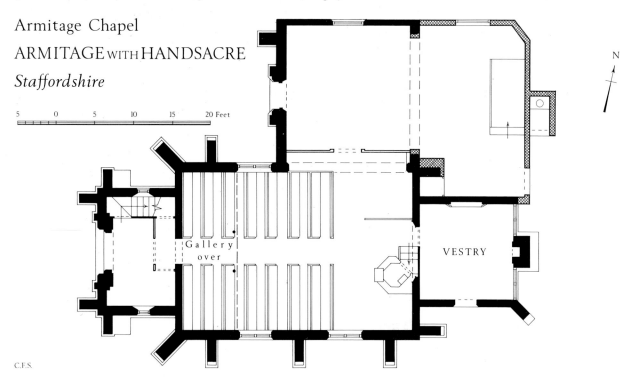

5   0   5   10   15   20 Feet

Gallery over

VESTRY

C.F.S.

The interior of the chapel has a segmental barrel-vaulted ceiling with two exposed tie-beams surmounted by arcading; a four-centred arch at the E end, resembling a small chancel arch, is closed by a pair of panelled wooden doors opening to the vestry with the pulpit in front of the S door. A four-centred arched opening to the N aisle has been closed by a later wooden screen. At the W end is a gallery with panelled front approached by a staircase in the W porch.

Fittings – *Clock*: on front of gallery, brass face, signed 'Parkinson, London', early 19th-century. *Monuments*: on W wall of N aisle (1) Thomas Birch of Armitage Lodge, 1837; (2) Mary, widow of Thomas Birch, 1842, pair of white marble tablets surmounted by urns; in burial-ground S of chapel (3) James Matthews, 1841, Mary his wife, 1830, *et al.*, table-tomb; (4) Louisa Ibotson, 1825. *Pulpit*: octagonal, with panelled sides, moulded base and cornice, *c*.1820. *Seating*: in gallery, original pews with panelled backs; lower seating renewed late 19th century.

ASHLEY

(8) CONGREGATIONAL (SJ 759367). Brown brick and tile with simple pediments to front and rear and date-tablet of 1841.

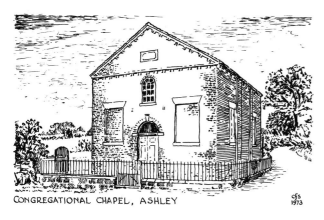

CONGREGATIONAL CHAPEL, ASHLEY

cfs 1973

Lower vestry wing behind built 1868. *Monuments*: in burial-ground (1) William Furnival, 1848, and James Unett Furnival, 1849 died at Forzapore, Bengal; (2) Alice Dunn, 1849; (3) Thomas Ward, 1849, William his son, 1845, *et al.*

(9) WESLEYAN, Wesley Road (SJ 753368). Originally three bays. Large tablet of 1860 over former entrance records gift of land by T. Astin.

(10) INDEPENDENT METHODIST, Hookgate (SJ 746351). Brick with four-centred arched windows; tablet 'Providence Chapel 1881' above entrance incorporates clock face.

(11) PRIMITIVE METHODIST, Hookgate (SJ 744353). Gabled front inscribed 'Primitive Methodist Jubilee Chapel 1860'.

AUDLEY RURAL

(12) WESLEYAN, Old Road, Audley (SJ 803511). Pedimented front with round-arched windows; dated 1876.

BAGNALL

(13) CONGREGATIONAL, Tompkin (SJ 944513). Built 1865, on site of chapel opened 1837. *Monument*: in burial-ground, to William Turner, 1839, and Ann his wife, 1838. (URC)

BARTON-UNDER-NEEDWOOD

(14) WESLEYAN (SK 187188). Rendered brick walls and slate roof hipped to front. Two round-arched windows with intersecting glazing bars and oval tablet ' . . . Ebenezer 1828', above later porch.

BLORE WITH SWINSCOE

(15) PRIMITIVE METHODIST, Swinscoe (SK 132481). Rubble and tile, lean-to porch against E gable wall covers original entrance, tablet over dated 1835.

BRADNOP

(16) WESLEYAN, School Lane (SK 012552). Squared stone with ashlar dressings. Large tablet above S entrance dated 1840. (Much altered since 1973)

BRANSTON

(17) CONGREGATIONAL (SK 222211). Rendered front with lancet windows; dated 1834. Small Sunday-school opposite *c*.1860. (URC)

BREWOOD

(18) WESLEYAN, Coven (SJ 909065). Low gabled front dated 1839.

BURTON UPON TRENT

(19) Former CONGREGATIONAL, High Street (SK 252232). The church which met here until *c*.1973 originated as a Presbyterian congregation gathered in the late 17th century by Thomas Bakewell, ejected Rector of Rolleston, Staffs. In 1803 the meeting-house was let to Independents and the trust deed was subsequently altered in their favour. The present chapel, opened 20 September 1842 to replace a building registered in 1708, is said to incorporate some re-used materials from the recently demolished racecourse grandstand.

The chapel has walls of brick with an ashlar front and a slated

roof. The E front has an arched centre bay flanked by buttresses perhaps once surmounted by pinnacles, opening to a porch with a four-light traceried window at the back and entrances in the return walls to N and south. *Monuments*: in front of chapel, slate headstones, (1) Rev. James Peggs, 1850, former missionary at Cuttack, Orissa, and four years General Baptist pastor in Burton; (2) Elizabeth Bakewell, 1838, 'lineal descendant of the Revd. Thos Bakewell, Rector of Rollestone... ejected 1661'.

CHST III (1907–8) 81–7: *Evangelical Magazine* (Nov. 1842) 550: Matthews (1924) III, 168–9, 219 and *passim*.

CANNOCK

(20) WESLEYAN, Chapel Lane, Cannock Wood (SK 042123). Rendered walls, round-arched windows. Opened 1834.

CHAPEL AND HILL CHORLTON

(21) Former WESLEYAN, Hill Chorlton (SJ 801394). Rendered brick walls and slate roof. Oval tablet inscribed 'Wesleyan Chapel. The land kindly granted by his Grace the Duke of

Sutherland. 1834'. Converted to house 1971 and chapel windows altered.

CHEADLE

(22) CONGREGATIONAL, Tape Street (SK 010433). The original chapel standing behind the present building is a plain structure of brick with a tiled roof ($30\frac{1}{4}$ft by $26\frac{3}{4}$ft externally); it was erected in 1799 and the remains of a round-arched window of this date survive in the NW wall; it was enlarged by $6\frac{1}{2}$ft to the SW and refronted in 1821.

Present chapel.　　　　　　*Photograph © Staffs. C.C.*

The present chapel, which like its predecessor is named 'Bethel', was built in 1850 in a simple Gothic style to the designs of John Holmes, 'architect and builder' (see monument (3) below). The walls are of red brick with stone dressings and the roof is slated. A shield-shaped tablet in the main gable bears the date of erection. *Monuments*: in burial-ground (1) John Mellor, 1830; (2) William Bennett, 1835, *et al.*; (3) John Holmes, 1858, builder, Lucy his first wife, 1852, and Hannah his second wife, 1867, slate headstone.

CYB (1851) 258–9.

(21) CHAPEL AND HILL CHORLTON. Former Wesleyan chapel. Before and after conversion to house.

CHEBSEY

(23) Former WESLEYAN, Norton Bridge (SJ 871301). Dated 1859. Original cast-iron railings in front. (Windows altered and railings removed since 1973)

CHECKLEY

(24) PRIMITIVE METHODIST, Fole (SK 044374). Brown brick with hipped tiled roof; three-bay front, dated 1850.

(25) PROVIDENCE CHAPEL, New Road, Upper Tean (SK 009396). Congregational services commenced in 1770 and the present chapel was built in 1822. Three-bay gabled front of red brick with central doorway and two tiers of windows. *Monument*: in front of chapel, to Mary, wife of James Burton, 1834.

(26) WESLEYAN, New Road, Upper Tean (SK 009397). Brick and slate; dated 1843.

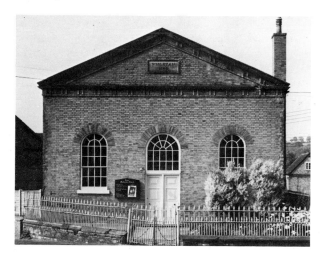

CHEDDLETON

(27) Former FRIENDS (SJ 989512), SW of Basford Hall. The meeting-house was built in 1695–7 on a site acquired in 1693. It

is a small building (20¾ft by 15¼ft) with stone walls and a tiled roof. The entrance is centrally in the W wall and traces of original windows remain in the N and S gable walls.

The former *burial-ground* to the S, initially 20 yards by 10 yards, was granted to Friends in 1667 and continued in use until 1828. It is now an irregular enclosure with low stone boundary walls rising a few feet above the surrounding ground; there are no monuments.

Stuart (1971) 40–1.

(28) WESLEYAN (SJ 971523). Brick and tile, mostly concealed behind later building. Original doorway and windows in N wall. Date-tablet, loose, inscribed 'Wesleyan Chapel, 1849'.

COLWICH

(29) MOUNT ZION CHAPEL, Great Haywood (SJ 999225). Congregational, of red brick with stone dressings and a tiled roof, built 1845. Gabled front with round-arched doorway in plain gabled stone surround and two tiers of round-arched windows, the upper pair blind, with moulded labels. The design similar to (95) below. *Monuments*: S of chapel, to James Whittle, 1849.

DENSTONE

(30) PRIMITIVE METHODIST, Stubwood (SK 096400). Stone and slate; dated 1841.

DUDLEY   *West Midlands*

(31) THE OLD MEETING-HOUSE, Wolverhampton Street, Dudley (SO 943902). The first meeting-house of the Presbyterian (latterly Unitarian) society, built in 1702, was destroyed in the Sacheverell riots of July 1715, in an account of which reference is made to 'the two great pillars that beare up the roofe'. The meeting-house was rebuilt at public expense and re-opened in 1717. It was drastically altered in 1869 when a new entrance was made at the NE end and the interior refitted.

The walls are of rubble with ashlar facing to the NW and a hipped slated roof. The NW wall has a stone plinth, platband and moulded eaves cornice; two windows in the end bays replace original entrances. The SE wall is similarly fenestrated but with timber lintels to the windows. Two tall round-arched windows

at the SW end replace two tiers of windows of which the upper lintels remain. The NE wall was rendered and an entrance-porch and organ-chamber added in 1869.

The interior (38ft by 48ft) has a gallery around three sides and pulpit at the SW end. Some 18th-century fielded panels are re-used as a dado and behind the gallery fronts. *Plate*: includes a pair of two-handled cups of 1751.

Evans: (1897) 77–8: Evans (1899) 101–21: *UHST* VI (1935–8) 158–9.

(32) CONGREGATIONAL, King Street, Dudley (SO 944901). The church (now URC) was formed in 1792. The chapel, of brick and slate rendered at the front with stucco, is dated 1840.

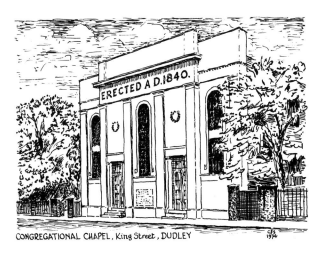

CONGREGATIONAL CHAPEL, King Street, DUDLEY

(33) BAPTIST, Ebenezer Street, Coseley (SO 940937). 'Ebenezer Chapel', brick and slate with rendered three-bay pedimented and pilastered front, is dated 1857. Side wall facing Birmingham New Road originally of four bays with two tiers of windows round-arched in blue and yellow brick.

(34) BAPTIST, Hospital Lane, Coseley (SO 937935). The former 'Providence Chapel', alongside Providence Row, of brick and slate, with simple pedimented front of three bays with two tiers

of round-arched windows, is dated 1809. Present chapel to W, 1870–1, by T. Richards.

(35) RUITON CHAPEL, Hermit Street, Lower Gornal (SO 919921), built in 1830 for a Congregational Church (now URC) formed in 1778, has walls of ashlar and a slated roof. The

SE front has terminal pilasters supporting a moulded cornice and pedimental gable. The previous chapel, built in 1778, had a broad front to the S with two doorways, a segmental-arched window between and gallery windows above.

SE of the chapel is a former school building of two stories with a fragmentary inscription reset close to the foot of an external stair with the date 1827.

Barnett, F. A. *et al.*, *Ruiton Congregational Church* (1972).

(36) METHODIST NEW CONNEXION, Ruiton Street, Lower Gornal (SO 918915). Rendered front with two tiers of round-arched windows; dated 1841.

(37) WESLEYAN, Mount Pleasant, Merry Hill (SO 924862). Rendered front much altered in late 19th century inscribed '1828/WESLEY'.

(38) METHODIST NEW CONNEXION, Northfield Road, Netherton (SO 950878). 'Providence Chapel', opened 1837, has brick walls covered with modern rendering. The gabled front, of three bays, has a central entrance with pilasters and two tiers of round-arched windows with cast-iron frames. A gallery around three sides is supported by slender fluted columns. (Re-erected 1978 in the Black Country Museum, Dudley. SO 948917)

(39) METHODIST NEW CONNEXION, St John Street, Netherton (SO 944881). Built 1848, enlarged to the rear in 19th century and refronted 1903.

(40) METHODIST NEW CONNEXION, High Street, Pensnett (SO 914892). Three-bay front with recessed centre inscribed 'ST. JAMES' CHAPEL 1837'. Sunday-school behind, built 1839, rebuilt 1928. (Demolition proposed 1982)

ECCLESHALL

(41) Former CHAPEL, The Horsefair (SJ 831290). Round-arched windows with intersecting glazing bars, and defaced tablet above altered entrance. Mid 19th-century.

FAWFIELDHEAD

(42) Former PRIMITIVE METHODIST, Hulme End (SK 103593). Limestone with sandstone dressings. Gabled front with rusticated quoins, round-arched doorway with fanlight, and partly defaced tablet of 1834. Side walls each with two windows with rusticated jambs.

(43) WESLEYAN, Newtown (SK 061633). Stone and tile, S front with tablet dated 1841. *Sundial.*

WESLEYAN CHAPEL, NEWTOWN, FAWFIELDHEAD
cfs 1973

(44) WESLEYAN, Rewlach (SK 094617). Stone and tile with contemporary porch dated 1849.

WESLEYAN CHAPEL, REWLACH, FAWFIELDHEAD
cfs 1973

FORSBROOK

(45) WESLEYAN, Boundary (SJ 982426). Brick and tile. Tablet on gabled side dated 1827.

HAMMERWICH

(46) PRIMITIVE METHODIST, Springhill (SK 072056). Gabled S front originally had central doorway between two round-arched windows. Entrance re-sited and inscribed tablet of 1844 altered.

HEATHYLEE

(47) PRIMITIVE METHODIST, Morridge Top (SK 032654). Small chapel at 1,500ft altitude, with stone walls and stone slate roof.

Opened 1850. Gabled entrance to S, two plain windows in each side wall.

(48) WESLEYAN, Upper Hulme (SK 013610). Gabled front with large tablet below upper window inscribed 'UPPERHULME/ *SUNDAY SCHOOL*/1838'.

HEATON

(49) WESLEYAN, Danebridge (SJ 965651). Stone and slate, on steeply sloping site with chapel at upper level. Two blocked windows in W wall suggest a major alteration or subdivision in the late 19th century. Tablet on E gable wall dated 1834.

HILDERSTONE

(50) WESLEYAN (SJ 949342). Built 1894; oval tablet inscribed 'J.WESLEY/Methodist Chapel/1822' reset in front wall.

HOLLINGSCLOUGH

(51) WESLEYAN (SK 065666). Walls of coursed rubble with ashlar dressings and a stone slate roof. The gabled front of three bays has two tiers of round-arched windows and a central doorway with rusticated surround; a tablet below the middle upper window is inscribed 'BETHEL/J * L/1801', and in the gable is an oval recess pierced at the centre, perhaps intended to take the drive for a public clock. The interior has a rear gallery returning half-way along one side, with panelled front and early 19th-century seating. *Chandelier*: brass, six branches reduced to three, surmounted by a dove, early 19th-century. *Monument*: John Lomas, 1823, and Sarah his widow, 1833.

HORTON

(52) WESLEYAN, Gratton (SJ 934562). Three-bay chapel opened 1822, refronted with banded red brick in late 19th century.

IPSTONES

(53) 'CHAPEL HOUSE' (SK 005499) was built *c*.1790 as a private chapel by John Sneyd of Belmont Hall following a temporary dispute with the incumbent of St Leonards Church and subsequently converted to domestic use. It has walls of sandstone and a tiled roof, and comprises a nave and W tower. The nave has a large E window, now blocked, of four lights with cusped intersecting tracery in a two-centred arched head. Some traces of

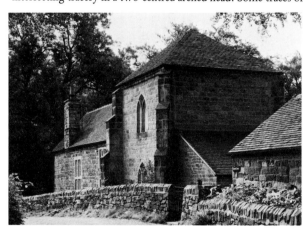

former windows remain in the N wall. On the S side is a central doorway with chamfered jambs and two windows to the W with Y-tracery in two-centred arched heads; the lower of two windows to the E is also probably original. The W tower is of two stages with stepped buttresses and a pyramidal roof; the N and S walls have in each stage a pointed-arched window with Y-tracery.

(54) Former PRIMITIVE METHODIST (SK 023501). Stone walls with brick front and hipped tiled roof. The broad NW front of three bays has been altered but the tops of two pointed-arched windows with keystones remain flanking a tablet inscribed with the name and date 1837.

KINGSLEY

(55) PRIMITIVE METHODIST, Whiston (SK 036472). The former chapel of *c.*1840, standing opposite its successor of 1907–8, has stone walls with a brick front and tiled roof. The gabled front, now altered, originally had a parapet with ball finials and a round-arched doorway with tablet above.

LAPLEY

(56) CONGREGATIONAL, Wheaton Aston (SJ 852127). 'Zion Chapel', dated 1814, was enlarged to rear and much altered 1908.

LEEK

(57) CONGREGATIONAL, Derby Street (SJ 985565). Built 1862–3 in Decorated Gothic Style by William Sugden of Leek has a tower and spire above the principal entrance. It stands on the site of the formerly Presbyterian meeting-house occupied from the late 17th century which was rebuilt in 1780. (URC)
    CHST III (1907–8) 4–19; *CYB* (1864) 282–3: Matthews (1924) 132–3, 150–1.

(58) FRIENDS, Overton Bank (SJ 982566). Quaker meetings commenced in the mid 17th century; in 1693 land called 'Tranter's Croft' and some old buildings were bought and by 1697 the present meeting-house had been built. It was extensively altered in 1794 and enlarged to the E but traces of the former fenestration remain. The walls are of stone and the roof is tiled. The original building (approx. 30ft by 17ft) is aligned E–W. In the gabled W wall is a wide doorway and three-light mullioned window, both now blocked; in the N wall is a second narrower doorway with two windows to the W and two above, also blocked, and on the S side further windows at two levels probably replace original mullioned openings. The interior, now much altered, has at the W end the remains of a stand with a large hung-sash window behind it, and a gallery at the E end.
    Stuart (1971) 42: Sturge (1895) 19.

(59) WESLEYAN, Mount Pleasant (SJ 982567). Large chapel of brown brick with slate roof hipped to N, built 1811 and enlarged 1877 and 1891. The N front, of five bays, has a stone plinth, platband and cornice, and two tiers of round-arched windows; a central doorway has been inserted between the two original entrances and a pair of Tuscan columned porches in front of the latter have been united. The side walls have each four bays of windows with stone lintels. *Monuments*: in forecourt to N,

seven ledger stones including (1) Rev. Edward Jones, Wesleyan Minister, 1837; (2) Samuel Rowley, 1818; (3) William, son of William and Catherine Arnott, 1816, with indent of brass inscription plate.

LICHFIELD ST MARY

(60) CONGREGATIONAL, Wade Street, Lichfield (SK 118094). Opened 18 March 1812 by a congregation (now URC) formerly meeting in a room in Tunstall's Yard, Sandford Street. Brick

walls and a slated roof; front with a simple pediment and two tiers of windows. Gallery around three sides with panelled front. The pulpit and lower pews renewed, some original seating remains in gallery.
    Monuments: in chapel (1) Rev. David Griffiths, 1848; (2) Rev. William Salt, 1857; (3) William Daniel, 1829, 'one of the first members of the church assembling in this place'. (Demolition proposed 1978)
    Matthews (1924) 186–90.

LONGDON

(61) LONGDON GREEN CHAPEL (SK 087136), built by a Presbyterian, latterly Congregational, society and registered in 1696, was a plain brick building (30ft by 20½ft) with a tiled roof. It was demolished for road construction *c.*1965–70. Existing photographs show two late 17th-century windows in the N wall; a pair of taller windows on the S and a pointed-arched doorway in the W gable wall, apparently of *c.*1800, indicate later alterations for which George Birch of Armitage may have been responsible. *Monument*: William Edwards, 1775, 'Clerk of this Chappel', headstone.
    CHST III (1907–8) 33–47: Matthews (1924) 106, 125.

LONGNOR

(62) WESLEYAN, Buxton Road (SK 088650). Stone and slate, pedimented front with rusticated quoins and round-arched windows to lower stage; dated 1853 but perhaps incorporating part of an earlier structure.

(61) LONGDON. Longdon Green Chapel. *Photograph © Staffs C.C.*

MADELEY

(63) Former WESLEYAN (SJ 771442). Blue brick and tile, gabled front with oval tablet dated 1831.

(64) PRIMITIVE METHODIST (SJ 773449). 'Ebenezer Chapel' dated 1856.

MARCHINGTON

(65) PRIMITIVE METHODIST (SK 132308). Gabled front with small lancet windows. Dated 1841.

MILWICH

(66) WESLEYAN, Garshall Green (SJ 969341). Gabled front with narrow round-arched windows. Dated 1835.

MUCKLESTONE

(67) PRIMITIVE METHODIST, Knighton (SJ 730402). Low three-bay front with later porch and altered tablet dated 1834.

NEWCASTLE-UNDER-LYME

(68) THE OLD MEETING-HOUSE, Lower Street (SJ 846461). The Presbyterian, now Unitarian, congregation originated in the later 17th century when it was assisted by Rev. George Long, one of the ejected ministers. In 1694 a building 'on ground called the Fulatt' was registered as a meeting-house and this was superseded in 1717 by the present building, the former having been

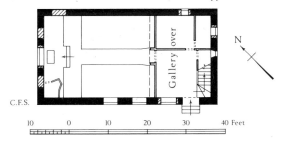

The Old Meeting-house,
NEWCASTLE-UNDER-LYME, *Staffordshire*

destroyed by rioters on 14 July 1715. The congregation has had a very chequered existence, dying out and being re-formed on several occasions and the meeting-house was closed or put to other uses 1804–8, 1810–20, 1850–2, 1872–6 and *c*.1895–8. As a result the building has undergone numerous refittings and alterations, the latest in 1926 being the addition of an upper storey, and little of the original work remains visible.

The meeting-house, standing close NW of St Giles Church and claiming a right of access through the churchyard, has brick walls covered with a modern rendering and a tiled roof. The front wall facing SW has three segmental-arched windows and a doorway to the south-east. The interior ($42\frac{3}{4}$ ft by $20\frac{1}{2}$ ft) has a SE gallery with fielded panelled front of *c*.1717 and a staircase of similar date with moulded balusters and straight string; the pulpit and partitioning below the gallery incorporate re-used 18th-century panelling. A window centrally in the NW wall inserted *c*.1926 and containing late 19th-century glass from the Unitarian 'Church of the Saviour', Whitchurch, Shropshire, replaces two smaller windows.

Monuments: none now visible, but Pegler records, in floor below gallery (1) Hannah, wife of Tho. Astbury, 1729; (2) Lydia, wife of Humphry Borrow, 1731. *Sculpture*: on gallery front, portrait of Josiah Wedgewood, carved oak in enriched oval frame, by F. J. Saunders, 1910.

Pegler, G., *A History of the Old Meeting House, Newcastle-under-Lyme* [*c*.1924]: UHST V (1931–4) 393–410.

(69) CONGREGATIONAL, King Street (SJ 852462). Of 1859, by R. Moffat Smith. Built on a new site to replace 'the Marsh Chapel' occupied since *c*.1784 by a church formed in 1777 through the preaching of Captain Jonathan Scott. The walls are of yellow brick with bands of blue brick and stone dressings. In front is a large wheel-window above the entrance and a thin octagonal tower and spire at one corner.

CYB (1860) 245: Matthews (1924) 132, 234.

(70) Former WESLEYAN, Merrial Street (SJ 850462). 'Ebenezer Chapel' of 1857–8 by James Simpson has walls of red brick with

stone dressings and a slate roof. The front has a stone plinth, platband and pediment. Inside is a continuous rounded gallery. (Converted to commercial use since 1978)

A former Wesleyan chapel, later United Methodist, in Lower Street, perhaps late 18th-century, has been demolished.

(71) PRIMITIVE METHODIST, Higherland (SJ 846457). Brick and tile with pedimented centre bay inscribed 'Rebuilt A.D. 1853'; perhaps incorporating work of the early 19th century. Sunday-school behind dated 1836.

NEW CHAPEL

(72) WESLEYAN, Mow Cop (SJ 856570). Large chapel of ashlar with a hipped roof, broad S wall of three bays with two tiers of round-arched windows and tablet above entrance inscribed

'WESLEYAN/1852'; a second, larger, entrance at a higher level at the W end is flanked by two tall windows.

OAKAMOOR

(73) BOLTON MEMORIAL CHAPEL (SK 054451), opened 21 April 1878, was built by Alfred Sohier Bolton, proprietor of a local brass and copper wire works, for an Independent church

which originated in 1867. It is a highly finished 'patronage chapel' of stone in the Gothic style of Edward F.C. Clarke, comprising a continuous nave and chancel, N vestry, S organ-chamber and porch, W vestry and W porch, with a bell-cote above the W gable. Original fittings include a stone pulpit and font and a carved wood eagle lectern.

Glass: in E window with symbolic figures of Life, Immortality and Hope, given 1878. *Inscription*: in W vestry on painted board, recording the erection and opening of the chapel and inclusion of the 'Te Deum' in the order of service. *Monuments*: in chapel on W wall (1) A.S. Bolton 'founder of this Chapel', 1901; W of chapel (2) A.S. Bolton, 1901, *et al.*, tall Celtic cross of granite.

ONECOTE

(74) PRIMITIVE METHODIST (SK 049550). Gabled front with tablet dated 1822, porch added 1934; tablet of 1843 on S wall perhaps records a refacing.

QUARNFORD

(75) WESLEYAN, Flash (SK 024672). Stone with hipped slate roof, broad three-bay front with two tiers of chapel windows

above basement storey and central doorway approached by double flight of steps. Tablet above entrance dated '1784 . . . rebuilt 1821'. Two blocked windows in side wall perhaps remain from earlier chapel.

ROCESTER

(76) Former GENERAL BAPTIST (SK 107393). Brown brick with

hipped slate roof and three-bay front; altered tablet above entrance, dated 1837. Now Roman Catholic.

Wood (1847) 230.

RUGELEY

(77) WESLEYAN, Brereton (SK 053165). Built 1872; oval stone tablet from former chapel of *c.*1809 reset in gable.

RUSHTON

(78) PRIMITIVE METHODIST, Cloud (SJ 910624). A low building of stone with a tiled roof, opened in 1815 and one of the earliest to be built by this denomination. It has three windows in

the E wall and an entrance in the S gable wall now covered by a recent extension. The N and S gables have shaped kneelers.

Kendall (1905) I, 170.

STAFFORD

(79) PRESBYTERIAN, Mount Street (SJ 920234). The congregation (now URC) originated in the late 17th century when they were supported by the Rev. Noah Bryan, an ejected minister. In the late 18th century a minister was appointed from

the Church of Scotland and in 1836 the building was referred to as the 'Scotch Church'. The meeting-house built in 1689 still remains although damaged by rioters in 1715 or 16, enlarged to the N in 1835–6 and to the S in 1899–1901. The walls are of brick with stone dressings and the roofs are tiled, except the N wing which is slate covered.

The original meeting-house, aligned E–W, is greatly obscured by the later work but the W end is unaltered apart from the substitution of a large traceried window and has a moulded plinth, ashlar quoins, moulded eaves cornice and a hipped roof. A gable has been added to the E end. The original broad S front remained until 1899 and had a pair of windows flanking the pulpit and entrances at each end. The interior (20¾ft by 41¾ft) had E and W galleries, now removed. The 1835–6 extension designed by Messrs Boulton and Palmer produced a T-shaped plan with a N wing equal in length to the older part and at right angles to it, with tall round-arched windows and an entrance at the N end. In the enlargement begun in 1899 a square S wing was added with a tower and short spire above a SE entrance, the seating pattern was reversed, the N wing was subdivided leaving a short chancel with schoolroom beyond and the interior refitted. *Royal Arms*: in glazed frame, after 1837.

Black (1906) 294–5: Drysdale (1889) 561–6.

(80) THE ROOM, St Mary's Place (SJ 921231), 50 yards SW of St Mary's Church, is one of the earliest meeting-rooms to be built for the Brethren. The assembly originated in 1838 and soon attracted the support of the Presbyterian minister, Rev. Alexander Stewart, who transferred his allegiance to the new society. 'The Room', built 1839–40, has brick walls and a slate roof, with wide eaves and a pediment at the N end. A modern N porch supersedes two segmental-arched entrances in the end bays of the E wall facing Church lane; the three intermediate bays on

the E side project slightly and have two tiers of windows with stone lintels. Minor rooms to the S were added in 1906 and 1927 and the interior was entirely refitted in 1930.

Monuments: loose in yard N of N porch, headstones, include (1) Charles Rowley, 1840, and Charlotte Rowley, 1846; (2) William Bayley, 1848.

Rowdon, H. H., *The Origins of the Brethren* (1967) 176.

(81) FRIENDS, Foregate Street (SJ 920237). The meeting-house, built in 1730 to the designs of Edward Frith on land which had been in use as a Friends' burial-ground since the late 17th century, is a small building of brick with a tiled roof, gabled to N

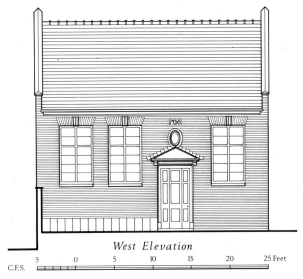

Friends' Meeting-house ,   STAFFORD
Staffordshire

West Elevation

C.F.S.   5   0   5   10   15   20   25 Feet

and south. The W front wall has windows with shaped keystones and a doorway with original frame and shaped brackets supporting a renewed pedimented canopy over which is an oval window and the date 1730 in raised characters. The E wall is mostly covered by a hall added in 1892 but one original window remains internally at the N end.

The interior (27¾ft by 18½ft) has a gallery at the S end with panelled front and staircase at the SW corner with turned balusters and a straight string. The stand at the opposite end is of one stage with two steps E and west. An attic room approached from the gallery by a winding stair in the SE corner is lit by a single window in the S wall and has a small fireplace adjacent. The roof has one truss with tie-beam and collar-beam.

Sturge (1895) 19–20.

(82) Former PRIMITIVE METHODIST, Gaol Road (SJ 921235). Three-bay pedimented front with giant pilasters, and pediments to former central entrance and lower windows. Built 1848; now Masonic Hall.

STANTON

(83) PRIMITIVE METHODIST (SK 125463). Above entrance'. . . Erected at the sole Expence of David Smith A.D. 1824'.

STOKE-ON-TRENT

(84) Former METHODIST NEW CONNEXION, Waterloo Road, Burslem (SJ 871495). 'Bethel Chapel' dated 1824 with rendered brick walls and slate roof has a front of five bays with pedimented centrepiece, round-arched upper windows, and wide porch. Two wings each of three storeys were added in 1835 and 'The Dr Coke Memorial School' at the rear, in polychrome brickwork, dates from the late 19th century.

(85) FREE METHODIST, Westport Road, Burslem (SJ 866498). The large 'Hill Top' Methodist chapel, also designated 'Burslem Sunday School' of brick with a slate roof, is of three storeys with the principal entrance approached by a double flight of steps and covered by a colonnaded porch of eight Greek Doric columns.

The front and sides are of five bays; a polygonal apse at the rear has a blocked Venetian window at the upper stage. Built 1836–7 to the designs of Samuel Parch. (Demolition proposed 1978–81)

(86) Former METHODIST NEW CONNEXION, Elder Road, Corbridge (SJ 876488). 'Providence Chapel', of 1884, now in industrial use, incorporates in the front wall an oval tablet of 1822 from the gable of its predecessor.

(87) WESLEYAN, Etruria Road, Etruria (SJ 868471). Three-bay rendered front with circular tablet dated 1820, stucco dressings later.

(88) HOPE CHAPEL, New Hall Street, Hanley (SJ 881478), built in 1812 for an Independent congregation which had recently seceded from The Tabernacle, was altered internally in 1891. The

walls are of brick and the roof is slated. The front wall has two doorways with fanlights and columned surrounds. (Reported demolished *c*.1975)

(89) METHODIST NEW CONNEXION, Albion Street, Hanley (SJ 882473). The large 'Bethesda Chapel' occupies the site of a preaching-house erected in 1798 soon after the formation of the Connexion. That building was enlarged in 1813 by about 10 yards with a circular end and gallery behind the pulpit. This is reported to have been replaced in 1819–20 by the present building for which the plans were drawn up by Mr Perkins, a schoolmaster. In 1856 the pulpit and communion-rail were renewed to designs by Robert Scrivener and in 1859–60 the chapel was refronted.

The walls are of red brick with yellow brick headers in Flemish bond and the roof is slate covered; the front wall is rendered in stucco. The rear part of the building, which is wider than the front, has a curved back wall with two tiers of windows in eight bays and five-bay sides with round-arched entrances in

the foremost bays. The narrower front section, perhaps added in 1859, is four bays in length and has a burial crypt below; the elaborately detailed facade is of five bays with bracketed cornice, two tiers of windows and open pediment above a central Venetian window. The front entrances, now partly rearranged, are covered by a loggia with colonnade of eight Corinthian columns reminiscent of that at Burslem Sunday-school (85). The interior, refitted in the late 19th century, has a continuous round-ended gallery and octagonal pulpit in an oval communion area.

Beyond the extensive burial-ground to the S is the School; of twelve bays with central pediment and octagonal lantern, and pedimented W end with inscriptions recording its erection in 1819 and enlargement in 1836. *Monument* in crypt, Rev. William Driver, 1831.

Smith, H. & Beard A., *Bethesda Chapel, Hanley* (1899).

(90) INDEPENDENT, Caroline Street, Longton (SJ 912437). Rebuilt 1905, circular tablet of 1819 from former chapel reset in side wall. (URC)

(91) METHODIST NEW CONNEXION, Lightwood, Longton (SJ 923415). Three-bay gabled front with circular tablet inscribed 'MOUNT ZION/1816'.

(92) Former INDEPENDENT, Aquinas Street (previously Thomas Street), Stoke-on-Trent (SJ 874453). Built in 1823 but sold to the Society of Friends in 1832 who continued to use it until 1951. It is of a single storey with brick walls, gabled to the N, with two windows in this wall and three at the E side with the entrance at the S end of the E wall. Burial-ground to E with flat marker-stones. (Derelict 1973)

Stuart (1971) 44–5: Sturge (1895) 20–1.

(93) WESLEYAN, Epworth Street, Stoke-on-Trent (SJ 875452). A large chapel of brick and slate, dated 1816, stands on a sloping site with windows to basement rooms at the E end. The W wall has a wide round-arched entrance flanked by pairs of windows. The longer N wall facing Hide Street is of five bays with two tiers of windows; the three slightly projecting middle bays are pedimented and have a former doorway at the centre from which a flight of steps has presumably been removed.

The interior has a continuous gallery with an organ recess at the E end, perhaps the site of a communion area behind the pulpit. The *pulpit* is an unusually elaborate structure of wood in

(93) STOKE-ON-TRENT. Wesleyan chapel, Epworth Street. Interior from W.

the Gothic manner supported by clustered pillars and ogee arches with vaulting beneath, and approached by twin staircases (see p. 224). The small *communion table* is in a similar style. *Fontlet*: pottery, copy of St Mary Magdalene, Oxford. *Monument*: David Bostock, 1820, 'ironfounder of this town', Mary his widow, 1830, *et al.*

(94) Former METHODIST NEW CONNEXION, Tower Square, Tunstall (SJ 859512). Rendered pedimented front of three bays, lower story converted to shops, built 1823–4.

STOWE

(95) Former CONGREGATIONAL, Hixon (SK 001257). The chapel, latterly Wesleyan, with altered date-tablet of 1842, closely resembles that at Great Haywood (29). It has red brick walls and a tiled roof. The gabled N front has a round-arched doorway in a gabled surround and two tiers of windows all with round-arched heads and moulded brick labels.

TAMWORTH

(96) THE NEW MEETING-HOUSE, Victoria Road (SK 209041). The Presbyterian, latterly Unitarian, society founded in the late 17th century erected their new meeting-house in 1724 on a site behind houses on the NE side of Colehill, which street long remained its principal or only approach. The building was re-roofed and drastically altered internally in 1879–80, and more recently a new entrance has been made in the SE side and the whole of that wall, exposed by the demolition of adjoining buildings, rendered and the window frames renewed.

The walls are of brown brick with darker glazed headers in Flemish bond and the roof is hipped and slate covered. The original entrance at one corner of the SW wall has been blocked, as has a corresponding doorway at the opposite side which led to the burial-ground and a new entrance and porch substituted c.1880 above which is a tablet inscribed 'THIS HOUSE/WAS BUILT/1724'. The NW wall is largely unaltered and has two tiers of segmental-arched windows with wooden cross-frames, three of which have opening lights with fretted escutcheons to the latches.

The interior (24ft by $42\frac{1}{4}$ft) may have had the pulpit against the SE side and galleries around, but no certain evidence remains. In 1879–80 the pulpit was re-sited at the NE end with a wooden screen of three pointed arches demarcating the line of the final bay.

Fittings – Monuments: on NW wall (1) John Lakin, 1860, and Elizabeth his widow, 1865; (2) Henry Lakin, 1846, and Anne Isabella his widow, 1863; (3) John Lakin, 1825, and Elizabeth his wife, 1824; (4) Sarah Lakin, 1831; (5) Rev. William Parkinson, 1857, 20 years minister; (6) Benjamin Shelton, 1833, and Catherine his wife, 1829; on SW wall (7) marble surround with urn, inscription panel lost; (8) Rev. John Byng, 1827, 53 years

Exterior from W.

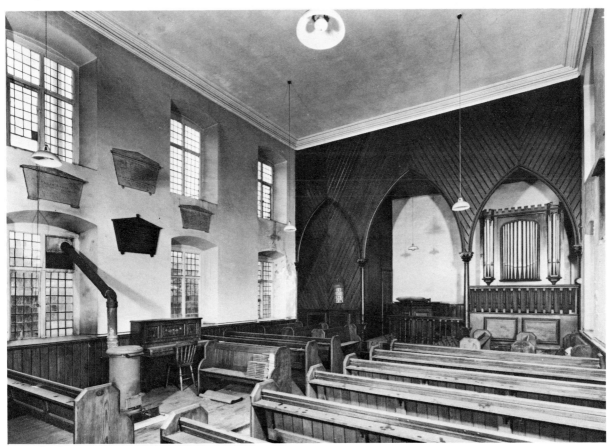

Interior from S.
(96) TAMWORTH. The New Meeting-house, Victoria Road.

The New Meeting-house , TAMWORTH
Staffordshire

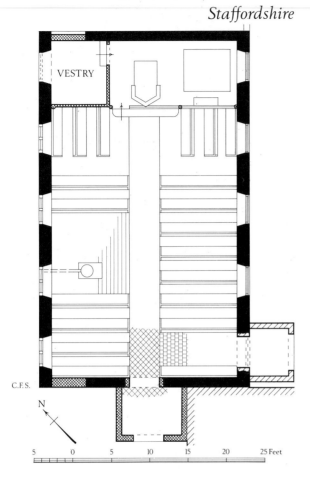

VESTRY

C.F.S.

N

5   0   5   10   15   20   25 Feet

TUTBURY

(99) CONGREGATIONAL, Monk Street (SK 212290). 'Ebenezer Chapel', built 1804–5, with brick walls rendered to the S and a slate roof, replaces a barn fitted up in 1799. It stands behind a forebuilding of brick with stone dressings and a central projecting turret (altered) added in the late 19th century when the chapel was refitted. Sunday-school to S dated 1884. *Monuments*: in burial-ground slate headstones, signed Brunt of Burton; Longhurst of Alrewas; and Shaw of Longford, include (1) Rev. Joshua Shaw, 1842, 32 years pastor at Ilkeston and Moorgreen, Derbys, and 12 years here, and Mary his widow, 1843; (2) Job Banister, 1839.

Matthews (1924) 183–5, 241.

(100) Former WESLEYAN, High Street (SK 213289). Three-bay gabled front with shaped tablet dated 1838.

UTTOXETER

(101) CONGREGATIONAL, Carter Street (SK 091334). Built 1827–8 superseding a meeting-house of 1792 in Bridge Street.

Brick and slate; front entrance with two Doric colums *in antis* to a formerly open lobby. Interior refitted 1887. (URC)

Elkes, L. M., *History of Congregational Church and Sunday School, Uttoxeter, 1788–1960* (1960).

(102) FRIENDS, Carter Street (SK 090333). The meeting-house built in 1705 on land given to the Society in 1700 was replaced by the present small building in 1770. The walls are of brick and the roof is tiled. The entrance was originally in the centre of the S wall facing the burial-ground flanked by two segmental-arched windows; in the 19th century the doorway was re-sited in the E gable wall and the former converted to a window. The E wall was partly rebuilt in 1961–2 when other major repairs were carried out. The interior (25¼ft by 18ft) has a gallery at the E end

pastor; (9) Henrietta, daughter of Rev. John Byng, 1827; on SE wall (10) Charles Harding, 1868, *et al.*; (11) Thomas Brittan Willcox, 1840; (12) William Harding, 1802, and Thomas son of William and Martha Harding, 1801; (13) Thomas Byng, 1822, Anne daughter of Thomas and Martha Byng, 1827, Thomas Gwyllym Byng, 1829, and Elizabeth Byng, 1829; (14) Joseph Clarson, 1831, Sarah his widow, 1860, and David their son, 1827. Nine of the above are signed by Mitchell of Tamworth.

Panelling: below side arches of NE arcade, four fielded panels with bolection-moulded edges, *c*.1724. *Pulpit*: four panelled sides with moulded cornice and base, from original pulpit; the railings in front incorporate 18th-century moulded balusters.

Evans (1897) 237: Evans (1899) 203–12.

(97) CONGREGATIONAL, Aldergate (SK 206042). Brick and slate dated 1827 but entirely refenestrated. Traces of two pedimented doorways remain on front wall now replaced by windows.

Sibree & Caston (1855) 336–44.

TITTESWORTH

(98) PRIMITIVE METHODIST, Thorncliff (SK 015584). Dated 1839.

S front.

and a staircase with turned balusters and shaped finial to the bottom newel. The stand at the W end, removed 1961–2 and replaced by a single raised seat, formerly had a central entrance flanked by benches with shaped ends and tall backs of plank-and-muntin partitioning with newels as on the staircase. *Monuments*: in burial-ground (1) Samuel Botham, 1828 (father of the authoress Mary Howitt); (2) Harrison Alderson of Burlington, New Jersey, 1871.

Friends' Meeting-house, UTTOXETER

Staffordshire

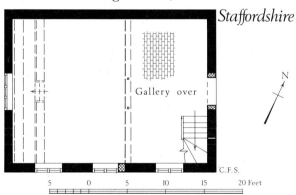

(103) WESLEYAN, High Street (SK 091335). Brick, with three-bay gabled front; centre bay recessed with semicircular arch over, enclosing pedimented entrance, upper window and tablet dated 1812. Side walls of two bays extended one bay to rear. Interior with continuous gallery on iron columns partly refitted but with early 19th-century pulpit.

WALSALL   *West Midlands*

(104) WESLEYAN, Union Street, Willenhall (SO 964985). Built *c*.1836, front of five bays with domed corner towers added 1863–4; greatly altered. *Monument*: E of chapel, to James Carpenter, 1844, *et al.*

(103) UTTOXETER. Wesleyan chapel.

WEST BROMWICH   *West Midlands*

(105) PRIMITIVE METHODIST, Bell Street, Tipton (SO 951922). Opened 1823, much altered and extended to rear.

WOLVERHAMPTON   *West Midlands*

(106) Former STRICT BAPTIST, Temple Street (SO 913983). On S side of street. Brick and slate; opened 1796 by a church which, after suffering mixed fortunes and being re-formed on several occasions, was finally dissolved in 1955. The front wall has been entirely rebuilt but the rest remains little altered. The W wall has three arched recesses at an upper level. Two windows have been added at the S end. Now in industrial use.

Chambers (1963) 15–17.

(107) WESLEYAN, Darlington Street (SO 912986). Large chapel of brick and slate with rusticated stone dressings, built 1900–1 to designs by Arthur Marshall to replace a chapel of 1825. Pedimented N front between staircase bays surmounted by domed turrets. Galleried nave and transepts with apsidal choir gallery at S end and large lantern dome with mosaic-decorated pendentives above the crossing.

(108) PRIMITIVE METHODIST, Bath Street, Cinder Hill (SO 926943). Dated 1850. Brick and slate with round-arched windows; extended to rear.

WOOTTON

(109) Former PRIMITIVE METHODIST (SK 106451). The former chapel behind Tollgate Cottage has an ashlar front of three bays; the main windows, which had pointed-arched heads, have been altered and the doorway and a small window to the left blocked. Perhaps the conversion of an 18th-century cottage.

(93) STOKE-ON-TRENT. Wesleyan chapel, Epworth Street. Pulpit.

Outside the principal centres of population around Birmingham and Coventry and some of the smaller towns, surviving nonconformist buildings are generally unremarkable, whilst in the two major centres some severe losses have been sustained. Three Quaker meeting-houses of the late 17th century remain of which that at Ettington (38), in existence by 1689, is outstanding not only as one of the smallest meeting-houses in the country but for the retention of much of the fittings and atmosphere of its period; the others, at Shipston on Stour (65) and Warwick (79), have suffered greatly by the loss of all interior fittings. Of Friends' buildings of the 18th century, several of which remain in the county, only Armscote (75), of 1705, survives in generally unaltered form; nothing of consequence is now visible from the following century although the Bull Street meeting-house in Birmingham, of 1857, had it not been demolished in 1931 would have served to indicate the continued strength of the movement in that city, the power of which is still evinced by the notable meeting-house in Bournville (22), of 1905, erected under the patronage of George Cadbury.

The chequered history of Presbyterian societies, at times torn by doctrinal differences and at others encouraged by popular support, has left few of their earlier meeting-houses standing in recognizable form. The only substantial building remaining from the early 18th century, the Old Meeting-house at Bedworth (10), of 1727, although much altered, is a reminder that not all such societies left the paths of orthodoxy, a fact which may be reiterated in reference to the remains of the Rother Market Chapel at Stratford-on-Avon (68) and the much later chapel at Stretton-under-Fosse (70), of 1780–1, which is the least altered of the larger 18th-century meeting-houses. The full extent of the loss sustained by the dispersal of fittings may be judged by the published description of the Alcester meeting-house (2), now surviving only in the final stages of decay. Of those societies which in the 19th century had come to support the Unitarian position only Warwick (77) retains its late 18th-century meeting-house although in an altered state. At Coventry (29) the Great Meeting-house of 1700–1 disappeared c.1937 and in Birmingham (13–15), where much damage was caused by rioters in the 18th century, both the Old and New Meetings built large and impressive Gothic chapels in the late 19th century which have now in their turn been demolished; a fortunate survival is the New Meeting-house of 1802 which, con-

verted to Roman Catholic use, still retains to a remarkable extent its original character and fittings. Particularly notable in the field of non-subscribing congregations, is the former chapel at Kenilworth (47), built in 1845 as the direct result of a thank offering for the passage of the Dissenters' Chapels Bill. Although unrelated to the older societies the former Presbyterian chapel in Broad Street, Birmingham (23), should here be mentioned as an unusual and strikingly monumental building of 1849.

The development of Congregationalism throughout Warwickshire, which was recorded in detail by Sibree and Caston, has left a considerable number of chapels, mainly of early 19th-century date, some of which derive from earlier Presbyterian foundations, others being the homes of new causes following in the wake of the religious revival of the late 18th century. Although Vicar Lane, Coventry (34), has gone and Carrs Lane, Birmingham (18), has been rebuilt, the chapel at Warwick (78) still occupies the site and may retain part of the structure of the first meeting-house built for the orthodox seceders from the Old Meeting, but in its present form the chapel can only be regarded as representative of the early 19th century. The late 18th-century chapel in Foleshill Road, Coventry (35), is now principally notable as an example of the extent to which the character of such a building may be affected by modern additions and alterations. Spencer Street, Leamington (52), of 1836, is outstanding for its size and the use of fashionable Classical details at a popular resort while at Southam (66) the chapel of 1839 is a particularly successful and relatively early essay in the Gothic style.

The only early Baptist meeting-house recorded, at Alcester (1), survives as an appendage to a later chapel, and examples from the early 19th century are generally unrewarding. The portico at Stratford-on-Avon (69) should, however, be noted as an attempt to give monumental character to an otherwise undistinguished building, and the few chapels of the General Baptist New Connexion, at Austrey (7), Polesworth (61), and Longford (32, 33), are interesting representatives of this branch of the denomination. The principal Baptist monument, 'Christ Church', Umberslade (73), of 1877, is important as a token of the successful patronage of nonconformist architecture by a wealthy client; the loss of the equally notable and architecturally more imaginative 'Church of the Redeemer' in Birmingham (17), of 1881–2 by James Cubitt, must be regretted.

Other denominations have not produced buildings of particular note. Methodist chapels, principally Wesleyan, are generally small and utilitarian, although the earliest, at Harbury (41), of 1804, is relatively unaltered and at Fenny Compton (39) the situation of the chapel entrance at the end of a narrow passage between houses indicates the difficulty sometimes experienced in obtaining a suitable site. The Moravian chapel in Priors Marsden (63) and the Salvation Army citadel in Leamington (53), of the late 19th century, are also listed as representative of their date and denomination.

The majority of buildings recorded here have brick walls and are roofed with tile or slate, but stone is found in a few restricted areas, the soft blue lias laid in alternately deep and shallow courses being particularly noticeable at Bidford (12) and Temple Grafton (74). No timber framing was recorded although the earlier Presbyterian meeting-house in Warwick (77) was evidently of this material.

ALCESTER

(1) BAPTIST, Church Street and Meeting Lane (SP 092575). The Particular Baptist church in existence by 1655 drew its members from a wide radius including, by the early 18th century, meetings at Henley in Arden and Bengeworth (Evesham). A meeting-house 'lately built' in Tibbett's Lane, now Meeting Lane, was registered 11 January 1737 and enlarged in 1817. A new chapel contiguous with the last but facing Church Street was built in 1859.

The chapel of c.1736 which remains in use as a hall has brick walls and a hipped tiled roof. The present entrance at the NE end replaces a window and has a blocked segmental-arched window above. The NW wall has three round-arched windows with the site of a former doorway below that next to the NE end. The SE wall, which has a stone plinth, has been partly masked by the addition of a two-storied Sunday-school wing of 1817; the original fenestration may have provided two regularly spaced round-arched windows of which one remains; a second window near the corner of the surviving wall has been altered or inserted.

The interior (35¾ft by 21½ft) has no original fittings; the pulpit was latterly between two small round-arched windows at the SW end but it is possible that prior to 1817 it may have been on the NW side. A gallery, probably of 1817, has been removed

From E.

from the NE end. There is a coved plaster ceiling with a moulded cornice. The Sunday-school has shutters opening to the chapel at both levels, the staircase to the upper floor was originally external.

The present chapel, SW of the former, is dated 1859; it has a rendered front wall with pedimented centre between wings.

Monuments: in former chapel (1) Rev. Thomas Skinner, 1782, 'Minister of this Congregation for More than 17 Years', Mary his widow, 1801, and Elizabeth their daughter, 1793, marble tablet with apron and shaped top surmounted by a dove; (2) John Hopkins, 1802, Elizabeth his wife, 1794, and William their son, 1811, oval tablet with urn on octagonal backing; (3) Joshua Hopkins, 1798, deacon almost 30 years, and Anna his wife, 1782, similar to last; (4) John Cox, 1799, and Ann his widow, 1821; in burial-ground NW of former chapel (5) Job Cox, 1775, Ann his wife, 1744, and William Goffe, 1787, headstone with winged cherubs' heads and sunburst.

(2) Former PRESBYTERIAN, Bull's Head Yard (SP 089575). The chapel, now largely demolished, was built in 1721 behind houses on the W side of High Street to replace a meeting-house in use by 1693. The congregation, which traced its origin to Samuel Ticknew, ejected vicar of Alcester, became Unitarian by the 19th century. The meeting was closed c.1900 and the building and contents were sold by auction 28 August 1901. The chapel was derelict by 1947 and in 1960 was severely damaged by fire. The structure remaining in 1971 comprised parts of the E and N walls and NE vestry. The walls were of brick with a stone plinth

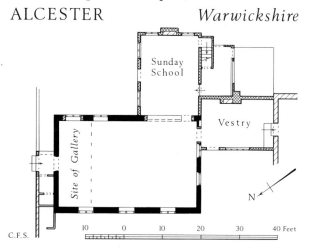

Former Baptist Chapel,
ALCESTER   *Warwickshire*

Sunday
School

Vestry

Site of Gallery

N

10   0   10   20   30   40 Feet

C.F.S.

and had brick pilasters at the corners. The front wall faced south. The E wall had two flat-arched windows with wooden cross-frames below a platband and a later vestry to the N which probably replaced a third window; there may have been three similar upper windows and identical fenestration on the W side. The N wall had two wide windows flanking the pulpit.

The interior (28ft by 40¼ft) was entirely gutted in 1901. Details of the fittings recorded by G.E. Evans suggest that these were of unusual interest and included a two-decker pulpit with square sounding board, brass chandelier of nine branches with dove, stone font, and communion pews designed to form 'long narrow tables by half folding over the backs of the seats'. *Monument* to Rev. Joseph Porter, 1721, see Evesham, Worcs. (16).

Evans (1897) 2: Evans (1899) 9–18: *UHST* IV (1927–30) 60–2.

ANSLEY

(3) CONGREGATIONAL, 'Providence Chapel' (SP 297918) dated 1822. Pointed-arched windows flank later porch. (URC)

ATHERSTONE

(4) CONGREGATIONAL, North Street (SP 310979). A Presbyterian meeting which existed from the late 17th century built a meeting-house in Long Street in 1725 where by the 19th century Unitarian preaching prevailed. A new Independent cause (now URC) was commenced in the late 18th century and between 1794–1801 had the use of the Long Street building although a small chapel is also said to have been built for their use in 1792 in the Coach and Horses Yard. The Long Street meeting-house was also used *c.*1848–55 by seceders from this congregation before erecting a chapel in North Street; the two societies have since re-united. The former meeting-house was demolished *c.*1970 or after, but no description of the building is available.

The present chapel, built in 1826–7, is of brick with a three-bay front with two tiers of round-arched windows and a central doorway with rusticated sub-arch supported by two Ionic columns which flank the entrance. A rendered parapet is inscribed 'INDEPENDENT CHAPEL 1827'. *Monuments*: in burial ground, slate headstones re-sited as boundary fence.

CYB (1857) 238–9: Evans (1899) 19–30: *Inquirer*, 15 Nov. 1980: Sibree & Caston (1855) 234–50.

(5) Former FRIENDS, Long Street (SP 312977). The meeting-house, standing behind houses on the NE side of the street, was built by Nathanial Newton the younger on land acquired about 1729 and probably completed in that year although the property may not have been formally transferred until 1740; it was registered in 1741. The building, which had been extended to the front by the early 19th century, was closed in 1846 and has since been used as a workshop.

The meeting-house, behind 174 Long Street, has brick walls and a tiled roof with gabled ends. The original building (19¾ft by 30¼ft) of three bays has been extended by 16½ft to the south-west. In the original NW wall are four closely set windows with wooden cross-frames and in the NE wall is a segmental-arched window with a similar 18th-century frame. Some traces of

Exterior from W.

Interior looking towards gallery.

blocked windows are visible in the SW wall. The interior has in the older part three roof trusses with king-posts and braces, ceiled at mid-height, and a gallery with boarded but formerly balustraded front at the SW end.

Hodson (1953) cvii: Sturge (1895) 9–10: White (1894) 103.

(6) WESLEYAN, Coleshill Road (SP 308977). Brick and slate. Opened 1836, porch later.

AUSTREY

(7) GENERAL BAPTIST (SK 297065). The chapel was built in 1819 for a church formed in 1808. Brick and slate with two tiers of round-arched windows with keystones and impost blocks. Three-bay gabled W front with wide central entrance reduced in size. Interior has a W gallery; at E end is a vestry with school-room above and shutters opening to chapel over which at a high level is an upper gallery with open railed front. The pulpit, with arched and keyed front panel, has been reduced in height. Seating comprises plain open-backed benches. *Monuments:* externally on front wall, Martha, wife of Joseph Burton of Netherseal, 1825, three children 1823–5, and later inscription to Joseph Burton, 1863, slate, signed C. Cooper Sculp. Edengale; also, in burial-ground, several slate headstones, some loose.

Taylor (1818) II, 337, 369–72: Wood (1847) 207.

BADDESLEY ENSOR

(8) Former FRIENDS (SP 272982). A meeting-house given to the society in 1669 was superseded by one on the present site in 1722. This building, which records suggest may have been rebuilt *c.*1768, stands behind a red brick Wesleyan chapel of 1895. Friends meetings ceased in 1847 and the building was later leased and eventually sold to the Wesleyans; it now serves as a Sunday-school. The walls are of brick and the roof tiled. The

front wall, facing W, has segmental-arched openings formerly with external shutters for the windows; at the N end are the remains of a cottage. The interior (34ft by 18¼ft) has two king-post roof trusses ceiled at mid height; wall benches and a boarded dado date from the 19th century. *Pulpit:* seven-sided with canopy, incorporating 17th-century panelling.

Hodson (1953) cvii–cviii: Sturge (1895) 8–9: White (1894) 96–9.

BEDWORTH

(9) ZION CHAPEL, High Street (SP 360868), was built in 1798 for a Strict and Particular Baptist church which had met from 1796 in a room in Millerships Yard, the scene of William Gadsby's first sermon. The chapel (33ft by 27ft externally) has brick walls, rendered and embellished in the late 19th century, and a hipped slate roof. A Sunday-school was added to the rear *c.*1860. The front wall is of three bays with two doorways and two tiers of round-arched windows; there are two bays of similar windows at the sides. Interior refitted 1910.

Chambers (1963) 50–1.

(10) THE OLD MEETING-HOUSE (SP 360872) was built for a Presbyterian, later Congregational church (now URC) formed in 1686 for which the first known meeting-house was registered in 1705. The present building was described as 'lately erected' when it was registered for Presbyterians in 1727. In 1808 the walls were heightened, a gallery probably inserted and the roof rebuilt. The walls are of brick and the roof is hipped and slated. The front wall is of four bays with a platband, continuous around the building, between two tiers of windows round-arched above and segmental-arched below, and two doorways in the end bays. In the rear wall are two tall round-arched windows with a later vestry between and windows above and below the ends of the galleries. The return walls are of three bays; school-rooms were added at one end in 1840. The interior (38¼ft by 45¼ft), largely refitted *c.*1891, has a gallery around three sides supported by cast-iron columns. The plaster ceiling is coved on all sides.

Fittings – *Books:* Matthew Henry, *Commentary*, 4 vols (1721), and two vols *Sermons*, with chains formerly attached to

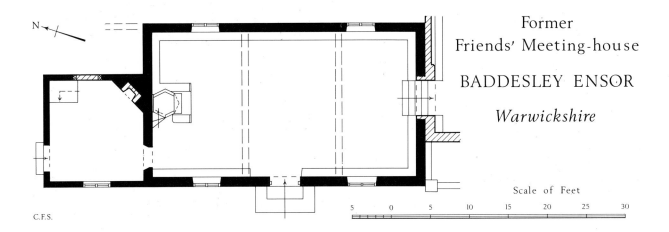

Former
Friends' Meeting-house

BADDESLEY ENSOR

Warwickshire

Scale of Feet

5   0   5   10   15   20   25   30

C.F.S.

communion table. *Inscriptions*: on bricks in front wall with initials and dates 1726, 1808. *Monuments*: in chapel, (1) Rev. Julius Saunders, minister 1687–1730, buried below table-pew, and Rev. Thomas Saunders, his grandson, minister 1764–85, buried in Bunhill Fields, London, modern tablet; (2) Elizabeth wife of Rev. John Hewitt, 1801; (3) Thomas Goodyer, Gent., of Exhall, Coventry, recording legacies of £200 and £500 to the trustees under will dated 1820; in burial-ground (4) Ann wife of Samuel Drakeford, Independent pastor at Marple Bridge, Derbys., 1852, and children; (5) C.M. Cullen, daughter of J. Cullen of Lacock, Wilts., 1845.

Hodson (1953) lxxxviii–ix: Mann, A., *History of the Pastorate of the Old Meeting Church, Bedworth* (1966): Sibree & Caston (1855) 146–73.

(11) CONGREGATIONAL, Bulkington (SP 393866). Brick and slate 'erected 1811, restored 1883'. Gabled front with round-arched windows above altered entrance. A minister's house was added at the back in 1821. *Monuments*: in manse garden (1) William Smith, 1869, and Elizabeth his wife, 1842; against side of chapel (2) William Clewer, 1874, and Catherine his wife, 1846, slate headstone signed J. Lee, Bedworth.

Sibree & Caston (1855) 291–2.

BIDFORD-ON-AVON

(12) WESLEYAN (SP 097519). Dated 1837; walls of soft blue lias in alternating courses, brick N front and dressings, hipped slate roof. Three round-arched windows front and rear, two plain windows at W end above and below gallery, blocked window in E wall behind pulpit. (Disused 1971)

Cox (1982) 8.

BIRMINGHAM   *West Midlands*

(13) THE OLD MEETING-HOUSE, Bristol Street (SP 069858), destroyed by bombing in 1940, was a stone building by J.A. Cossins in the Gothic style with tower and spire; it was built in 1885 to replace the former meeting-house in Philip Street, later Old Meeting Street, built 1689, rebuilt 1715 and 1795 after damage by rioters, and finally demolished for the erection of

New Street station. The society, originally Presbyterian, became Unitarian by the early 19th century and in 1928 adopted the name 'Society of Free Catholics'.

Beale, C.H., *Memorials of the Old Meeting House and Burial Ground* (1882): Evans (1897) 17–18: Evans (1899) 45–51: Sibree & Caston (1855) 174–7: *UHST* IV (1927–30) 160–3; XII (1959–62) 53–68: VCH *Warwickshire* VII (1964) 474, 476.

(14) THE NEW MEETING-HOUSE, Moor Street (SP 074869), was built in 1802 to replace a building of 1732 destroyed by rioters in 1791. In 1861 the original Presbyterian, latterly Unitarian, congregation moved to a new chapel (see (15) below) and sold the former meeting-house to the Roman Catholics who still use it as 'St Michael's Church'.

The building has brick walls with ashlar facing to S and E and a hipped slate roof. The E front has an open loggia entrance incorporating the gallery staircases. The side walls are of five bays with round-arched upper windows. The interior retains its original gallery around three sides, except for the W bay which has been altered to form a sanctuary, and much contemporary seating.

Evans (1897) 19–20: Evans (1899) 52–62: Little, B., *Catholic Churches, Since 1623* (1966) 200–1: *UHST* IV (1927–30) 163–4: VCH *Warwickshire* VII (1964) 409, 475.

(15) CHURCH OF THE MESSIAH, Broad Street (SP 062867), built 1860–1 to supersede the foregoing was replaced in 1974 by a new meeting-house in Ryland Street. The building, designed by J.J. Bateman in the Decorated style, has stone walls and a slate roof, tower and spire at one corner, triple-gabled entrance and separate gables above the side windows. To the rear stands a brick school dated 1861. *Monument*: to Joseph Priestley, 1804, from former meeting-house, now removed to Ryland Street.

Inquirer, 23 Nov. 1974.

(16) Former UNITARIAN, Newhall Hill (SP 061873). Built 1839–40 for a recently-formed congregation derived from the New Meeting Sunday School; closed 1910 and fittings removed to a new chapel in Handsworth. Brick and slate with later rendering; gabled front divided by two plain buttresses rising to square stone finials, lancet windows grouped above central doorway. Schoolrooms below. Architect D.R. Hill (*cf* Coleshill (28) below).

CF (1872) 104–5: Evans (1897) 21–2: Evans (1899) 63–9: *UHST* IV (1927–30) 164: VCH *Warwickshire* VII (1964) 475–6.

(17) CHURCH OF THE REDEEMER, Hagley Road (SP 046860), was built 1881–2 for a Particular Baptist church which originated in 1828 and previously met in a chapel in Graham Street. The new chapel in Hagley Road was designed by James Cubitt and is a notable exemplar of his published work on the adaptation of the Gothic style for auditory worship (*Church Design for Congregations*, 1870). The building, of stone with slate

Interior looking towards apse.

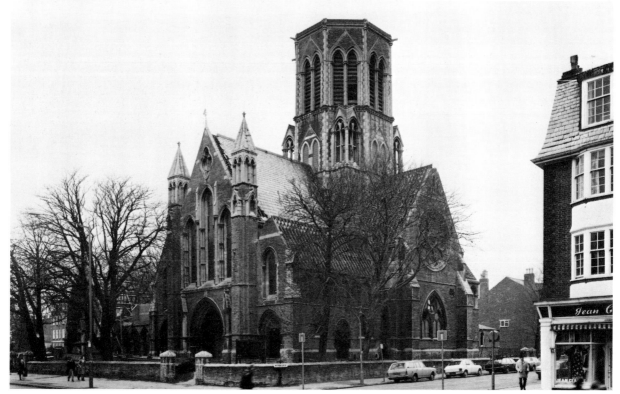

(17) BIRMINGHAM. 'Church of the Redeemer'.

roofs, comprises a short nave of three bays with transepts, apse and octagonal crossing tower formerly having a parapet and pinnacles (removed 1930). Galleries in the transepts and at the end of the nave are separated from the body of the building by two-centred arches partly filled with plate tracery. The pulpit stands at one corner of the crossing. There is an open baptistery in the apse. (Demolished 1975)

Hutton, T.W., *Church of the Redeemer, 1882–1957* (1957): Langley (1939) 90–4, 102–7: VCH *Warwickshire* VII (1964) 438.

(18) CONGREGATIONAL, Carrs Lane (SP 074869). This site close to the New Meeting-house has been occupied since 1747–8 when a new congregation (now URC) was formed by secession from the Old Meeting and a new meeting-house erected. A new chapel, built 1802, was superseded in 1820 by a larger building designed by Thomas Stedman Whitwell which had a pedimented front and Doric columns carrying a wide arch above the entrance. In 1876 the chapel was refronted and in 1884 the interior was altered, reseated, and cast-iron arcades inserted to support the roof. This building was replaced *c*.1970 by a polygonal chapel.

Monuments: (1) John Angell James, 1859, pastor 55 years; (2) Rev. Gervas Wilde, 1766, Rev. John Punfield, 1791, and Rev. Edward Williams, 1813, erected 1837; (3) Rev. Robert William Dale, 1895, brass.

Driver, A.H., *Carrs Lane 1748–1948* (1948): Little, B., *Birmingham Buildings* (1971) pls 40 and 109: Sibree & Caston (1855) 174–83: VCH *Warwickshire* VII (1964) 448–9.

(19) CONGREGATIONAL, 'Lozells Chapel', Wheeler Street (SP 067893), built in 1839, was converted for Sunday-school use in 1863 when a new chapel was built nearby. The latter, which was a notable building by Poulton and Woodman with a wide round-arched portal and two stages of galleries, suffered severe bomb damage in 1942 and was demolished after 1961. The earlier chapel has brick walls rendered at the front with two tiers of windows, the upper ones round-arched. (URC)

CYB (1862) 293–6: Sibree & Caston (1855) 181, 193: VCH *Warwickshire* VII (1964) 454.

Front of 1863 chapel, from 'Congregational Year Book' (1862)

(20) Former CONGREGATIONAL, 'Highbury Chapel', Graham Street (SP 062874), built 1844–5 for a section of a church which seceded from Carrs Lane in 1802, has been used since 1879 by a variety of denominations and now serves as a Sikh temple. Brick walls with rendered dressings, front of three principal bays with altered gable, central doorway with pediment and tall round-arched windows.

Sibree & Caston (1855) 188–9: VCH *Warwickshire* VII (1964) 450, 454.

(21) CONGREGATIONAL, High Street, Erdington (SP 111921). Built 1839 for a church which previously met in a small former Wesleyan chapel of 1814. Brick walls rendered at front, slate roof. Gabled front with projecting centre bay having octagonal corner buttresses, central entrance with crocketed gable, and three graduated lancets above. *Monuments*: in burial-ground (1) Joseph Allen, 'artist', 1839, and his sisters Ann, 1842, and Elizabeth, 184[?9]; (2) Thomas Gibbins, 1843. (Closed by 1976)

Sibree & Caston (1855) 310–4: VCH *Warwickshire* VII (1964) 450–1.

(22) FRIENDS, Linden Road, Bournville (SP 045813). Built 1905 to serve the model village then under construction next to George Cadbury's factory. The meeting-house, designed by W. Alexander Harvey and intended for general community use, is of brick with stone dressings and a tiled roof; it has a round-arched entrance in the gabled front wall between low wings and an

octagonal stair turret. Fittings – *Clock*: on gallery front, octagonal face dated 1723, and another of similar period in rear room. *Organ*: given 1905 by George and Elsie M. Cadbury. *Statue*: in external niche, George Cadbury, 1837–1922. *Sundial*: on front gable. *Table*: 17th-century.

VCH Warwickshire VII (1964) 487.

(23) Former PRESBYTERIAN, Broad Street (SP 061866). Orthodox Presbyterians built an octagonal chapel in Graham Street in 1824 but were unable to support it and sold the building to the Baptists in 1827; it has since been demolished. A fresh start was then made in smaller premises, the first chapel on the Broad Street site was built in 1834 and superseded by the present building in 1849. Since 1924 it has been used by a Christian Science church. The chapel, designed by J.R. Botham, has walls of blue Staffordshire bricks with stone dressings. At the front is a

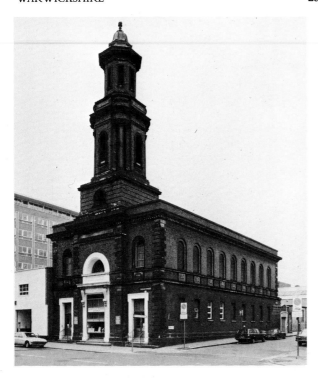

two-stage tower rising from a podium above the general level of the walls; at the centre is a tall former entrance and minor entrances to right and left leading to gallery staircases. The side walls are of nine bays with two tiers of windows all originally blind. Roof lights and a wide window in the rear gable give overhead illumination.

Little, B., *Birmingham Buildings* (1971) pl. 43: Owen, J.M.G., *Records of an Old Association* (1905) pls opp. 145, 153: VCH *Warwickshire* VII (1964) 476.

BISHOP'S ITCHINGTON

(24) CONGREGATIONAL (SP 391577). Brick and slate with gable tablet inscribed '1836 INDEPENDENT CHAPEL'. Opened 1837; interior partly refitted in late 19th century.

Sibree & Caston (1855) 372–4.

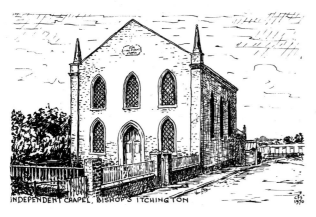

INDEPENDENT CHAPEL, BISHOP'S ITCHINGTON

BURTON DASSETT

(25) WESLEYAN, Knightcote (SP 399545). Low three-bay gabled front dated 1837; porch added 1914.

(26) WESLEYAN, Northend (SP 392525). Gabled front with arched gallery windows and tablet dated 1831. Sunday-school adjacent built 1900.

(27) Former PRIMITIVE METHODIST, Northend (SP 393526). Gabled front dated 1855; now a cottage.

COLESHILL

(28) CONGREGATIONAL (SP 199892). Brick and slate; front divided by plain buttresses rising to rendered turrets with broach pinnacles. Built 1834. The design is comparable with (16) above and may be the same architect. (Disused 1973)

Sibree & Caston (1855) 379–84.

COVENTRY   *West Midlands*

(29) THE GREAT MEETING-HOUSE, Smithford Street (SP 332791), built in 1700–1 for a Presbyterian society, was demolished after 1937 when the then Unitarian congregation removed to a new building in Holyhead Road. The building was of red brick with stone dressings and had a five-bay pedimented front with two tiers of windows.

Evans (1897) 57–8: Sibree & Caston (1855) frontis., 45: *UHST* V (1931–4) 473–4: VCH *Warwickshire* VIII (1969) 393–4.

(30) Former PARTICULAR BAPTIST, Cow Lane (SP 339789). Built in 1793 for a church formerly meeting in Jordan Well which in 1884 removed to a new chapel in Queens Road. The

(29) COVENTRY. The Great Meeting-house, Smithford Street.
(Sibree & Caston, 1855)

former chapel, which had been altered in the mid 19th century
and later, was subsequently used for school and social purposes
and in 1948 was further altered for use as part of the City Library.
VCH describes this as 'the only early nonconformist place of
worship to survive in central Coventry', and states that 'the red
brick front has a central doorway, round-headed windows, and a
tablet in the gable commemorating the building's erection in
1793'. A photograph in Morris (1926) shows the two entrances
with mid 19th-century porches, and the tablet above a central
lower window with a lunette ventilator in the gable. (Demolished before 1981)

Hodson (1953) lxxix–lxxx: Morris I, *Three Hundred Years of
Baptist Life in Coventry* (1926): Sibree & Caston (1855) 113–6:
VCH *Warwickshire* VIII (1969) 382–3.

(31) BAPTIST, Lenton's Lane, Hawkesbury (SP 368840). 'Zion
Chapel', dated 1845, has rendered brick walls and a slate roof.
The front was rebuilt in 1921 but the original side walls remain
of two bays with two tiers of iron-framed windows in round-
arched recesses. At the rear is a lower schoolroom wing of the
mid 19th century.

VCH *Warwickshire* VIII (1969) 384.

(32) GENERAL BAPTIST, Lady Lane or Canal Road, Longford
(SP 349838). 'Salem Chapel', first built in 1765 for a section of
the church at Barton in the Beans, Shackerstone, Leicestershire
(72), was enlarged in 1776, rebuilt in 1807, again enlarged in
1825 and replaced by the present chapel in 1872. Red brick with
blue brick dressings and slate roof, bays divided by rendered
pilasters. Two tiers of windows above a basement. *Monuments*:
in burial-ground include some early 19th-century slate headstones.

Godfrey (1891) 69–70, 76: Sibree & Caston (1855) 261–2:
VCH *Warwickshire* VIII (1969) 382: Wood (1847) 181.

(33) GENERAL BAPTIST, Union Place, Longford (SP 350841). A
new chapel, built in 1827 for seceders from the foregoing, has
rendered brick walls and a hipped slate roof. The wide W front
has two tiers of windows and a rendered platband; the two
entrances are at the rear.

Sibree & Caston (1855) 262–3: VCH *Warwickshire* VIII (1969)
384–5: Wood (1847) 228.

(34) CONGREGATIONAL, Vicar Lane (SP 333790). Built 1724 for
seceders from the Great Meeting; extended to the front and
partly rebuilt in 1823. The church moved to a new chapel in
Warwick Road in 1891 and the Vicar Lane buildings were sold
in 1897; they were destroyed by bombing in 1941.

Sibree & Caston (1855) frontis., 57–78: VCH *Warwickshire*
VIII (1969) 387–8.

(35) CONGREGATIONAL, Foleshill Road (SP 347823). Built in
1795 for a congregation (now URC) gathered by Rev. Jonathan
Evans, and greatly altered by external rendering, replacement or
alteration of window frames and the erection of a large vestibule.
The walls (50½ft by 40½ft externally) are of brick and the roof is
slated. The side walls each have two tiers of segmental-arched
windows. The former British School to the NW is dated 1848.

Sibree & Caston (1855) 253–61: VCH *Warwickshire* VIII
(1969) 386.

(36) Former WESLEYAN, Old Church Road, Foleshill (SP
355824). Rendered brick with slate roof, built 1848 to replace a
chapel of 1813, enlarged to rear 1910; three-bay pedimented
front with two tiers of round-arched windows.

VCH *Warwickshire* VIII (1969) 392.

(37) FREE METHODIST, Alderman's Green Road, Foleshill (SP
359833). Adjoining the present chapel of 1898 is the small
former chapel of brick with gabled front and two pointed-arched
windows with elaborate cast-iron frames of the mid 19th
century.

ETTINGTON

(38) FRIENDS (SP 268488). The meeting-house stands on a
concealed site 300 yards SSE of the parish church. Quakers were
active in Ettington by 1660 and meetings were held at the house
of Samuel Lucas who in 1681 left the present site on trust 'with
the intent that a Meeting House for the use of the congregation
of the people called Quakers should be built thereon'. The
meeting-house, built *c*.1684–9 and registered in 1689, has walls
of soft grey stone with dressings of ironstone; it has been little

Friends' Meeting-house, ETTINGTON
Warwickshire

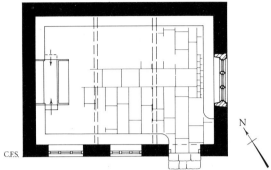

5   0   5   10   15 Feet

C.F.S.

N

altered except for the insertion of a window in the E gable and the substitution of slate for stone as a roof covering in 1894.

The S front has two original windows with wooden frames each of three lights with leaded glazing and decorative iron plates to the casements of the opening lights; the doorway to the right (see p. 244) has a timber frame and contains an original boarded and nail-studded door with wrought-iron strap hinges (replaced 1976, original door loose inside). The interior (23ft by 16ft) comprises a single room having two roof-trusses with inserted double collars below a later plaster ceiling. The stand at the W end has shaped arm rests to the principal seat with disc ornament. Wall benches are of 19th-century date and have a dado formerly panelled but now replaced by rush matting against the walls; four wooden benches of earlier date remain but the seats have been widened. In the burial-ground to the S the graves are marked by grass mounds.

Arnold (1960) 103, 108, 117: Hodson (1953) cxvii: Sturge (1895) 14: White (1894) 134–5.

FENNY COMPTON

(39) WESLEYAN, High Street (SP 417523). The chapel has a narrow frontage, barely exposed between two houses. The stone wall is rendered above the entrance and has a round-arched upper window and a tablet dated 1838. The rear walls are of brick and the roof is slated. The interior, largely refitted in the late 19th century, has a single gallery.

(40) Former PRIMITIVE METHODIST (SP 417523), SW of the foregoing. Three-bay front dated ?1843.

HARBURY

(41) WESLEYAN (SP 372599). The chapel, opened 1804, has walls of roughly squared and coursed rubble and a slated roof gabled to N and south. The central S doorway has a flat-arched head above which two rectangular gallery windows have been blocked and a round-arched window inserted at a higher level. The side walls

(38) ETTINGTON. Friends' meeting-house.

have each one wide window and at the N end two windows flank the pulpit. A vestry at the NE corner has been extended to the north. The interior (30¼ft by 24ft), partly refitted, has a gallery at the S end. *Monuments*: in chapel (1) John Flecknoe, 1849, and Ann his widow, 1872; (2) John Flecknoe, Gent., 'by whom this chapel was founded in 1800', 1835, and William, his grandson, son of John and Ann Flecknoe, 1837; in burial-ground to N (3) Ann daughter of Timothy and Hannah Fairfax, 1823; (4) Elizabeth wife of William Coles, 1836; E of chapel (5) vault with stone wall and moulded plinth to S, uninscribed.

HARTSHILL

(42) CONGREGATIONAL, Chapel End (SP 325934). Rendered front with tall round-arched windows and pedimental gable, was built in 1840 to replace a chapel of 1807–8. Side galleries for the Sunday-school children were added in 1853. *Monument*: in burial-ground, to John Dagley, pastor, 1840.

Sibree & Caston (1855) 280–8.

(43) Former FRIENDS (SP 326946). Built in 1740 to replace a meeting-house of 1720 which had been destroyed by rioters; a new meeting-house was erected nearby *c*.1972 and the former building has been converted to a house. Before alteration the building had exposed brick walls (37ft by 16½ft externally) with a gabled front having traces of an earlier central entrance and an upper window which cut across a brick platband. There was also an upper window in the rear gable. Two roof trusses, removed during conversion, had king-posts and braces. *Monument*: in burial-ground Thomas Rathbone, senior, 1867, and Thomas Rathbone junior, 1870.

Hodson (1953) cxi: Sturge (1895) 9: White (1894) 99–101.

(44) WESLEYAN, Grange Road (SP 327947). Dated 1836.

HENLEY-IN-ARDEN

(45) BAPTIST (SP 151659). Stone with Gothic details including small corner tower, octagonal turret with gablets and spire. Built 1867 probably by George Ingall who gave a water colour sketch of the former chapel which had two arched doorways, three front windows and gable lunette. Interior refitted after fire in 1936.

ILMINGTON

(46) WESLEYAN (SP 212435). Dated 1848.

KENILWORTH

(47) Former PRESBYTERIAN, Rosemary Hill (SP 288723). Built for a congregation which originated about 1700 and whose first meeting-house was erected in 1705. The present chapel, which was closed in 1891 and has since been converted for use as the 'Priory Theatre', was built in 1845 by which date the society was regarded as Unitarian. The new building was paid for in part by Edwin Wilkins Field, son of the then minister, with money collected for him in recognition of his services as a solicitor on the successful passage of the Dissenters' Chapels Bill (1844); the architect was Horace Field.

The chapel is a modest building of sandstone with a gabled front having a three-light traceried window and the motto above 'Soli Deo'. Considerable extensions have recently been made for theatrical use. Several monuments of the late 19th century remain in the forecourt.

Evans (1897) 116–7: Evans (1899) 134–42: Sibree & Caston (1855) 215–21.

(48) BAPTIST, Albion Street (SP 291723). 'Albion Chapel' was built in 1829.

Trinitarian seceders from the Rosemary Hill meeting commenced separate meetings in 1817 in a barn on Abbey Hill some of them formed a Particular Baptist church in 1820–1; the church ceased to exist after 1874 and the chapel was let to Plymouth Brethren until 1914 when it was re-opened by the West Midland Baptist Association.

The chapel has brick walls and a slate roof. The front of three round-arched bays enclosing two tiers of windows with a pedimental gable above, is partly covered by a later rendered porch.

Leamington, Warwick & County Chronicle, 24 Sept. 1914: Owen, J. M. G., *Records of an Old Association* (1905) 159–60: Sibree & Caston (1855) 219–22.

(49) CONGREGATIONAL, Abbey Hill (SP 288721). The paedo-baptist section of the seceders from the Rosemary Hill meeting (see above) separated before 1820 and in 1828–9 built a chapel which still stands behind its successor of 1872. The former chapel of brick has two tiers of windows with two-centred arched heads and intersecting glazing bars set in tall pointed-arched recesses. A brick at one corner of the SW wall is inscribed 'ME 1828'. (URC)

Sibree & Caston (1855) 215–23.

KINGSBURY

(50) WESLEYAN, Bodymoor Heath (SP 199963). Gabled front with two short pointed-arched gallery windows; dated 1844.

LEAMINGTON

(51) BAPTIST, Warwick Street (SP 318660). The chapel, which was built in 1833 to designs of William Thomas, of brick and stucco with a gabled front, lancet windows and pinnacles, has suffered drastic alteration in recent years. A few early 19th-century monuments remain at one side.

(52) CONGREGATIONAL, Spencer Street (SP 319654). The chapel was built in 1836 to designs of J. Russell for the majority of a congregation formerly meeting in Union Chapel, Clemens Street, where an Independent church was formed in 1828. The

walls are of brick and the roof slated; the rendered S front has a central portico with Ionic columns. The flanking bays and the side walls have tall round-arched windows with altered glazing. An organ-chamber was added at the rear in the later 19th century. The interior is lofty and has galleries around three sides with panelled fronts supported by fluted cast-iron columns, and an upper gallery at the S end with balustraded front. The original pulpit, with fluted columns at the corners, has been reduced in height. (URC)

    Sibree & Caston (1855) 293–302.

(53) SALVATION ARMY, Park Street (SP 319660). Typical late 19th-century citadel of red brick with battlemented towers flanking a three-storied elevation.

(54) PRIMITIVE METHODIST, Warwick Street (SP 320661). Built c.1840. Long narrow interior with late 19th-century gallery. (Derelict 1970)

LONG COMPTON

(55) CONGREGATIONAL (SP 289325). 'Ebenezer Chapel', built 1824–5, has brick walls with some later rendering and a modern tiled roof. Gabled front with stone finials, two tiers of round-arched windows with renewed frames, and a small porch. Gallery at entrance; low vestry at rear.

    Sibree & Caston (1855) 315–8.

(56) Former FRIENDS (SP 289329). This site was acquired in 1670 for use as a burial-ground together with three bays of building then occupied as a meeting-house. The meeting-house was closed c.1830 and sold in 1860 but repurchased by Friends in 1869; by 1895 it was in use as a barn although not finally disposed of until 1949. The present building has walls of coursed rubble and the roof is covered by stone slates. Three segmental-arched windows face the road and two towards the former burial-ground at the rear. The interior ($38\frac{1}{2}$ft by 17ft) has three roof trusses of 19th-century date. The outline of an earlier, possibly 17th-century, gable is visible in the E wall, otherwise the meeting-house appears to have been rebuilt in the late 19th century.

    Hodson (1953) cxviii: Sturge (1895) 1: White (1894) 132–4.

(57) WESLEYAN, East Street (SP 289327). Rubble and tile (replacing slate) with gabled front having two windows with timber lintels flanking a later porch and a segmental-arched upper window with iron frame. Opened 1807.

MARTON

(58) CONGREGATIONAL (SP 405686). The chapel, opened 1866, replaces a small building of 1833. Red brick with dressings of blue brick and stone; gabled front with wooden bell-cote with one bell at corner, formerly with a spire.

    CYB (1866) 318; (1867) p. after 368: Sibree & Caston (1855) 354–61.

MORETON MORRELL

(59) WESLEYAN (SP 312561). Dated 1843; four-centred arched windows with iron frames and intersecting glazing bars.

NUNEATON

(60) CONGREGATIONAL, Chapel Street (SP 362917), by Ingall and Son of Birmingham, built 1903 for the reunited congregations (now URC) of the Old Meeting-house (rebuilt on this site 1793) and a seceding congregation of 1817 which met in Bond Street. Brick and terra-cotta with elaborate free Gothic details and prominent ventilator.

    CYB (1904) 150–1: Sibree & Caston (1855) 207–11.

POLESWORTH

(61) GENERAL BAPTIST, The Gullett (SK 260020). Built in 1828 as a preaching station for the church at Austrey. Brick with two tiers of round-arched windows with keystones and impost-blocks. Burial-ground to N contains some slate headstones.

    Taylor (1818) II, 371–2: Wood (1847) 207.

(62) CONGREGATIONAL, High Street (SK 262025). Brick and tile, gabled N front of three bays with two tiers of round-arched windows and date 1828 on a stone above the entrance; adjacent properties have been demolished. This is claimed by Sibree and Caston to be a dwelling-house fitted up for use as a chapel in 1829. Parts of the structure may be of slightly earlier date, but the front wall appears to be at least in part of 1828–9; a long lower wing has been built at the back at a later period. The interior is small with an early 19th-century gallery at the entrance having a panelled front and some original box-pews.

Sibree & Caston (1855) 251.

PRIORS MARSTON

(63) MORAVIAN (SP 490578). Meetings commenced in 1801 and in 1806 a large barn was fitted up for use as a meeting-house. The present chapel, opened in 1862 and 'thoroughly renovated' in

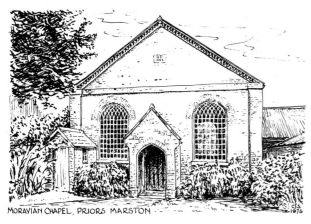

MORAVIAN CHAPEL, PRIORS MARSTON

1883, is of rubble with a brick front; the windows have cast-iron frames and intersecting glazing-bars. *Chandelier*: brass, with ten branches, inscribed 'THE GIFT OF JAMES OLDHAM OF LONDON / TO THE UNITED BRETHREN OF FAIR-FIELD LANCASHIRE', late 18th-century, from Moravian chapel at Droylsden, Lancashire.

England (1886) I, 5, 6, pls viii, ix.

RADWAY

(64) Former FRIENDS (SP 371482). The meeting-house, now 'Oriel Cottage', was built 1702–3; meetings ceased in 1851 and a few years later it was sold and converted to a cottage with the addition of a wing to the north. The walls are of stone (35ft by 20½ft externally) and the roof is thatched. The S wall, which faces away from the road, has a central doorway between two windows, that to the E having a flat-arched head the other a timber lintel, and two dormers in the roof. In the gabled E and W walls are two tiers of windows, only the latter having voussoired stone heads. The interior has been refitted.

Hodson (1953), cxviii–ix: White (1894) 136.

SHIPSTON ON STOUR

(65) Former FRIENDS, Church Street (SP 259405). The meeting-house, built c.1690 and now used as a public library, has stone walls and a tiled roof. The entrance, off-centre in the gabled N

Friends' Meeting-house
SHIPSTON ON STOUR
Warwickshire

N

wall, has a flat stone head with keystone and a decayed date-stone above. The W wall facing the street continues beyond the limits of the meeting-house to incorporate the doorway of an adjacent cottage; centrally in this wall is a stone-mullioned window of three lights. The E wall originally had two gables replaced c.1887 when the roof was entirely reconstructed in altered form. The wall has more recently been refaced in brick with five lower windows in the original positions and five above replacing two wider windows formerly in the gables.

The interior (26ft by 30ft), now divided into two stories with a large upper room of c.1887, retains the structure of a continuous gallery supported by two turned wood columns with octagonal plinths and moulded capitals. The columns were re-sited E of their original positions probably in the late 19th century when the stand, presumably at the W side, was repositioned at the S end. Fittings include three old forms with backs added. There is a small burial-ground at the rear.

Hodson (1953) cxvi: Sturge (1895) 14.

SOUTHAM

(66) CONGREGATIONAL, Wood Street (SP 419619). Brick with a rendered front and slate roof; built 1839. The gabled front has a central doorway beneath a two-centred arched head with crocketed label and blind tracery above the doors; the windows

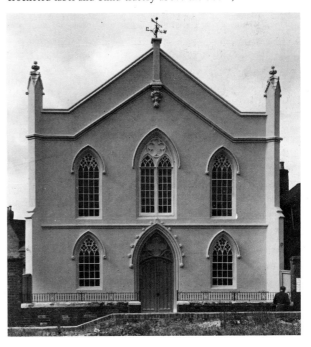

have deeply splayed reveals and traceried cast-iron frames. *Weather vane*: on apex of front gable.

Sibree & Caston (1855) 346–53.

STOURTON

(67) WESLEYAN (SP 296370). Built 1809 on a retired site approached by a footpath. Gabled front with two tiers of four-centred arched windows, blind lunette in gable and inscribed stone tablet with moulded cornice. *Monument*: S of chapel, William Jaques, 1838.

STRATFORD-UPON-AVON

(68) ROTHER MARKET CHAPEL, Rother Street (SP 198548). A Presbyterian society in existence by the late 17th century traced its origins to the ejection of the vicar, Alexander Beane, in 1662, and the presence of a Presbyterian conventicle was noticed in 1669. The history of the congregation in the mid 18th century is obscure but in 1783 it was re-formed as an Independent church. 'The New House lately erected in the Rother Markett' was registered for Presbyterian use in 1714. About 1824 major alterations were made to the building including extension to the front, heightening of the walls and re-roofing, and the erection of a schoolroom at the rear to house the newly formed British School. A further programme of 'renovation and improvement' was carried out in 1859, and in 1880 a new Congregational chapel (now URC) designed by H. J. Paull was built on a new site in the same street. The former chapel was then converted for use as a public hall.

The original chapel of 1714 was a small building (about 25ft by 36ft) of brick with a tall hipped roof. The side walls which remain in the enlarged building have been refenestrated: the SW wall has a brick platband with two former windows above and below it; the opposite wall, covered by a single storied vestry, later heightened, also had two upper windows. In the early 19th-century enlargement two tiers of round-arched windows were inserted into the side walls, and a new front wall was built and later rendered, with a central doorway and three bays of windows with intersecting glazing bars. The schoolroom of *c*.1824, of a single storey with segmental-arched windows at the back, had an upper room added in the mid 19th century.

The interior, entirely altered after 1880, has a flat plaster ceiling and retains traces of galleries around three sides. The roof, which is hipped and slated, is supported by queen-post trusses. *Monument*: re-used as door-step between schoolroom and NE vestry, Daniel Pardoe, 1840. (Demolished 1976)

Barber, A., *A Church of the Ejectment, Stratford-on-Avon* (1912): *CYB* (1879) 410–11: Hodson (1953) xcvi–xcvii: Sibree & Caston (1855) 195–203.

(69) BAPTIST, Payton Street (SP 203552). Plain building of 1835; monumental Doric portico and pediment.

STRETTON UNDER FOSSE

(70) Former PRESBYTERIAN (SP 451815). The chapel, built 1780–1 for a society which had existed since the late 17th century, was registered as a 'new erected building at Stretton-under-Fosse, Monks Kirby parish, for Presbyterians', on 24 April 1781. The church, which became Congregational in the 19th century, was dissolved *c*.1965. The chapel has brick walls and a hipped roof covered with Swithland slates. The walls are in English bond brickwork with a platband and brick dentil eaves

Congregational Chapel, STRETTON UNDER FOSSE *Warwickshire*

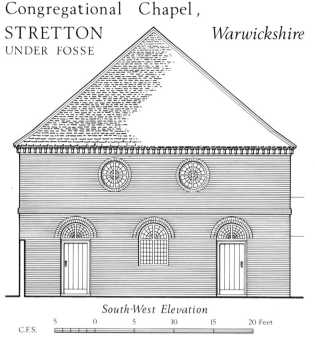

South-West Elevation

C.F.S. 5 0 5 10 15 20 Feet

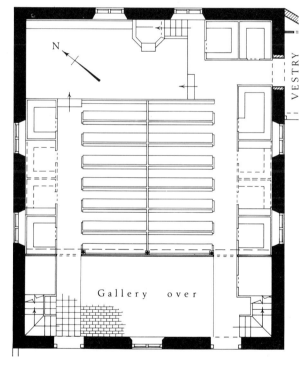

Gallery over

VESTRY

wood columns with high moulded bases. Original box-pews remain in the gallery and in part below, but the centre pews were replaced in the late 19th century.

Monuments: in burial-ground, many slate headstones including (1) Mary, daughter of John and Frances Smith, 1798; (2) John Adnott, 1803; (3) Jane wife of John Adnott, 1790; (4) John Bradford, 1797.

Hodson (1953) xcvii–xcviii: Sibree & Caston (1855) 224–33.

STUDLEY

(71) BAPTIST, New Road (SP 074632). Dated 1847. Brick with cast-iron window frames.

SUTTON COLDFIELD   *West Midlands*

(72) Former FRIENDS, Wiggins Hill (SP 168931). Built in 1724 on a site which had been acquired in 1711 by Friends who seem to have met earlier at Wishaw. Meetings ceased *c*.1825–30 and by the end of that century the meeting-house was described as 'in a very dilapidated condition'. The building, which is of brick with a tiled roof, has been greatly altered and extended to the E in recent years on conversion to a house. The original structure (28½ft by 18¼ft externally) retains in the S wall the segmental-arched head of a tall window to the main room and to the left a small dormer window which lit a gallery at that end. The W wall, which has been much rebuilt, has an external chimney breast; a stable reported to have stood at that end next to the road has been removed.

Sturge (1895) 9–10: White (1894) 101–2.

TANWORTH

(73) CHRIST CHURCH, Umberslade (SP 147721), was built in 1877 by George Frederick Muntz of Umberslade Hall who, having become a Baptist, formed a church of that persuasion which first met at the Hall. The chapel, standing in an isolated park-like setting with a long drive approach from the N, is a large Gothic building by George Ingall of Birmingham, of coursed stone with a blue slate roof. It comprises a polygonal chancel at the E end, shallow gabled transepts, nave, and SW tower and spire. The transepts have each a rose window with cusped circular tracery; other windows are traceried lancets. Buttresses at the corners of the transepts and chancel rise to tall pinnacles and the gables of the transepts and the E end of the nave

cornice. The front wall has two doorways with a window between and two circular windows above; the sides have each two round-arched lower windows and one circular upper window. In the back wall two round-arched windows flank the pulpit. A small vestry projects on the SE side.

The interior (39¼ft by 31ft) has a flat plaster ceiling. The gallery along one end only is supported by three original turned

From S.

Interior from W.
(73) TANWORTH. 'Christ Church'. Umberslade.

TREDINGTON

(75) FRIENDS, Armscote (SP 245447). A meeting was in existence by 1673 in which year a conventicle held at the barn of John Halford was the cause of George Fox's last arrest and imprisonment. The barn, described as 'three bays of a building', together with a piece of land 32yds by 31yds, was acquired in or about 1672 for use as a meeting-house and burial-ground. The present building appears to be a new structure erected in 1705 on the site of the barn. The walls are of coursed grey stone with some brown stone in the quoins; the roof, formerly covered by stone slates, is now tiled. The S front, partly obscured by a wooden loggia of c.1900, has a central doorway with original oak frame, flanked on each side by windows with wooden cross-frames moulded internally and leaded glazing; external shutters have been removed.

The interior (18¾ft by 32ft) retains many original fittings, including a stand along the N wall with raised centre having a panelled front and shaped ends to the seats. A formerly continuous wall-bench remains at the W end. The roof is supported by two trusses with tie-beams and king-posts and is ceiled at mid height. No monuments are visible in the burial-ground. (Reported sold c.1982)

Hodson (1953) cxvi: Sturge (1895) 15: White (1894) 137–8.

Friends' Meeting-house at Armscote
TREDINGTON   *Warwickshire*

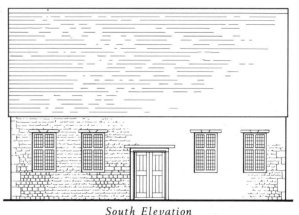

South Elevation

C.F.S.   5   0   5   10   15   20 Feet

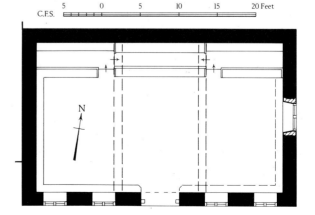

have geometrical stone finials. The tower has a vice at the SE corner rising to a battlemented turret; stepped buttresses at the corners are finished with crocketed pinnacles. There is a parapet around the base of the spire.

The interior has an open timber roof with trusses springing from carved stone capitals. The nave, which is without aisles, is of four bays W of the transepts and has one narrow bay to the east. The pulpit, of wood with a later reredos, stands centrally in the chancel and has an open baptistery in front.

Fittings – *Bells*: in tower, carillon of eight bells with striking mechanism only. *Clock*: in tower, by Gillett and Bland of Croydon, 1877. *Glass*: in rose windows of transepts, non-representational patterns of coloured glass; other windows have obscured plain glass with light green borders. *Monuments*: in N transept (1) brass tablet to George Frederick and Sarah Matilda Muntz, erected by the church and congregation; in burial-ground to SW (2) George Frederick Muntz, 1898, Marianne Lydia his first wife, 1864, buried at Kings Norton, Sarah Matilda his second wife, 1918, and two children, table-tomb.

Langley (1939) 206–9: *The Freeman*, 28 Sept. 1877.

TEMPLE GRAFTON

(74) BAPTIST (SP 127549). Built about 1841 for a church formed in that year; the walls are of soft blue lias in alternating courses and the roof is tiled. The front wall has a gabled porch at one end enclosing a stone staircase to the gallery, and two round-arched windows which are repeated in the opposite wall. The rostrum pulpit is of late 19th-century date.

WARMINGTON

(76) WESLEYAN (SP 411477). The chapel, dated 1811, was refronted in the late 19th century. Attached at one end is an early 18th-century cottage of stone and thatch half of which serves as a vestry and schoolroom and which may have been the original preaching-house. The chapel has stone walls with later rendering and a slate roof. The rear wall, possibly heightened, has a small square window at the centre, blocked in stone, and two later round-arched windows. The interior has a single gallery of 1811 with contemporary seating. In the vestry is an 18th-century fire-place with moulded cornice.

WARWICK

(77) HIGH STREET CHAPEL (SP 28116477). A Presbyterian society was in existence by 1691; an orthodox secession occurred in the mid 18th century after which the meeting became increasingly Unitarian in character and so remains. Prior to 1780 the meeting-house stood on a site now enclosed within the grounds of the castle: it is described as 'an old building of timber in squares, plastered over, and whitewashed: it was a converted house, the floors having been removed and only the shell left'. The present building, on a site given in exchange for the former, was registered in 1781. The front and rear walls are of sandstone ashlar, the side walls are of brick and the roof, originally tiled, is now slated. A brick and tiled chancel was added in 1862–3. The NW front has a moulded string-course at the base of the gable; a

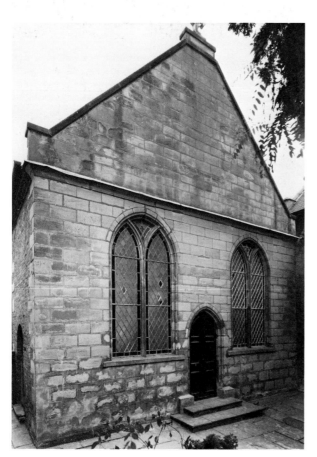

central doorway with pointed-arched head and large flanking windows with Y-tracery were altered in 1862. In the gable a rectangular upper window has been carefully blocked and at the apex a cross finial replaces an urn which was blown down in 1835. The side walls have each two windows with stone Y-tracery in altered frames and near the front a doorway with round-arched brick head. Traces of former windows remain in the rear wall.

The interior ($39\frac{1}{4}$ft by $28\frac{1}{4}$ft) has been much altered in the late 19th century and the chancel, which originally housed the organ, has been refitted on several occasions. A rear gallery with panelled front supported by two columns has been enclosed and one staircase removed. The main floor of the chapel which slopes down towards the pulpit probably dates from 1818 when work was carried out in 'raising the floors in the chapel and under-building them'. The seating is in box-pews which incorporate some late 18th-century panelling; the side pews were re-aligned on a raking plan in the late 19th century. (Interior refitted and floor levelled 1983)

Fittings – *Library*: some 930 volumes from the library of the Rev. W. Field were presented *c*.1843–52 to form a minister's library; unlocated. *Monuments*: in chapel (1) Mary wife of Edwin Wilkins Field, 1831; (2) Catharine Mabbatt, 1844; (3) Emily (Field) widow of William Venning, 1835; (4) Rose Dunsford, 1836; (5) Joseph Brookhouse, 1831, and Mary his widow, 1833; (6) Rev. William Field, 1851, descendant of Oliver Cromwell, minister 1789–1843, and Mary (Wilkins) his wife, 1848; (7) Sarah, daughter of James Benton, 1841; (8) Arabella Anne, daughter of Samuel and Arabella Brown, 1847; (9) Francis Bott, 1833, and Arabella his widow, 1845; (10) William Parkes, 1806, Anne his first wife, 1800, and Sarah his second wife, 1830.

Evans (1897) 251–2: Evans (1899) 222–9: Hodson (1953) xcviii–xcix: Sibree & Caston (1855) 121–44: VCH *Warwickshire* VIII (1969) 536–7.

(78) CONGREGATIONAL, Brook Street, formerly Cow Lane (SP 281648). Seceders from the Presbyterian society in the mid 18th century first met in a room in High Street and in 1758 built a chapel in Cow Lane. The chapel was enlarged in 1798 and further enlarged to the front and heightened in 1826 to the designs of Thomas Stedman Whitewell. The building, described in a conveyance of 1772 as 43ft by 34ft, is now $62\frac{1}{4}$ft by $40\frac{1}{2}$ft externally. The walls are of brick with a rendered front and the roof is slated. The side walls, now of five bays with two tiers of windows round-arched above and segmental-arched below gallery level, show signs of heightening and an enlargement by 20ft to the front. The front wall of 1826 has a pediment across five bays with tall round-arched upper windows and a three-bay porch, formerly open, with two Greek Doric columns *in antis* and gallery staircases inside the porch. The interior of the chapel, which has galleries around three sides supported by cast-iron columns, was reseated and the porch enclosed in 1866 and further altered in 1874. Two round-arched windows formerly flanking the pulpit have been blocked. (Chapel closed, seating removed and demolition proposed *c*.1981)

Fittings – *Gates*: at entrance from street, two, cast-iron with Gothic details and matching standards, *c*.1826 (temporarily removed for road widening *c*.1974). *Monuments*: in chapel (1)

Rev. Joseph Wilcox Percy, 1870; (2) Sarah Groves Satchell, 1822, *et al.*; (3) Mary, wife of Thomas Snape, 1842, *et al.*; (4) Edward Gardner Glanville, co-pastor 1857; (5) Rev. James Moody, 25 years pastor, 1806, signed 'J. Bacon Junr. Ft. 1808' described by Sibree & Caston (1855) as 'a handsome tablet, given

by his admiring friend, Bacon, the great sculptor of the day, who had frequently heard him on his visits to London'; in the vestibule (6) William Goold, 1835, Elizabeth his wife, 1834, and Sarah their daughter, 1847; on external wall (7) Ebenezer Heathcote, ?1840, and Ann his daughter, ?1832; (8) John Burton, 1834, *et al.*

Hodson (1953) xcviii–xcix: Sibree & Caston (1855) 121–44. VCH Warwickshire VIII (1969) 537.

(79) FRIENDS, High Street (SP 28096472). The site was acquired in 1671, although it may have been in use as a burial-ground since *c.*1660, and a building on it was used as a meeting-house until 1694 when this and part of the town was destroyed by fire. The existing building (42½ft by 20¾ft externally) which replaced it in 1695 at a cost of £116 17s. 8d. was closed by 1912 and not re-opened for regular use until 1954. The walls are of brick with a stone plinth and quoins and the roof is tiled. A cottage was built at the NW end in the 18th century. The SW front appears to have had a wide central doorway and upper window, flanked by two segmental-arched windows with wooden cross-frames; in the late 18th century a central window replaced the doorway which was re-sited at the end next to the cottage, the former window at that end was superseded by two smaller windows,

one lighting the gallery, and a fireplace with external chimney-breast was built between the two other windows. An upper window in the SE end wall has been altered. Outside the front wall is a deep stone-lined well. The interior, with a gallery at the NW end with panelled front inserted in the 18th century, has otherwise been entirely refitted in recent years.

Southall (1974) 54–5: Sturge (1895) 2: White (1894) 112–8.

WOLSTON

(80) BAPTIST, Main Street (SP 413755). Rendered front with pedimented gable and round-arched windows; mid 19th-century probably replacing an earlier building.

Sibree & Caston (1855) 393–7.

WOLVEY

(81) GENERAL BAPTIST, School Lane (SP 430879). Brick in Flemish bond with light headers, and a hipped slate roof; probably built in 1803 when a chapel of 1789 is said to have been 'enlarged' having 'become too small for the congregation'. Some refenestration was carried out and a baptistery recess built behind the pulpit in the late 19th century. The front is of four bays with two tiers of round-arched windows and two door-ways in later brick surrounds. A rear gallery of the early 19th century has some contemporary seating. *Inscription*: on brick in front wall 'W + P H + P G + P'. *Monument* in burial-ground, Mary Ann, daughter of William and Sarah Crofts, 1838, *et al.*

Taylor (1818) II, 166, 244, 354–7: Wood (1847) 209.

(38) ETTINGTON. Friends' meeting-house. Original door, 17th-century.

WORCESTERSHIRE
(Hereford and Worcester)

Although the number of monuments recorded in the county is not great, one in three date from the 18th century or before and in most of the larger towns some evidences of the early development of dissent are to be found. The Presbyterian divine, Richard Baxter, who played a leading role in the religious politics of the Restoration is particularly remembered in Kidderminster, the scene of his earlier labours, where the Old Meeting-house (26) now bears his name and the New Meeting-house (27) harbours his pulpit. Presbyterian congregations existed from the 17th century in Worcester, and at Evesham where Oat Street Chapel (16), of 1738, is notable, but most congregations of this name are to be found in the manufacturing districts to the north. Several Presbyterian meeting-houses were damaged in the Sacheverell riots of 1715 and at Kingswood (58) the effects of the Birmingham riots of 1791 were also felt. The late 18th-century chapel at Bewdley (4) is particularly remarkable for its unique oval plan while Park Lane Chapel, Cradley (20) of 1796 is amongst the few of that period that possessed a tower. The Presbyterian chapel at Stourbridge (41) is also noteworthy and retains many original fittings.

The earliest meeting-houses in the county are those of the Friends at Bewdley (2) and Stourbridge (40), both small and typical of their kind, and at Worcester (55), of 1701, where a larger building was required. The Baptist meeting-house at Upton upon Severn (44), of 1734, is of interest for its date and concealed siting and the former

Methodist preaching-house in the same place (45) is of historical note. The former Methodist chapel in Worcester (56), of 1772, is of greater importance despite subsequent alterations and that at Stourport (43), of 1788, is illustrative of the cumulative effects of enlargement.

Several chapels of the Countess of Huntingdon's Connexion occur; those at Evesham (18) and Cradley (21), both of 1789, retained evidence of an attempt at architectural grandeur in the coved ceiling of the former and the square tabernacle-style design of the latter, but the chapel in Worcester (54), of 1804–15, is perhaps the most elaborate associated with this denomination. Most of the early 19th-century chapels in the county are undistinguished but the Baptist at Atch Lench (14), of 1829, is a good example, retaining most of its contemporary fittings, and that of the same denomination at Astwood Bank, Redditch (35), of 1822, should also be noted. Of the few late 19th-century chapels recorded those of the Baptists and Congregationalists in Worcester, (52), (53), illustrate the two principal architectural styles then in use, while the polychrome-brick 'Ebenezer Chapel' at Halesowen (23) of 1868 and the battlemented 'Salvation Army Fort' at Warley (47) of 1893 are minor buildings of character.

Walls are predominently of brick, the only possibly early use of stone being at Bromsgrove (12). Roofs are now generally slate covered although the use of plain tiles was noted in several places throughout the county.

BEWDLEY

(1) BAPTIST, High Street (SO 787751). The church was formed *c.*1649 by John Tombes who, although a Baptist, was minister of Bewdley Chapel until his re-appointment in 1650 as vicar of Leominster. The present chapel, set back behind a range of other buildings and concealed by a later Sunday-school standing immediately in front of it, was built *c.*1764 but has been greatly altered and refitted. The former front wall, of large bricks, has a gable with a platband at eaves level; a segmental-arched doorway is flanked by two tall round-arched windows with a third window above. A gallery at one end has an early 19th-century panelled front and is supported by two cast-iron columns. At the rear of the chapel is a small burial-ground.

Clock: on gallery front, by Jos'h Young, Bewdley, 19th-century. *Plate*: includes a two-handled cup of 1757 or 1763 given

by Josiah Stockwell.

BQ XIII, 116–24: Ivimey IV (1830) 547: Palmer (1802) II, 293–6.

(2) FRIENDS, Lower Park (SO 789750). The meeting-house built in 1706, superseding one acquired in 1691, has brick walls and a tiled roof. The NW and SE walls are gabled with brick dentil cornices and upper windows, that in the NW wall now blocked, and a doorway at the SE end which replaces a window. The NE wall has two principal cross-framed windows separated by a narrow doorway blocked at an early date, and a smaller window near the E corner. The SW wall, partly covered by a short later 18th-century wing, has a brick platband which descends above a wide former entrance, now replaced by a window, and formerly had a window in place of the present internal doorway. The original structure ($32\frac{3}{4}$ft by $22\frac{3}{4}$ft externally) comprises a single

Former Presbyterian Meeting-house
BEWDLEY   *Worcestershire*

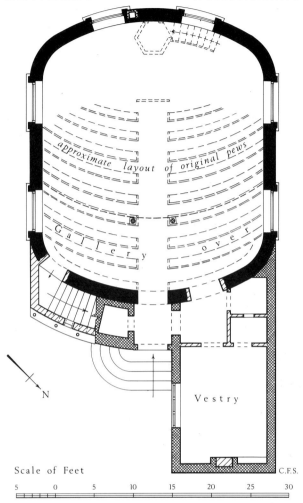

Scale of Feet

5   0   5   10   15   20   25   30

C.F.S.

room with a gallery at the SE end having an open balustraded front and shutters below. The stand at the opposite end was replaced in the late 19th century. Further accommodation was added at the NW end in 1963–4.

Southall (1974) 41–2.

(3) WESLEYAN, High Street (SO 787752). The chapel, opened in 1794, has brick walls rendered at the front and a hipped slated roof; a basement apparently comprising two former dwellings, descends to two stories at the rear. The front wall is of three bays with two tiers of round-arched windows with keystones and a central doorway with open pediment; the basement also has a central entrance at the front flanked by segmental-arched windows.

(4) Former PRESBYTERIAN, High Street (SO 786752). The congregation originated in the late 17th century under the ministry of Henry Oasland who, in 1650, succeeded John Tombes as minister of Bewdley Chapel whence he was ejected in 1662. The first permanent meeting-house was built c.1696 by Joseph Tyndall with money raised by public subscription and placed in trust 10 February 1700, the site being described as '24 yards in length and 14 yards in breadth, in Upper Street, Bewdley'. The present building, which succeeded it c.1778, con-

tinued in the occupation of the original society, which eventually became Unitarian, until c.1894. It was subsequently used as a builder's store, but after repairs it was re-opened in 1952 as the Roman Catholic 'Church of the Holy Family'.

The meeting-house, which stands behind the former manse, No. 63 High Street, has brick walls and a slated roof; it has unusual rounded ends, a continuous moulded stone eaves cornice and, on three sides, two round-arched windows with stone surrounds. The NE front is partly covered by a low vestry added in the late 18th century and to the left of the entrance by an external gallery staircase with roof supported by widely-spaced turned wood columns, now closed by a modern wall and altered to provide internal access. The interior ($33\frac{3}{4}$ft by $28\frac{1}{4}$ft) has a moulded plaster cornice and a late 18th-century gallery with segmental fielded panelled front. Some fragments remain of the curved box-pews and the hexagonal pulpit with fielded-panelled backboard flanked by fluted pilasters, hexagonal sounding board and curved staircase; all in a nearby outbuilding. Reset in two modern doors in the vestry wing are fragments of window glass, one with the scratching 'JT/1778'. Evans (1899) records a monument to Samuel Kenrick, 1811, with Latin inscription.

Evans (1897) 15: Evans (1899) 38–44: *UHST* IV (1927–30) 158–9.

BISHAMPTON

(5) BAPTIST (SO 989514). Brown brick and slate, with dentil eaves cornice to gabled front and open porch; dated 1844. Original pulpit and open-backed benches.

Cox (1982) 8.

BREDON

(6) BAPTIST, Kinsham (SO 934356). Built *c*.1871 for seceders from the Seventh-day Baptists at Natton, Glos. (2), reopened in 1904 by the present First-day church. Three-bay front with pulpit to left of entrance facing open-backed benches.

Former SEVENTH-DAY BAPTIST CHAPEL, KINSHAM

(7) BAPTIST, Westmancote (SO 938376). A chapel opened in 1771, was replaced in the late 19th century. The burial-ground, 50 yards N behind former manse, appears to have been first used by an earlier Independent congregation and includes the following early *Monuments*: (1) Anne wife of William Kent, 1702; (2) Margaret Westmacott, 1706, with Latin inscription; (3) Samuel Jenkes, 1694; (4) John Kent, 1713.

Ivimey IV (1830) 549–50.

BROADHEATH

(8) COUNTESS OF HUNTINGDON'S CONNEXION, Lower Broadheath (SO 813570). Brick with round-arched windows. Dated 1825.

BROADWAY

(9) Former CONGREGATIONAL, High Street (SP 097374). A small chapel concealed behind other buildings on S side of street, was built in 1798 but enlarged and largely rebuilt in 1811. After the erection of the present chapel in 1842–3 it served as a British School. The walls are of coursed stone and the roof is slated with half hips to N and south. The E front has a combined ogee-arched doorway and window, the latter with Gothic-traceried

reveals, between two plain windows. There are two similar windows at the S end and two in the W wall.

Morris, J., *The Annals of a Village Church* (1896).

(10) CONGREGATIONAL, High Street (SP 101375). Built in 1842–3 to the designs of J. and R. Vardy, superseding the foregoing. Prior to drastic alterations *c*.1960–70 involving a reduction in height and the elimination of all windows in the front wall it had a N front of rusticated masonry with pediment, inscribed frieze, three round-arched windows and central entrance. The pulpit and pews are of *c*.1843. (URC)

Morris, *op. cit*.

(11) WESLEYAN, High Street (SP 099376). Rubble and slate; opened 1812. The original wide entrance in the W side wall, now blocked, has a window to the left altered *c*.1860 with the addition of semicircular-arched head. The gabled S front has two windows, similarly altered, and a small later porch.

Cox (1982) 9.

BROMSGROVE

(12) CONGREGATIONAL, Chapel Street (SO 961708). The congregation originated with the ejection in 1662 of the vicar, John Spilsbury, who in 1672 took out a licence as an Independent teacher. The chapel is mainly of *c*.1833 but parts of the NE side are of earlier date. The principal walls are rendered in stucco and the roof is hipped and slated. The NW front is of three bays with Greek Doric columns and entablature to the entrance, a small

window above and two tall round-arched windows each side. The NE side, of sandstone, has a lean-to aisle with a re-cut triangular date-stone of 1693 at the NW end (a newly-built meeting-house was registered in that year) and a wooden cross-framed window of 18th-century character in the return wall.

Monuments: in burial-ground include (1) Rev. Thomas Morgan, 'Pastor of a dissenting Church at Oswestry in Shropshire', late 18th-century; (2) Edwin, son of Edward and Mary Giles, 'accidentally killed', 1838. (URC)

(13) PRIMITIVE METHODIST, Fairfield Road, Bournheath (SO 951738). Opened 1837, enlarged.

CHURCH LENCH

(14) BAPTIST, Atch Lench (SP 034508). The chapel, opened in 1829, has walls of locally made red brick and a slate roof. The windows have cast-iron frames; two round-arched windows in each side wall have intersecting glazing bars. The interior retains most of its original fittings, with rear gallery, box-pews, and large table-pew in front of a small pulpit with single post support. Behind the pulpit are two shuttered openings from the Sunday-school. *Monument*: in chapel, to Joseph Bomford, 1858, 'one of the originators ... of the cause of God in this place', Letitia his wife, 1848, *et al.*

Bomford, F.E., *A History of the Baptist Church at Atch Lench, Worcestershire, 1825–1925* (1925).

DORMSTON

(15) BAPTIST, Stock Green (SO 978584). Small three-bay chapel opened 1846.

DUDLEY (see Staffordshire)

EVESHAM

(16) OAT STREET CHAPEL (SP 038439). Although the minister of All Saints Church was ejected in 1662, no direct connexion can be traced with the emergent Presbyterian (latterly Unitarian) congregation. The first known meeting-house was a converted barn off the W side of High Street, hired in 1696, bought in 1701 and sold in 1738 following the erection of the chapel in Oat Street on a site acquired the previous year.

The chapel has brick walls, faced on the S with ashlar, and a

hipped tiled roof. The wide S front has a moulded plinth and eaves cornice; two pilasters divide the wall into three unequal bays having a central entrance with later pedimented porch and four windows with semicircular-arched heads, keystones and impost blocks. The N wall, similarly fenestrated and with two corresponding pilasters of brickwork, has traces of a former opening below and to the right of the easternmost window. The E and W ends have against them respectively an organ-chamber of 1875 and a later 19th-century vestry; a round-arched upper window at the W end has been blocked in stone.

The interior (27ft by 48¼ft), altered in 1820, 1862–3 and 1874–5, has the pulpit at the W end with a former doorway behind for direct access from the previous vestry built 1862. A gallery, erected at the E end in 1820 and removed when the organ-chamber was built may have replaced a smaller gallery perhaps matching one at the W end, with the pulpit against the N wall, but corroborative evidence is lacking.

Fittings – Font: stone, with baluster stem and circular bowl with stone cover, perhaps early 19th century. *Monument*: in vestry, Joseph Porter V.D.M., 1721, with Latin inscription, marble with gadrooned base and moulded cornice, from former Presbyterian chapel, Alcester, Warwicks. (2). *Plate*: includes a two-handled cup of 1747 given 1838. *Pulpit*: fielded-panelled front, early 18th-century – loose in vestry: wooden eagle, gilt, with olive branch in beak, from former canopy removed 1862. *Seating*: box-pews, 18th-century, reduced in height.

Evans (1897) 81: Evans (1899) 122–33: Smith, K.G., *The Story of an Old Meeting House, 1737–1937* (1937): *UHST* VI (1935–8) 252–3.

(17) BAPTIST, Cowl Street (SP 03924380). Baptist meetings were held from the beginning of the 18th century in Bengeworth, E of the river Avon; by 1704 a barn had been converted to a meeting-house, this was replaced in 1722 by a brick building which was rebuilt in 1760 after a fire. The church was constituted in 1732, the adherents being formerly in membership with the church in Alcester. Meetings W of the river were commenced in 1783, the present site was bought in 1787 and the chapel erected in the following year. The former meeting-house, on the N side of Port Street (SP 044436), retained for occasional use, was demolished about 1845; a 'Memorial Building' of 1874 stands near the site.

The chapel has rendered brick walls and a slate roof. The external appearance, with three windows in each side wall, is entirely of 1870–1 when major alterations were carried out including the substitution of a S porch for the original entrances in the W wall. The interior (48ft by 40¼ft) was also much altered but the galleries date in part from 1830 (demolished 1979). *Monument*: to Rev. Lawrence Butterworth M.A. 'under whose direction and by whose active exertions this chapel was erected', pastor over 60 years, 1828.

Cox (1982) 7–8, 13: *Evesham Baptist Church; Bi-centenary Celebrations 1732–1932* [1932]: *Evesham Journal*, 28 Jan. 1871: Ivimey IV (1830) 550–4.

(18) Former COUNTESS OF HUNTINGDON'S CONNEXION, Mill Street (SO 039438). The chapel, registered in October 1789, was built by a recently formed society which first met in an upper room in the High Street. It was later occupied by a seceding Baptist church until 1857 when the two Baptist congregations reunited, and has since been used as the Meeting Room of a Brethren assembly and latterly by Elim Pentecostal Church.

The walls are of brick, rendered at the front and sides, and the roof is hipped and slated. The broad SE front has a slightly projecting pedimented centre with two tall windows flanking the site of the original entrance now blocked and re-sited in the SW bay; the doorway has a flat moulded hood and shaped and enriched brackets. The rear wall has two tall original windows with external shutters. In the SW wall is a centrally-placed door-way, now blocked and replaced by a later entrance to the right.

The interior (27¾ft by 44¾ft) has a coved plaster ceiling with moulded and bracketed cornice. The fittings were much altered in the 19th century when the pulpit, probably against the NW wall, was re-sited at the NE end and side and rear galleries erected. The galleries have box-pews of the early 19th century. (Demolished 1979)

(19) FRIENDS, Cowl Street (SP 03854382). Quaker meetings commenced in 1655 and, until the acquisition of the present site in 1676, were mainly conducted at the house of Edward Pitway (site of Northwick Arms Hotel, Waterside) behind which was a *burial-ground* (SP 040434) in use from 1675 to 1838. The meeting-house standing within a second burial-ground behind buildings on the W side of Cowl Street, drastically reconstructed in 1870, is reported to have been rebuilt in 1892–4. Some older panelling is reset as a dado to the wall-benches. The three principal ceiling beams are supported by thin cast-iron columns of quatrefoil section of early 19th-century type.

Brown, A.W., *Evesham Friends in the Olden Time* (1885).

HALESOWEN   *West Midlands*

(20) PARK LANE CHAPEL, Netherend, Cradley (SO 935851). The Presbyterian congregation (latterly Unitarian) originated in 1704; their first meeting-house at Pensnett in Staffordshire, opened in 1707, was destroyed by rioters in 1715 and rebuilt

Exterior from S before 1864 enlargement. Early 19th-century engraving.

with government assistance in the following year. The present site (approx. 3 miles SSE of the former) was bought in 1794 and the chapel opened 15 May 1796, the previous meeting-house being sold to 'a society of Mr. Wesley's Methodists'. The chapel was enlarged to the front and partly refitted in 1864. The walls

the N and S walls. The E entrance front is of three bays with canted wings formerly flanking a pedimented centrepiece but now separated by a tower built in 1876. A chancel was added at the W end in 1933.

The interior (originally 57½ft by 53ft) has galleries around three sides with fielded panelled fronts. The original seating remains in the N and S galleries. *Monuments*: in chapel, below S gallery (1) Rev. Thomas Best, 1821, 'first minister of this church', marble tablet 'erected by the Seat-holders', signed W. Hollins, Birmingham; in burial-ground, E of tower (2) Mark Jones, 1833, 'Architect of this Chapel when erected in 1789', *et al.*, headstone laid flat.

Stevens, F., *A Short History of Cradley Chapel Commonly called the Parish Church of St Peter, Cradley, Staffs., from 1798–1933* [1933].

(22) METHODIST NEW CONNEXION, Stourbridge Road, Halesowen (SO 964836). Methodist chapel dated 1842, of brick with three-bay gabled front and two tiers of windows above a basement storey.

(23) EBENEZER CHAPEL, Birmingham Street, Halesowen (SO 968835). Primitive Methodist, dated 1868; three-bay front in red brick with blue and white polychrome decoration.

are of brick, made on the site, and the roof is slated. The original building was of three bays with round-arched windows with intersecting wooden tracery and a short tower above the SE entrance. The two bays added in 1864 have windows reproducing the earlier work and a similarly placed tower which rises to a short pyramidal spire.

The interior (originally 43¼ft by 32¼ft) has a gallery at the SE end now divided and altered, incorporating late 18th-century panelling. At the opposite end a short chancel has been taken out of the projecting NW vestry and a semicircular arch inserted in the former end wall. Fittings – *Inscription*: in SE porch, 'Erected 1796 Enlarged 1864'. *Monuments*: in chapel (1) Thomas Pargeter, 1849, Caroline his wife, 1840, and Thomas their son 1806; (2) Thomas Pargeter, 1796, and Nicholas Hancox Pargeter, 1797; (3) John Pargeter, 1829, Thomas Pargeter, 1831, *et al.*; (4) Henry Shaw, 1846; (5) Rev. James Scott, 1827, 38 years pastor. *Plate*: includes a pair of two-handled cups of Sheffield plate dated 1796. *Pulpit*: segmentally-bowed front, fluted corner pilasters and moulded cornice, 1796, lowered and re-sited.

Evans: (1897) 60: Evans (1899) 89–100: *UHST* VI (1935–8) 51–3.

(21) CRADLEY CHAPEL, High Street, Cradley (SO 942851). A Methodist chapel built on this site in 1768 was purchased for the Countess of Huntingdon's Connexion in 1785 and replaced by the present building in 1789. In 1798 the chapel was transferred to the Church of England, the minister, Thomas Best, remaining as Perpetual Curate. The chapel, of brick with stone dressings, is approximately square with three tall round-arched windows in

INKBERROW

(24) BAPTIST, Cookhill (SP 056582), on W side of Ridge Way, built c.1840. Brick with pointed-arched windows and double-gabled rear wing. Two-storied cottage adjacent.

KEMERTON

(25) WESLEYAN (SO 948376). Stone with hipped tiled roof. Former entrance at W end with window over; two windows in S wall with stone mullions added and lozenge-shaped tablet between inscribed 'W + M/1819'. Present E entrance built in mid 19th century. Rostrum at W end incorporates round front of former pulpit.

KIDDERMINSTER BOROUGH

(26) THE OLD MEETING-HOUSE, Bull Ring, Kidderminster (SO 830576675). The Presbyterian Old Meeting, latterly Congregational (now URC), originated indirectly with the preaching of Richard Baxter at the Parish Church throughout the Commonwealth and more directly with that of Thomas Baldwin, ejected minister of Chaddesley Corbett. The first meeting-house on the present site was built in 1693, rebuilt 1753 and again in 1824; it was superseded by the existing 'Baxter Church' in 1884–5, a building of stone in the Gothic style by F.W. Tarring. This has a N chancel, nave, E and W aisles and SW tower and spire, four-bay nave arcades with cast-iron columns and timber arches with galleries above the aisles and at the S end.

Fittings – *Chest*: carved wood, 17th-century. *Communion Table*: oak, with four turned columnar legs, 6¾ft long, reputedly

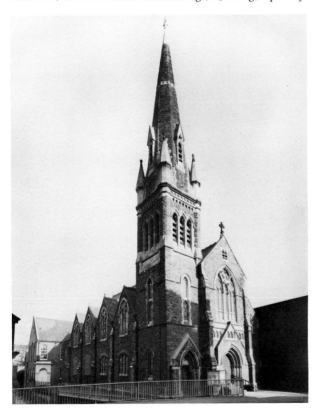

from parish church, 17th-century. *Paintings*: (1) portrait of Richard Baxter, oil on canvas, dated 1669; (2) smaller portrait on wood, probably Baxter; (3) in vestry, portrait of a minister, late 17th-century.

Blanchford, F.H., *Bi-centenary Memorials of Baxter Church, Kidderminster* (1893): Hunsworth, G., *Memorials of the Old Meeting Congregational Church, Kidderminster* (1874).

(27) THE NEW MEETING-HOUSE, Church Street, Kidderminster (SO 831768). A second Presbyterian society (now Unitarian) was formed in 1782 following dissatisfaction over the appointment

of a minister at the Old Meeting. The New Meeting-house was opened 18 October 1782, altered internally 1863–70, further altered and a chancel added in 1879 and enlarged to the front and entirely refitted in 1883. The brick side walls of the original building remain (48ft by 44¼ft externally) but with altered windows; the former front wall was of three bays with a central doorway and flanking windows set in tall four-centred arched recesses and low rectangular windows above with intersecting glazing bars. The present front of stone in the Perpendicular Gothic style by Payne and Talbot of Birmingham had an open stone parapet with a crocketed turret above the apex of the gable and pinnacles over the flanking buttresses, all of which have been removed.

Fittings – *Plate*: includes three mugs of 1721, 1726 and 1793. *Pulpit*: octagonal with gadrooned base, two tiers of panelling, lower panels with floral ornament in low relief, upper panels inscribed 'MTRS ALICE DAWKX WIDOW GAVE THIS PULPIT'; back-board with low relief ornament and date ANNO 1621; octagonal canopy, star painted on soffit, edge inscribed 'PRAISE:THE.LORD/AND.CALL.UPON/HIS. -NAME.DECLARE/HIS.WORKS.A/MONG.THE.PEOP-LE/PSALMS.THE.CV/VERS.THE.IST.'. The pulpit was removed as lumber from the parish church c.1780 and acquired by Nicholas Pearsall, one of the founders of the New Meeting; it is associated with the preaching of Richard Baxter. A carved wood crown and cushion formerly attached to the back-board has been removed.

Evans (1897) 117: Evans (1899) 143–58: Evans, E.D.P., *A History of the New Meeting House, Kidderminster 1782—1900*, (1900).

(28) WESLEYAN, Mill Street (SO 829767). Rendered front. Continuous round-ended gallery on cast-iron columns, late 19th-century pulpit, and pews with padded and buttoned backs. Built 1803, enlarged to rear 1821; closed 1974 prior to demolition.

WESLEYAN CHAPEL, Mill Street, KIDDERMINSTER CFS 1972

LEIGH

(29) COUNTESS OF HUNTINGDON'S CONNEXION, Leigh Sinton (SO 782506). Dated 1831. Long brick front with dentil eaves cornice and hipped slate roof. Contemporary manse behind.

(30) WESLEYAN, Smith End Green (SO 775523). Centenary chapel dated 1839.

COUNTESS OF HUNTINGDON'S CHAPEL, LEIGH SINTON 1973

LINDRIDGE

(31) WESLEYAN, Frith Common (SO 690697). Rubble with hipped slate roof, two pointed windows in W wall and doorway opposite. Opened 1811.

PEBWORTH

(32) WESLEYAN (SP 130468). Yellow brick with hipped slate roof; pointed-arched windows. Opened 1840.
Cox (1982) 16.

PENDOCK

(33) WESLEYAN (SO 787326). Red brick with hipped slate roof, three-bay front with two tiers of flat-arched windows with fluted keystones; circular tablet dated 1824.

PERSHORE

(34) BAPTIST, Broad Street (SO 949457). The church, founded in 1658, long met in a converted malthouse on the present site. This was replaced in 1841 by the existing chapel now concealed from the road by schoolrooms added at the front in 1889. The walls are of brick and the roof slated; windows have pointed-arched heads. The interior, which retains many contemporary fittings, has a gallery around three sides with cusped panelled front supported by cast-iron columns. The baptistery is unusually sited at the opposite end from the pulpit. *Monuments* and *Floorslabs*. *Monuments*: (1) Richard Hudson, 1804, and Eleanor his widow, 1818, signed Lewis, Cheltenham; (2) Benjamin Risdon, 1846, Clementina his wife, 1822, and Eliza Hood Risdon, 1870, signed Lewis, Cheltenham. *Floorslabs*: several of late 18th century, including one to Elizabeth [ ], 1771. *Organ*: in gallery, with traceried Gothic case of 1849.
Ivimey IV (1830) 555–62.

REDDITCH

(35) BAPTIST, Astwood Bank (SP 042622). Red brick and slate; three-bay front, pedimental gable with urns, two tiers of flat-arched windows with rusticated voussoirs and lunette above with border inscription 'ERECTED 1822'. Sides originally of three bays, extended to rear and interior altered in the late 19th century. *Monument*: Rev. James Smith, 1850.
Ivimey IV (1830) 545–6.

(36) CONGREGATIONAL, Evesham Street (SP 040675). Red brick with E front of three bays divided by panelled pilasters and two tiers of windows in round-arched recesses. Central porch with two Greek Doric columns *in antis*, now altered. Built *c*.1827, closed prior to demolition 1976. *Gate*: reset at SE corner, cast-iron with crescent-shaped finials, early 19th-century. *Monuments*: in front of chapel (1) Mary Thomas, 1843, *et al.*, stone tomb-chest with urn; (2) Rev. Henry Humphreys, 1851, 22 years pastor, and Maria his daughter, 1854.

(37) WESLEYAN, Bates Hill (SP 040677). Brick with pedimented front and stone porch with paired Roman Doric columns. Built 1842, enlarged 1881.

(38) WESLEYAN, Crabbs Cross (SP 042644). Built in 1812, extended to rear and altered in later 19th century.

STOURBRIDGE   *West Midlands*

(39) CONGREGATIONAL, Lower High Street (SO 900846). The Independent congregation (now URC) seems to have originated *c*.1743. It had a meeting-house at Brettell Lane where, in 1788, it was joined by seceders from the Presbyterian meeting. From 1791 to 1810 it occupied the former Presbyterian meeting-house and in 1810 built the present much-altered brick chapel which lies behind a five-bay frontage of 1841.

Worthington, A.W., *Early History of the Presbyterian Congregation, Stourbridge* (1886–8) pt 1, 9.

(40) FRIENDS, Scott's Road (SO 899845). The meeting, in existence since 1668, acquired the present site in 1688 on a 1,000 year lease. The meeting-house, of this date, has brick walls much altered by external rendering, and a tiled roof. The N wall is blank and the W gable wall has been rebuilt. The E wall, also gabled, has a modern entrance with older casement windows above and to the left. The rear S wall has a brick dentil cornice,

two wood-framed windows of three lights with leaded glazing to the principal room and a third window at a lower level to the right with a dormer window over to light an E gallery.

The interior (41¼ft by 18¼ft) comprises a single room with shuttered lobby below the gallery. The gallery has a balustraded front of shaped flat balusters and is closed with later shutters. A narrow stand at the W end has steps to N and south. The principal roof-truss has king and queen-struts of plank-like proportions. A second truss incorporated in the front of the gallery is enclosed by later boxing but appears to include braces rising from an intermediate beam.

Sturge (1895) 11.

(41) PRESBYTERIAN, Lower High Street (SO 900845). The congregation originated *c*.1696 when George Flower came as chaplain to Philip Foley, ironmaster of Prestwood, Staffs. (2 miles NW), who supported nonconformist preaching in a private chapel on his estate. A meeting-house built in Stourbridge in 1698, behind a house in Coventry Street, was damaged by rioters in 1715 but repaired and remained in use until the erection of the present chapel on a new site in 1787–8. The former building was used by Independents from 1791–1810; it still stood, as a warehouse, in 1886. A small orthodox secession in 1788 left the new building firmly in non-subscribing hands.

The chapel, designed by Thomas Johnson of Worcester and built by Blackburn and Burchell of Studley, Warwicks., is of red brick with stone dressings and a slated roof. The pedimented E front is of three bays with tall round-arched windows (iron frames inserted 1823) and a wide porch inscribed above the entrance 'A.D. 1788 Hoc TEMPLUM aedificatum'. The side walls have each four windows matching those at the front. The interior (56¼ft by 34¼ft) has a flat plaster ceiling with moulded cornice. An organ-chamber was added at the W end in the late 19th century and the pulpit removed to the SW corner, but most of the original seating remains.

Fittings – *Gallery*: erected 1794 to accommodate organ, singers and scholars, between windows at E end, panelled front painted with records of benefactions, supported by two fluted Roman Doric columns. *Monuments*: in chapel (1) Michael

E front.

Interior from SE.
(41) STOURBRIDGE. Presbyterian chapel. Lower High Street.

Beasley, 1831; (2) Thomas Beasley, 1835; (3) Rev. Alexander Paterson M.A., 1852; (4) Samuel Parkes, 1811, 'one of the first trustees'; (5) Frances Lucy, wife of E.J. Kendall, 1824; (6) Rev. James Scott, 1827; (7) Francis Witton, 1792, and Mary his widow, 1803: (8) John Scott, 1788, Elizabeth his widow, 1800, William Scott, 1792, and Ann his widow, 1813; (9) Robert Scott, 1856, son of Charles Wellbeloved of York and Sarah his widow, 1874, daughter of John Scott, M.P. for Walsall 1841–7; (10) Alice (Pynock), wife of William Scott, 1826; (11) John Scott, 1832, and Sarah his widow, 1836; (12) William Scott, 1834; (13) Benjamin Carpenter, 1816, pastor 1778–95, 1807–16. *Pulpit*: rounded front with applied mouldings; pediment and fluted columns from former back-board re-used on vestry doorway. *Seating*: box-pews with fielded panelled sides and numbered doors.

Evans: (1897) 234: Evans (1899) 194–202: *UHST* IX (1947–50) 175–6: Worthington, A.W., *Early History of the Presbyterian Congregation, Stourbridge*, 2 pts (1886–8).

(42) LYE CHAPEL (SO 925844) was first built 1805–6 to serve the inhabitants of Lye Waste where a colony of nailmakers was established in the 18th century. The church, founded by Rev. James Scott pastor of Pensnett Chapel (see (20) above) and later of the Presbyterian chapel, Stourbridge (41), has always supported a Unitarian ministry. A new chapel was built alongside the former in 1861 to the designs of Francis Smallman Smith of Stourbridge.

The original chapel of brick and slate has two round-arched windows in the S wall. The second chapel, of similar materials, has a contemporary clock-tower, formerly with a spire, not part of the intended design but added as a memorial to the founder. The roof, of four, bays has open timber trusses resting on stone corbels carved with foliage, one incorporating a skull. *Monument*: to Rev. James Scott, 1827, with details of his early patron-

age of the society and a benefaction of £200, erected by the Trustees, 1828. *Painting*: portrait of Rev. James Scott, oils, by Jonah Child of Dudley.

Evans: (1897), 160: Evans (1899) 168–71: Simpson, C., *The Story of the Unitarian Chapel, Lye, 1790–1961* (1961).

STOURPORT-ON-SEVERN

(43) WESLEYAN, High Street (SO 811714). A Methodist society was formed in 1781 within a few years of the opening of the canal and the origin of the town itself. The chapel, registered in 1788 and enlarged to the SW in 1872 is of brick with a slated roof; the NE wall facing the street, rendered and embellished in the later 19th century, has two tiers of windows and an open pediment to the original end wall. The interior (initially 27ft by 44¾ft) has a horse-shoe-shaped gallery of 1812 with box-pews. An unusually elaborate alabaster pulpit and the adjacent fittings and statuary date from 1896.

Locke, E., *Stourport Methodist Church* (1970).

UPTON UPON SEVERN

(44) BAPTIST, Old Street (SO 852404). The church claims to have originated in the mid 17th century and to have formerly met in a house in Dunn's Lane. The present meeting-house, built in 1734, stands behind a row of houses on the E side of the street. It was enlarged to the rear by 16ft and much refitted in 1863–4. The walls are of brick and the roof is tiled. The W front of three bays is rendered and has a central doorway with a flat canopy supported by long scrolled brackets flanked by two round-arched windows. The original side walls have each two similar windows with a third in the N wall of the rear extension. The roof has double gables to E and W with a central valley at collar level.

The interior (52¼ft by 28¼ft) has a W gallery with a 19th-century panelled front projecting at centre and supported by a single post and bracket; the S staircase has 18th-century moulded balusters and handrail. *Monuments*: in chapel (1) Rev. Isaac Stephens, 1785, white marble oval tablet in fluted stone surround surmounted by urn in low relief; (2) Benjamin Lloyd, 1834, deacon, and Sophia his wife, 1819; (3) John Hinton, 1791.

Cox, W., *A Short History of the Upton Baptist Church* (1953).

(45) Former METHODIST, Court Row (SO 853405). A plain brick and tile building, now a garage, has been identified as the 'new room' in which John Wesley preached 14 March, 1770. The gabled E wall formerly had a central entrance. In the longer N wall are two pointed-arched windows, now blocked, and traces of two similar windows remain in the surviving fragment of the original W wall. The interior (30¾ft by 16¼ft) has a flat plaster ceiling; there is a storage cellar beneath.

Cox, *op. cit.*, 14.

WARLEY   *West Midlands*

(46) WESLEYAN, Junction Street, Brades Village (SO 985900). Brick and slate, three-bay pedimented front with tablet of 1849 above entrance. Pilasters and entablature all round. Iron-framed windows with semicircular-arched heads. *Clock-face*: in front pediment, stone with numerals carved in relief. (Derelict 1974)

(47) THE SALVATION ARMY FORT, Newtown Lane, Cradley Heath (SO 947862). Red brick with blue and yellow dressings and battlemented front, dated 1893. 'The Junior Soldier Barracks', of 1900, in similar style, behind.

(48) THE OLD CHAPEL, Birmingham Street, Oldbury (SO 992895). The Presbyterian, latterly Unitarian, congregation claims to have occupied the parochial chapel (Christchurch, rebuilt 1840) until the early 18th century, building the first meeting-house on the present site in 1708 following their ejection from the former building. The meeting-house was damaged by rioters in 1715 and replaced by the existing chapel of brick and slate in 1807. This has a three-bay pedimented front with round-

arched windows and an elaborately detailed brick cornice probably added in 1862 when extensive alterations and refitting took place; it was further altered in 1889. A fragment of early 18th-century brickwork remains in the wall behind the pulpit. The 'Oldbury Free School' dated 1851 stands at the rear of the chapel. *Pulpit*: square, with panelled corners, bolection-moulded panels to front and side, and moulded cornice, *c*.1708.

CF (1870) 136–8: Evans (1897) 193: Evans (1899) 172–80.

(49) INDEPENDENT, Talbot Street, Oldbury (SO 989895). Built 1843 by seceders from the Methodist New Connexion. Two tiers of round-arched windows with iron frames above a basement.

(50) METHODIST NEW CONNEXION, Dudley Road West, Tividale (SO 969907). Rendered pedimented front; dated 1840.

(51) WESLEYAN, Tipton Road, Tividale (SO 974907). Rebuilt 1931, incorporating tablet from 'Wesleyan Centenary Chapel, 1839'.

WORCESTER

(52) BAPTIST, Sansome Walk (SO 850554). The chapel, built 1863–4 in the Gothic style by Pritchett and Son of Darlington, succeeded one of 1797 which stood in Silver Street, a site occupied by the congregation since the 17th century. Stone walls with tapered corner tower and spire, nave with timber arcades supported by tall cast-iron columns, galleried transepts and chancel with organ gallery above vestries.

(53) CONGREGATIONAL, Angel Street (SO 849549). The church, which originated as a Presbyterian congregation in the late 17th century, built a meeting-house in Angel Street in 1708. The present chapel by Poulton and Woodman which superseded

it in 1858–60 (latterly URC, closed *c*.1980) has an ashlar front dominated by a semicircular portico with four tall Corinthian columns. The interior, which is square with rounded corners, has a coved and panelled ceiling with a twelve-sided central lantern and pendant ventilator with original gas lighting fittings. A gallery with panelled front extends around three walls with an upper gallery at each side with open cast-iron front supported by iron brackets. The pulpit stands in front of an arched organ recess opposite the entrance.

Monument: Rev. Thomas Badland 'a faithfull & profitable preacher of the Gospel in this City for the space of 35 Years', 1698, with added inscription 'This Chapel Founded 1708 Rebuilt 1858'.

CYB (1859) 257; (1860) 240–1: Urwick, W., *Nonconformity in Worcester* (1897).

(54) COUNTESS OF HUNTINGDON'S CONNEXION, Birdport (SO 849548). A congregation of 'nearly 200 persons' existed by 1769 and in 1773 the first chapel was built on part of the present site; this was rebuilt to a larger size in 1804 and again enlarged in 1815 to seat two thousand. The chapel is an unusual example of the development of a restricted site and the fittings of the pulpit and communion area are especially notable.

The building stands at the end of a courtyard on the E side of the street with the former manse adjacent to the S corner. It has brick walls and a hipped tiled roof with central valley to the earliest portion and slate to the later parts. The older W arm, principally of 1804, follows irregular site boundaries but it is possible that the major section at the E end of this arm covers the area and may include part of the walling of the 18th-century chapel. A round-ended transept at the E extremity represents the 1815 enlargement and the seating and galleries throughout are contemporary with this work.

The W front, with three upper windows and a central doorway, is partly covered by a mid 19th-century external staircase to the gallery; the principal windows in this wall and on the N and S sides are round-arched with tripartite wood frames and have segmental-arched windows below. The E transept is rendered to the N and has at this end a secondary entrance with a wooden porch having fluted Doric columns and a simplified entablature with incised ornament on the frieze. Two tall round-arched windows flanking this entrance are balanced by two at the S end and repeated on the E wall.

The interior, lightly divided at the junction of the parts by two cast-iron columns, arched between and carrying the wall-plate, has a continuous gallery and a full complement of box-pews. The pulpit stands in an oval enclosure at the centre of the E transept

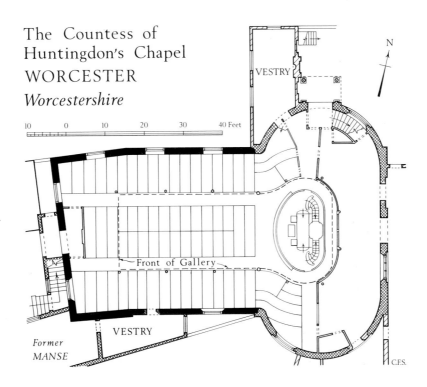

The Countess of
Huntingdon's Chapel
WORCESTER
Worcestershire

10   0   10   20   30   40 Feet

VESTRY

N

Front of Gallery

VESTRY

Former
MANSE

C.F.S.

W front.

Interior from W.
(54) WORCESTER. Countess of Huntingdon's chapel, Birdport.

flanked by eagle lecterns with tables of the creed and decalogue behind attached to a screen wall built below the front of the E gallery in the late 19th century.

Fittings – *Benefaction Boards*: two, on wall of E gallery, with records from 1818. *Christening Bowl*: marbled pottery bowl, light blue with blue and white veining on green marbled stand with gilt claw feet, bowl inscribed with references to *Matthew* xxviii.19 and *Mark* x.14. *Collecting Plates*: fifteen, pewter. *Communion Rail*: mahogany, formerly with plain square balusters replaced by cast-iron standards in late 19th century. *Glass*: in E windows, coloured glass including figures of Christ, inserted 1858. *Lecterns*: pair of cast-iron eagles on fluted and marbled wooden pedestals (see p. 260). *Organ*: in E gallery, first erected 1840 by John Nicholson of Worcester, rebuilt 1896. *Pulpit*: square with rounded corners and panelled sides, supported by eight Roman Doric columns and with twin staircases N and S, balusters replaced in late 19th century.

Urwick, *op. cit.*, 155–9.

(55) FRIENDS, Sansome Place (SO 851551). Meetings which commenced in 1655 were held *c*.1670 in Cooking Street (Copenhagen Street), from 1681 in a house in Friars Street, and transferred to the present site in 1701. The meeting-house, of this

date, is of brick with a hipped slated roof. The S front has a brick platband above four segmental-arched windows and a central entrance with later pedimented porch; there are two windows in the N wall. About 1823 a two-storied annexe was built to the E including a small meeting-house on the upper floor and the original meeting-house partly refitted. The interior (49½ft by 36¼ft) has a narrow gallery at the E end facing the stand. The original entrance has on the N face a moulded wood architrave and pediment of the 18th century. (Major internal alterations proposed 1981)

Noake, J., *Worcester Sects* (1861) 191–296.

(56) Former METHODIST, New Street (SO 851549). This, the first permanent Methodist preaching-house in Worcester, was opened in 1772. It was superseded in 1796, after becoming too small for the congregation, by a new chapel in Pump Street (since rebuilt) on the site of a former Independent meeting-house. The New Street building was then converted to a manse and later divided and shops built on the ground floor.

The former preaching-house is a square building with brick

walls and a tiled roof. The W front of three bays has two shop fronts, one with a bow window and doorway of the early 19th century, and segmental-arched windows to the two upper floors. The rear E wall is gabled and has a pair of segmental-arched windows to the first floor.

Noake, *op. cit.*, 297–341.

WYRE PIDDLE

(57) WESLEYAN, Chapel Lane (SO 970474). Built 1840, concealed behind two-storied extension of 1890.

WYTHALL

(58) KINGSWOOD MEETING-HOUSE, Hollywood (SP 078770). The Presbyterian (latterly Unitarian) meeting-house, built *c*.1708 and damaged in the Sacheverell riots of 1715, was entirely

destroyed in the Birmingham riots of 1791 and replaced by the present building opened October 1793. The nickname 'Dollax Chapel' also applied to the building derives from the name of one of the 1715 rioters who was executed for his part in the affair. The meeting-house (32ft by 28¾ft) has brick walls and a slated roof. It was refenestrated and largely refitted *c*.1860–74 when a two-storied S porch and a N chancel were added and the roof renewed. The gabled S front has two brick platbands and a pair of doorways inside the porch.

Fittings – *Inscriptions*: on E wall, externally, four bricks dated 1792 with names John Bardill and Thos., B.S., and Wm. Greves. *Monuments*: in chapel (1) Emma Greves, 1842, *et. al.*; (2) Rebecca (Greves) wife of Rev. Rees Lewis Lloyd of Belper, Derbys, 1849; (3) Richard Greves, 1843, and Emma his widow, 1861; (4) Harry Van Wart, drowned at Llandudno 1874; in S porch (5) Richard Greves, 1843, *et al.*; in burial-ground (6) Esther, daughter of Thomas and Mary Chellingworth, 1794; (7) Rev. Rees Lloyd, 1839, and Mary (Blackburne) his widow, 1844, buried at Croft, Lancs.

CF (1870) 24–5: Evans (1897) 122: Evans (1899) 159–67.

(54) WORCESTER. Countess of Huntingdon's chapel, Birdport. Eagle lectern.

ABBREVIATIONS

NMR   National Monuments Record
RCHM   Royal Commission on the Historical Monuments of England
URC   United Reformed Church

BIBLIOGRAPHICAL SOURCES
other than those fully titled in the text

Alger, B. A. M. 1901	*History of the Derby and District Affiliated Free Churches.*
Arnold, H. G. 1960	'Early Meeting Houses', *Trans. Anc. Monum. Soc.*, NS VIII (1960) 89–139.
Barker, J. *c.* 1910	*Shrewsbury Free Churches* [*c.* 1910].
Belden, A. D. *c.* 1930	*George Whitefield – The Awakener* [*c.* 1930].
B. Hbk	*The Baptist Hand-book* (Baptist Union of GB & Ireland), from 1861.
Black, K. M. 1906	*The Scots Churches in England.*
Blake, S. T. 1979	*Cheltenham's Churches and Chapels AD 773–1883.*
Bolam, C. G. 1962	*Three Hundred Years, 1662–1962; The Story of the Churches Forming the North Midland Presbyterian and Unitarian Association.*
BQ	*The Baptist Quarterly* (from 1922). Incorporating *Trans. Baptist Hist. Soc.*
Bright, T. 1954	*The Rise of Nonconformity in the Forest of Dean* [1954].
BRSP	*Bristol Record Society Publications* (from 1930).
Bull, F. W. 1900	*A History of Newport Pagnell.*
Caston, M. 1860	*Independency in Bristol.*
CF	*Christian Freeman* (from 1856).
Chambers, R. F. 1963	*The Chapels of the Industrial Midlands*: vol. IV of *The Strict Baptist Chapels of England* (5 vols, 1952–68).
CHST	*Transactions of the Congregational Historical Society*, 21 vols (1901–72).
Coleman, T. 1853	*Memorials of the Independent Churches in Northamptonshire.*
Cox, B. G. 1982	*Chapels and Meeting Houses in the Vale of Evesham.*
Crosby, T. 1738–40	*The History of the English Baptists*, 4 vols.
CYB	*The Congregational Year Book* (Congregational Union of England & Wales), from 1846.
Deacon, M. 1980	*Philip Doddridge of Northamptonshire, 1702–51.*
Dolbey, G. W. 1964	*The Architectural Expression of Methodism: The First Hundred Years.*
Drysdale, A. H. 1889	*History of the Presbyterians in England.*
Durley, T. 1910	*Centenary Annals of . . . Wesleyan Methodism in Aylesbury and the Surrounding Villages.*
Eayrs, G. 1911	*Wesley and Kingswood and its Free Churches.*
Elliot, E., ed. 1898	*A History of Congregationalism in Shropshire.*
EM	*The Evangelical Magazine* (1793–1904).
England, J. 1886–7	*The Western Group of Moravian Chapels . . . The West of England and South Wales*, in 2 parts.
England, J. 1888	*Moravian Chapels and Preaching-houses . . . Lancashire, Cheshire, The Midlands and Scotland.*
Evans, G. E. 1897	*Vestiges of Protestant Dissent.*
Evans, G. E. 1899	*Midland Churches: A History of the Congregations on the Roll of the Midland Christian Union.*
Evans, S. 1912	*Bradwell: Ancient and Modern.*
Gibbs, R. 1885	*A History of Aylesbury.*
Gill, J. 1909	*The History of Wesleyan Methodism in Melton Mowbray and the Vicinity: 1769–1900.*
Godfrey, J. R. 1891	*Historic Memorials of Barton and Melbourne General Baptist Churches.*
Hindmarsh, R. 1861	*Rise and Progress of the New Jerusalem Church.*
Hodson, J. H. 1953	'Warwickshire Nonconformist and Quaker Meetings and Meeting Houses, 1660–1750', *Warwick County Rec.* VIII (1953) lxix–cxxxviii.

Ivimey, H.   1811–30   *A History of the English Baptists*, 4 vols.
Kendall, H. B.   1905   *The Origin and History of the Primitive Methodist Church*, 2 vols [1905].
Langley, A. S.   1939   *Birmingham Baptists Past and Present.*
Ledger, R.   1915   *Worksop Wesleyan Methodist Circuit 1818–1915.*
Lidbetter, H.   1961   *The Friends Meeting House.*
Lindley, K.   1969   *Chapels and Meeting Houses.*
Little, B.   1966   *Catholic Churches Since 1623.*
LRCU   1962   *The Story of Our Churches 1662–1962*, Leics. & Rutland Congregational Union.
LRSP   *London Record Society Publications* (from 1965).
Matthews, A. G.   1924   *The Congregational Churches of Staffordshire.*
Matthews, A. G.   1934   *Calamy Revised.*
Murch, J.   1835   *A History of the Presbyterian and General Baptist Churches in the West of England.*
NBAP   *Proceedings and Report of the North Bucks. Association of Independent Churches and Ministers* (from 1819).
Oliver, R. W.   1968   *The Chapels of Wiltshire and the West*, vol. V of *The Strict Baptist Chapels of England*, 5 vols (1952–68).
Palmer, S.   1802   Revision of Edmund Calamy's *The Nonconformist's Memorial* (2nd edn, 3 vols).
Pevsner, N., ed.   1970   *Gloucestershire* (Buildings of England Series), Pevsner N., ed. and Verey, D., 2 vols.
RB   *Records of Buckinghamshire* (from 1858).
RCHM   County Inventories: *Buckinghamshire*, 2 vols (1912, 1913); *Herefordshire*, 3 vols (1931–4).
Reavley, J.   1925   *Presbyterianism in Shrewsbury and District, 1647–1925.*
Seymour, A. C. H.   1839   *The Life and Times of Selina, Countess of Huntingdon* [A. C. H. Seymour], 2 vols.
Sibree, J. & Caston, M.   1855   *Independency in Warwickshire.*
Snell, B., ed.   1937   *The Minute Book of the Monthly Meeting of the Society of Friends from the Upperside of Buckinghamshire, 1669–1690*, Rec. Branch, Bucks. Archaeol. Soc., I.
Southall, K. H.   1974   *Our Quaker Heritage: Early Meeting Houses Built Prior to 1720 and In Use Today.*
Stanley, J.   *c.* 1935   *The Church in the Hop Garden* [*c.* 1935].
Stell, C. F.   1977   'The Eastern Association of Baptist Churches, 1775–1782', *BQ* XXVII (1977) 14–26.
Stuart, D. G.   1971   'The Burial-grounds of the Society of Friends in Staffordshire', *Trans. South Staffs. Archaeol. & Hist. Soc.*, XII (1970–1) 37–48.
Sturge, C. D. *et al.*   1895   *An Account of the Charitable Trusts... Belonging to Friends of Warwick, Leicester and Stafford Quarterly Meeting.*
Summers, W. H.   1905   *History of the Congregational Churches in the Berks., South Oxon. and South Bucks. Association.*
Summers, W. H.   1906   *The Lollards of the Chiltern Hills.*
Taylor, A.   1818   *The History of the English General Baptists*, 2 vols.
Thompson, D. P.   1967   *Lady Glenorchy and Her Churches.*
Tibbutt, H. G., ed.   1972   *Some Early Nonconformist Church Books (Publs. Beds. Hist. Rec. Soc.,* LI).
UHST   *Transactions of the Unitarian Historical Society* (from 1917).
Urwick, W.   1884   *Nonconformity in Hertfordshire.*
VCH   Victoria History of the Counties of England *Gloucestershire*, 6 vols (1907–81), in prog.; *Oxfordshire*, 11 vols (1907–83), in prog.; *Leicestershire*, 5 vols (1907–64), incomplete; *Rutland*, 2 vols (1908–35); *Shropshire*, 4 vols (1908–79), in prog.; *Warwickshire*, 8 vols (1904–69); *Worcestershire*, 4 vols (1901–24).
White, B. R.   1971–4   *Association Records of the Particular Baptists of England, Wales and Ireland to 1660*, in 3 pts (Baptist Hist. Soc.).
White, W.   1894   *Friends in Warwickshire in the 17th and 18th Centuries* (3rd edn).
Whitley, W. T., ed.   1912   *The Church Books of Ford or Cuddington and Amersham.*
WHSP   *Proceedings of the Wesley Historical Society* (from 1897).
Wicks, G. H.   1910   *Free Church Life in Bristol from Wycliffe to Wesley.*
Wood, J. H.   1847   *A Condensed History of the General Baptists of the New Connexion.*

INDEX